MANUFACTURING IDEOLOGY

MANUFACTURING IDEOLOGY

SCIENTIFIC MANAGEMENT IN
TWENTIETH-CENTURY JAPAN

William M. Tsutsui

PRINCETON UNIVERSITY PRESS   PRINCETON, NEW JERSEY

Library of Congress Cataloging-in-Publication Data

Tsutsui, William M.
Manufacturing ideology : scientific management in twentieth-century
Japan / William M. Tsutsui.
p.   cm.
Includes bibliographical references and index.
ISBN 0-691-05808-3 (cloth : alk. paper)
1. Industrial engineering—Japan.   2. Industrial management—Japan.
I. Title.
T55.77.J3T78   1998
658'.00952'0904—dc21   97-48505   CIP

This book has been composed in Times Roman

For My Mother

Contents

Librarians were essential to the writing of this study.

One afternoon in the autumn of 1991, I was sitting in the lobby of the National Diet Library in Tokyo, waiting for a few more dusty volumes on factory management to be brought up from the closed stacks. My spirits were not high, as my research appeared to have hit a dead end. Exploring the diffusion and application of Scientific Management (also known as Taylorism) in twentieth-century Japanese industry had once seemed such a promising and timely topic. Yet over the preceding few weeks, a string of Japanese scholars had warned me that my project was pure folly, that American models like Scientific Management—characterized by a cold, mechanistic rationality— had had little influence on the evolution of "Japanese-style" work practices. My Japanese adviser had similar worries: he had gently suggested on several occasions that I switch to a "safer" study like a company history or biography of a businessman. Even nonexperts found my project woefully misguided. *"Everyone* knows," the teenaged daughter of my Tokyo landlord once informed me, "that we Japanese learned all our management secrets from the Germans."

With such sobering admonitions echoing in my head, I waited dejectedly for my books to be delivered. As the minutes dragged by, I began—for the first time in many months of visits to the Diet Library—to observe the staff working behind the large circulation desk. Each of the librarians was engaged in a specific task: one officiously collected book orders, another brusquely called out the names of readers whose materials were ready, a third checked out the books, while yet another gathered and organized the returns. Even in my disheartened mood I could see the fundamentally Taylorite nature of this work routine. With each job standardized, specialized, and simplified, the librarians worked with daunting efficiency, processing books and paperwork with almost mechanical regimentation. Even without the obligatory time-and-motion expert, stopwatch in hand, this seemed a virtually textbook example of classic Scientific Management in action.

And yet, as I watched closely, I began to see that the library staff did not entirely fit the familiar stereotype of the Taylorized worker, the slave of the assembly line sentenced forever to repeating a single, mind-numbing task. Indeed, the librarians changed jobs at regular intervals: every thirty minutes, in a kind of bureaucratic musical chairs, each member of the crew shifted to a different station behind the desk. Over the course of a workday, each librarian thus rotated through all of the jobs in the circulation department.

Here surely was something that lay beyond the traditional Scientific Management paradigm. By reducing worker monotony while maintaining high productive efficiency, the librarians' system appeared to offer real relief from the dehumanizing grind of the Taylorized workplace. At the same time, the system seemed as much an intensification of Taylorism as an escape from its excesses: instead of performing one simple, repetitive task, the librarians were expected to undertake a series of equally mindless clerical functions. Was this Taylorism transformed or Taylorism perfected?

I left the library that day in 1991 assured that tracing the history of Scientific Management in Japan was a far more worthwhile project than I had been advised. I hope that this book will bring home to its readers what an afternoon at a circulation desk brought home to me: that an appreciation of Japan's Taylorite heritage is essential to understanding the contemporary phenomenon of "Japanese-style management." In any case, to the efficient (and inspiring) staff of the National Diet Library, I extend my profuse thanks.

Without the encouragement and assistance of many other individuals, this study would never have come to fruition. I am particularly indebted to Sheldon Garon, whose knowledge and guidance have been invaluable throughout this project. His unfailing enthusiasm has made my work easier; his incisive comments have made my work better. I owe special thanks as well to Marius Jansen, whose generosity and good humor made the long process of research and writing far less harrowing than it might have been. Miles Fletcher, Andrew Gordon, David Howell, and Kent Calder all suffered through the manuscript at various stages in its evolution: their careful readings and many suggestions for improvement have immeasurably enriched this work. Among the many Japanese scholars who gave unsparingly of their time and expertise, I wish to thank Watanabe Osamu, Sugayama Shinji and, above all, Nakamura Masanori, my long-suffering sponsor at Hitotsubashi University. I would also like to express my appreciation to past and present colleagues in the Department of History at the University of Kansas, especially Dan Bays, John Dardess, Grant Goodman, Cappy Hurst, and Tom Lewin: their patience and support have been extraordinary. Bill Towns helped me sharpen my thinking on the contributions of W. Edwards Deming to the quality control movement. Beth Tsunoda provided me with a variety of useful sources, including a copy of her insightful dissertation on the rationalization movement. Brigitta van Rheinberg of Princeton University Press guided this book through the publication process with boundless enthusiasm, energy, and expertise. Madeleine Adams and Gavin Lewis saw this book through production and copyediting with meticulous care and professionalism. Funding for my research in Japan was provided by the Japan-U.S. Educational Commission (Fulbright Program) and for that, needless to say, I am extremely grateful.

Portions of chapter 6 were previously published as "W. Edwards Deming and the Origins of Quality Control in Japan," *Journal of Japanese Studies* 22, no. 2 (Summer 1996): 295–325. Parts of chapter 1 appeared as "Rethinking the Paternalist Paradigm in Japanese Industrial Management," *Business and Economic History* 26, no. 2 (Winter 1997): 561–72. I thank the Society for Japanese Studies and the Business History Conference for permission to use this material.

On a more personal note, my thanks go to my cousin, Tsutsui Shigeo, who put up with many annoying requests during my year in Japan, and to Selina Man, who made Princeton and Tokyo warmer places. The ability of my wife, Marjorie Swann, to find split infinitives, holes in my arguments, and humor in the darkest moments has sharpened my work and buoyed my spirits throughout this project.

This book is dedicated to my mother, Ethel Ashworth Tsutsui, who died suddenly in January 1998.

Abbreviations

CCS   Civil Communications Section
HR   Human Relations
IE   Industrial engineering
JNR   Japan National Railways
JPC   Japan Productivity Center
JUSE Union of Japanese Scientists and Engineers
MTP   Management Training Program
QC   Quality control
QCC   Quality control circle
TQC   Total quality control
TWI   Training Within Industry

MANUFACTURING IDEOLOGY

Introduction _____

During the 1980s, scholars and business leaders began to herald the demise of assembly-line mass production. For more than half a century, the model of manufacturing pioneered by Henry Ford and acclaimed as the engine of American economic might had been the world's dominant paradigm of industrial production. Indeed, the Fordist assembly line seemed the very manifestation of modernity writ in steel and sweat: in Aldous Huxley's "brave new world," time itself began with the advent of mass production, "the year of our Ford." Yet in the last two decades, confronted by a new array of economic realities and organizational challenges, mass production and its pervasive technological and ideological dictates have seemed headed inexorably for the scrap heap. And ironically enough, those attributes of the assembly line system which once made it the archetype of efficiency—standardized tasks, dedicated machinery, deskilled labor, and strict supervision—now appear to be its greatest liabilities.[1]

The heir presumptive to traditional mass production is the Japanese model of industrial management. Labeled "flexible" or "lean" manufacturing, the Japanese approach, with its distinctive structures of shop-floor labor relations and production management, has been celebrated as the new global benchmark. The champions of this rising Japanese paradigm describe its economic value and social benefits in almost utopian terms. Compared to the stifling rigidity of the assembly line, Japanese methods promise high productivity, superior quality, technological adaptability, and keen responsiveness to market conditions. Even more startlingly, the Japanese approach appears to transcend the Fordist conception of work: in place of drudgery and alienation, the Japanese model offers a vision of empowered, multiskilled employees working in teams and participating actively in shop-floor decision making. In light of Japan's conspicuous economic successes, the Japanese "post-Fordist" system is now widely extolled as the optimal prototype for a sweeping international restructuring of industrial production methods.[2]

----

[1] Michael Piore and Charles Sabel, *The Second Industrial Divide: Possibilities for Prosperity* (New York: Basic Books, 1984); James Womack, Daniel Jones, and Daniel Roos, *The Machine that Changed the World* (New York: Rawson Associates, 1990); Ulrich Jurgens, Thomas Malsch, and Knuth Dohse, *Breaking from Taylorism: Changing Forms of Work in the Automobile Industry* (Cambridge: Cambridge University Press, 1993).

[2] Martin Kenney and Richard Florida, "Beyond Mass Production: Production and the Labor Process in Japan," *Politics and Society* 16, no. 1 (March 1988): 121–58; Martin Kenney and Richard Florida, *Beyond Mass Production: The Japanese System and Its Transfer to the U.S.*

Yet despite the recent enthusiasm for Japanese management, not all observers have acknowledged the Japanese model as a revolutionary break from past practice. Some commentators have suggested that beneath a well-tended aura of warm human relations and technical virtuosity, Japanese production strategies are only superficially different from the dynamics of the Fordist assembly line. Critics charge that the participative rhetoric of the Japanese workplace is hollow, and that Japanese workers face jobs as repetitive, fragmented, closely supervised and mind-numbing as do their American counterparts. Some have even asserted that the Japanese system goes beyond the assembly line in its exploitation of labor, damning Japanese practices as "management by stress" and "ultra-Fordist."[3] Trenchant support for such conclusions has come from scholars studying Japanese transplant factories in the United States: expecting to discover industrial bliss in Japanese firms, they have found instead a management regime even more repressive and rigid than that associated with traditional Fordist mass production.[4] To many, then, the Japanese model is less a vision of progress, regeneration, and redemption than an enhanced, refined (and perhaps even perfected) reformulation of the classic assembly-line order.

Why does the Japanese factory seem so different and yet so familiar to Western observers, at once the rejection of the assembly line and its apotheosis? Is the Japanese approach a complete departure from the logic of Western mass production—a radical reinterpretation of modern industrial work—or is it merely an evolutionary advance on the now antiquated Fordist model? How has the Japanese paradigm become, to some, a beacon of enlightened labor management and responsible technological development,

---

(New York: Oxford University Press, 1993); Robert E. Cole, *Work, Mobility and Participation* (Berkeley: University of California Press, 1979). Although W. Mark Fruin does not adopt the "post-Fordist" idiom in his recent study, *Knowledge Works: Managing Intellectual Capital at Toshiba* (New York: Oxford University Press, 1997), his conclusions are consistent with the celebratory view of Japan's "lean" manufacturing methods.

    [3] Mike Parker, "Industrial Relations Myth and Shop-Floor Reality: The 'Team Concept' in the Auto Industry," in *Industrial Democracy in America: The Ambiguous Promise,* ed. Nelson Lichtenstein and Howell Harris (Cambridge: Cambridge University Press, 1993); Katō Tetsurō and Rob Steven, *Is Japanese Capitalism Post-Fordist?,* Papers of the Japanese Studies Centre, Monash University, no.16, (Melbourne, 1991); Knuth Dohse, Ulrich Jurgens, and Thomas Malsch, "From 'Fordism' to 'Toyotism'? The Social Organization of the Labor Process in the Japanese Automobile Industry," *Politics and Society* 14, no. 2 (1985): 115–46; Stephen Wood, "The Transformation of Work?" in *The Transformation of Work?* ed. Stephen Wood (London: Unwin Hyman, 1989), esp. 32–34. For evocative descriptions of Japanese management from the workers' perspective, see Kamata Satoshi, *Japan in the Passing Lane,* trans. Akimoto Tatsuru (New York: Pantheon, 1982) and Akamatsu Tokuji, *Toyota zankoku monogatari* (Eeru shuppansha, 1982).

    [4] Laurie Graham, *On the Line at Subaru-Isuzu: The Japanese Model and the American Worker* (Ithaca, N.Y.: ILR Press, 1995); Joseph J. and Suzy Fucini, *Working for the Japanese* (New York: Free Press, 1990). For a provocative (and far less critical) appraisal, see Paul Adler, "Time-and-Motion Regained," *Harvard Business Review* 71, no. 1 (January–February 1993): 97–108.

while others excoriate it as an intensified Fordist purgatory, Charlie Chaplin's *Modern Times* restaged with quality control circles and morning calisthenics? How can these seemingly contradictory interpretations of the Japanese management system be reconciled? Moreover, what of the common message of these two polarized perspectives, that (at least from the corporate vantage point) Japanese practices have proven remarkably successful in the international rivalry with assembly-line mass production? After all, as one group of scholars has acutely observed, "The new interest in work organization in Japan is not the result of a search for a more humane alternative to Fordism but of the superiority of the Japanese automobile industry in world market competition."[5]

Most previous attempts to explain the attributes, achievements, and paradoxes of the Japanese management system have led only to dead ends or incomplete answers. Culturalist interpretations, which have long dominated popular perceptions on both sides of the Pacific, sustain the notion that Japan's management customs are fundamentally different from American ways.[6] Yet this approach, which ascribes the distinctive nature of Japanese methods to a unique legacy of social organization, has repeatedly proven itself a limited conceptual framework for analyzing the Japanese experience of industrial production. An increasingly prevalent view downplays Japanese cultural exceptionalism, stressing instead Japan's proficiency at imitating management techniques once revered (but now apparently forgotten) in the United States. Emphasizing the contributions of Americans like quality guru W. Edwards Deming, many analysts have asserted that Japan's recent managerial advances were, in fact, "Made in the U.S.A."[7] But however provocative the conclusion that American firms were beaten at their own game by the Japanese, the casting of Japanese managers as peerless mimics is ultimately as stereotyped and unconvincing as the culturalists' dogma. Meanwhile, organizational sociologists and labor process theorists, undoubtedly the most prolific commentators on the current flux in industrial management regimes, have become bogged

---

[5] Dohse, Jurgens and Malsch, "From 'Fordism' to 'Toyotism'?" 118.

[6] The culturalist approach was originally popularized in the West by James Abegglen's *The Japanese Factory: Aspects of its Social Organization* (Glencoe, Ill.: Free Press, 1958). Other landmark works in this tradition are Thomas P. Rohlen, *For Harmony and Strength* (Berkeley: University of California Press, 1974); William G. Ouchi, *Theory Z* (New York: Avon Books, 1981); Richard T. Pascale and Anthony G. Athos, *The Art of Japanese Management* (New York: Warner Books, 1981). For a Japanese perspective, see Hayashi Shuji, *Culture and Management in Japan,* trans. Frank Baldwin (Tokyo: University of Tokyo Press, 1988).

[7] For example, the standard American textbook on the history of management notes that "the managerial revolution that occurred in Japan after World War II was made in the United States." Daniel A. Wren, *The Evolution of Management Thought,* 4th ed. (New York: Wiley, 1994), 361. On the Deming legend, see W. Edwards Deming, *Out of the Crisis* (Cambridge: Cambridge University Press, 1982); Lloyd Dobyns and Clair Crawford Mason, *Quality or Else: The Revolution in World Business* (Boston: Houghton Mifflin, 1991).

down in semantic arguments and appear unable to reach a clear consensus on the origins or implications of the ascendant Japanese model.[8]

What seems to unite the great majority of commentators on Japanese management, whether they trumpet cultural transcendence or argue that "we taught them all they know," whether they condone or condemn, is the failure to examine Japanese practices from a historical perspective. Until quite recently, the discourse on Japanese management has been dominated by business experts, journalists, and social scientists, some of whom have gone beyond the existing preconceptions, but few of whom have sought historical affirmation for their views. In the past decade, however, several important works on the history of Japanese labor relations, industrial organization, and production techniques have appeared in English.[9] Although these contributions afford valuable insights into the institutional context of the Japanese factory, they provide only fragmentary and tangential accounts of the evolution of the Japanese management paradigm. Notably, by concentrating on workers and labor unions, government bureaucrats, or the outspoken "captains of industry," historians have tended to overlook the central role played by managers themselves, those most intimately involved in the conception and implementation of industrial management methods. Business historians, meanwhile, by establishing artificial barriers between the firm and the external sociopolitical environment, have often ignored the larger cultural and ideological implications of Japan's emergent managerial structures. Furthermore, in seeking to emphasize the distinctiveness of the Japanese experience, many scholars have disregarded the influence of Western models on Japanese managerial practices and neglected promising comparative perspectives.

Nevertheless, by addressing the deficiencies in the existing historical literature and establishing a more comprehensive genealogy of Japanese manage-

---

[8] See, for example, Stephen Wood, "The Japanization of Fordism," *Economic and Industrial Democracy* 14 (1993): 535–55; Paul Thompson, *The Nature of Work: An Introduction to Debates on the Labour Process,* 2d ed. (Basingstoke: Macmillan, 1989).

[9] Chalmers Johnson, *MITI and the Japanese Miracle* (Stanford, Calif.: Stanford University Press, 1982); Andrew Gordon, *The Evolution of Labor Relations in Japan: Heavy Industry, 1853–1955* (Cambridge, Mass.: Harvard University Press, 1985); Michael A. Cusumano, *The Japanese Automobile Industry: Technology and Management at Nissan and Toyota* (Cambridge, Mass.: Harvard University Press, 1985); Sheldon Garon, *The State and Labor in Modern Japan* (Berkeley: University of California Press, 1987); W. Dean Kinzley, *Industrial Harmony in Modern Japan: The Invention of a Tradition* (London: Routledge, 1991); Andrew Gordon, "Contests for the Workplace," in *Postwar Japan as History,* ed. Andrew Gordon (Berkeley: University of California Press, 1993); John Price, *Japan Works: Power and Paradox in Postwar Industrial Relations* (Ithaca, N.Y.: ILR Press, 1997). Although not dealing specifically with industrial, labor, or management issues, another important source is Eleanor Westney, *Imitation and Innovation: The Transfer of Western Organizational Patterns to Meiji Japan* (Cambridge, Mass.: Harvard University Press, 1987). See also W. Mark Fruin, *The Japanese Enterprise System: Competitive Strategies and Cooperative Structures* (Oxford: Clarendon Press, 1992), and Byron Marshall, *Capitalism and Nationalism in Prewar Japan* (Stanford, Calif.: Stanford University Press, 1967).

ment thought, the confounding ambiguities and ostensible contradictions of the Japanese model can be clarified and reconciled. As this study will demonstrate, constructing a new narrative of the evolution of Japanese methods can bring meaningful relief from the fractured and polarized readings which dominate the current discourse on Japanese industrial management, the ill-informed and unproductive debates—traditional versus modern, native versus imported, liberating versus oppressive, "post-Fordist" versus "ultra-Fordist"—which have led to the continuing interpretive deadlock. By examining Japanese management in its full historical complexity, and specifically by reconceiving it as the product of a century-long dynamic of foreign inspiration and indigenous adjustment, this work seeks to provide a new coherence to contemporary understandings of the Japanese model and its origins.

The reception and adaptation of American managerial ideas in Japan will be the prism through which the development of the Japanese management paradigm is scrutinized in this study. Until very recently, American industrial management was almost universally regarded as the yardstick of progress, and was a source of inspiration and contention among managers, businessmen, bureaucrats, and intellectuals throughout the world. As the most influential and controversial management model to emerge from the United States prior to World War II— and as the methodological and intellectual foundation of Fordist mass production—Taylorism (also known as Scientific Management) was of pivotal importance in this international diffusion.[10] Originally articulated by the mechanical engineer Frederick Winslow Taylor, Scientific Management has constituted the backbone of American managerial thought and practice since the

---

[10] On Taylorism, see Hugh Aitken, *Scientific Management in Action: Taylorism at Watertown Arsenal, 1908–1915* (Princeton, N.J.: Princeton University Press, 1960); Samuel Haber, *Efficiency and Uplift: Scientific Management in the Progressive Era* (Chicago: University of Chicago Press, 1964); Harry Braverman, *Labor and Monopoly Capital: The Degradation of Work in the Twentieth Century* (New York: Monthly Review Press, 1974); David F. Noble, *America by Design: Science, Technology and the Rise of Corporate Capitalism* (New York: Knopf, 1977); Daniel Nelson, *Frederick W. Taylor and the Rise of Scientific Management* (Madison: University of Wisconsin Press, 1980); Judith A. Merkle, *Management and Ideology: The Legacy of the International Scientific Management Movement* (Berkeley: University of California Press, 1980); Stephen P. Waring, *Taylorism Transformed: Scientific Management Theory Since 1945* (Chapel Hill: University of North Carolina Press, 1991); Daniel Nelson, ed., *A Mental Revolution: Scientific Management Since Taylor* (Columbus: Ohio State University Press, 1992); John M. Jordan, *Machine-Age Ideology: Social Engineering and American Liberalism, 1911–1939* (Chapel Hill: University of North Carolina Press, 1994); Robert Kanigel, *The One Best Way: Frederick Winslow Taylor and the Enigma of Efficiency* (New York: Viking, 1997). Interesting literary perspectives on the pervasiveness of Taylorism in American society are provided by Martha Banta, *Taylored Lives: Narrative Productions in the Age of Taylor, Veblen, and Ford* (Chicago: University of Chicago Press, 1993); James Knapp, *Literary Modernism and the Transformation of Work* (Evanston, Ill.: Northwestern University Press, 1988); Cecilia Tichi, *Shifting Gears: Technology, Literature, Culture in Modernist America* (Chapel Hill: University of North Carolina Press, 1987).

late nineteenth century. Rejecting unsystematic workshop methods based on customary practice—the "rules of thumb" wielded by skilled craftsmen—as well as the "arbitrariness, greed, and lack of control" that characterized factory management in industrializing America,[11] Taylorism championed the scientific analysis of the manufacturing process by a professional managerial elite. Seeking the "one best way" of organizing production, Scientific Management aimed to maximize efficiency by intricately dissecting work routines, standardizing shop-floor procedures, and simplifying the tasks assigned to workers. The key to such reforms, Taylorites insisted, was the complete separation of planning (management) from execution (labor), with full authority over the workplace invested in a cadre of trained managerial experts. "To work according to scientific laws," Frederick Winslow Taylor declared in 1911, "the management must take over and perform much of the work which is now left to the men; almost every act of the workman should be preceded by one or more preparatory acts of the management which enable him to do his work better and quicker than he otherwise could."[12]

To equip the new ranks of scientific managers, Taylor and his associates devised a formidable arsenal of techniques for determining optimal production methods and ensuring worker compliance. Although now associated primarily with these workshop methodologies—notably time-and-motion study and elaborate incentive wage schemes—Taylorism offered more than technical innovations and increased productivity. Indeed, Scientific Management looked toward a permanent reconciliation between labor and capital—the so-called "Mental Revolution"—made possible by the objectivity of scientific methods and the promise of untold plenty brought by the diffusion of Taylorite techniques. Assured that employers and employees alike would profit materially from the "apolitical" application of science to industrial management, Taylorites maintained that the pacification of labor relations in the factory would lead to broader social harmonization. Thus conceived as more than a shop-floor regimen, Scientific Management came to encompass a complex set of values and imperatives—an ideology—which ultimately assumed an importance far beyond the sphere of factory management. In the United States (and indeed in much of the industrial world), the assumptions, prescriptions and implications of the Taylorite framework would suffuse political discourse, intellectual debate and even popular culture throughout the twentieth century.

Although the importance of Taylorism in Europe has long been recognized,[13] historians have generally discounted the significance of Scientific

---

[11] Mauro Guillen, *Models of Management: Work, Authority, and Organization in a Comparative Perspective* (Chicago: University of Chicago Press, 1994), 8.

[12] Frederick Winslow Taylor, *The Principles of Scientific Management* (New York: Harper, 1911), 26.

[13] On Taylorism in Europe, see Charles Maier, "Between Taylorism and Technocracy: European Ideologies and the Vision of Industrial Productivity in the 1920s," in *In Search of Stabil-*

Management in Japan. While acknowledging that Japan was swept up in the worldwide mania for "efficiency" in the 1920s, most Western observers have dismissed the popularity of American models as a passing fad and condemned the Japanese understanding of Taylorism as "curious," "diluted," "distorted" and "poorly digested."[14] The mainstream of Japanese scholarship (following on the work of Hazama Hiroshi) has assumed that indigenous traditions of hierarchy, group responsibility, and emotionalism made Scientific Management untenable in Japanese factories.[15] As one influential historical overview describes it, U.S. methods like Taylorism proved so unsuited to Japanese conditions and so dissonant with Japanese cultural proclivities that they could not be transplanted; in the end, Scientific Management was rejected, and contemporary "Japanese-style management" was constructed independently from a "revolutionary inheritance of tradition."[16]

In recent years, however, a number of scholars have begun to reappraise the received wisdom on the impact of Taylorism in Japan.[17] Although such work

---

ity: Explorations in Historical Political Economy (Cambridge: Cambridge University Press, 1987; originally published 1970); Mark R. Beissinger, *Scientific Management, Socialist Discipline, and Soviet Power* (Cambridge, Mass.: Harvard University Press, 1988); Joan Campbell, *Joy in Work, German Work* (Princeton, N.J.: Princeton University Press, 1989); Perry R. Willson, *The Clockwork Factory: Women and Work in Fascist Italy* (Oxford: Clarendon Press, 1993); Mary Nolan, *Visions of Modernity: American Business and the Modernization of Germany* (New York: Oxford University Press, 1994). A fascinating study of Scientific Management in Latin America is Barbara Weinstein, *For Social Peace in Brazil: Industrialists and the Remaking of the Working Class in São Paulo, 1920–1964* (Chapel Hill: University of North Carolina Press, 1996).

[14] Tessa Morris-Suzuki, *The Technological Transformation of Japan* (Cambridge: Cambridge University Press, 1994), 122; Cole, *Work, Mobility and Participation*, 111; Kinzley, *Industrial Harmony*, 104; Johnson, *MITI*, 105.

[15] See, for example, Hazama Hiroshi, *Nihon ni okeru rōshi kyōchō no teiryū* (Waseda daigaku shuppanbu, 1978), esp. chap. 4; Hazama Hiroshi, *Nihon rōmu kanrishi kenkyū* (Daiyamondo, 1964); Nakase Toshikazu, "The Introduction of Scientific Management in Japan and its Characteristics," in *Labor and Management,* ed. Nakagawa Keiichirō, Proceedings of the Fourth International Conference on Business History (Tokyo: University of Tokyo Press, 1977); Chokki Toshiaki, "Teiraa shisutemu no dōnyū," in *Nihon keieishi o manabu 2,* ed. Kobayashi Masaaki et al. (Yūhikaku, 1976), 154–56.

[16] Hashimoto Jurō, "1955-nen," in *Nihon keizai shi 8: Kōdo seichō,* ed. Yasuba Yasukichi and Inoki Takenori (Iwanami shoten, 1989), 85.

[17] Among Japanese scholars, the contributions of Okuda Kenji, Sasaki Satoshi, Nakaoka Tetsurō, and Takahashi Mamoru have been particularly important. Among their many works, see Okuda Kenji, *Hito to keiei: Nihon keiei kanrishi kenkyū* (Manejimento-sha, 1985); Sasaki Satoshi, "Scientific Management Movements in Pre-War Japan," in *Japanese Yearbook on Business History: 1987,* ed. Yasuoka Shigeaki and Morikawa Hidemasa (Tokyo: Japan Business History Institute, 1987), 51–76; Nakaoka Tetsurō, "Senchū, sengo no kagakuteki kanri undō," pts. 1, 2, and 3, *Keizaigaku zasshi* 82, no. 1 (May 1981): 10–27, 82, no. 3 (September 1981): 43–60, and 83, no. 1 (May 1982): 43–61; and Takahashi Mamoru, *"Kagakuteki kanrihō" to Nihon kigyō* (Ochanomizu shobō, 1994). In English, see Andrew Gordon, "Araki Tōichirō and the Shaping of Labor Management," in *Japanese Management in Historical Perspective,* ed. Yui Tsunehiko and Nakagawa Keiichirō, Proceedings of the Fifteenth International Conference on Business History (Tokyo:

points the way toward a broad reevaluation, the new literature on Japanese Taylorism has remained limited in scope and tentative in tone. As with most historical writings on Japanese management, this preliminary research has emphasized the uniqueness of Japan's experience and has not considered the Japanese reception of Scientific Management in a larger comparative context. As a consequence, any deviations from Taylorite doctrine have commonly been assumed to constitute distinctive, "Japanese" adaptations, a view which overlooks the fact that European (and even American) responses to Scientific Management were often substantially the same. Furthermore, even revisionist scholars have been inclined to view American managerial thought very narrowly, conceiving Taylorism as a technique rather than an ideology, as an interwar phenomenon rather than a transwar one, as the idiom of the assembly line rather than an expansive language of political, economic, and social reform. By thus figuring Scientific Management as stopwatches and piece rates, as a methodology marooned on the shop floor and frozen in a prewar moment, previous attempts to reassess its broader significance in Japan have been handicapped from the start.

This work will rechart the history of Scientific Management in Japan, amending the customary assumptions of the thwarted, limited—or else all-powerful—role of American models in the shaping of Japanese managerial practice. On the most basic level, this study seeks to document the importance of Taylorite methods and mind-sets in Japan before, during and after the Second World War. Tracing the application of Scientific Management from its introduction in 1911, through the "efficiency movement" of the 1920s, Depression-era "industrial rationalization," the mobilization campaigns of World War II, the postwar drive for "productivity," and the quality control initiatives of "miracle economy" Japan, this study will demonstrate that Taylorism was progressively embraced as the logical and natural model for Japanese industry. Although Taylorite procedures spread unevenly through Japanese workshops prior to World War II—with some methods adopted, others adapted, and a few abandoned—the generalization of Scientific Management techniques was apparent during the postwar transition to a mass production, mass consumption economy.

Furthermore, as in the United States and Europe, Taylorism extended far beyond workshop methodologies to constitute a broadly defined ideology of management, an ideology which transcended the factory to structure debates over economic policy, social stabilization, industrial relations, and bureaucratic authority.[18] Taylorite visions—progress premised on science, politically

University of Tokyo Press, 1989), 173–91; Malcolm Warner, "Japanese Culture, Western Management: Taylorism and Human Resources in Japan," *Organization Studies* 15, no. 4 (1994): 509–33.

[18] On the concept of ideologies of management and the significance of management systems as ideologies, see Reinhard Bendix, *Work and Authority in Industry: Ideologies of Management in*

transcendent expertism, "objective" social engineering, class reconciliation through the "Mental Revolution"—clearly resonated with many Japanese audiences. As this study will argue, Scientific Management has proven a potent ideological template in Japan throughout the twentieth century. During the interwar decades, Taylorism lay at the intellectual core of a spreading technocratic humor, an emergent bureaucratic authoritarianism which culminated in the wartime "New Order" of statist economic management. After defeat in 1945, the Taylorite message was resuscitated and recast as a comprehensive ideological framework for class harmonization and economic growth. Under the banner "productivity," this reincarnation of Scientific Management thought proved a durable basis for accord among capitalists, managers, and workers in "high-growth" Japan.

Significantly, Scientific Management was neither rejected nor "distorted" in its transmission across the Pacific. Instead, this study suggests that the Japanese experience of Taylorism paralleled those of the United States and Europe in numerous ways. At the same time, it is apparent that Japanese Scientific Management was not simply a mindless regurgitation of American prototypes. In the particular economic, social, political, and technological context of twentieth-century Japan, the practice of Taylorism was subtly reshaped into a specifically Japanese approach to modern management. Seeking an enhanced formulation—a "revised" Taylorism—that combined mechanistic efficiency with a "humanized" appeal to labor, Japan's industrial managers experimented with a variety of institutional forms, rhetorical tactics, and methodological innovations. The Japanese refinement of Scientific Management, eventually systematized and disseminated as the total quality control concept of the 1960s, allowed firms to exploit the technical benefits of Taylorism while avoiding the determined opposition of workers and labor unions. Thus, while remaining consistent with Taylorite imperatives, the Japanese practice of modern management ultimately traced a distinct trajectory of development.

---

the Course of Industrialization (New York: Wiley, 1963); Merkle, Management and Ideology; Maier, "Between Taylorism and Technocracy." An important recent work, following on Bendix, is Mauro Guillen's Models of Management: Work, Authority, and Organization in a Comparative Perspective (Chicago: University of Chicago Press, 1994). Although Guillen downplays the impact of Taylorism and his model fails to account for the Japanese case, his comparative historical approach (which examines the application of management paradigms within specific institutional frameworks) is consistent with the approach adopted here. What this study considers "ideologies of management" corresponds to what Guillen calls "organizational ideologies": "The concept of organizational ideology includes, but is not limited to, a discourse, demagoguery, rhetoric, language, public-relations effort, or sheer talk. Similarly, an organizational ideology is more than a mere creed, philosophy, style, or fad. Managers use organizational ideologies to inform perception and action as well as to justify their authority. Organizational ideologies can serve as cognitive tools that managers use to sort out the complexities of reality, frame the relevant issues, and choose among alternative paths of action" (4).

By figuring the evolution of Japanese industrial management as an ongoing interchange between foreign models and domestic constraints, a long-term process of imitation and innovation, this work seeks to challenge simplistic popular notions of the origins of the Japanese paradigm. Neither culturalist essentialism nor a genius for mimicry can account adequately for the apparent contradictions of contemporary Japanese management. Yet by recognizing the ways in which Japanese practices both derived and deviated from imported Taylorite nostrums, the deadlocked contemporary debate over the categorization of Japanese management—the semantic tangle of hyphenated Fordisms—can be surmounted. As this study will suggest, the Japanese management paradigm must be seen *both* as an evolutionary advance upon classic mass production *and* as a potentially revolutionary departure from the orthodoxy of the American assembly line.

A final word regarding definitions and approach is in order. Stephen Wood and John Kelly have noted perceptively that "The broader one's definition of Taylorism, the more one sees it as all pervasive . . . , while a narrower definition suggests a lesser degree of influence."[19] Students of management history are notoriously—and often calculatingly—vague in their definitions of Taylorism. In much of the historical and sociological literature, aphoristic definitions jostle with conceptions so commodious as to be useless analytically: on one end of the spectrum, Taylorism is synonymous with the separation of planning and execution, while on the other, Taylor's *Principles of Scientific Management* becomes a codex to which virtually all the attributes of modernity can be traced. To some extent, this study follows in the scholarly tradition of ambiguity: by not delineating at the start an explicit normative definition of Scientific Management, it begs charges of manipulative vagueness. Yet by not establishing a rigid taxonomy of what is Taylorite and what is not, by attempting to perceive Scientific Management as its proponents, practitioners, critics, and subjects in Japan have understood it, and by placing the Japanese experience in a broad comparative context, this work seeks to avoid preconceiving Taylorism as straw man (or superman) in the formation of the Japanese management paradigm.

The focus here will not be on the business community, leading industrialists or Japan's high-profile economic federations, the groups which have typically preoccupied scholarly treatments of management issues in Japan. Nor will the emphasis fall on the commercial and financial aspects of corporate management—the usual terrain of business history—or on the roots of the Japanese employment system, which have been meticulously documented by

[19] Stephen Wood and John Kelly, "Taylorism, Responsible Autonomy and Management Strategy," in *The Degradation of Work?* ed. Stephen Wood (London: Hutchinson, 1982), 74. See also Chris Wright, "Taylorism Reconsidered: The Impact of Scientific Management Within the Australian Workplace," *Labour History* 64 (May 1993): 34–53.

labor historians. Instead, the stress will be on production management—the deployment of labor, technology, and resources in the process of manufacturing—and on those individuals directly connected with the production management function: engineers, factory heads, consultants, management experts, and scholars, those to whom the principles of Taylorism had the most immediacy and relevance. Moreover, in a further departure from the standard methodologies of Japanese business historians, this study will deal less with how the methods of modern management were used than with how American managerial models were "sold"—publicized, packaged, and disseminated—to the corporate elite, industrial labor, and the general public.

In short, this book will center on the various broad and active (but little studied) movements to modernize industrial management in twentieth-century Japan. More specifically, it will examine the efforts of those individuals and organizations that were the main interpreters of U.S. management ideas and that most actively propounded the reform of Japanese managerial practice along American lines. By analyzing the rhetorical approaches and ideological constructs arrayed by such reformers—and the ultimate embedding of Taylorite models in Japanese conceptions of production management—the following chapters will testify to the complex and mixed intellectual heritage of the Japanese paradigm. The industrialist Honda Sōichirō reputedly once remarked that Japanese management and American management are 95 percent the same, yet different in all important respects. As it recharts the history of Taylorism in Japan, this study will reveal just how illuminating Honda's observation can be in discerning the origins, evolution, and implications of "Japanese-style management."

1

The Introduction of Taylorism and the Efficiency Movement, 1911–1927

As SCHOLARS have long appreciated, habits of industriousness have deep roots in Japanese society. During the Tokugawa period (1603–1868), attention to questions of productive efficiency was widespread, both in the predominant agrarian sector and in the preindustrial craft economy. Japanese peasants were keen managers of time and resources, and rural prophets of productivity (like Ninomiya Sontoku) enjoined the farming populace to be thrifty, methodical, and proficient. Tokugawa handicraft production displayed a similar penchant for economy, and was characterized by a sophisticated division of labor, exacting quality standards, and refined, specialized technology.[1] In the decades after the Meiji Restoration of 1868, as Japan was rapidly propelled into the ranks of the world's industrial powers, these traditional patterns were readily and fruitfully aligned with a new socioeconomic order. At the same time, systematic learning from Western models was central to Japan's modern transformation: in the Meiji drive for *fukoku kyōhei* ("rich nation, strong army"), the technological achievements, organizational forms, and ideological constructs of the industrial West were feverishly studied and earnestly emulated. Thus long-standing preoccupations with productivity and empiricism came to complement and support Japan's newfound determination to master the secrets of modern industry.

Seen in this context, early twentieth-century Japan would appear to have been fertile ground indeed for the introduction of Scientific Management. Yet the dominant historical narratives of Japanese industrial management, conveniently overlooking the Tokugawa passion for efficiency and the Meiji experi-

---

[1] Susan Hanley describes Tokugawa Japan as a "resource-efficient culture": "In Japan the seventeenth-century peak of prosperity was accompanied by rapid population growth and pressure on resources, leading to an affluence that not only made the most of scarce resources, but also made a virtue of necessity and continued a form of luxury in austerity." Susan Hanley, *Everyday Things in Premodern Japan: The Hidden Legacy of Material Culture* (Berkeley: University of California Press, 1997), 58. On agriculture, see Thomas Smith, *Native Sources of Japanese Industrialization, 1750–1920* (Berkeley: University of California Press, 1988), esp. chap. 8, "Ōkura Nagatsune and the Technologists," and chap. 9, "Peasant Time and Factory Time in Japan." On craft production, see Tessa Morris-Suzuki, *The Technological Transformation of Japan* (Cambridge: Cambridge University Press, 1994), chap. 2. On the development of scientific thought in Tokugawa Japan, see James Bartholomew, *The Formation of Science in Japan* (New Haven, Conn.: Yale University Press, 1989), chap. 2.

ence of institutional learning, suggest that Taylorism's alien sensibilities thwarted its penetration of Japanese factories. Instead, elaborate schemes of corporate paternalism, emotive familial rhetoric, and the arbitrary exercise of management authority—practices often figured as the cultural residue of other aspects of Japan's preindustrial past—are usually taken to characterize Japanese management throughout the prewar period. Nevertheless, the introduction of Taylorite methods and ideological axioms was crucial to the evolution of Japanese management during the 1910s and 1920s. Over what has been tagged the "era of proselytization," the "germination period of Scientific Management," and, perhaps most aptly, the "age of efficiency,"[2] Taylorism was elaborated, debated, and in many cases championed by Japanese businessmen, academics, and bureaucrats. Furthermore, although the process of Taylorism's diffusion and integration in Japanese industry was distinctive, by the time of the Great Depression, the impact of Scientific Management in Japan was comparable in extent and in form to its influence in the United States and Europe.

Industrial Management in Japan before Taylor

The organization of the work process and the management of labor in the pre-Taylor Japanese factory and the pre-Taylor American factory were remarkably similar. As Andrew Gordon has noted, Japanese and U.S. shop-floor labor arrangements seem to have resembled each other more in the nineteenth century than they did in the 1950s.[3] In the modern heavy industries of Meiji Japan—shipbuilding, munitions, metals—production was based on an indirect system of management: company managers contracted for intermediate goods with semiautonomous, skilled foremen (*oyakata*) who held broad authority over the pace and methods of work as well as the employment conditions and training of subordinate workers. To the nineteenth-century Japanese manager (as to his American counterpart), there were few if any alternatives to this indirect structure of control: operating at a low level of mechanization and lacking a large cadre of trained technical personnel, he could not avoid depending on the individual abilities of traditional skilled workers.[4]

[2] Hōchi shinbun keizaibu, *Nōritsu zōshin jidai* (Chikura shobō, 1930).

[3] Andrew Gordon, *The Evolution of Labor Relations in Japan: Heavy Industry, 1853–1955* (Cambridge, Mass.: Harvard University Press, 1985), 413. On management practices in the Meiji textile industry, see E. Patricia Tsurumi, *Factory Girls: Women in the Thread Mills of Meiji Japan* (Princeton, N.J.: Princeton University Press, 1990), esp. 241–54.

[4] On the U.S. case, see Daniel Nelson, *Frederick W. Taylor and the Rise of Scientific Management* (Madison: University of Wisconsin Press, 1980), 4–10; on Japan, Nishinarita Yutaka, *Kindai Nihon rōshi kankeishi no kenkyū* (Tokyo daigaku shuppankai, 1988), 23–31; Gordon, *Evolution,* 38–46; Chokki Toshiaki, *Nihon no kigyō keiei* (Hōsei daigaku shuppankai, 1992), 84–89.

The weaknesses of the *oyakata* system from the managerial perspective are obvious: as Gordon has succinctly put it, "Indirect management was inefficient."[5] When dealing with multiple foremen, coordination was difficult and the attainment of uniform quality problematic; lack of managerial knowledge regarding the work process frustrated efforts to systematize operations; technical advances were hindered by the dominance of rule-of-thumb methods; decentralized control over labor engendered divisive variations in worker treatment and remuneration. Management dissatisfaction with the *oyakata* system grew most acute during periods of rapid economic growth (such as the late Meiji war booms) and when new technology was being introduced. At Hitachi, for example, one observer lamented that "while some departments were frantically busy, other departments had nothing to do," even when the order books were full.[6] At Oki Electric, "Differences in the speed of production [of the various *oyakata* groups] were common. Errors also cropped up because gauges and jigs [templates used to ensure uniform assembly] were all homemade. In the case of something like a telephone switching apparatus, which had to pass through dozens of processes and was fabricated from hundreds of individual components, a delay in one gang could cause an entire unit to go unfinished and an error in the production of a single component could cause the whole machine to malfunction."[7]

As early as the 1890s, however, managers in some industries began to extend their direct control over the production process and employment conditions. As the government's landmark labor survey *Shokkō jijō* (The Conditions of Factory Workers) reported in 1902, "the advance of the division of labor is gradually leading to the eradication [of internal contracting] from the current factory system."[8] Writing in 1910, noted social commentator Yokoyama Gennosuke confirmed the trend away from *oyakata* "workers' control": "These days it's hard to find any old-style foremen, either in the arsenals or in any other machine shops. As a result of this decline in *oyakata,* the factory owner-foreman-worker style of employment relationship has all but disappeared, replaced by a new, one-to-one relationship between the owner and the employees."[9] In most firms, the dismantling of the *oyakata* system began with the assertion of management control over wages and worker evaluation, and ended with the integration of the once independent foremen into managerial hierarchies. The introduction of new production technologies and the rise of a

    [5] Gordon, *Evolution,* 51.

    [6] Sugayama Shinji, "The Bureaucratization of Japanese Firms and Academic Credentialism: A Case Study of Hitachi, Ltd.," *Japanese Yearbook on Business History: 1991* (Tokyo: Japan Business History Institute, 1991), 76.

    [7] Chokki, *Kigyō keiei,* 91.

    [8] Quoted in Okuda Kenji, *Hito to keiei: Nihon keiei kanrishi kenkyu* (Manejimento-sha, 1985), 31.

    [9] Quoted in Hyōdō Tsutomu, *Nihon in okeru rōshi kankei no tenkai* (Tokyo daigaku shuppankai, 1971), 253.

new class of manager-technicians conversant with them were critical to this transformation in factory organization. As Morikawa Hidemasa has demonstrated, the assertion of direct control in the workplace was paralleled by the rapid ascent of "professional" managers and engineers, that is to say, those trained in universities or higher schools.[10] This dynamic and its implications for industrial progress were obvious to contemporary observers as well. One Japanese National Railways technician recalled that "when I was appointed to my post [in 1908] there were just a few school graduates on the staff. Management of the shop floor was entrusted to foremen. After that time, though, school graduates gradually took over that role, the factory finally got rid of the old system and we came to see rapid advances."[11]

Between the turn of the century and the 1920s, and particularly in the decade following the Russo-Japanese War, the *oyakata* system was largely eliminated from Japan's modern industries.[12] As had been the case in the United States several decades earlier, this spread of direct managerial responsibility over factory work provided a powerful stimulus to the development of systematic approaches to labor and production management. The swelling ranks of professional middle managers and technicians required suitable methodologies and ideologies to guide them in their newly established duties. Corporate bureaucratization and the decline of internal contracting were, however, not the only factors spurring interest in management ideas during the first decades of the twentieth century. The prolonged debate over the Factory Law and its phased implementation (beginning in 1916) created considerable interest in managerial methods for maintaining international competitiveness under the new legislation's restrictions.[13] Economic downturns—notably those following the Russo-Japanese War, the 1912–14 "Imperial Mourning" slump, and the sharp "Panic of 1920"—also stimulated business interest in management techniques, especially those designed to bolster profits by reducing costs. Not least, a surge in labor unrest after the Sino-Japanese War and the stirrings of an organized labor movement in the 1910s placed pressure on factory managers to reconsider their handling of workers and seek a systematic, managerial response to the "labor problem."[14]

---

[10] Morikawa Hidemasa, *Nihon keieishi* (Nihon keizai shinbunsha, 1981), chaps. 2 and 3. See also Uchida Hoshimi, "Gijutsusha no zōka, bunpu to Nihon no kōgyōka," *Keizai kenkyū* 39, no. 4 (October 1988): 289–97.

[11] Quoted in Okuda, *Hito to keiei,* 34.

[12] The process did not advance uniformly through all sectors and in all firms, however. Internal contracting was eliminated from Hokkaidō Colliery in 1893, Shibaura Manufacturing in 1900, Mitsubishi Nagasaki Shipyard in 1908, and Oki Electric in the mid-1920s. See Chokki, *Kigyō keiei,* 89–92.

[13] Taira Koji, "Factory Legislation and Management Modernization during Japan's Industrialization, 1886–1916," *Business History Review* 44, no. 1 (Spring 1970): 84–109.

[14] Andrew Gordon, *Labor and Imperial Democracy in Prewar Japan* (Berkeley: University of California Press, 1991), chap. 3. Okuda, *Hito to keiei,* 42–50. For the experience at Toyoda Loom,

Thus, when accounts of the Taylor System first began to appear in Japan in 1911—the same year as the publication of *The Principles of Scientific Management*—a receptive audience already existed. Although it can hardly be denied that the subsequent spread of Taylorism was, as Nakase Toshikazu has characterized it, "rapid" and "sensational,"[15] it would be hasty to conclude that 1911 marked the start of the "modernization" of Japanese factory management, or even of the importation of American administrative methods. Indeed, as the decline of the *oyakata* system indicated, efforts to rationalize the production process and systematize employment relationships in Japan antedated the introduction of Taylorism by a decade or more in some cases. American models figured to a considerable extent in these early management initiatives. At Nippon Electric, for example, a functionally differentiated management structure was in place by 1909 and, as was the custom in U.S. factories at the time, officials called "tracers" were appointed to coordinate the flow of production.[16] American premium wage systems were also well known and widely used, even before the turn of the century. Kanda Kōichi's *Jissen kōjō kanri* (Practical Factory Management), published in 1912 and regarded as the first comprehensive work on business administration in Japan, contained detailed descriptions and evaluations of the Rowan and Halsey systems as well as Taylor's differential piece rate.[17] In short, just as Taylorism in the United States was built on the foundations of the "systematic management" movement, so in Japan its "sensational" introduction was prefaced by a variety of managerial efforts to restructure the industrial workplace.[18]

Preaching the Taylorite Gospel

The early days of what might well be called Japan's first "management boom" are rather murky, although Taylorism's first missionary seems to have been one Ikeda Tōshirō, a journalist and sometime employee of Wrigley Chewing Gum's Japan branch. In 1911, Ikeda returned from a tour of the United States and published a series of articles on Taylorism in the *Sakigake shinbun*. Their

where in 1907 an American engineer named Charles Francis standardized workshop routines and instituted a system for manufacturing interchangeable parts, see William Mass and Andrew Robertson, "From Textiles to Automobiles: Mechanical and Organizational Innovation in the Toyoda Enterprises, 1895–1933," *Business and Economic History* 25, no. 2 (Winter 1996): 8–9.

[15] Nakase Toshikazu, "The Introduction of Scientific Management in Japan and its Characteristics," in *Labor and Management,* ed. Nakagawa Keiichirō, Proceedings of the Fourth International Conference on Business History (Tokyo: University of Tokyo Press, 1977), 173.

[16] Chokki, *Kigyō keiei,* 86–88.

[17] Gordon, *Evolution,* 45; Kanda Kōichi, *Jissen kōjō kanri* (Kōbunkan, 1912). On American incentive wage schemes, see Nelson, *Frederick W. Taylor,* 14–16.

[18] See Daniel Nelson, "Scientific Management in Retrospect," in *A Mental Revolution: Scientific Management since Taylor,* ed. Nelson (Columbus: Ohio State University Press), 7.

popularity inspired Ikeda to write a longer introduction to the new management methods, which he entitled *Mueki no tesū o habuku hiketsu* (The Secrets of Eliminating Wasted Work) and had privately printed in January 1913. Ikeda's account was a far from perfect elaboration of Taylor's ideas. In fact, being recounted in a narrative and somewhat didactic style, it resembled the Horatio Alger stories and Meiji "success literature" more than *The Principles of Scientific Management*.[19] Nevertheless, Ikeda's folksy tale of a boy named Tarō and his battle against "soldiering" and waste was an instant bestseller. The pamphlet is said to have sold 1.5 million copies, with Iwasaki Hisaya reputedly distributing 20,000 copies to his employees at Mitsubishi Gōshi, and Matsukata Kōjirō providing over 50,000 to the workers at Kawasaki Shipbuilding.[20]

Others soon followed in Ikeda's footsteps. Hoshino Yukinori, an official of the Kajima Trust Bank who traveled through North America in 1910–11, secured Taylor's permission and published a Japanese translation of the *Principles* in mid-1913. Hoshino proclaimed in his preface that "A great revolution in work has recently swept through the United States, from the shop floor to the front office. This has come from the application of what is known as Scientific Management."[21] Translations of Frank Gilbreth's *Motion Study* and Taylor's *Shop Management* appeared in short order and accounts of American managerial advances came to figure prominently in Japan's nascent business press.[22] As early as 1915, one observer could write that the term "efficiency increase" (*nōritsu zōshin*), which in Japan as in America was closely tied to the ideas of Scientific Management, "has lately become an expression much in vogue."[23]

Despite the faddish air that surrounded its introduction, Taylorism continued to attract considerable attention through the economic boom of the First World War, and even in the bust which followed. The spread of instruction in Scientific Management in Japanese universities and technical schools gave

[19] On the Meiji "success literature," see Earl Kinmonth, *The Self-Made Man in Meiji Japanese Thought* (Berkeley: University of California Press, 1981). For selections from Ikeda's work, see Katō Takabumi, ed., *Nihon keiei shiryō taikei 3: Soshiki, gōrika* (San-ichi shobō, 1989), 49–50.

[20] Nakase, "Scientific Management," 172; Ueno Yōichi, ed., *Nōritsu handobukku,* 3 vols. (Dōbunkan, 1939), 1:70. The reception given to Ikeda's pamphlet by the workers is not recorded, though in at least one case the effect of reading Tarō's story was formative. Inoue Yoshikazu, an employee at Kawasaki in 1913, was so taken with the new management ideas that he dedicated himself to the study of the American methods. Inoue later became a prominent proponent of Scientific Management in Japan and a leader in the efficiency movement in the Osaka area.

[21] Frederick Winslow Taylor, *Gakuriteki jitsugyō kanrihō,* trans. Hoshino Yukinori (Sūbunkan, 1913), translator's preface, 1.

[22] Okuda, *Hito to keiei,* 56. *Jitsugyōkai* (Business World), for example, published several special issues on Scientific Management, while Ikeda became a columnist for the journal *Daiyamondo* (Diamond).

[23] Morito Tatsuo, "Kagakuteki kanrihō no shakai seisakuteki kachi," pt. 1, *Kokka gakkai zasshi* 30, no. 11 (1916): 77.

one indication of the deepening of interest in the American techniques. Lectures on the Taylor System were given at Tokyo University from 1919, while Kanda Kōichi taught classes in modern factory management at the Tokyo College of Commerce and Keiō University in 1921 and 1922. A 1925 study reported that Scientific Management courses had been or were being offered at eight technical and commercial colleges, eight higher commercial schools, and more than seventy-five vocational schools (*jitsugyō gakkō*).[24] Public lecture series and seminars on the philosophy and methods of efficiency were also common, some drawing hundreds and even thousands of participants.[25] An "efficiency exposition" (*nōritsu tenrankai*) held in Osaka in 1924 featured dozens of displays on the new management practices and is said to have attracted 98,000 visitors, half again as many as attended a similar 1914 event in New York.[26] Short courses for the training of personnel able to advise firms on the application of Scientific Management methods also proliferated, especially in the Kansai region. In 1923 and 1924 alone, over four hundred of these "efficiency engineers" (*nōritsu gishi*) graduated from a series of sessions held in Osaka and funded by local business leaders. Study groups, research associations, and roundtables dedicated to modern management and efficiency flourished in the years immediately following World War I as well, with five organized groups (totaling over five hundred members) recorded in 1925 in Tokyo alone.[27]

Prior to the 1920s, the dissemination of information on Scientific Management in Japan was left mainly to journalists and those like Ikeda and Hoshino who had firsthand knowledge of American practices. Corporate engineers and managers subsequently came to lead the promotion efforts, although interest in advanced management methods also spread rapidly in the fledgling field of psychology. Several of Taylorism's strongest proponents came to it from that perspective, notably Ueno Yōichi, an energetic and eccentric individual who would later be tagged the "father of efficiency" and the "Taylor of Japan." Ueno received a degree in psychology from Tokyo Imperial University in 1908 and played an important role in introducing the work of Dewey, Binet, and Freud to Japan before turning his attention to the question of efficiency. During the 1910s and 1920s Ueno was Japan's most insistent advocate of Taylorism, and it was largely through his initiative and under his leadership that the early mania for Taylorism eventually developed into a wide-ranging,

---

[24] Ueno Yōichi, ed., *Sangyō nōritsu kenkyū ni kansuru naigai no jōkyō* (Sangyō nōritsu kenkyūjo, 1925), 98–106.

[25] Osaka furitsu sangyō nōritsu kenkyūjo, *Nōken 50-nen shi* (Osaka: Sangyō nōritsu kenkyūjo, 1976), 21–22.

[26] *Nōritsu tenrankai shi* (Osaka: Nōritsu tenrankai sōmubu, 1924); Samuel Haber, *Efficiency and Uplift: Scientific Management in the Progressive Era* (Chicago: University of Chicago Press, 1994), 60.

[27] Ueno, *Sangyō nōritsu kenkyū*, 109–12.

structured, and lasting movement for the promotion of Scientific Management.[28]

Interestingly, the spread of the Taylorite gospel received relatively little direct support from the Japanese state, at least until the late 1920s. Although government-owned enterprises were among the pioneers in the implementation of Scientific Management and their engineers and managers were often vocal proselytizers, the state sponsored no organized, long-term efforts to promote and publicize modern management techniques. An Efficiency Section (Nōritsu-ka) was formed in 1920 in the Ministry of Agriculture and Commerce, with the original intention of underwriting lecture and consulting tours by American managerial experts. Among its staff was Yoshino Shinji, who later in the decade would be one of the architects of Japan's rationalization movement. The department was short-lived, however, and no consultants were invited, as it was decided that the scale of Japanese industry was still too small for the wholesale introduction of Scientific Management.[29] Extensive efficiency research did occur in the Ministry of Communications from an early date, with officials in the Deposits Bureau and the Post Office investigating work design, psychological testing, and labor fatigue.[30] The results of these studies were not widely publicized, however, and as with the other direct government initiatives prior to the Depression, had a limited impact on the management reform movement.

The government's indirect role in the early promotion of Taylorism was probably more significant that its direct one. Between 1896 and 1916, for example, the Ministry of Agriculture and Commerce sponsored six hundred overseas fellowships for training personnel in the practical skills of Western commerce and industrial technology.[31] Over two hundred of these recruits were dispatched to the United States, among them Katō Shigeo (who apprenticed in American machine shops and subsequently introduced the Taylor System into Niigata Ironworks) and Araki Tōichirō (who studied at the University

[28] Ueno Yōichi, *Ueno Yōichi den,* ed. Misawa Hitoshi (Sangyō nōritsu tanki daigaku, 1967); Saitō Takenori, *Ueno Yōichi—hito to gyōseki* (Sangyō nōritsu daigaku, 1983); William M. Tsutsui, "The Way of Efficiency: Ueno Yōichi and Scientific Management in Twentieth-Century Japan," *Modern Asian Studies* (forthcoming).

[29] Ueno, *Nōritsu handobukku,* 1:71; Takahashi Mamoru, *"Kagakuteki kanrihō" to Nihon kigyō* (Ochanomizu shobō, 1994), 69, 82–83.

[30] Hugo Munsterberg's *Psychology and Industrial Efficiency,* for example, was translated in 1915 by a member of the Deposits Bureau's General Affairs Section who was studying psychological selection of workers and improved methods for using the abacus. Wakabayashi Yonekichi conducted fatigue research and work study in the Post Office and was a noted commentator on Taylorism in the 1920s.

[31] Sasaki Satoshi, "Scientific Management Movements in Pre-War Japan," in *Japanese Yearbook on Business History: 1987,* ed. Yasuoka Shigeaki and Morikawa Hidemasa (Tokyo: Japan Business History Institute), 55.

of Akron and ultimately became one of Japan's most influential management consultants). In fact, a large proportion of the leaders of the efficiency movement had formative experiences in the United States and not a few, like Katō, returned to Japan with trunkloads of the most recent materials on factory management. Muramoto Fukumatsu, one of the staunchest academic proponents of Taylorism, boasted of being the first Japanese graduate of Harvard Business School. Godō Takuo and Yamashita Okiie, engineers in state-owned factories and later leaders of the Scientific Management movement, both considered visits to advanced American workshops as turning points in their professional careers. Ueno, who toured Taylor's Philadelphia estate in 1927, even reported being "deeply moved" by the experience of sitting at Taylor's desk and viewing his private bathroom.[32]

The stream of Japanese engineers and managers that flowed through American factories and universities in the 1910s and 1920s was only one aspect of the web of connections which Japanese Taylorites formed with their Western counterparts. American management luminaries were frequent visitors to Japan in the 1920s: Carl Barth toured in 1924 and lectured to a crowd of one thousand at the Osaka Efficiency Exposition; in 1929, Harrington Emerson visited as a guest of the South Manchurian Railway and King Hathaway as a consultant for Mitsubishi Electric. In the same year, the World Engineering Congress was convened in Tokyo and papers on Scientific Management were delivered by Lillian Gilbreth and Francesco Mauro, chairman of the Comité International de l'Organisation Scientifique. Japanese delegates attended the 1925 International Management Congress in Brussels and the 1927 Geneva International Economic Conference, both of which focused on the dissemination and implementation of Scientific Management methods.[33] On his two trips to America, Ueno Yōichi met most of the notables of the U.S. movement and attended meetings of the Taylor Society, whose Japanese branch he founded in 1925. In short, over the course of the 1920s, Japanese advocates of Taylorism and Japan's drive for efficiency were increasingly closely tied to the international Scientific Management movement.[34]

The trend toward internationalization was only one of several tendencies which became more pronounced as the modern management movement began

---

[32] Ueno, *Ueno Yōichi den,* 100–105. On corporate-sponsored missions to the United States and Europe to study modern technology and management methods, see Fukasaku Yukiko, *Technology and Industrial Development in Pre-war Japan: Mitsubishi Nagasaki Shipyard 1884–1934* (London: Routledge, 1992), 51–55, 153–61.

[33] Sasaki Satoshi, "Tokyo bankoku kōgyō kaigi ni okeru kagakuteki kanri mondai," *Meiji daigaku daigakuin kiyō* 22, no. 6 (February 1985): 129–41.

[34] On the international movement, see Judith Merkle, *Management and Ideology: The Legacy of the International Scientific Management Movement* (Berkeley: University of California Press, 1980). For a contemporary perspective provided by one of Taylor's American disciples, see Horace King Hathaway, "Scientific Management in Japan," *Bulletin of the Taylor Society* 14, no. 4 (August 1929): 182–86.

to mature and grow more structured after World War I. The most significant of these was a rift that developed between two groups of Scientific Management proponents who had entered the movement with different backgrounds, had different perspectives on Taylorism, and ultimately came to stress different aspects of its message. The distinction between the two camps was subtle through most of the Taishō period (1912–26), although the split grew more obvious during the 1920s before coming to a head in the rationalization movement of the early 1930s.[35] On one side stood what might be labeled the "practical" stream or the "technicians," those advocates of U.S. methods who had direct experience organizing the shop floor or handling machinery and who thus approached Taylorism as active practitioners of factory management. For the most part, these individuals were engineers or professional managers in large private firms and government-owned enterprises, which were most suited for the application of Taylorism and where its methods were applied most quickly. Kanda Kōichi was the first of these "practical" advocates of Scientific Management to gain prominence as a managerial expert, although many followed—notably Yamashita Okiie, Godō Takuo, Katō Shigeo, and Katō Takeo—and they would eventually come to form the mainstream of the drive to modernize Japan's industrial management.

While the pragmatic stream tended to emphasize the technical aspects of Scientific Management (such as work study, standardization, and systematic planning), the other wing of the modern management movement took a more eclectic approach to Taylorism. Fastening onto the concept of "efficiency" rather than the methodological specifics of the Taylor System, these advocates sought "efficiency increase" (*nōritsu zōshin*) not only in business administration but in all aspects of day-to-day life and social intercourse. Ueno Yōichi summed up this holistic approach: "It goes without saying that the principles of Scientific Management should be spread widely, into individual households and through all areas of national society."[36] Dedicated to the popularization of Taylorite ideas and the spread of the gospel of efficiency, this stream—perhaps best tagged the "efficiency experts"—spoke more to the general public and to small businessmen than to trained engineers and corporate functionaries. Comprising a variety of individuals—self-styled management consultants, educators, journalists, and, most prominently, Ueno and his disciples—the "efficiency experts" attracted considerable attention, especially in what Ueno called their "high tide" between 1923 and 1926.[37]

To a large extent, the divide that appeared in the Japanese Scientific Management movement paralleled a rift which characterized its American counter-

[35] Sasaki Satoshi and Nonaka Izumi, "Nihon in okeru kagakuteki kanrihō no dōnyū to tenkai," in *Kagakuteki kanrihō no dōnyū to tenkai—sono rekishiteki kokusai hikaku,* ed. Hara Terushi (Kyōto: Shōwadō, 1990), 246–47.

[36] Ueno, *Nōritsu handobukku,* 1:14.

[37] Ibid., 1:75.

part. Although the mainstream of American Taylorism was solemnly led by Taylor's colleagues, industrialist supporters of the Taylor Society, and professional engineers, a vigorous "efficiency craze" raged in the United States from 1910 to World War I.[38] The work of Ueno and the "efficiency experts" was just beginning to wax as the American craze was on the wane, yet its Japanese proponents came to absorb much of the spirit and many of the ideas of their U.S. predecessors. Ueno earnestly subscribed to virtually every efficiency fad: he owned (and very soon junked) one of the first electric cars in Japan, he was a staunch advocate of writing simplification and the use of arabic numerals, and was a strict practitioner of Fletcherism, a nutritional regimen premised on the extended mastication of food.[39] Ueno was not alone in his obsessions, however. Serious studies were conducted on the most efficient arrangements for kitchens, the most efficient golf swing, and the "one best way" in pearl diving.[40] Although in Japan, as in America, the mania for efficiency was relatively short-lived—eventually being subsumed by the industrialists' and technicians' view of Scientific Management—its contribution to the dissemination of Taylorism and its role in enriching Scientific Management's message were considerable.

Whether "technicians" or "efficiency experts," advocates of Taylorism in Japan were highly dependent on U.S. and European literature for their philosophies and methodologies. In 1940, Andō Yaichi, an expert on clerical work and former employee of Niigata Ironworks, wrote caustically that "the period from the introduction of Scientific Management into our country up to now should be called the 'age of translated mimicry' [honyakuteki mohō jidai]."[41] Indeed, through the 1910s and 1920s the air of "literal translation" was strong: not only were many published accounts of Scientific Management direct renderings of Western tracts, but a number of reputedly original texts were nothing more than paraphrases of foreign management literature.[42] In addition, much of the early Japanese writing on Taylorism was strong on rhetoric and light on substance. Regarding Taylorism as a newly uncovered secret of America's conspicuous economic success, Japanese observers had high, often exaggerated, expectations for the new methods. One Finance Ministry bureau-

[38] Haber, *Efficiency and Uplift.*

[39] Ueno, *Ueno Yōichi den,* 125, 149.

[40] Perhaps the greatest publicity for the Japanese craze was achieved by Araki Tōichirō who, declaring that he sought to further world peace and "give a demonstration of Scientific Management in practice," used modern planning methods to win a 1928 international contest to see how quickly the world could be circled using only public transportation. Araki accomplished the feat in 33 days, 16 hours, 33 minutes, and 29 seconds. Araki Tōichirō, *Nōritsu ichidaiki* (Nihon nōritsu kyōkai, 1971), 23–33.

[41] Andō Yaichi, *Kōjō kaizen—Nihon no kagakuteki kōjō kanri* (Daiyamondo, 1940), 132.

[42] Hazama Hiroshi, for example, contends that 60–70 percent of Kanda Kōichi's *Jissen kōjō kanri* was cribbed from a 1911 American management textbook. Hazama, *Nihon ni okeru rōshi kyōchō no teiryū* (Waseda daigaku shuppanbu, 1978), 38.

crat proclaimed, "I believe that if information about efficiency is disseminated and if at the same time the strengths of the Japanese people are developed, we will stand second to none in economic efficiency just as we do in military efficiency."[43] And Ikeda Tōshirō lamented in 1930 that "ninety-nine out of a hundred people regard Taylor's methods as some sort of specially concocted miracle drug or magic potion. They expect that this sorcery can resuscitate a store or factory that has fallen on hard times due to old-fashioned, wasteful management, transforming it overnight (or at most within a week) into a first-rate, profitable enterprise."[44]

Even if Taylorism could not live up to such inflated expectations, most observers of the 1910s and 1920s recognized the pressing need to improve management methods and instill a spirit of efficiency in Japanese industry. In one commentator's view, "Japan is certainly not well endowed with resources and its population is constantly increasing. . . . How should we extricate ourselves from this dilemma? In my opinion there is no way but to reform our production methods and increase the efficiency of our people."[45] To the majority of Japanese managers, however, nightmares of resource poverty and Malthusian crises were probably not what made the new U.S. methods so compelling. Ikeda spoke for most advocates when he enumerated the four best reasons for adopting Taylorism as increasing profits, satisfying the customer, improving relations with labor, and reducing production costs.[46] To Japanese industrialists, the first and last items of this list were very likely the most persuasive arguments for the adoption of Scientific Management, and accounts of Taylorism in the business press invariably stressed its salutary effects on productivity and profitability. Yet Taylorism was not perceived in Japan as simply another cost-cutting device: Ikeda's third point—Taylorism's implications for factory workers and labor management—was certainly not overlooked by Japanese observers. The founding statement of the Japan Efficiency Association (Nihon Nōritsu Kenkyūkai, the largest of the early efficiency research groups) suggested the attention given to this aspect of the Taylorite message: "This organization aims: (1) to endeavor to reduce production costs, promote the welfare of workers, and strengthen the foundations of our nation's industry through efficiency methods; (2) to investigate theories

[43] Preface by Yabashi Masakichi to *Nōritsu dokuhon,* ed. Uenaka Kōdō (Chūgai sangyō chōsakai, 1926), 8. To many commentators, the debate over industrial efficiency was continuous with the debate over "national efficiency," a turn-of-the-century English obsession with national competitiveness, both economic and military. Japan (with its cult of *bushidō* and its reputedly docile populace) enjoyed a vogue in Britain as a model of this particular conception of efficiency, peaking with the publication of Alfred Stead's *Great Japan: A Study of National Efficiency,* in 1905. See G. R. Searle, *The Quest for National Efficiency* (Oxford: Blackwell, 1971), 57–60.

[44] Ikeda Tōshirō, *Muda seibatsu no hiketsu* (Shūbunkaku shobō, 1930), 221–22.

[45] Preface by Takebe Yoshikazu to Uenaka, *Nōritsu dokuhon,* 9.

[46] Ikeda Tōshirō, *Kagakuteki keieihō* (Jitsugyō no sekaisha, 1923), 137–38.

regarding industrial labor and determine methods for their application. . . ."[47] In fact, Japanese proponents presented Taylorism as being much more than just the latest technique in systematic factory management, highlighting from the very start its promise in alleviating the intensifying "labor problem," both at the factory level and in society as a whole. As Wakabayashi Yonekichi stressed, "Although there are those who see [Scientific Management] as just a convenient tool for capitalists to squeeze the last drop of blood from the workers, they are greatly mistaken."[48]

The Taylorite approach to class reconciliation and the harmonization of workshop labor relations was deceptively simple in outline. As Hoshino Yukinori crisply summarized the Taylorite social gospel, "the employers get greater production, the workers get better wages, and both end up being very contented. In short, if people, motions, time, machinery, and methods are thoroughly researched scientifically, then each person will realize his greatest abilities and will be suitably highly rewarded for them."[49] The promise of industrial efficiency was that increased productivity and lower manufacturing costs could give rise to both high wages for labor and large profits for capitalists. As Taylor stated eloquently in 1912:

> Now, in its essence, scientific management involves a complete mental revolution on the part of the workingman . . . a complete mental revolution on the part of these men as to their duties toward their work, toward their fellow men, and toward their employers. And it involves the equally complete mental revolution on the part of those on the management's side—the foreman, the superintendent, the owner of the business. . . .
>
> The great revolution that takes place in the mental attitude of the two parties under scientific management is that both sides take their eyes off of the division of the surplus as the all-important matter, and together turn their attention toward increasing the size of the surplus until this surplus becomes so large that it is unnecessary to quarrel over how it shall be divided. . . . It is along this line of complete change in the mental attitude of both sides; of the substitution of peace for war; the substitution of hearty brotherly cooperation for contention and strife . . . that scientific management must be developed.[50]

The commonsensical logic of Taylor's vision—that cooperation and science could deliver so much wealth as to make moot the thorny questions of distribution—resonated with Japanese audiences. As in the United States and Europe, the ideal that the factory could be denatured politically, that the pre-

---

[47] Ueno, *Sangyō nōritsu kenkyū,* 109.

[48] Quoted in Okuda, *Hito to keiei,* 127.

[49] Taylor, *Gakuriteki jitsugyō kanrihō,* translator's preface, 2.

[50] "Taylor's Testimony Before the Special House Committee" (1912), in Frederick Winslow Taylor, *Scientific Management* (New York: Harper, 1947), 27–30.

sumed inevitability of capital-labor confrontation could be subverted by the application of Scientific Management, was seductive to many in Japan.

However, as Muramoto Fukumatsu observed, "both the average business-man and the wage worker are completely dubious of the actual compatibility of high wages and low production costs."[51] Cheap labor was widely assumed to be the root of Japan's competitive advantage in international trade, and business interests generally balked at any suggestion of a high-wage strategy, even if larger payrolls were linked with increased labor productivity. Not surprisingly then, questions regarding the distribution of the surplus generated by Taylorite reforms—the "ever-increasing pie" presumed by the "Mental Revolution"—received less rhetorical attention than the appeal for labor-management cooperation. "Harmony" and "cooperation" became keywords of Japan's Scientific Management movement. Ueno Yōichi was a particularly enthusiastic spokesman for this aspect of the "Mental Revolution":

> Cooperation is absolutely necessary in all organizations. In business, success is doubtful without cooperation. If all, from the president down to the lowest function-ary, can pool together their various personal abilities, work together for the common good of the company's prosperity, and devote themselves as a group, then great increases in results are possible. If, however, capitalists live in fear of labor offen-sives, workers label capitalists as the enemy, and there is never anything but quarrel-ing, then the company will decline day by day. Where there is no diligent coopera-tion there is no prosperity.[52]

Ueno's ideas, and the Taylorite ideology from which they were derived, overlapped in many ways with the philosophy of the Kyōchōkai (Harmoniza-tion Society), a think tank founded in 1919 by the state and big business interests, and dedicated to the nurturing of *kyōchōshugi* ("harmonious cooper-ation") in industrial relations. In 1922, Ueno was named head of the organiza-tion's new Industrial Efficiency Institute (Sangyō Nōritsu Kenkyūjo) and charged with disseminating information on Scientific Management methods and the Taylorite philosophy of class reconciliation. As the institute's activ-ities were not well coordinated with the Kyōchōkai's program and the Tay-lorite message did not mesh smoothly with the *kyōchōshugi* "organicist, com-munitarian view of factory and social organization,"[53] the affiliation was severed in 1923.[54] Nevertheless, Ueno and many other Taylorites continued to

[51] Muramoto Fukumatsu, "Horie hakase oyobi Teruoka gakushi no kagakuteki keieihō ni kan-suru hihan o yomite," *Shōgyō oyobi keizai kenkyū* 20 (October 1920): 31.

[52] Ueno Yōichi, *Nōritsugaku genron* (Kihōdō, 1956), 49.

[53] W. Dean Kinzley, *Industrial Harmony in Modern Japan: The Invention of a Tradition* (London: Routledge, 1991), 104.

[54] After 1923, the institute continued operation as an independent research and consulting organization, with Ueno as director and funding provided by Nakayama Taichi, the president of

preach the mutual benefits of labor-management cooperation and the model of the "Mental Revolution" thoughout the interwar period.

As Japanese proponents came to recognize, the "hearty brotherly coopera- tion" Taylor promised was not necessarily spontaneous or organic, and the attainment of a Taylorite paradise of plenty was premised on the mobilization of science in the workshop. In the logic of Scientific Management, the implicit corollary of the harmonization of management and labor interests was the neutrality of science and its acolytes—engineers and modern managers—in industry. Not only was the application of scientific methods essential in the making of an "ever-increasing pie" but, as Japanese and American Taylorites alike affirmed, the objective dictates of science transcended the political di- vides of the shop floor. Ikeda, for example, maintained that "Engineers have a connection with industry above and beyond their official responsibilities. They consequently have a keen understanding of a number of problems in industry and are in the position of always being able to provide impartial and disin- terested advice."[55] According to Kiribuchi Kanzō, "Management [kanri] is a technical intermediary between engineering and the economy, and a social intermediary between capital and the masses."[56] Perhaps most vehement in this regard was Yamashita Okiie, the influential engineer who sponsored Tay- lorism in the National Railways. In words that might have come from Taylor's mouth, Yamashita proclaimed at a 1930 mechanical engineering conference that "we hear a good deal about labor-management harmony [rōshi kyōchō] but there are a great many people who think it isn't of much concern to us engineers [wareware enjinia]. This certainly isn't so. . . . We engineers must understand it. This is, I believe, our greatest mission."[57]

Implementing Scientific Management in Taishō Japan

The "mission" of scientific managers and the actual practice of Taylorism were, of course, not necessarily the same. Nevertheless, the application of Scientific Management in Japanese factories progressed hand in hand with the spread of Taylorite ideas and the "efficiency boom" during the 1910s and 1920s. As a number of contemporary observers recognized, in Japan as in the United States, "there are no workshops where the teachings of Taylor and Gantt have been put into practice exactly."[58] The methods of Scientific Management—even if not

Nakayama Taiyōdō and a major benefactor of the prewar efficiency movement. Kinzley, *Indus- trial Harmony*, 102–5; Ueno, *Ueno Yōichi den*, 107–17.

[55] Ikeda, *Kagakuteki keieihō*, 250.

[56] Kiribuchi Kanzō, "Kagakuteki kanri no jūten to sono dōkō," *Keiei kenkyū* 3, no. 2 (Septem- ber 1934): 48.

[57] "Tōron," *Kikai gakkai shi* 33, no. 163 (November 1930): 703.

[58] Kitazawa Shinjirō, "Kagakuteki kanrihō to rōdōsha," *Kaihō* 4, no. 3 (March 1922): 53. As

the entire technical regimen prescribed by Taylor—were widely utilized, however, particularly in four sectors of industry: state-owned enterprises such as arsenals and the railways; companies having joint ventures or licensing agreements with foreign firms, especially in the electrical machinery industry; large, technologically sophisticated firms, often associated with zaibatsu interests, in the vanguard of modern Japanese industry (including textiles and metals); and small- and medium-sized concerns of various types that engaged the services of "efficiency engineers" and management consultants like Ueno Yōichi and Araki Tōichirō.

The first implementation of Scientific Management in Japanese factories appeared almost simultaneously with Taylorism's debut in the business press. The earliest reforms on the new American model were virtually all directed by Japanese engineers who had closely observed U.S. workshops. Katō Shigeo, for example, apprenticed for over a year at the Tabor Manufacturing Company, one of the most famous "model factories" of Taylorism. On his return to Japan in 1914, Katō drew heavily on this American experience, and his rigorous application of Taylorite labor and production management turned the newly founded Kamata factory of Niigata Ironworks into what many hailed as the most complete example of Scientific Management in practice in the nation.[59] Takeo Toshisuke performed a similar role at Karatsu Ironworks, introducing advanced production methods (originally developed at Stevens Institute of Technology) which he had observed in operation in the United States. Taylorism also began to enter the textile and electrical machinery industries before the First World War: from 1912 to 1915 Mutō Sanji promoted the introduction of Scientific Management methods at Kanegafuchi Spinning, while Nippon Electric, which established the first Japanese-American joint venture in its industry, dispatched technicians to Western Electric factories from as early as 1905.[60]

After the World War I boom, which brought increases in the scale and complexity of production in many industries, a growing number of companies began to experiment with Scientific Management. Taylorite methods spread particularly rapidly among spinning firms, where mechanization and specialization were already highly advanced. Apprehension surrounding the impact of the Factory Law, however, accounted for much of the enthusiasm over

---

Daniel Nelson has noted regarding the United States, "Although the popularity of industrial engineering was due in large measure to the writings of Taylor and other pioneers, few executives took those statements literally or introduced all or most of the changes that Taylor and other industrial engineers advocated. Their customary approach was pragmatic and selective." Daniel Nelson, "Industrial Engineering and the Industrial Enterprise, 1890–1940," in *Coordination and Information: Historical Perspectives on the Organization of Enterprise,* ed. Naomi Lamoreaux and Daniel Raff (Chicago: University of Chicago Press, 1995), 47.

[59] Okuda, *Hito to keiei,* 82–84; Andō, *Kōjō kaizen,* 75–79.

[60] Sasaki, "Scientific Management Movements," 52; Chokki, *Kigyō keiei,* 85.

management reform in the textile sector. The cotton spinners expected to lose the most from the prohibition of night labor for women and minors (scheduled to take effect in 1929) and they sought to prepare themselves for the inevitable rise in labor costs through managerial and technological improvements.[61] Work study began at Tōyō Spinning (Tōyōbō) in 1917; technicians at Nisshin began developing standard motions, unifying measurements and attempting to stabilize quality from 1921; at Kurashiki, Taylorization progressed from 1923, with particular attention to functional organization, "thorough standardization," explicit planning, cost accounting, and a system of "efficiency auditing."[62] In some cases the results were spectacular: at Tōyōbō, for example, it was reported that the elaboration of precise standard motions allowed a worker who had previously tended only a single machine to serve nine simultaneously.[63]

Scientific Management procedures also progressed quickly in the electrical goods sector, where the large number of foreign tie-ups and intense competition during the 1920s promoted high levels of managerial (as well as technical) transfer from the United States. Through General Electric's links with Tokyo Electric and Shibaura Machine Works, Westinghouse's with Mitsubishi Electric, and Siemens's with Fuji Electric, exchanges of engineering personnel and the transplanting of advanced management practices were widespread.[64] Perhaps the most famous example of Taylorization in the Japanese electrical products industry took place at Mitsubishi in the mid-1920s, when elaborate time-and-motion studies were carried out at the company's Kobe works by Katō Takeo (a recent graduate of the Westinghouse apprentices school) and his cousin Noda Nobuo.[65] Significantly, Scientific Management methods appear to have spread broadly through electrical goods manufacturers, even into firms without foreign linkages that championed "self reliance in technology." At Hitachi, for example, Taylorite innovations in shop-floor management organization began in 1919, with standardization, time study,

[61] Takahashi, *"Kagakuteki kanrihō,"* 53–61.

[62] Chokki, *Kigyō keiei*, 118–124.

[63] Okuda, *Hito to keiei*, 92–104.

[64] Yoshida Masaki, "Seisan kanri no keieishi—senzen no jūdenki seisan o chūshin ni," *Keiei shigaku* 5, no. 1 (October 1970): 41–67; Shinomiya Masachika, "Senzen Nihon ni okeru kigyō keiei no kindaika to gaishikei kigyō," *Keiei shigaku* 29, no. 3 (October 1994): 35–72. See also Mark Mason, *American Multinationals in Japan: The Political Economy of Capital Controls 1899–1980* (Cambridge, Mass.: Harvard University Press, 1992), chap. 1.

[65] Sasaki Satoshi, "Mitsubishi denki ni miru kagakuteki kanrihō no dōnyū katei," *Keiei shigaku* 21, no. 4 (January 1987): 29–66; an English-language version of this article has been published as "The Introduction of Scientific Management by the Mitsubishi Electric Engineering Company and the Formation of an Organised Scientific Management Movement in Japan in the 1920s and 1930s," *Business History* 34, no. 2 (1992): 12–27. Sasaki Satoshi, "Shibaura seisakujo ni miru waaren-shisutemu dōnyū no kokoromi," *Keiei shigaku* 30, no. 2 (July 1995): 48–71; Noda Nobuo, "Kagakuteki kanrihō kara seisansei undō e," *Keiei to rekishi* 9 (1986): 4–5.

and wage reform (based on the Taylor and Gantt models) introduced progressively over the next several years.[66]

Despite the accomplishments of the new American methods in private industry, Scientific Management's most celebrated achievements in Taishō Japan occurred in state-run enterprises, specifically in the National Railways (JNR) and the naval arsenals. In the case of the former, the impetus to reform managerial arrangements came from nationalization in 1906 and the subsequent need to assimilate and standardize various technological and organizational approaches. According to Gotō Shinpei, the dynamic first president of the merged railway, "rather than strict adherence to bureaucratic rules, we must emphasize the realization of efficiency."[67] Toward this end, JNR engineers made a close study of American and European management schemes and from the early 1910s, Scientific Management methods were being widely applied in the railway's repair workshops. Specialization of repair facilities, standardization of parts, machinery, and procedures, improved inventory control and record keeping, and, perhaps most importantly, the rationalization of planning and production process control using a "master schedule" based on the Gantt chart[68] all contributed to spectacular increases in productivity. Between 1914 and 1926, for example, the number of man-hours required to overhaul a locomotive declined from over 800 to 350 and the total in-shop time for such servicing was cut from more than a month to less than a week. The JNR gained national and even international acclaim for the speed and efficiency of its repairs. In fact, in 1930, many decades before "Japanese-style management" would be the subject of widespread Western attention, the Soviet railways invited a JNR delegation to advise them on shop management procedures.[69]

Although managerial reform at Japan's state-run arsenals never attracted such worldwide attention, Scientific Management was implemented even more thoroughly there than at the JNR. Kure Naval Arsenal in particular was renowned for the use of Taylorite mass production methods, its "limit gauge" system becoming one of the most influential production management methods in interwar Japan. Scientific Management techniques first entered Kure in about 1915, when navy engineer Saitō Haruchika experimented with time study methods he had learned at Vickers in Britain. Serious efforts at managerial modernization only began in 1919, however, with the government's com-

[66] Sugayama, "Bureaucratization," 78.

[67] Quoted in Okuda, *Hito to keiei*, 64.

[68] The Gantt chart—named for its inventor, the Taylor disciple Henry L. Gantt—was a graphical device used for production scheduling and performance evaluation. See Daniel A. Wren, *The Evolution of Management Thought*, 4th ed. (New York: Wiley, 1994), 137–39.

[69] On Taylorism in the JNR, see Konno Kōichirō, "Kokutetsu kōsaku kōjō ni miru kagakuteki kanri no ayumi," pts. 1–4, *Rōmu kenkyū* 29, nos. 10, 11, 12 (1976), 30, no. 1 (1977); Daitō Eisuke, "Railways and Scientific Management in Japan, 1907–1930," *Business History* 31, no. 1 (January 1989): 1–28; Okuda, *Hito to keiei*, 64–74.

mitment to fleet expansion and the arrival at Kure of Godō Takuo, a veteran engineer just returned from a two-year tour of wartime munitions factories in the United States and Europe. Godō had been greatly impressed by the accomplishments of Taylorism and spent the years from 1919 to 1921 formulating an American-style mass production system for use at Kure. The "limit gauge" system which resulted was in a narrow sense little more than a framework for standardizing measurements and machining tolerances. Looked at more broadly, however, Godō's system called for a revolution in the production process, with provision for accelerated division of labor, centralized planning, stopwatch time study, cost accounting, Gantt chart tracking, and instruction card procedures. Covering the full range of Scientific Management techniques, the "limit gauge" even embraced controversial Taylorite prescriptions like "functional foremanship," a complex organizational program which divided shop-floor administrative duties among a number of specialized overseers. Yet Godō could boast of impressive results. In the manufacture of fourteen-centimeter artillery pieces, for example, costs were cut 30 percent, man-hours were halved, and quality greatly improved. The heyday of the "limit gauge" at Kure was short-lived, however, as cutbacks under the Washington Treaty brought to an end the conditions required for the mass production of heavy armaments. Several key elements of the new production order were scrapped as a result of naval limitation, yet due to Godō's forceful public advocacy of his system, the "limit gauge" model continued to attract the attention of managers through the Second World War.[70]

Although Scientific Management in 1920s Japan appeared mainly in large, highly mechanized factories and was spread primarily by company engineers with overseas experience, Taylorism also flourished in a number of smaller firms which employed "efficiency experts" to rework their managerial methods. The first and most prominent of these Taishō managerial consultants was Ueno Yōichi, who in 1920 agreed to reorganize the Lion Toothpowder Company's chronically inefficient packing department. In Ueno's own retelling:

> The time and motion study was tried by me at the first time in my life, as exactly as it was explained in textbooks of Scientific Management. Side by side with female workers, I myself tried the operation among a pretty cloud of the powder for some time. A plan of improvement hit upon me. I asked the plant manager to lend me 15 of the female workers to see how this plan would work. This was consented. I remember that I could hardly sleep the night before the improved operation would be put into practice, lest I should find what I had studied might prove an academic theory impracticable in [fact].[71]

[70] On Taylorism at Kure, see Konno Kōichirō, "Kure kaigun kōshō ni miru kagakuteki kanri no ayumi," pts. 1–4, *IE* 17, nos. 6, 7, 8, 9 (1975); Saguchi Kazurō, *Nihon ni okeru sangyō minshūshugi no zentei* (Tokyo daigaku shuppankai, 1991), 115–121; Okuda, *Hito to keiei*, 60–64.

[71] Quoted from a speech delivered (and translated) by Ueno in 1953 in Ronald Greenwood and

Through work study, layout reform, and a system of more frequent rest periods, Ueno achieved remarkable cost savings. His success at Lion led to a number of commissions from small- and medium-sized producers of consumer goods (notably Fukusuke Tabi and Nakayama Taiyōdō) and a variety of other enterprises (such as the Osaka Mint and Shirokiya Department Store). Ueno was a tireless self-promoter and his accomplishments in implementing basic Taylorite methods at Lion and Fukusuke came to garner almost as much renown as the elaborate Scientific Management schemes at JNR and Kure.[72]

Several points regarding the process and the results of the implementation of Scientific Management in Japanese industry in the 1910s and 1920s are worth noting briefly. First, there was a significant interchange of information and experience regarding "best method" in modern management, both among private companies and between state enterprises and the private sector in Taishō Japan. Beyond the formal institutions for disseminating new techniques (study groups, research journals, consultancy practices, and so forth), a number of informal, ad hoc means for diffusing managerial expertise—what Tessa Morris-Suzuki has described as "social networks of innovation"—also appeared.[73] For example, large firms which made improvements in production management commonly passed the new techniques on to their subcontractors in the hope of reducing costs, improving quality, or stabilizing the supply of contracted components. This was the case at several of the large electrical goods manufacturers as well as at Kure Arsenal and with the National Railways.[74] Touring managerially advanced factories was also a common practice in the 1920s. The Osaka Efficiency Research Association (Osaka Nōritsu Kenkyūkai), for one, sponsored a number of outings for local businessmen to famous Taylorite workshops throughout Japan.[75] Business organizations also occasionally assumed the role of propagator. The Japan Spinners Association (Dai Nihon Bōseki Rengōkai), for instance, is said to have taken the lead in

---

Robert Ross, "Early American Influence on Japanese Management Philosophy: The Scientific Management Movement in Japan," in *Management by Japanese Systems,* ed. Sang Lee and Gary Schwendiman (New York: Praeger, 1982), 47.

[72] Ueno, *Ueno Yōichi den,* 88–93. Ueno was not Japan's only management consultant, however, as a number of consulting practices were maintained by Japanese proponents of Taylorism before World War II. The most successful of these was the Araki Nōritsu Jimusho, founded in 1923 by Araki Tōichirō, a former subordinate of Ueno at the Kyōchōkai and future round-the-world travel contestant. Working mainly in relatively small firms, though also taking contracts at major manufacturers like Nippon Kōkan and Yokohama Dock, Araki played a significant role in spreading Scientific Management practices directly to the shop floor in interwar Japan. Gordon, "Araki Tōichirō"; Araki, *Ichidaiki,* esp. 11–23.

[73] Morris-Suzuki, *Technological Transformation,* 5–7.

[74] Daitō, "Railways," 20–24; Okuda, *Hito to keiei,* 92.

[75] Inoue Yoshikazu, "Osaka ni okeru nōritsu undō o kaerimite" (1950), in *Kagakuteki kanrihō no dōnyū,* ed. Hazama Hiroshi, Nihon rōmu kanrishi shiryō kashū, vol. 8 (Gosandō shoten, 1987), 18–20.

spreading cost-accounting procedures through the textile industry.[76] Perhaps most intriguing, however, was a web of informal ties, linking practitioners of Scientific Management in large firms and state enterprises, which served as a conduit for advances in managerial methods. Sumitomo Steel, for example, maintained close relations with Kure managers and hired an engineer from the arsenal to advise its managers on Taylorism in 1923. Even more strikingly, Noda Nobuo and Katō Takeo, whose reforms at Mitsubishi Electric drew closely on Kure's "limit gauge" system, were in turn asked to advise JNR engineers in 1929 when the railways embarked on systematic time-and-motion study.[77] Clearly, beneath the media popularization of Scientific Management lay less conspicuous but nonetheless very dynamic informal structures for sharing expertise and exchanging information on Taylorite methods.

Second, as in the United States, some elements of the Taylor System were implemented more extensively and more successfully than others in Japan. Great accomplishments were noted in some areas: functional organization of administrative hierarchies, planning and process control, shop layout, worker selection methods, and, in particular, time-and-motion study.[78] Yet some facets of Scientific Management proved quite problematic. For example, Taylor's functional foremanship was as confusing to Japanese managers as it was to their American counterparts. At Kure it was one of the first of Godō's reforms to be scuttled; at JNR's Ōi Works, Yamashita Okiie implemented the system in 1922, but his successor quickly reverted to the prior arrangements only a year later.[79] Wage systems were also a thorny issue. Although incentive pay systems flourished in the 1920s, both managers and workers showed considerable dissatisfaction with existing American premium plans and methods for determining wage standards. A number of influential models based to varying degrees on American practice were introduced by Japanese proponents of Scientific Management: the Mitsubishi Electric system (using Westinghouse methods and local wage level standards); Godō's proposed Kure wage scheme (combining seniority, skill, and incentive portions); and Araki's

---

[76] Okuda, *Hito to keiei,* 102.

[77] Nakase, "Scientific Management," 186; Konno, "Kokutetsu," pt. 3, 31–32. A detailed account of technological information gathering and sharing is provided in Fukasaku, *Technology and Industrial Development,* chaps. 3–4.

[78] Kiribuchi Kanzō, for example, observed in 1934 that "the value of work study has been widely recognized as a matter of course in Japan for a number of years." Kiribuchi, "Kagakuteki kanri," 53. Suzuki Yoshitaka's statistical studies show that in 1920, out of the 93 firms in Japan with over 1,000 employees, 44 were organized on a "line structure," 27 on a "functional/line" basis, 7 by "production unit," and 15 were functionally departmentalized. By 1940, only 8 out of the 108 firms of such a scale still had a line structure, indicating the spread of functional organization. Suzuki Yoshitaka, *Japanese Management Structures, 1920–1980* (London: Macmillan, 1991), 19–20.

[79] Okuda, *Hito to keiei,* 68. On functional foremanship in the United States, see Daniel Nelson, *Managers and Workers* (Madison: University of Wisconsin Press, 1975), 69.

Yokohama Dock system (a complex blend of "living wage" and incentive considerations).[80] A comprehensive, workable wage system acceptable to both labor and capital remained elusive through the 1920s, and despite much managerial groping for an efficient and balanced approach, there was ultimately no consensus on what wage structure should be adapted to complement the increasingly Taylorized production process in Japan.

Thirdly, as Chokki Toshiaki has concluded, "In Japan the Taylor System was used more for the sake of the maintenance of the firm (rationalization) than for the realization of the mutual goals of labor and capital (high wages and low labor costs)."[81] Chokki's assessment is valid, and even contemporary proponents of Taylorism chided Japanese businessmen for their helter-skelter adoption of Scientific Management methods, their unwillingness to learn about the entire Taylor System, and their cynical use of the new management techniques to increase profits and "sweat" labor.[82] This was, needless to say, largely the case in the United States as well, where despite Taylor's claim to be offering a "partial solution to the labor problem," in actual practice Scientific Management's production techniques were emphasized more than its appeal to the workers.[83]

Although, as noted earlier, many Japanese Taylorites tried to sidestep the materialistic message of the "Mental Revolution," the goal of a "high-wage/low-cost" economy were not scorned by all Japanese business leaders, at least on a philosophical level. In 1921–22, for example, a blue-ribbon group of Japanese industrialists (led by Dan Takuma and including Hoshino Yukinori) toured the United States and England surveying postwar industrial, financial, and labor conditions. After an itinerary that included visits to Westinghouse factories and meetings with Elbert Gary, Herbert Hoover, and Charles W. Eliot, the delegation returned to Japan much impressed by American economic arrangements. The mission's final report fulsomely praised the accomplishments of Scientific Management and U.S. labor-management cooperation and indicated an uncommon receptivity to the "high-wage/low-cost" ideal.[84] Nevertheless, these well-traveled business leaders appear to have been the exception rather than the rule. The managers at Lion Toothpowder were apparently more representative: when Ueno suggested in good Taylorite fashion that a portion of the gains in productivity realized by his

---

[80] Gordon, *Evolution,* 164–72; Minami Manshū tetsudō, *Naichi ni okeru kōjō chingin seidō no chōsa kenkyū* (Minami Manshū tetsudō, 1930); Okuda, *Hito to keiei,* 242–54.

[81] Chokki, *Kigyō keiei,* 128.

[82] See, for example, Noda Nobuo, "Kagakuteki kanrihō to rōdōsha no fukuri," *Shakai seisaku jihō* 41 (February 1924): 48–76.

[83] Haber, *Efficiency and Uplift,* 17.

[84] Sheldon Garon, *The State and Labor in Modern Japan* (Berkeley: University of California Press, 1987), 190–91; Sakai Tokutarō, ed., *Ei-bei hōmon jitsugyōdan shi* (Nihon kōgyō kurabu 11-nen kai, 1926), esp. 588–90.

reforms should be passed on to the workers as higher wages, the management flatly refused.[85]

Overall, it would seem that Scientific Management's career in Japanese factories in the 1910s and 1920s was not as abortive as most observers have concluded.[86] Although some experiments with the new American methods ended in failure, many instances of the successful implementation of Taylorism became widely known and much discussed in the Taishō business community. To suggest that Scientific Management practices were generalized throughout Japanese industry in the Taishō period would certainly be an exaggeration. Through the interwar decades and even well after World War II, the lack of a sufficient scale for mass production in many industries, a lower level of mechanization than in the United States, and, perhaps most importantly, cheaper labor than in North America or Europe all worked against the spread of Scientific Management practices in Japan. Despite these obstacles, Taylorite methods did diffuse through much of modern industry by the 1920s and, in most of the documented cases, the application of Scientific Management was effective in advancing systematic administrative procedures and in reducing the costs of production.

Accurately gauging the degree of Taylorism's impact on Japanese (or indeed on American) industry is almost certainly impossible, however. In a 1917 international survey, for example, Taylor disciple C. Bertrand Thompson recorded more Taylorized firms in Japan than in either Germany or France.[87] The implausibility of this result merely underlines the practical and methodological difficulties of attempting to quantify the diffusion of Scientific Management practices. Nevertheless, from the extensive impressionistic evidence available, it would appear that the employment of Taylorism in interwar Japan was not particularly retarded, abridged, or truncated in comparison to its course in the industrialized West. Especially as business historians have come to scale back their estimates of the scope of Scientific Management's penetration of the American workplace in the 1920s, it seems that the extent of Taylorism's use in Japan was much in line with its progress in U.S. or European workshops.[88]

---

[85] Ueno, *Ueno Yōichi den,* 91.

[86] Nishinarita, *Rōshi kankeishi,* 62; Hazama, *Rōshi kyōchō,* 170; Hazama Hiroshi, *Nihonteki keiei no keifu* (Bunshindō, 1989; originally published 1963), 186–89.

[87] Quoted in Hazama, *Keifu,* 123.

[88] Nelson, "Scientific Management in Retrospect," 5–39; Nelson, "Industrial Engineering," 35–50; Daniel Nelson, "Scientific Management and the Workplace, 1920–1935," in *Masters to Managers,* ed. Sanford Jacoby (New York: Columbia University Press, 1991), 88; David M. Gordon, Richard Edwards, and Michael Reich, *Segmented Work, Divided Workers* (Cambridge: Cambridge University Press, 1982), 146; Stephen P. Waring, *Taylorism Transformed: Scientific Management Theory since 1945* (Chapel Hill: University of North Carolina Press, 1991), 11.

Workers, Intellectuals, and the Question of Taylorism

As David Montgomery has noted regarding the United States, "opposition to Scientific Management spread much faster than did its practice."[89] In Japan, as in America and Europe, the accomplishments of Scientific Management practitioners and the claims of Taylorite proponents engendered immediate and stiff criticism. Indeed, Scientific Management was a focus of intellectual contention and the target of much vitriol throughout the interwar period. As Anson Rabinbach has characterized the European experience—and this can as easily be said of Japan—"the debate *about* the Taylor System was in many ways far more important than the *extent* of its application."[90]

A distinctive aspect of the Japanese reaction to Taylorism in the 1910s and 1920s was the apparent indifference accorded Scientific Management by Japanese workers and labor unions. In the United States and much of Europe, the introduction of Taylorite methods—notably motion study, incentive wage schemes, work specialization and simplification—provoked intense hostility from labor. But while American techniques spread broadly through Japanese industry in the 1920s, only a handful of examples of direct worker opposition to the Taylorization of factory production have been documented. Of the famous "model factories" of Scientific Management, only one appears to have suffered from notable labor unrest prior to 1930: the workers at Niigata Ironworks struck for sixty days in 1923, protesting (among other things) the application of a "scientific" hourly wage system.[91] A short 1916 walkout at Sumitomo Steel also grew out of Taylorite wage reforms, as did a more serious 1927 dispute at the Tsurumi factory of Shibaura Machine Works. Some observers have also argued that the two major strikes at Noda Soy Sauce in the 1920s (including the 1927–28 "great" strike) derived in part from the introduction of Scientific Management production routines.[92] Unorganized resistance to managerial reforms or opposition that did not progress to the point of industrial action was presumably more common than full-blown strikes, yet very little activity of this nature has been documented. Although a number of managers boasted of introducing American techniques without worker criticism, labor dissatisfaction in several recorded cases—such as at Nippon Kōkan and in some shops of the JNR—led to the modification or abandonment of the reform schemes.[93] Although most labor complaints appear to have cen-

---

[89] David Montgomery, *The Fall of the House of Labor* (Cambridge: Cambridge University Press, 1987), 247.

[90] Anson Rabinbach, *The Human Motor* (New York: Basic Books, 1990), 240.

[91] Okuda, *Hito to keiei,* 284–86.

[92] Ibid., 296–306; Gordon, *Evolution,* 175–79; Sasaki, "Shibaura," 67–68; W. Mark Fruin, *Kikkoman* (Cambridge, Mass.: Harvard University Press, 1983), chaps. 5 and 6.

[93] Araki, *Ichidaiki,* 11–23; Shōji Yukihiko, "Sangyō gōrika no sagyō shūdan to rōmu seisaku," *Keizaigaku kenkyū* 33, no. 3 (December 1983).

tered on wage system modifications, resistance was also expressed vehe-
mently in some cases by skilled workers (like those at Tōyōbō in the
mid-1920s) who stood to lose the most under Taylorization.[94]

Nevertheless, impressionistic evidence suggests that Scientific Management did not attract the same widespread worker detestation or strong union
response (either pro or con) which it did in the United States and Europe.
Something of the indifference and ambivalence of Japanese workers and
unionists toward Taylorism is apparent in the writings of Nishio Suehiro, the
prominent social democrat and labor leader, who had his first strike experience representing the employees during the Sumitomo Steel dispute of 1916.
Looking back on the experience Nishio recalled that "the company announced
it was replacing the existing piece-rate system with the Taylor system. The
workers didn't understand the new arrangements very well. They were uneasy
because the wage rate per unit decreased once a certain level of production
had been reached. [After the strike, however,] when they actually gave it a go,
they found the system really wasn't too bad after all."[95]

The reasons for labor's apparently passive attitude toward Taylorization are
by no means obvious, although several factors appear relevant in this regard.
First, historically weak craft organization in Japan allowed Taylorite reforms
to progress with less resistance than in the West, where horizontal linkages
between skilled laborers provided for more effective resistance to the specialization and simplification of factory work. The impression that most direct
resistance to Scientific Management in Japan focused on wage issues rather
than on the reform of the production process or the preservation of craft prerogatives suggests this was the case.[96] Second, Scientific Management does
not appear to have gained a reputation for being a "union-busting" device in
Japan. With a variety of corporate, governmental, and social structures in
place to discourage (and suppress) labor organization, and in the absence of a
widespread, assertive labor movement, Japanese managers did not come to

---

[94] Okuda, *Hito to keiei,* 98–99, 106, n. 26. Not only workers had reason to be suspicious of
Scientific Management. In some cases, managers feared they would lose their authority to new
technical staff, and registered their disapproval. See Morikawa, *Keieishi,* 112–13.

[95] Quoted in Okuda, *Hito to keiei,* 286–87. For an instructive analysis of the response of
Brazilian workers to Scientific Management, see Barbara Weinstein, *For Social Peace in Brazil:
Industrialists and the Remaking of the Working Class in São Paulo, 1920–1964* (Chapel Hill:
University of North Carolina Press, 1996). As Weinstein reveals, Brazilian workers, like their
Japanese counterparts, proved generally receptive to Taylorite ideology.

[96] Gordon, *Evolution,* 22–35; Okuda, *Hito to keiei,* 316–17. According to Okuda, "it can be
said that [Japan's] trade unions traditionally were committed to the 'fostering of a well-disciplined
factory labor force,' the same objective which scientific management was aimed at achieving.
Unlike the craft unions of skilled workers in the advanced Western nations whose basic policy
was to preserve their 'right to a trade,' however, Japanese trade unions directed their efforts
primarily toward improving the worker's lot through various programs designed to increase his
own productivity." Okuda Kenji, "Managerial Evolution in Japan III," *Management Japan* 6, no.
1 (1972): 35.

look upon Taylorism as an offensive weapon in industrial relations. Moreover, it appears that many Japanese Taylorites, who were well aware of the initial union opposition to Scientific Management in America, sought to introduce workshop reforms in an intentionally less contentious fashion.[97]

Third, some scholars have suggested that Japanese workers—exhibiting a distinctive concern with the dignity and social status of their labor—actually considered themselves elevated by the Taylorization of the production system. According to Okuda Kenji, shop-floor employees stood to gain public respect as "modern factory workers" under Scientific Management, while Konno Kōi-chirō has noted that some JNR workers considered it a great honor to be the subject of time-and-motion study.[98] Finally, the possibility that Scientific Management actually delivered on its materialistic promise of high wages must be considered as a source of labor acceptance of Taylorite reforms. As many Japanese proponents bragged (and as Nishio's metalworkers attested), the application of Scientific Management could and sometimes did lead to wage increases. No firm conclusion can be made regarding the extent or validity of such claims—aggregate statistical evidence is ambiguous[99]—yet the possibility that Japanese workers accepted Taylorism for its pecuniary rewards should be acknowledged.

Despite its quiet reception on the shop floor, however, the introduction of Scientific Management did not go unchallenged in Japan. Academics and labor experts were not nearly as muted in their reaction to Taylorism as the factory workers who experienced managerial restructuring firsthand. Four aspects of the new system—its effects on individual workers, its implications for the labor movement, its social consequences, and its claims to be scientific—attracted the most attention from Japanese intellectuals in the 1910s and 1920s.

---

[97] When introducing Scientific Management at Mitsubishi Electric's Kobe factory, for example, Noda Nobuo and Katō Takeo were well aware of local labor tensions and carefully ensured that their new premium wage system would not cause any worker to suffer a decrease in real income. Their extensive reforms were implemented without any reported labor opposition. Sasaki, "Mitsubishi denki," 37–47. Okuda has suggested that worker opposition to Taylorism was stifled: "the function of labor unions to act as a mouthpiece for workers to whom the scientific management system was applied was seriously weakened under the suppressive labor policy of prewar Japan." Okuda Kenji, "Managerial Evolution in Japan I," *Management Japan* 5, no. 3 (1971): 18. Okuda does not, however, present convincing evidence of workers repressing their hostility to Scientific Management.

[98] Okuda, *Hito to keiei,* 318; Konno, "Kokutetsu," pt. 4, 50. See also Okuda Kenji, "Managerial Evolution in Japan II," *Management Japan* 5, no. 4 (1972): 21–22.

[99] According to Nishinarita's figures, wage levels in large firms in heavy industry (where Scientific Management was comparatively advanced) increased steadily over the 1920s, the companies pursuing what Nishinarita describes as a "relatively high wage" policy. Nevertheless, wages in the textile sector (reputed to be Japan's most Taylorized) stagnated over the same period. Nishinarita, *Rōshi kankeishi,* 53–56.

On the first count, Scientific Management's detractors argued that the new American methods ignored the physiological limitations and psychological needs of the laborer, leading unavoidably to the degradation of work and the redoubling of capitalist exploitation. According to Morito Tatsuo, the noted Marxist economist, Taylorism was a "method for squeezing the utmost efficiency from workers under the guise of 'harmony' and 'science.'"[100] Standardization, specialization, and the concentration of technical skills in management were purported to deskill and dehumanize, Taylorism's "theft from the laborers of their knowledge and their experience" leading to a loss of worker autonomy and an enhancement of managerial control over the production process.[101] "Artisans," social commentator Hosoi Wakizō mourned, "have lost forever the joy of creation."[102] With the employers' ability to "drive" workers thus intensified and with work made increasingly tedious by simplification and detailed motion study, critics charged, overwork became the norm and workers were ever more hindered by physical and mental fatigue.[103] The Taylorite future was painted as one of physical degradation and grinding monotony. Horie Kiichi saw "the human being [becoming] just another machine, with no sense of purpose, no powers of imagination or invention, untiringly performing its alloted work, knowing nothing else."[104] As one observer aptly noted, Taylorism "overlooks completely those aspects of 'human nature' that cannot be quantified or predicted."[105]

Critics were thus damning in their estimates of Scientific Management's effects on workers. Kitazawa Shinjirō, a scholar closely associated with the Yūaikai (Friendly Society) labor federation, averred in no uncertain terms that "the principles of Scientific Management have been put forward to bolster the capitalistic economic structure and increase the profits of capitalists . . . [and] have undoubtedly been injurious to workers, not furthering their welfare even one iota."[106] In Taylor's view, of course, labor's aspirations were to be fulfilled and unions were to be rendered unnecessary in the new era of plenty spawned by cooperation in the workplace and the application of scientific methodology. As many observers noted, however, Taylor was conveniently vague on how and by whom the reputedly ever-increasing pie was to be divided. "The prime cause of strikes," Morito explained, "is disputes over how

[100] Morito Tatsuo, "Kagakuteki kanrihō no shakai seisakuteki kachi," pt. 2, *Kokka gakkai zasshi* 30, no. 12 (1916): 109.

[101] Ibid., 111.

[102] Quoted in Okuda, *Hito to keiei*, 327, n. 4.

[103] Isobe Kiichi, "Teiraa shisutemu to sono genkai," pt. 2, *Shōgyō oyobi keizai kenkyū* 47 (September 1927): 182–83; Teruoka Gitō, "'Gōriteki rōdō' no kenchi yori mitaru Taylorism no hihan," *Chūō kōron* 35, no. 5 (May 1920): 35.

[104] Horie Kiichi, "Kagakuteki keieihō to rōdō kumiai," *Mita gakkai zasshi* 14, no. 7 (1920): 96.

[105] Teruoka, "'Gōriteki rōdō,'" 35.

[106] Kitazawa, "Kagakuteki kanrihō," 60.

the surplus produced jointly by workers and capital is to be distributed. There will always be contention surrounding this as long as there is no fair and mutually acknowledged standard for determining the distribution beyond that of social power relationships. . . . If someone were to discover a scientific law regarding the question of distribution, one would have to say that person was a sage who had solved the modern-day 'riddle of the Sphinx.'"[107]

To many commentators, a powerful labor movement offered the only hope of equitable distribution, yet organized labor stood to fare even worse under the new American management regime than individual workers did. Japanese observers were well aware of union opposition to Taylorism in the United States. Many of their negative evaluations of it were in fact based on readings of Robert Hoxie's 1915 report on labor under the Taylor System. Nakatsumi Tomokata, for example, charged that "The laws of Scientific Management are undemocratic" and are "incompatible with and destructive toward" labor unions and collective bargaining. Like a number of others, Nakatsumi recognized that Taylorite reforms of the workplace threatened the foundations of labor strength: "[Scientific Management] wage systems appeal to the profit motive of workers, consequently undermining their moral values as well as their sense of mutual solidarity, and giving rise to antagonisms and jealousy among them."[108]

A number of critics worried that the resentments and hostilities created by the application of Scientific Management to industry would spill over and destabilize the entirety of society. While proponents asserted that Taylorism would pacify not only the workplace but society as a whole, detractors warned that "those who think that we won't need any sort of social policy if we employ [Taylorism] are sorely mistaken."[109] Opponents warned that the implementation of Taylorism and the consequent increases in industrial efficiency would "provoke excess production and cause unemployment. This is the greatest problem of Scientific Management in actual practice."[110] Taylorism, they argued, would lead to the division of the working class, as "first-class men" staffed the Taylorized factories while the vast majority labored in unreformed workshops, if they had work at all.[111] Despite Scientific Management's promise to share the gains of increased productivity with the workers involved, it offered no guarantee that this surplus would trickle down to those workers outside Taylorized concerns. At any rate, the critics stressed, Scientific Management offered no equitable, "scientific" formula for distributing

---

[107] Morito, "Kagakuteki kanrihō," pt. 2, 102.

[108] Nakatsumi Tomokata, "Kagakuteki kanrihō ni taisuru gensei hihan," *Kokka gakkai zasshi* 36, no. 2 (1922): 130. See also Horie, "Kagakuteki keieihō"; Muramoto Fukumatsu, "Horie hakase," 29–33.

[109] Morito, "Kagakuteki kanrihō," pt. 2, 113.

[110] Nakatsumi, "Kagakuteki kanrihō," 131.

[111] Morito, "Kagakuteki kanrihō" pt. 2, 99–100.

gains, even to the "first class" workers. As Morito put it, "The argument of efficiency experts that a greatly increased surplus is the finish line in the search for a solution to social problems is greatly mistaken. In fact, the creation of a surplus is the starting point in the appearance of social problems. Scientific Management, however, provides no firm and disinterested scientific methodology for distributing the surplus. Even under these new managerial methods, then, current social problems (which derive from problems in distribution) are likely to continue."[112]

In prewar Japan, as in most industrializing societies, appeals to "science" were rhetorically potent and ideologically charged. As a result, Japanese critics of Taylorism repeatedly railed against its bold claims to scientific neutrality and exactitude. After deriding Taylorites for their lack of a "fair and disinterested" methodology for sharing the spoils of increased efficiency, Morito warned that "Under the current power relationships in society, the 'colorless' managerial methods propounded by the efficiency experts are actually tinged with a capitalist hue."[113] Nakatsumi Tomokata was more explicit, stating that "treating humans just like machines is certainly not scientific" and that the scientific foundations of Taylorism were "flimsy."[114] Furthermore, Nakatsumi asserted, "Science must not be the monopoly of managers and factory owners. Just as a craving for peace is different from working peacefully under the surveillance of managers, so aspiring to the spread of science in industry is different from entrusting to employers the laws of Scientific Management."[115]

The most strident objections to Taylorism's scientific pretensions, however, came from the nascent field of labor science and, in particular, from its Japanese pioneer Teruoka Gitō. Teruoka was a physician and physiologist—as well as the first member of Tokyo University's left-wing New Man Society (Shinjinkai) from the Faculty of Medicine—and began his career researching public health in the impoverished districts of Japan's cities. In 1919 he came to the attention of the progressive textile executive Ōhara Magosaburō, who was then in the process of organizing his Institute for Social Research (Ōhara Shakai Mondai Kenkyūjo). Ōhara persuaded Teruoka to turn his attention from the urban poor to industrial workers and installed him as the director of a newly founded sister organization, the Labor Science Research Institute (Rōdō Kagaku Kenkyūjo).[116] Teruoka and his associates' work lay in the

[112] Ibid., 105.

[113] Ibid., 111. On the power of the concept of science, see Sheldon Garon, "Rethinking Modernization and Modernity in Japanese History: A Focus on State-Society Relations," *Journal of Asian Studies* 53, no. 2 (May 1994): 350–54.

[114] Nakatsumi, "Kagakuteki kanrihō," 127.

[115] Ibid., 130.

[116] On Teruoka, see Miura Toyohiko, *Teruoka Gitō,* Minkan Nihon gakusha, vol. 31 (Riburopōto, 1991).

tradition of the European "science of labor," a discipline which developed in the late nineteenth century and was based on the premise that fatigue was the greatest ill of industrial society.[117] Using a variety of techniques from psychology and physiology, labor science researchers believed their approach to the problems of the working class—unlike that of Taylorism—was rational and purely scientific. In a series of noted articles—one in the influential magazine *Chūō kōron* (Central Review), another as the flagship article of his institute's research journal *Rōdō kagaku kenkyū* (Labor Science Studies)—Teruoka lit into Taylorism and its appropriation of the term "scientific." Noting that most Taylorites were engineers and experts in law or economics "who are lacking in scientific knowledge," Teruoka maintained that "proponents of Taylorism, despite their protestations of being 'scientific,' have an Achilles' heel when it comes to certainty [*kakujitsusa*], that most esssential element in science. Though they call themselves scientific, their methods are based on unscientific formulations and reckonings. [Their] fundamental problem . . . is that they have no conception of physiological facts and pay no heed to the physiological dictates of managing labor."[118] Arguing that Taylorism was in many ways no more scientific than the rule-of-thumb arrangements which preceded it, Teruoka concluded that "while Taylorites avow their respect for science and proclaim that their methods are based on scientific research, in actual fact they are unwittingly causing problems due to their lack of psychological and physiological expertise. Our concern is that workers will fall victim to fatigue, grow unhealthy, age prematurely, and sink quickly into decay [under Scientific Management]."[119]

Although Teruoka's critiques attracted widespread attention, he was not the most celebrated commentator on Taylorism in Taishō Japan. According to most observers, the prolific and well-connected Kanda Kōichi deserved this distinction, due less perhaps to the originality of his ideas than to his skill in synthesizing and elucidating the arguments of others.[120] Kanda, a graduate of the Miyagi Prefectural School of Agriculture, had no training in engineering or commerce prior to joining the state-run Tobacco Monopoly Bureau in 1897. By 1909, he had risen to head of the bureau's newly established Yodobashi factory, a large modern facility where he gained the first-hand experience that informed his writings on management. Kanda was definitely a "technician," one of the "practical" men of the Scientific Management movement and unlike most of the critics of Taylorism, Kanda's perspective was not academic, scientific, or overtly politicized.

---

[117] Rabinbach, *Human Motor.*

[118] Teruoka, "'Gōriteki rōdō,'" 35–36.

[119] Teruoka Gitō, "Rōdō kagaku ni tsuite," *Rōdō kagaku kenkyū* 1, no. 1 (1924): 36.

[120] Okuda, *Hito to keiei,* 129–32; Katō, *Nihon keiei shiryō taikei 3,* 63–64; Bae Boo-gil, *Keieigaku hattatsu shi* (Gakubunsha, 1990), 12–34.

Although most of Kanda's writings touched on Scientific Management, his 1922 study *Rōdō nōritsu kenkyū* (Research on Labor Efficiency) dealt with it in depth and presented most clearly his approach to the new American management techniques. According to Kanda, "While Scientific Management's goal is the increase of production, it is now becoming clear that its philosophical basis is rooted in the progress of capitalism."[121] Echoing other critiques, Kanda proceeded to fault Taylorism for its tendency to overwork laborers, its dehumanizing aspects, its ill effects on product quality, and its antidemocratic proclivities (going so far as to call Scientific Management "militaristic" and "despotic").[122] Kanda's main objection to Taylorism, however, was with its view of the worker and the workplace, and in this Kanda went beyond most of his contemporaries. To Kanda, Taylorism not only showed scorn for the workers' minds (in assuming that only technical staff had the knowledge to determine the production process) but also denigrated their hearts. In stressing materialistic rewards, Taylorism "neglected to look at the spiritual element."[123] Perhaps even more importantly to Kanda, Taylor's assumptions of materialistic motivation and his strategy of promoting competition on the shop floor derived from a view of the worker which focused narrowly on the individual and individual efficiency. Taylorism consequently neglected collective behavior and collective efficiency: this was not surprising, Kanda reasoned, since Scientific Management "naturally came to display tendencies and attributes which derived from the characteristically excessive individualism of its native land, America."[124] Thus, in Kanda's view, not only the human element but also the social element, the dynamic of humans working in groups, was sadly lacking in the Taylorite approach to labor management.

When one steps back to look at the Taishō debates over Taylorism as a whole, three points are worth noting. First, the imported ideas of Scientific Management were not "poorly digested" or "distorted" as some have suggested.[125] While the faddish excesses of the efficiency movement may appear to contradict this, its eccentricites and its exaggerations of Scientific Management closely mirrored those of the U.S. "cult of efficiency." In fact, both the proponents and opponents of Taylorism in Japan appear to have had a firm grasp of its methods and its philosophy, although early explications were often inaccurate and Japanese translators tended to be unselective in their choice of Western texts. Ueno Yōichi complained that "there are a great many scholars in this country who debate Taylorism and criticize it without ever having read Taylor. Many only come to know of Scientific Management by way of the

---

[121] Kanda Kōichi, *Rōdō nōritsu kenkyū* (Tōjō shoten, 1922), 25.

[122] Ibid., 25–32.

[123] Ibid., 27.

[124] Ibid., 28.

[125] Chalmers Johnson, *MITI and the Japanese Miracle* (Stanford, Calif.: Stanford University Press, 1982), 105; Kinzley, *Industrial Harmony,* 104.

writings of German academics and, gobbling down these critiques, they come to espouse them as their own."[126] Ueno's rebuke was justified: most Japanese detractors relied on a small number of Western sources (particularly Robert Hoxie, C. Bertrand Thompson, and J. Ermanski), with Teruoka's famous assessments of Taylorism depending almost entirely on recent French and German studies. Nonetheless, the depth and precision of many Japanese analyses of Taylorism compared favorably to contemporary American discussions. As the work of authors like Kanda Kōichi, Kunimatsu Tarō, Kaneko Rihachirō, and Wakabayashi Yonekichi suggests, the Japanese discourse on Taylorism during the 1920s had progressed beyond mindless "literal translation" and displayed neither a befuddled nor a warped understanding of American Scientific Management.

Second, it is important to note that not all critics of Taylorism were completely dismissive of its value. Most had to admit Scientific Management's economic worth. Morito, for example, conceded that Taylorism's application "leads in virtually all cases to a large increase in productive power, usually doubling or tripling it but, in extraordinary cases, boosting it seven- or even tenfold."[127] Nakatsumi concurred, stating, "It is difficult to conclude that Scientific Management is a completely bad system. . . . There is probably no one who would be opposed to increased output, reduced expenses, and the improvement of production methods."[128] One opponent even had to admit that, at least in comparison to existing management methods, "it is not unreasonable" to call Taylorism "scientific."[129]

Significantly, Samuel Haber's observation that "many who vigorously disparaged [Taylor's] accomplishment came to share his aspiration" held true in Japan as well as in America.[130] Many of Taylorism's critics (and a number of its advocates as well) subscribed to the notion that Scientific Management was much more flawed in practice than it was in theory. Morito echoed broader sentiments when he stated, "Scientific Management has been adopted by the capitalist class as a convenient tool in its efforts to preserve its status. This is probably not the use which Taylorism's founders originally intended for it, however. Many of them were men earnestly devoted to the uplift of workers and the welfare of human beings."[131] While the authoritarian and exploitative use of Scientific Management was widely denounced, Japanese commentators on Taylorism (both for and against) appear to have reached a broad consensus on its "aspirations"—the application of science to business administration, the

---

[126] Ueno Yōichi, ed. and trans., *Taylor zenshū,* 2 vols. (Dōbunkan, 1932), 1:2, preface.
[127] Morito, "Kagakuteki kanrihō," pt. 1, 86.
[128] Nakatsumi, "Kagakuteki kanrihō," 129; see also Kitazawa, "Kagakuteki kanrihō," 60.
[129] Isobe, "Teiraa shisutemu" pt. 2, 174.
[130] Haber, *Efficiency and Uplift,* xi.
[131] Morito, "Kagakuteki kanrihō," pt. 2, 110.

systematization of the work process and labor management, the formation of a cooperative and mutually beneficial labor-capital relationship.

Third and finally, it should be noted that most Japanese critics were tilting against the windmill of "original" Taylorism, the managerial schema developed by Taylor at the turn of the century and given its purest theoretical exposition in *The Principles of Scientific Management*. The vast majority of the academic commentators did not fully recognize that Scientific Management as it was being introduced in Japan was not identical to Taylor's archetype, at least after the initial mania of the mid-1910s. While detractors blasted the new management methods for their neglect of psychology, their indifference to the "human element" and group dynamics, and their antagonism to organized labor, Scientific Management proponents were busily championing many of the very elements which critics argued they ignored or opposed.

In a 1925 survey of modern management reforms conducted by Muramoto Fukumatsu, for example, the categories grouped under Scientific Management included not only motion study and incentive wage schemes but also welfare facilities, aptitude tests, and fatigue research.[132] Similarly, all three of the major "efficiency engineer" training courses held in the early 1920s dedicated significant portions of their curricula to unconventionally Taylorite topics such as "labor medicine," "experimental psychology," and "works councils."[133] A number of Scientific Management advocates stressed the humanity of the workers and suggested new approaches to motivation, labor input on the production process, and group efficiency. Araki Tōichirō's much-discussed Nippon Kōkan and Yokohama Dock wage systems, for example, deviated from the classic Taylor model and included incentive components for work group (as well as individual) productivity.[134] Ueno Yōichi called for an entirely new approach, a "total human engineering" (*kanzen na ningen kōgaku*) that would be true to Taylor's ideals while "encompassing the entire human character."[135] One 1924 study on modern office management was more down-to-earth, advising that "the manager who does not bid 'good morning' to his employees will find it difficult to get the best out of them. A smile and a word of encouragement are often more precious than wages. . . ."[136]

Some Japanese Scientific Management supporters were exploring decidedly un-Taylorite approaches to the "labor problem," such as worker representation and collective bargaining, even as detractors were blasting Taylorism's anti-union bias. Works councils based on English and American models began appearing in large Japanese factories after World War I and were endorsed by many Taylorites for their contributions to increasing efficiency and

---

[132] Quoted in Nakase, "Scientific Management," 195.

[133] Ueno, *Sangyō nōritsu kenkyū*, 113–16.

[134] Gordon, "Araki Tōichirō," 182–85.

[135] Ueno Yōichi, *Ueno Yōichi senshū* (Chōbunkan, 1941), 188.

[136] Quoted in Katō, *Nihon keiei shiryō taikei 3*, 68.

promoting harmonious labor relations. A number of the "model factories" of Japanese Scientific Management instituted such bodies in the early 1920s, notably the JNR repair shops, Mitsubishi Electric's Kobe works, and the military arsenals, including Kure.[137] In some firms, including Ishikawajima Heavy Industries, special councils were even formed to discuss issues of labor efficiency and workshop management.[138]

A few Japanese Taylorites were thinking beyond such "conservative reform" in the workplace (as Gordon characterizes the works councils) and proposed more progressive approaches. Foremost among these was Noda Nobuo, an economist in the research department of Mitsubishi Gōshi and a collaborator in the introduction of work study into Mitsubishi Electric. In a strongly worded 1924 essay in the Kyōchōkai's organ publication *Shakai seisaku jihō* (Social Policy Review), Noda argued that Taylorism and collective bargaining were not incompatible and, moreover, that a significant labor voice in managerial decision making was essential, lest capital come to monopolize and misuse the power of "science." Noda seemed to go beyond the idea of works councils yet did not explicitly support the recognition of unions in Japan, concluding that the necessary elements for the successful advancement of Scientific Management were "(1) good faith on the part of managers, (2) the sound development of worker representation systems, and (3) suitable laws and regulations."[139]

A number of observers have interpreted the apparent broadening of the Taylorite message as something peculiarly Japanese, the unique result of Scientific Management (embodying the modern, individualism, hierarchy, and rationalism) colliding head-on with Japanese society and its traditions (identified with the feudal, groupism, anti-elitism, and emotionalism). According to Okuda Kenji, "In the case of Japan, the methods of U.S. Scientific Management were introduced but the contemptuous view of the worker which underlay it was denied."[140] While it appears clear that a "revised" version of Taylorism—encompassing a broadened conception of Scientific Management and a new emphasis on the "human element"—was increasingly espoused over the course of the Taishō period, the assertion that this was a distinctively Japanese adaptation is dubious.[141] In both the United States and Europe, Sci-

---

[137] Nishinarita, *Rōshi kankeishi,* 200–20; Garon, *The State and Labor,* 53–54; Gordon, *Imperial Democracy,* 130–31.

[138] Takahashi, *"Kagakuteki kanrihō,"* 111–12. Takahashi also details the structure of a similar council, instituted by consultants from the Osaka Industrial Efficiency Research Institute (Osaka Furitsu Sangyō Nōritsu Kenkyūjo), at an unnamed dyestuffs factory (123–24).

[139] Noda, "Kagakuteki kanrihō to rōdōsha," 75.

[140] Okuda, *Hito to keiei,* 73; see also Hazama, *Rōshi kyōchō,* 170–76.

[141] In arguing for the emergence of a "revised Taylorism" in Taishō Japan, I employ the same terminology as Okuda Kenji, who writes of a "Japanese revision of classic management thought" (*kotenteki keiei kanri shisō no Nihon-teki shūsei*) and "the revision of classic Scientific Management" (*kotenteki kagakuteki kanrihō no shūsei*). Nevertheless, our conceptions of what this

entific Management was far from monolithic during the 1910s and 1920s: changes in Taylorite rhetoric and in its approach to labor began to appear soon after the publication of the *Principles* and accelerated after Taylor's death in 1915. The First World War proved to be a critical period in this evolution, Scientific Management becoming "more popular and acceptable as Taylor's disciples adopted a broader view of the workers' role in the factory."[142] The wartime accord between the Taylor Society and the American Federation of Labor indicated a moderation in Taylorite hostility toward unions and a new willingness to consider the value of worker representation. Furthermore, according to Daniel Nelson, "Scientific Management by 1920 embraced the full panoply of personnel reforms, including personnel departments . . . as well as the new activities associated with industrial psychology."[143] As Anson Rabinbach has explained, "The European experience of Scientific Management in the 1920s—and to a large extent the Anglo-American—was a significant departure from the narrow application of the principles laid down by Taylor. . . . For the next generation of Taylorist managers, emphasis on the 'human factor' became an important corrective to Taylor's limited interest in the social consequences of Scientific Management."[144]

The notion of a "revised" Taylorism which emerged in Taishō Japan thus closely resembled the amended models of Scientific Management which evolved in the United States and Europe at approximately the same time.[145] Concluding, however, that Japanese responses to Taylorism only reflected foreign trends is as superficial as assuming that its modification was driven entirely by factors unique to Japan. While the close contacts between Japanese Taylorites and their Western counterparts in the 1920s provided a conduit for the direct introduction of a "humanized" Scientific Management, distinct in-

---

"revision" constituted—and especially how and when it was translated into actual shop floor practice—differ considerably. Specifically, I take issue with Okuda's culturalist reading of the "Japanese" reinterpretation of Taylorism, and I am skeptical of Okuda's suggestion that Scientific Management techniques were rapidly and easily "humanized" in the industrial workshops of prewar Japan. Okuda Kenji, "Nihon keiei kanrishi no ichi teiryū," *Nihon rōdō kyōkai zasshi* 29 (May 1987): 7–8; Okuda Kenji, "Datsu-koten no jidai ni okeru hito to keiei: sōhosei complementarity no genri ni tsuite," *Keiei shigaku* 30, no. 4 (January 1996): 3–7.

[142] Nelson, *Managers and Workers,* 142.

[143] Nelson, "Scientific Management in Retrospect," 15.

[144] Rabinbach, *The Human Motor,* 276.

[145] For fascinating comparative perspectives, see Perry Willson's discussions of a "revisionist Taylorism" in interwar Italy (Perry R. Willson, *The Clockwork Factory: Women and Work in Fascist Italy* (Oxford: Clarendon Press, 1993), 63–66), and Joan Campbell's treatment of the "humanization" of rationalized work in Weimar Germany (Joan Campbell, *Joy in Work, German Work* (Princeton, N.J.: Princeton University Press, 1989), chap. 7). See also Heidrun Homberg, "Scientific Management and Personnel Policy in the Modern German Enterprise 1918–1939: The Case of Siemens," in *Managerial Strategies and Industrial Relations,* ed. Howard Gospel and Craig Littler (London: Heinemann, 1983), 148–55.

digenous influences also had an effect on the evolving "revision" of Taylorism in Taishō Japan. The specific experience of implementing Scientific Management in Japanese workshops and its reception by Japanese labor were doubtless significant in this respect. However, particular attention must be given to Taylorism's encounter with Japanese paternalism, an amorphous set of beliefs and practices widely regarded as the foundation of Japanese managerial thought from the Meiji period to the present day. Approached from this perspective, the Japanese "revision" of Scientific Management can be seen to have paralleled, as well as directly derived from, the adaptation of the Taylorite message which occurred internationally around the time of the First World War.

Scientific Management and Japanese Paternalism

The importance of paternalism (*onjōshugi*) as the "guiding principle in labor management" in prewar Japan has been argued by many historians.[146] Hazama Hiroshi has been particularly vehement in this respect, asserting that contemporary "Japanese-style management" evolved from interwar notions of paternalism which had, in turn, derived from traditional models of the affective relationship between lord and retainer.[147] Institutions commonly associated with paternalistic management (such as worker dormitories) were as old as modern industry in Japan. Yet *onjōshugi* only gained rhetorical prominence and a sacred spot in the nascent national business ideology at the turn of the century, when industrialists brandished Japan's "beautiful customs" in employer-employee relations to counter pressure for Western-style factory legislation. In Hazama's telling, the subsequent decades witnessed the development of "systematic" paternalism, a distinctively Japanese model of labor management, adapted to modern factory production but based on traditions of "groupism, feelings of dependency, and a high regard for harmony and cooperation."[148]

In theory at least, such an approach—premised on the warm treatment of workers and emotionalism—would appear antithetical to the scientific, rational, and materialistic approach of Taylorism. Hazama has argued precisely

[146] Marshall, *Capitalism and Nationalism in Prewar Japan* (Stanford, Calif.: Stanford University Press, 1967), 63; W. Mark Fruin, "From Philanthropy to Paternalism in the Noda Soy Sauce Industry: Pre-Corporate and Corporate Charity in Japan," *Business History Review* 46, no. 2 (Summer 1982): 168–90.

[147] Hazama, *Rōshi kyōchō*; Hazama Hiroshi (with Jacqueline Kaminski), "Japanese Labor-Management Relations and Uno Riemon," *Journal of Japanese Studies* 5, no. 1 (Winter 1979): 71–106. Hazama's classic study of Japanese paternalism, *Nihon rōmu kanrishi kenkyū*, has recently been translated (in a much-abbreviated form) as *The History of Labour Management in Japan*, trans. Mari Sako and Eri Sako (Basingstoke: Macmillan, 1997).

[148] Hazama, "Uno Riemon," 104.

that, concluding that Scientific Management was eviscerated by the culturally rooted logic of paternalism and was consequently unable to gain the acceptance in Japan which it achieved in the West.[149] Hazama's analysis, however, overstates the influence of traditions and understates the impact of Taylorism: in fact, the rhetoric and institutions of Japanese *onjōshugi* were able to coexist anɑ overlap with the methodology and philosophy of Scientific Management to a remarkable degree. As in the West, the dichotomy between paternalism and Taylorism in prewar Japan appears to have been far less stark than many later observers have assumed.

On the most basic level, of course, Scientific Management and paternalism alike appealed to Japanese employers' closely related desires for labor peace and low costs. Both, in short, held out the promise of higher, more stable profits. At the same time, both strategies aimed to affirm and strengthen the authority of management in the industrial workplace. Whereas paternalism's approach was couched largely in moral terms and Taylorism's was premised on the managerial monopolization of "science," both sought to confirm management prerogatives by an ideological appeal to standards which transcended the shop floor.[150] The complementarity appears to have held on a more practical level as well. In the first place, *onjōshugi* was most powerful (and most frequently used) as a rhetorical device rather than as a comprehensive managerial strategy. Perhaps more importantly, Japanese paternalism prescribed no model of production management and gave no guidance in the design of the work process or the specifics of labor management (including wages), areas on which Taylorism focused. Scientific Management, meanwhile, paid little attention to the welfare facilities and cultural amenities which were the main institutional components of paternalistic appeals. *Onjōshugi* and Taylorism could, it seems, thus interlock (and even reinforce each other) in practical application as well as on a more abstract level.

The manner in which Scientific Management and paternalism could be intellectually reconciled is apparent in the writings of Uno Riemon, one of the most dedicated theorists of *onjōshugi* in prewar Japan. With a strong awareness of Japan's distinctive course of industrial development and a firm belief in a unique "Japanese spirit," Uno sought to create a systematic yet "humane" and culturally continuous model of paternalistic labor relations in Japan. Like many who approached management from a spiritual perspective, Uno was sharp in his evaluation of Taylorism:

---

[149] Hazama, *Rōshi kyōchō,* 170–86.

[150] On this point see Okuda, *Hito to keiei,* 392; Okuda Kenji, "Comments" on Andrew Gordon, "Araki Tōichirō and the Shaping of Labor Management," in *Japanese Management in Historical Perspective,* ed. Yui Tsunehiko and Nakagawa Keiichirō, Proceedings of the Fifteenth International Conference on Business History (Tokyo: University of Tokyo Press, 1989), 196.

Many books on the theory of increasing efficiency have already been published in Japan. However, since almost all of them are no more than translations of works originally written in America, their relevance to the situation of Japan's workers is highly tenuous. . . . There are many factories which have temporarily adopted scientific methods of management . . . but they have for the most part ended in failure, and few have been successful. The reason for these failures lies in having brought in American-style [practices] which attach much importance to material things, and using them in an unmodified form on Japanese workers, who are more inclined to be moved by things spiritual.[151]

While Uno criticized the "literal translation" of Taylorism and its excessive materialism, he did not take issue with any of its methods specifically and conceded its value in "increasing industrial efficiency." Uno even admitted that Taylorism could perform a constructive role in labor relations, listing Scientific Management (*gakuriteki kanrihō*) and its promise of "increasing profits while elevating workers' income" as "effective supplementary measures" in the "warm treatment of labor" (*shokkō yūgū*).[152] Indeed, Uno did not oppose the introduction of Taylorism so much as he questioned its efficacy in Japan without a more "spiritual" approach. Significantly, Uno recognized the presence of this element within Scientific Management: "Researchers and importers of the Taylor System misconstrue it as merely a scientific technique, a dry-as-dust intellectual framework. They are unable to grasp its true meaning, that the vitality of the system lies in its 'Mental Revolution' [*kōgyō dōtoku no kakumei*]."[153] From Uno's perspective, then, the Taylorite philosophy of labor-management cooperation could exist in accord with Japanese emotionalism and the techniques of American management could be introduced within the rubric of *onjōshugi*: in short, Taylorism was not antithetical to the spirit of Japanese paternalism.

If the example of Uno gives some indication of the intellectual compatibility of Taylorism and *onjōshugi*, then the case of Suzuki Tsunesaburō and the Nikkō Electric Copper Smelting Company suggests the extent to which the two approaches could mesh in actual practice. Suzuki was one of the early breed of Meiji professional managers: an employee of the Furukawa interests, he was a graduate of Keiō University and had studied accounting at Harvard. In 1912, he was appointed head of the Nikkō smelter, a subsidiary of Furukawa's Ashio mine, and was charged with improving its lackluster performance and legacy of labor problems.[154] Suzuki's success was legendary:

---

[151] Quoted from Uno's 1921 study, *Nōritsu zōshin no riron to jissai*, in Hazama, "Uno Riemon," 99–100.

[152] Quoted from Uno's *Shokkō yūgū ron* (1915) in Hazama, *Rōshi kyōchō*, 91–94.

[153] Quoted in Hazama, *Rōshi kyōchō*, 186.

[154] It was said, when Suzuki arrived, that "The relations between workers and managers were

within two years he had cut production costs by a third, halved the number of workers yet doubled the income of those who remained, greatly increased productivity and machine usage rates, and calmed labor discord. Nikkō became a model factory of paternalistic management practices and Suzuki one of the most celebrated proponents of *onjōshugi* in the 1910s and 1920s.

Suzuki's writings were rich with the standard paternalistic rhetoric: his essays dripped with praise for "beautiful customs" and emotionalism, and were generous with scorn for Taylorism's cold and dehumanizing edge.[155] Yet Suzuki's experience at Nikkō suggests that the practical distinction between Scientific Management and *onjōshugi* was far less extreme than the rhetorical dichotomy he later created. Suzuki did establish the usual welfare facilities at the smelter—safety devices, rest areas, workplace beautification, and so on—and he did show an uncommon interest in the economic well-being of his workers. Suzuki's factory was not, however, the "warm," familial, cooperative and group-oriented environment one would expect of a model paternalistic plant. In his first speech to the Nikkō workers, Suzuki sounded as much like Frederick Winslow Taylor selling the "Mental Revolution" as a feudal lord addressing his retainers:

> Although the facilities here are second to none in the world, . . . our products are expensive, their quality is inferior, and workers' wages are only one-quarter of those in other countries. This is a truly deplorable situation. I entreat all of you to work much more strenuously. If you do this, then we can without question make products just as good as those from foreign countries. . . . If you do this, your wages can be increased fourfold. The interests of capitalists and workers are not inevitably opposed. In advanced foreign countries there may be instances where profits for capital result in losses for labor, but this is not the case in undeveloped countries like Japan, where the interests of the two groups are as one. In other words, if efficiency increases then the profits generated by this increase can be split between labor and capital.[156]

Despite his critiques of Taylorite materialism, Suzuki was a firm believer in incentive wages, installing the Gantt system at Nikkō and putting his Harvard training to use by making the rate determination procedures as statistically precise as possible.[157] Regardless of his protestations of compassion and familialism, Suzuki—who, one admirer said, had a "warm spot in his heart for laborers"—emphasized competition on the shop floor and was ruthless in

extremely poor. Managers regarded the workers as hoodlums and the workers thought of managers as the enemy." Ishiyama Masakichi, "Nōritsu zōshin no mohan kōjō o miru," appended to Suzuki Tsunesaburō, *Kōjō kanri jitsugaku* (Daiyamondo, 1916), 3. On Suzuki, see also Hazama, *Rōshi kyōchō*, 118–28; Okuda, *Hito to keiei*, 340–45.

[155] See Suzuki Tsunesaburō, *Rōdō mondai to onjōshugi* (Yōrokusha, 1915).

[156] Suzuki, *Kōjō kanri*, 7–8.

[157] Ibid., 56–78, 273–83.

pruning the workforce at Nikkō. In what might well be cast as the Japanese version of Taylor's infamous "Schmidt experiment,"[158] Suzuki is reputed to have gathered half of the haulers at Furukawa's Akihabara warehouse and offered to split the gains in productivity with them if they could double the amount they carried in one day. The group, aided by some primitive work study, gladly obliged, whereupon Suzuki fired the now redundant other half of the haulers and distributed a portion of their wages to the more productive men who remained. Suzuki later tried to apply the results of this experiment to cargo handlers at the Nikkō factory, dismissing half the crew and ordering the remaining laborers to pick up their productivity proportionately. The Nikkō workers, however, refused to participate and, in the end, Suzuki blithely fired them all for insubordination.[159]

The case of Suzuki Tsunesaburō appears to confirm the impression that the reality of Japanese *onjōshugi* was hardly as warm and inviting as its propaganda. Even more revealing, however, is the light it sheds on the relationship between paternalism and Scientific Management in Japanese factories. It is important to note that Suzuki's smelter was far from being the only company to have championed *onjōshugi* while simultaneously applying classic Taylorite reforms to the work process. While JNR repair shops were among the most systematic users of Scientific Management methods in Taishō Japan, the National Railways was more widely renowned for its cult of familialism and its extensive range of worker welfare facilities. As a 1930 labor broadside indicated, workers recognized management's two approaches:

Brothers at the Ōmiya works!

How are your wretched lives these days?

It's intolerable that we can be driven 'til we drop by motion study, made to work for nothing by rate cutting, and threatened with being fired if we complain.

O paternalism [*onjōshugi*]! O familialism [*kazokushugi*]! We hear about them all the time but when have they actually improved our lives? It's all just a swindle that the management—which is afraid of our resistance—keeps pulling to make us obedient and really squeeze us!

Down with motion study! Down with rate cutting![160]

---

[158] During his work at Bethlehem Steel, Taylor conducted a series of experiments aimed at improving labor efficiency in pig iron handling. As recounted in *The Principles of Scientific Management,* Taylor promised a laborer (whom he called Schmidt) a 50 percent wage increase if he would submit to work study and increase his daily loading of pig iron from 12.5 tons to 47 tons. Schmidt, who Taylor described as "a man of the type of the ox . . . so stupid that he was unfitted to do most kinds of laboring work," easily accomplished this productivity target, which eventually led to the firing of most of the workers on the pig iron handling team. Taylor, *Principles of Scientific Management,* 41–64.

[159] Suzuki, *Kōjō kanri,* 7–8. See also Okuda, "Managerial Evolution III," 29–31.

[160] Konno, "Kokutetsu," pt. 4, 51.

Evidence of the coexistence of *onjōshugi* and Taylorism is provided even more strikingly by the prewar spinning industry, where both approaches reached high levels of advancement. At Kurashiki, for example, Ōhara Magosaburō's distinctive style of paternalism (its spirit captured best perhaps by the American Progressives' catchword "uplift") stood side by side with Scientific Management and Teruoka's labor science methods.[161] At Kanegafuchi Spinning (Kanebō), the most famous paternalistic firm of the 1910s and 1920s, the situation was quite similar. Despite president Mutō Sanji's commitment to the ambiguous concept of "spiritual operating methods" (*seishinteki sōgyōhō*) in 1915 and the provision of elaborate welfare and cultural facilities, Taylorization of the work process appears to have been as advanced at Kanebō as at any of the large textile concerns.[162] It may be significant to note that following his triumph at Nikkō, Suzuki Tsunesaburō moved on to work under Mutō at Kanegafuchi from 1915 to 1920.

As Okuda Kenji has argued, a number of prewar managers implemented Scientific Management—sometimes consciously, sometimes unwittingly—while simultaneously mouthing paternalistic platitudes and providing "warm" welfare facilities. In Okuda's view, paternalistic rhetoric and institutions functioned as complements and correctives to Taylorism: welfare facilities eased the physical strains of the new work regime, the ideology of familialism smoothed the transition to an increasingly stratified bureaucratic order in the factory. In other words, paternalism seemed to round the sharp edges of Scientific Management as it spread through Japanese industry.[163]

As Gramsci noted, the rationalization of industrial production required both the carrot and the stick, "a skillful combination of force . . . and persuasion (high wages, various social benefits, extremely subtle ideological and political propaganda)."[164] In Japan of the 1910s and 1920s, "persuasion" clearly took the form of paternalistic institutions and familial grandiloquence. Although Japanese management reformers could readily endorse the concept of the "Mental Revolution," the high-wage element of the Taylorite formula was seldom upheld in practice. Japanese firms thus came to utilize many of the techniques of Scientific Management, and the ideological core of Taylorism—the necessity of science in industry, the value of planning and expert guidance, the nullification of politics in the workplace—was widely espoused, but the embrace was not complete. As Okuda Kenji concluded, "the biggest problem

161 Chokki, *Kigyō keiei,* 123–24.

162 Okuda, *Hito to keiei,* 349–61; Hazama, *Rōshi kyōchō,* 176–79.

163 Okuda, *Hito to keiei,* 387–93. A similar point is made by Stephen Large, although he stresses the primacy of paternalism as a managerial strategy in the 1920s. Stephen Large, *Organized Workers and Socialist Politics in Interwar Japan* (Cambridge: Cambridge University Press, 1981), 73–74, 82–83.

164 Antonio Gramsci, *Selections from the Prison Notebooks,* ed. and trans. Quintin Hoare and Geoffrey Smith (New York: International Publishers, 1971), 285.

with the introduction of the scientific management system in the prewar days [was] the attitude of the industries which chose to adopt only the technical part of the system and sought to keep workers' wages at the previous low levels."[165] At least through the 1920s, Japanese managers' concern for the "human element" was almost invariably translated into "warm," enveloping familialism rather than cold, hard cash.

The extent to which the Japanese splicing of Taylorism and paternalistic "persuasion" was a conscious managerial strategy is unclear, as is its significance in explaining why Scientific Management was accepted so phlegmatically by Japanese workers. What is certain is that a similar path was being traced in the United States, where corporate paternalism (known as "welfare work") went from being a target of Taylorite contempt to a close adjunct of Scientific Management during the first decades of the twentieth century. According to Daniel Nelson and Stuart Campbell, "To an increasing number of employers, the differences between Scientific Management and welfare work, which appeared so wide to Taylor . . . seemed less important than the potential benefits of combining the systems. During World War I, elements of Taylorism were joined with welfare work to create the new field of personnel management."[166] The complementary and compensating nature of Japanese paternalism which Okuda noted also appears to have driven the American melding of the two approaches: "Personnel management was in no way seen as a replacement for Scientific Management. Rather, personnel management, with its various means of making workers feel part of a larger enterprise, was necessary precisely because Scientific Management and modern production techniques had, with few exceptions, reduced workers' control over their work and sentenced them to performing a series of repetitive, meaningless tasks."[167] In short, paternalistic approaches to labor management and Taylorism came to coexist and reinforce each other in the West much as they did in Japan: corporate avatars of modern management (like Ford) embraced corporate welfarism, while model shops of familialism (like the English candy manufacturer Cadbury) also adopted Taylorite techniques.[168]

[165] Okuda, "Managerial Evolution I," 19.

[166] Daniel Nelson and Stuart Campbell, "Taylorism Versus Welfare Work in American Industry: H. L. Gantt and the Bancrofts," *Business History Review* 46, no. 1 (Spring 1972): 165.

[167] Richard Gillespie, *Manufacturing Knowledge: A History of the Hawthorne Experiments* (Cambridge: Cambridge University Press, 1992), 26; see also Sanford Jacoby, *Employing Bureaucracy: Managers, Unions, and the Transformation of Work in American Industry, 1900–1945* (New York: Columbia University Press, 1985), chap. 2.

[168] On Ford, see Stephen Meyer III, *The Five-Dollar Day* (Albany: State University of New York Press, 1981), esp. 110 ff.; on Cadbury, Michael Rowlinson, "The Early Application of Scientific Management by Cadbury," *Business History* 30, no. 4 (1988): 377–95. Suzuki Tsunesaburō was much influenced by the paternalism of the "Chocolate King" Edward Cadbury, though it is unclear if he was aware that his Nikkō factory and Cadbury's Bournville works were

Japan's "revised" ideology of Scientific Management thus came to encompass a reconciliation with *onjōshugi* as well as a heightened concern for the "human element." Though the significance of this revision was lost on many contemporary observers, there were a few who seemed to recognize that the course of Taylorism in Taishō Japan was paralleling its path in the United States. In his 1923 speech to the Osaka Efficiency Exposition, for example, Godō Takuo confronted the arguments of some Japanese commentators that Scientific Management was in decline in America: while Godō acknowledged that "pure" Taylorism might be hard to find, he stressed that Scientific Management was evolving and advancing on both sides of the Pacific.[169] Muramoto Fukumatsu explained that while early Taylorites emphasized the rigorous application of centralized planning, a trend toward greater respect for the "human element" was undeniable and virtually all scientific managers had come to recognize the value of "tapping the inventive and creative powers of the workmen."[170] The recognition that Taylorism was being reconceived, its stark message broadened and softened, sometimes came from unlikely quarters. In 1926, Mutō Sanji aptly remarked that

> At first, research on the efficiency problem in Japan (just as in the United States) dealt only with issues directly related to production, such as the standardization of production facilities and worker routines. . . . On this basis, some people condemned it for turning men into machines. Recently, however, [efficiency] research has shown a more agreeable course of development: while still concerned with output, quality and so on, it is paying attention to human well-being and moving in tandem with psychological and physiological research on areas such as fatigue, motion, performance, and nutrition. I hope that from now on all people who seek to do research on efficiency will keep foremost in their minds that the efficiency problem is a human problem.[171]

If we recognize (as even Mutō did) that the Scientific Management of the 1920s had evolved greatly from the stark nostrums of Taylor's *Principles,* it is possible to understand how some observers, searching only for a pure, textbook form of Taylorism, have found little but distortion, subversion by tradition, and failure in Taishō Japan. Nevertheless, as the Taylorite "Mental Revolution" was intertwined with paternalistic spiritualism and *kyōchōshugi* harmonism, and as Scientific Management's methods grew to embrace welfare facilities, "hard" science, and a concern for the "human element," Taylorism was woven into the fabric of Japanese production and labor management

---

much alike in the blending of paternalism and Scientific Management. Hazama, *Nihon rōmu kanrishi kenkyū,* 482. See also Hazama, *History of Labour Management,* 158–59.

[169] *Nōritsu tenrankai shi,* 310–14.

[170] Muramoto, "Horie hakase," 33–34.

[171] Preface by Mutō Sanji to Uenaka, *Nōritsu dokuhon,* 23.

in the 1910s and 1920s. While the introduction of Scientific Management into Japan differed in its particulars from the process in the United States or Europe, the ideological and methodological paths taken by Japanese Taylorites were by no means unique. Indeed, the "revision" of Scientific Management in Japan both derived from and paralleled the transformation of Taylorism which was unfolding simultaneously in the West. Although conditioned by Japan's particular economic and intellectual context, Japanese managerial thought and "best method" practice came to reflect international trends far more closely than some indigenous repertoire of "tradition." In short, the epithet "Japanese-style" can be only loosely applied to the structures of industrial management which began to take root in Japan during the 1920s.

2

The Rationalization Movement and Scientific Management, 1927–1937

ACCORDING TO Ueno Yōichi, Japan's efficiency movement was at its most dynamic and influential between 1923 and 1926, the mid-decade doldrums of Japanese industry. Other observers have concurred, characterizing this period as the prewar apex of Scientific Management in Japan and concluding that, as the econoгıy subsequently slipped from stagnation into financial crisis and depression, Taylorism was increasingly driven to the periphery of managerial concerns. Scientific Management, most have assumed, was eclipsed and ulti-mately absorbed by industrial rationalization (*sangyō gōrika*), an amorphous but far-reaching movement of academics, bureaucrats, and businessmen that dominated the public discourse on industrial development and economic re-covery in early Shōwa Japan. Close scrutiny of Japan's rationalization drive and the course of the modern management movement suggests, however, that the message and methods of Taylorism were neither marginalized nor sub-sumed during the late 1920s and early 1930s. Rather, Scientific Management was regarded with newfound interest in Japan: its approach was broadened, its philosophy and rhetoric diffused more widely, and the organs for promoting it expanded and streamlined. Indeed, Taylorism was not so much rejected as reaffirmed in the Depression era. The fifteen-year legacy of Scientific Man-agement in Japan laid the intellectual and ideological foundations for *sangyō gōrika,* while the techniques of American management ultimately became a central component of rationalization initiatives. Although the rationalization movement has more often drawn attention as the ancestor of Japanese indus-trial policy than as the descendant of "efficiency increase," the histories of rationalization and of American management models in Japan are inextricably linked.

The Meanings of Rationalization

The spread of the idea of rationalization in Japan was even more "rapid" and "sensational" than the introduction of Scientific Management had been. Al-though industrial rationalization had emerged in Europe in the wake of World War I—the German Reichskuratorium für Wirtschaftlichkeit (National Board for Efficiency) was founded in 1921—the movement did not attract significant comment in Japan until the mid-1920s. At first, rationalization was discussed mainly in academic circles, but in 1927 it suddenly gained wide exposure in the press and among business leaders. One catalyst was the Geneva World Economic Conference (which was convened in that year and focused on the question of rationalization), but a more immediate stimulant was the "Shōwa financial crisis," a sobering panic in the banking system that foreshadowed the Great Depression in Japan. Interest in rationalization soon spread to the bureaucracy, although Yoshino Shinji, the Ministry of Commerce and Industry official who was to chart much of the state rationalization program, would later note that government attention was dilatory until 1929, when the extensive discussions of rationalization at the Tokyo World Engineering Congress inspired a number of bureaucrats to consider the movement more seriously.[1] At any rate, by the end of the decade the phrase *sangyō gōrika* had come into common usage and by 1930, when the Hamaguchi cabinet established the Temporary Industrial Rationalization Bureau (Rinji Sangyō Gōrikyoku), bibliographies of material on rationalization were already being published and the word was even appearing on higher school entrance examinations.[2]

Rationalization was considered an imported concept, and most observers have assumed that the country of origin was Germany. "By far the greatest influence on the Japanese theory of rationalization," Chalmers Johnson has noted, "came from the Germans."[3] Certainly German influence was great: the approaches associated with the German rationalization movement— specifically the use of state-sponsored trusts and cartels to restrain internecine competition and realize efficiency increases cooperatively—were fully integrated into the mentality and methods of *sangyō gōrika*. Nevertheless, "American-style" rationalization was avidly discussed in Japan, and the American experience appears to have influenced Japanese conceptions of rationalization at least as strongly as the German example did. The importance of the American model should hardly be surprising, as the concept of rationalization began to filter into Japan during a period when the United States was being described by many as the yardstick of industrial and social progress. Through the mid- and late 1920s, the Japanese business press chanted the praises of American prosperity and sought to tease out the "secrets" of that nation's unparalleled postwar growth.[4] Many of the factors identified in this search— notably the harmonious capital-labor relationship in the United States, the

---

[1] Yoshino Shinji, *Nihon kōgyō seisaku* (Nihon hyōronsha, 1935), 248. See also World Engineering Congress, *Proceedings,* vol. 38: *Scientific Management* (Tokyo: World Engineering Congress, 1931).

[2] Hirai Yasutarō, *Sangyō gōrika* (Kobe: Guroria sosaete, 1930), preface.

[3] Chalmers Johnson, *MITI and the Japanese Miracle* (Stanford, Calif.: Stanford University Press, 1982), 105–6.

[4] See, for example, Ueda Teijirō, "Beikoku no han'ei to sangyō gōrika," *Kigyō to shakai* 21 (December 1927): 633–44; Shimazaki Hikojirō, "Beikoku no sangyō gōrika o miru," *Tokyo kōjō konwakai kaihō* 50 (November 1930): 2–9.

professionalization of management, and the spread of Taylorism and mass production—were eventually absorbed into the emerging Japanese conception of rationalization.

In an eloquent graphical depiction of the history of rationalization (figure 1), Hirai Yasutarō portrayed the German and American movements as great and diverging rivers, the Japanese initiative as a small tributary, fed by both of the larger currents and flowing captive between them. To most contemporary observers, including Hirai, the American and German models were considered related although clearly distinct: "American-style" rationalization was taken to concentrate on the firm and shop-floor reforms, while the German movement looked to the industry or the national economy as its basis. As the confluence of these two streams, Japanese *sangyō gōrika* was thus perceived as a hybrid, the U.S. experience contributing the micro-level approaches (Scientific Management and technologies of production), the German tradition providing the macro-level strategies of concentration, cartelization, and state intervention in industrial organization.[5]

Although this anatomy of Japanese rationalization is valid to a considerable extent, the formula *sangyō gōrika* = German policy (industry-level) + American policy (firm-level) clearly has its limitations. For example, while Japanese observers did greatly admire the shop-floor strategies of "American-style" rationalization, many also looked to the Waste Elimination Movement and the work of Herbert Hoover as a model of dynamic bureaucratic policy and public-private cooperation.[6] Similarly, although American methods continued to dominate Japanese discussions of production management into the 1930s, German practice did attract some attention.[7] In short, the suggestion that state rationalization policy in Japan was German in inspiration and Japanese factory management reforms were American in origin is appealing conceptually, yet not entirely accurate.

While rationalization was a new concept in early Shōwa Japan and its provenance was distinctly foreign, the Japanese movement was built on strong domestic foundations. By 1930, the efficiency movement was nearly two decades old and the "revised" Taylorite message was well established in the business community. From the start, the concept of rationalization was per-

[5] See among others, Osaka furitsu sangyō nōritsu kenkyūjo, *Wagakuni ni okeru sangyō tōsei ni tsuite* (Osaka: Sangyō nōritsu kenkyūjo, 1931), 43; Andrew Gordon, "Araki Tōichirō and the Shaping of Labor Management," in *Japanese Management in Historical Perspective,* ed. Yui Tsunehiko and Nakagawa Keiichirō, Proceedings of the Fifteenth International Conference on Business History (Tokyo: University of Tokyo Press, 1989), 180.

[6] Yoshino Shinji, *Wagakuni kōgyō no gōrika* (Nihon hyōronsha, 1930), 31; Shimazaki, "Beikoku."

[7] Noteworthy in this respect is the *Refa-Mappe* system, a German adaptation of Scientific Management introduced into Japan by Noda Nobuo. Although Noda was a vocal proponent, the system did not take root. Noda Nobuo, "Kagakuteki kanrihō kara seisansei undō e," *Keiei to rekishi* 9 (1986): 10.

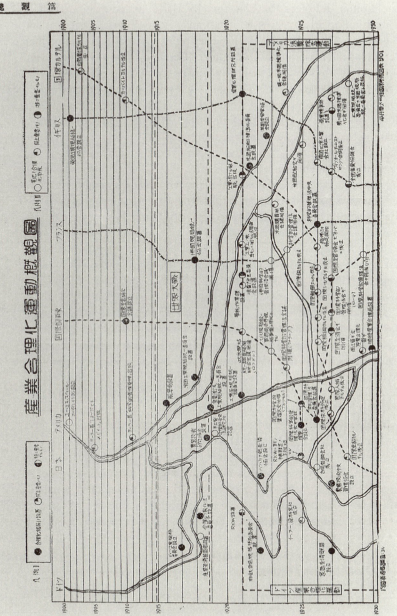

Fig. 1. "Sangyō gōrika undō gaikanzu" (An Outline of the Industrial Rationalization Movement). The broad but winding river at the left represents German rationalization, while the long and straight river diverging to the right represents the American movement. Japanese *sangyō gōrika* is depicted as the small—but growing—stream in the center. Source: Hirai Yasutarō, *Sangyō gōrika zuroku* (Shunyōdō, 1931), 10.

ceived in Japan as something novel and imported, yet at the same time as something familiar and accessible conceptually. Early Japanese commentators on rationalization invariably stressed its affinity with Scientific Management. "*Sangyō gōrika*," Minoguchi Tokijirō wrote pithily, "is nothing more than Scientific Management under another name."[8] Rationalization was presented as an outgrowth of Taylorism, a natural step forward in the application of the logic of Scientific Management. "The spirit and principles of rationalization and Scientific Management are the same," Ueno Yōichi assured his readers, but the scope of reform had been expanded from a single factory to an industry, the national economy and even the entire world.[9]

Although the continuity between the modern management movement and rationalization was taken as a given in Japan, there was less unanimity on what *sangyō gōrika* actually connoted and how (if at all) it should be put into practice. Almost all early accounts of rationalization sought inspiration in foreign models, and several standard definitions—all of them European in origin, epigrammatic, and unprovocative—came to be widely cited. Among the most popular was that proposed by the Reichskuratorium für Wirtschaftlichkeit: "Rationalization is the adoption and employment of all the means of increasing efficiency which are furnished by technical science and systematic organization. Its aim is to raise the general level of prosperity by cheaper, more plentiful, and better-quality goods."[10] Expansive and vague, definitions such as this provided little guidance to a Japanese audience seeking to understand the promise of the new movement. Such sweeping characterizations were apparently little consolation to European observers either, as Robert Brady reported that "Scarcely any term, concept, program or objective—whichever it may be considered— . . . has occasioned more discussion and dispute than 'rationalization.'"[11] The situation was to be much the same in Japan, as the definition of *sangyō gōrika* became a point of contention as soon as the term entered public discourse. Brady's conclusion that there was "considerable difference of opinion" regarding the movement seems a little mild, at least with respect to Japan. Writers from a wide range of political viewpoints sought to lay claim to the term and inscribe their preferred meanings upon it. Intellectuals, industrialists, and bureaucrats offered countless exegeses and vied to cast their interpretations as the "true" rationalization. One economist noted,

---

[8] Minoguchi Tokijirō, "Doitsu ni okeru sangyō gōrika no keizaiteki oyobi shakaiteki kokka," *Shakai seisaku jihō* 91 (April 1928): 11.

[9] Ueno Yōichi, "Amerika ni okeru gōrika undō," ibid., 86 (November 1927): 102.

[10] Robert Brady, "The Meaning of Rationalization: An Analysis of the Literature," *Quarterly Journal of Economics* 46 (May 1932): 527.

[11] Ibid., 526. See also Mary Nolan, *Visions of Modernity: American Business and the Modernization of Germany* (New York: Oxford University Press, 1994), 71.

with a certain frustration, that asking ten people for a definition of rationalization would yield "ten different answers."[12]

Although the term *sangyō gōrika* achieved remarkable rhetorical power, and the cluster of ideas and policies which came to adhere to it gained great exposure in Depression-era Japan, no definition more concrete than the Reichskuratorium's ever attained widespread acceptance. Writers at the time spoke of the "multiplicity of meanings" of "rationalization" and the more cautious academic commentators, rather than hazarding their own definitions, simply imposed taxonomies on others' attempts.[13] Within this context it is perhaps best to examine the Japanese conception of rationalization as a set of elements—assumptions, theories, and policies—which were acknowledged by virtually all parties as the ideological building blocks of *sangyō gōrika*. By recognizing that the multiplicity of definitions of rationalization derived from the relative stress that various commentators accorded these elements, it is possible to make sense not only of the concept of *sangyō gōrika* but also of the intellectual and methodological legacy of Scientific Management in early Shōwa Japan.

At the ideological heart of rationalization was the concept of science. " 'Rationally,' " Yoshino Shinji explained, "is interchangeable with 'scientifically' and means the management of an enterprise with a scientific spirit."[14] "Science and progress," another author observed, were synonymous with *sangyō gōrika*.[15] The power of science was perceived to be twofold. On the one hand, science was believed to be the source of economic growth and the engine of industrial development: America's production technology and Germany's applied research were credited for much of those nations' success in rationalization. On the other hand, science was assumed to be the optimum basis for the organization of economic life, from the household and factory up to the national and world economies. Rationalization was thus taken to be the application of science to industry and the industrial structure, "science" in this case connoting objectivity, the utmost efficiency, and the ascendance of "fact" over tradition and the rule of thumb.[16] As had been the case with Taylorism, however, such a claim to be "scientific" had more importance as an ideological

---

[12] Muramoto Fukumatsu, "Sangyō gōrika no hihan kijun to shite no tōsei no jūyōsei," *Shakai seisaku jihō* 116 (May 1930): 239.

[13] "Shasetsu: Wagakuni saikin no gorika undō," *Ekonomisuto,* 15 August 1928, 8; Hirai Yasutarō, *Sangyō gōrika zuroku* (Shunyōdō, 1931), 781–87.

[14] Yoshino, *Wagakuni,* 101.

[15] Nagaoka Yasutarō, "Sangyō no gōrika to rōdō kaikyū," *Shakai seisaku jihō* 91 (April 1928): 3.

[16] See Matsuoka Kinpei, *Sangyō gōrika ni maishin seyo* (Manejimento-sha, 1930), 93–95; on science and the concept of rationalization in Europe, see Robert Brady, *The Rationalization Movement in German Industry* (Berkeley: University of California Press, 1933), 3–4.

talisman than as a blueprint for policy. As science, rationalization was portrayed as natural, logical, and potent.

Although the appeal for scientific legitimation was common to both the efficiency and rationalization movements, the proponents of *sangyō gōrika* enhanced the concept of science used by Japanese Taylorites. Science (and thus rationalization), it was argued, was fundamentally at odds with what some called "economic individualism" and what others more bluntly labeled "selfishness." "Favoritism, custom, and blind self-centeredness," intoned Matsuoka Kinpei, a central figure in the Mitsubishi interests and a frequent commentator on *sangyō gōrika,* "are concepts fundamentally opposed to the spirit of industrial rationalization."[17] This particular gloss on "science" derived from the widely held belief that the world's economic problems during the 1920s stemmed from the narrow and self-serving behavior of certain economic actors: capitalists grasping after profits, firms falling into "excessive" competition, and organized labor demanding unreasonable rewards. The implications of this view were enormous: if the pursuit of self-interest had brought Japan and the world to an impasse, then the "invisible hand" was no more than a myth, and economic self-equilibration could not be assumed. The lesson to be learned from this realization seemed obvious, and virtually every Japanese commentator on *sangyō gōrika* took it on faith: the pursuit of rationalization required a "visible hand" to ensure efficiency and progress in industry.[18]

Recognizing the need for regulation in industrial development did not, however, answer the question of how the optimum economic adjustment was to be accomplished or what parties would direct the application of science and the restraint of "selfishness." On these issues there was much less consensus, and from the beginning of the rationalization movement the concept of "control" (*tōsei*) was highly charged. The specific point of contention was the role of the state in determining the structure and functioning of private industry. Many in the business community, especially those who spoke for small- and medium-sized producers, looked to the American model of an undemanding state that coordinated business self-regulation and promoted (rather than dictated) initiatives in standardization and waste elimination. A delegation of small businessmen that went to the United States in 1929, for example, recommended that the government's efforts in rationalization focus on the provision of trade offices abroad and the support of private efforts to boost exports and product quality.[19] This was hardly the role that most of the bureaucratic sponsors of

---

[17] Matsuoka, *Sangyō gōrika,* 94; see also Kishi Nobusuke, "Ōshū ni okeru sangyō gōrika no jissai ni tsuite," *Sangyō gōrika* 4 (January 1932): 30.

[18] For a persuasive presentation of this reasoning, see Yoshino, *Wagakuni,* 100 ff. For the view from a left-wing perspective, see Yamakawa Hitoshi, *Sangyō gōrika no hihan* (Shunyōdō, 1930).

[19] Kinoshita Otoichi, *Amerika no sangyō gōrika undō o miru* (Tenjinsha, 1930); Nakagawa Seisa, *Amerika no sangyō gōrika* (Tenjinsha, 1930).

sangyō gōrika dreamed of. The controlled economy may still have been just a glint in the eyes of young bureaucrats like Kishi Nobusuke in the early 1930s, yet the German experience provided a compelling model of a state that led rather than regulated, directed rather than nurtured, the process of rationalization.[20] In short, while the extent of state intervention in private industry was (and would continue to be) a focus of political controversy, the belief that the government must assume an active role in *sangyō gōrika* for the movement to be successful was a fundamental axiom in the Japanese conception of rationalization.[21]

The tools of rationalization were the subject of far less debate than the question of who should wield them. As Robert Brady attested, "There has been surprisingly little dispute on the scope and content of rationalization as a technical proposition."[22] On the macro level, rationalization was taken to mean horizontal and vertical integration—concentration, cartelization—with the goal of reducing "excessive" competition and allowing for cooperative efforts to eliminate waste, realize economies of scale, and lower costs. The need for such policies was felt particularly keenly in Japan, where the prevalence of small-scale industrial production and the pressure to maintain international competitiveness weighed heavily on the minds of policymakers. Nevertheless, it was recognized that integration alone would not ensure efficiency: structural adjustment had to be fused with reform of the production process to "rationalize" industry thoroughly. Despite the progress of the efficiency movement, the standards of business administration in Japan were much bemoaned by commentators on *sangyō gōrika*. Promoting the application of modern management methods was thus accorded new urgency as a central element of rationalization.

Despite the fact that Scientific Management had not fully penetrated Japanese workshops, some observers came to see Taylorization as only a first step in the rationalization of the factory. Over the course of the 1920s, Fordist mass production captured the imagination of industrialists, bureaucrats, and engineers around the world as a symbol of efficiency, technological progress, and the power of science. The mechanized assembly line, pioneered at Ford's Highland Park factory in the early 1910s, was a dramatic extension of the logic and the methodologies of Scientific Management. Like Taylorism, the Fordist vision was premised on the minute division of labor, the explicit segregation of planning from execution, and the standardization of all inputs, products, and processes. Yet in emphasizing economies of scale in manufac-

---

[20] Johnson, *MITI*, 103–9; Okuda Kenji, *Hito to keiei: Nihon keiei kanrishi kenkyū* (Manejimento-sha, 1985), 147–48.

[21] For example, see Matsuoka, *Sangyō gōrika*, 117–18; Ota Hidekazu, "Sangyō gōrika no shin-igi," *Sangyō* 7, no. 2 (February 1930): 38–39; Kojima Seiichi, *Sangyō gōrika* (Chikura shobō, 1929), 2.

[22] Brady, "Meaning," 539.

turing and the primacy of machine technology in determining the pace of factory work, Fordism went beyond the Taylorite agenda of managerial reform. As David Hounshell concludes, "The Ford approach was to eliminate labor by machinery, not, as the Taylorites customarily did, to take a given production process and improve the efficiency of the workers through time and motion study and a differential piecerate [*sic*] system of payment (or some such work incentive). Taylor took production hardware as a given and sought revisions in labor processes and the organization of work; Ford engineers mechanized work processes and found workers to tend their machines. . . . This was the essence of the assembly line. . . ."[23]

In theory at least, the Fordist model of high-volume, low-cost assembly-line production was the logical endpoint of the rationalization movement, the ultimate culmination of both industrial integration and the modernization of factory management. As many Japanese observers realized, however, the road to a Fordist paradise was not without its obstacles. In the first place, Fordist mass production required levels of technical mastery and capital investment that seemed beyond the capabilities of almost all sectors of Japanese industry at the time. Yet even had Japanese manufacturers been able to acquire sufficient financing and mechanical proficiency, the problem still remained of finding suitable markets for a new flood of mass produced commodities. Indeed, well over a decade after the end of World War II, Japanese industry continued to suffer from considerable excess capacity. Through the 1920s and the Depression years, in the context of a stagnant domestic economy and generally unstable, unpromising export markets, any corporate commitment to a high-volume production regime seemed premature—if not virtually suicidal—in the absence of an assured base of consumer demand.[24]

In the Fordist model, however, the dilemma of underdeveloped markets was hardly insurmountable. As the American experience seemed to prove, the mass consumption required by Fordist mass producers could be delivered by a corporate commitment to high wage levels. As Herbert Hoover attested, "High wages [are the] very essence of great production."[25] A few in the Japanese business community looked to the American example and promoted the development of domestic consumption as a viable economic recovery strategy.[26] Most, however, remained skeptical of a high-wage approach given Japan's

---

[23] David A. Hounshell, *From the American System to Mass Production, 1800–1932* (Baltimore: Johns Hopkins University Press, 1984), 252–53. See also Stephen E. Meyer III, *The Five Dollar Day* (Albany: State University of New York Press, 1981), chap. 2.

[24] For a detailed treatment of Japanese reactions to Fordism, and the economic circumstances which militated against Fordist reorganization in Japan, see Elizabeth P. Tsunoda, "Rationalizing Japan's Political Economy: The Business Initiative, 1920–1955" (Ph.D. diss., Columbia University, 1993), chap. 1.

[25] Quoted in Stuart Ewen, *Captains of Consciousness* (New York: McGraw-Hill, 1976), 28.

[26] Nakagawa Seisa, "Beikoku no sangyō gōrika o miru," *Tokyo kōjō konwakai kaihō* 51 (December 1930); Shimazaki, "Beikoku."

plentiful supply of inexpensive manpower and the comparative advantage this cheap labor provided in international competition. In any case, Japan's relative poverty and its dependence on imported raw materials clearly appeared to militate against an American-style consumer economy. Consequently, Japanese business and government leaders saw the expansion of overseas markets as the only possible alternative, the only path which could provide consumers for mass produced goods, yet would not necessitate a costly high-wage strategy. Thus in Japanese thinking on rationalization, an export drive was assumed to be an essential component—even a prerequisite—of any efforts to attain Fordist production practices.[27]

In short, although Japanese observers did come to regard Fordism as an evolutionary advance on Scientific Management, even an inevitable stage in the progress of modern industry, the Fordist reorganization of factory production was considered only a distant goal in Japan. In a small number of sectors, most notably textiles, extensive mechanization and the pursuit of advanced mass production methods did make economic sense in the 1920s and early 1930s. Yet under conditions of scarce capital, abundant labor, and uncertain markets, the high-volume, high-technology assembly line was acknowledged as an inappropriate model for most Japanese firms.

While Fordism thus turned out to be little more than a mirage in Depression-era Japan, its rejection did, if anything, reinforce the importance accorded Scientific Management in industrial circles. The application of Taylorite methods—which promised increased efficiency even to small-scale, labor-intensive workshops, and often required little new investment in production technology—seemed to address Japan's industrial ills in a manner that more elaborate Fordist reforms could not. Scientific Management was accordingly affirmed as an immediate priority—and a realistic objective—in Japan's rationalization offensive.

Although much of the writing on sangyō gōrika focused on its economic agenda and its effect on the business community, the social implications of rationalization were also addressed by many Japanese commentators. Proponents were unanimous in their insistence that the rationalization movement had to go beyond technical imperatives and high politics to cultivate a popular base of support. Well aware that progress could be checked by opposition or foot-dragging at any number of levels, the bureaucrats and business leaders

---

[27] Tawara Magoichi, "Sangyō gōrika seisaku yōkō," Shakai seisaku jihō 116 (May 1930): 1–6; Takahashi Mamoru, "Sangyō gōrika seisaku ni okeru kigyō tōsei," in Nihon shihonshugi—tenkai to ronri, ed. Hoshi Makoto (Tokyo daigaku shuppankai, 1978), 194. General Ugaki Kazunari explained in 1930 that "industrial rationalization will only increase unemployment and lead to social tragedy unless accompanied by expanded markets. . . . These markets will be won in economic competition over price and quality. But if foreign relations atrophy, the competition will be restricted." Quoted in Andrew Gordon, Labor and Imperial Democracy in Prewar Japan (Berkeley: University of California Press, 1991), 267.

championing rationalization endeavored to cast it as a mass mobilization of the Japanese people. "Rationalization," Minister of Commerce and Industry Tawara Magoichi declared in 1930, "must be a great popular movement with the cooperation of all."[28] Cooperation was considered crucial: the success of rationalization was taken to depend not only on public-private and interfirm cooperation, but also on a stable and harmonious capital-labor relationship. Many commentators interpreted this as a fundamental lesson of "American-style" rationalization and enjoined Japanese employers to redouble their efforts at harmonization (*rōshi kyōchō*).[29] As Matsuoka Kinpei noted, "It goes without saying that the most irrational element in industrial society today is the concept of class conflict."[30]

In the rhetoric of *sangyō gōrika,* "mutual sacrifice" went hand in hand with "mobilization" and "cooperation." Few observers could avoid the conclusion that rationalization would be detrimental to the interests of considerable portions of society. The editors of the business journal *Ekonomisuto* (Economist), while testifying to the need for rationalization, warned that it would almost certainly lead to increased unemployment, the "sweating" of labor, the collapse of many small businesses, and the artificial maintenance of high prices by cartels.[31] Proponents of *sangyō gōrika* argued that the ill effects of their program were transitory and that "mutual sacrifice" in the short run would bring "mutual gain" over time.[32] What exactly these future returns would be was somewhat vague, although proponents took great pains to stress that all classes should ultimately benefit from rationalization. Wakabayashi Yonekichi, for example, averred that "Rationalization is not for the benefit of capitalists. It is not for the sake of workers. It must truly be for the good of all human beings."[33] According to the industrialist Nakajima Kumakichi, an important spokesman on *sangyō gōrika,* the movement's goal was the "increase of national wealth and the people's well-being" (*kokuri minpuku no zōshin*).[34]

The protestations of concern for the common man which littered Japanese writings on rationalization were often far from convincing, especially in an environment of widespread layoffs and declining wage levels. The language of "mutual gain" was, after all, aimed in large part at deflecting the argument of left-wing intellectuals that the goal of *sangyō gōrika* was the buttressing of capitalism. Although much lip service was paid to "humanized" rationalization and the "welfare orientation" of the movement, little of this rhetoric ap-

[28] Tawara Magoichi, "Sangyō no gōrika to genseifu no kikaku," *Ekonomisuto,* 1 April 1930, 14; Kishi, "Ōshū," 35.

[29] Osaka furitsu sangyō nōritsu kenkyūjo, *Sangyō tōsei,* 23; Harada Shūichi, "Sangyō gōrika to shin rōshi kyōchō," *Shōgaku hyōron* 7, no. 4 (March 1929): 1–41; Yoshino, *Wagakuni,* 271.

[30] Matsuoka, *Sangyō gōrika,* 95.

[31] "Shuchō: Gōrika no hitsuzensei to sono tokushitsu," *Ekonomisuto,* 1 April 1930, 12.

[32] Osaka furitsu sangyō nōritsu kenkyūjo, *Sangyō tōsei,* 42.

[33] Wakabayashi Yonekichi, "Seishinteki dōsa no gōrika," *Shakai seisaku jihō* 116 (May 1930): 211.

[34] Quoted in Nakamura Seiji, *Nihon seisansei kōjō undō shi* (Keisō shobō, 1958), 39.

pears to have made the transition to policy.[35] The thorny issue of distribution was almost completely ignored, as proponents of rationalization avoided it much more scrupulously than Japanese Taylorites had. At the very least, vagueness on the nature of "mutual gain" seems to have betrayed the ambivalence of economic bureaucrats and industrialists regarding the goals of rationalization. Even if, as Nakajima claimed, the objective of the movement was *kokuri minpuku no zōshin,* attaining "national wealth" and increasing "the people's well-being" were by no means assumed to be the same thing. As shown graphically in a Ministry of Commerce and Industry report on industrial standardization (figure 2), although economic development and popular welfare were both seen as outcomes of rationalization, they were clearly perceived as distinct ends reached by distinct processes. Not surprisingly, while the rhetoric of rationalization exalted the benefits which would—eventually—be enjoyed by all, its practice tended to concentrate on the less expansive, more capitalistic goal of building "national wealth."

Overall, the extent to which the Japanese conception of rationalization grew out of the Taishō discourse of Scientific Management is striking. In the construction of *sangyō gōrika,* the Taylorite quest for efficiency within the factory was extended far beyond it: the "visible hand" of scientific managers on the shop floor was amplified to "control" (*tōsei*) on the industrial level; the long-standing appeal for mutually beneficial cooperation between capital and labor was drawn out to embrace cooperation among firms and between business and the state. On the ideological plane, "science" was central to both the efficiency movement and *sangyō gōrika,* as was the conception of reform as a sort of mass spiritual awakening. "The essential precondition for rationalization," Matsuoka concluded, "is a 'Mental Revolution' of our people just like the one Taylor called for regarding Scientific Management."[36] Not surprisingly, even the critiques of rationalization echoed earlier comment on Taylorism, Marxists denouncing it as exploitative, Teruoka Gitō condemning it as unscientific, Kanda Kōichi and others arguing for a "Japanese revision."[37] Industrial rationalization was, in short, an heir to the varied intellectual legacy of Japanese Taylorism and the Taishō efficiency movement.

In the West, a similar continuity of approach between the modern management movement and rationalization was apparent. Both German *Rationalisierung* and the American waste elimination and standardization movements

---

[35] See, for example, Watanabe Tetsuzō, "Rōdō no gōrika," and Taniguchi Yoshihiko, "Fukushi undō to shite no gōrika undō," both in *Shakai seisaku jihō* 116 (May 1930); Araki Tōichirō, "Kagakuteki kanrihō to rōdō sōgi," *Tokyo kōjō konwakai kaihō* 42 (June 1929): 59–71.

[36] Matsuoka, *Sangyō gōrika,* 114; see also Harada, "Sangyō gōrika," 34.

[37] Kawakami Hajime, "Rōdōsha kara mita sangyō gōrika," *Chūō kōron* 45, no. 6 (June 1930): 2–31; Teruoka Gitō, "Sangyō gōrika no konpon mondai," *Shakai seisaku jihō* 116 (May 1930): 145–60; Kanda Kōichi, "Nihon sangyō no gōrika to sangyō seishin no sakkō," *Tokyo kōjō konwakai kaihō* 55 (April 1931): 2–14.

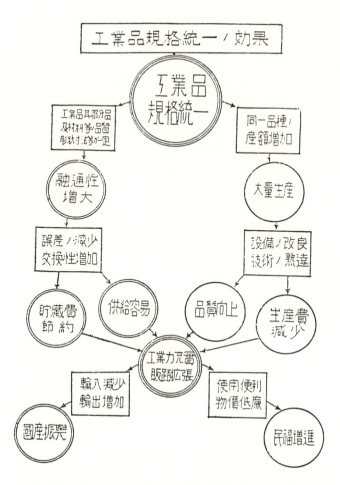

Fig. 2. "Kōgyōhin kikaku tōitsu no kōka" (The Results of Industrial Standardization). The chart shows how standardization leads, through mass production and "greater versatility" (*yūzōsei zōdai*), to the consolidation of industrial power and the expansion of markets. This, in turn, leads—via increased exports and decreased imports—to the "encouragement of domestic production" (circle at lower left). Meanwhile, lower prices and "convenience of use" (*shiyō benri*) are presumed to lead to "a betterment of the people's well-being" (circle at lower right). Source: "Kōgyōhin kikaku tōitsu oyobi shōhin tanjunka ni tsuite," *Sangyō gōrika* 2 (January 1931): 138.

drew heavily on previous experience in promoting Scientific Management.[38] At least in Europe, however, proponents of rationalization labored to divert attention away from their movement's roots and distance themselves ideologically from Taylorism and its considerable intellectual and political baggage. *Taylorismus* was increasingly portrayed as dated, exploitative and founded on self-interest, with rationalization and *Fordismus* appearing all the more dynamic and progressive as a consequence.[39] By contrast, while some in Japan sought to draw similar distinctions,[40] few indeed suggested that Scientific Management was discredited or that it was ideologically incompatible with *sangyō gōrika*. Given the provisional consensus on "revised" Taylorism in industrial and intellectual circles, Japanese proponents of rationalization did not feel compelled to distance themselves from the work of the efficiency movement. Furthermore, because Scientific Management did not attract the knee-jerk labor antipathy which it had in the United States, or acquire the "subversive" technocratic connotations which Charles Maier suggests it did in interwar Europe, the capitalist and bureaucrat champions of *sangyō gōrika* saw little need to deny their movement's Taylorite ancestry.[41] In any case, the Japanese conception of rationalization was based not on the rejection of Taylorite assumptions, strategies, and methodologies, but rather on their reaffirmation within a new political and economic context.

Rationalizing the Scientific Management Movement

As noted earlier, proponents of rationalization were keenly aware that modern management methods had not yet spread throughout Japanese industry. Depression-era observers recognized that, despite the progress of Taylorism in the 1920s, much room remained for increasing efficiency and reducing costs through managerial reform. "Regrettably," Matsuoka Kinpei noted, "there are still many aspects of factory management that must be judged to be unscientific."[42] As a Mitsubishi Economic Research Institute study stressed, the most pressing concern of *sangyō gōrika* at the firm level was the modernization of management: "The fact is that the problem of rationalization in this country cannot be understood as simply one of mechanization. Indeed, mechanization

[38] Judith Merkle, *Management and Ideology: The Legacy of the International Scientific Management Movement* (Berkeley: University of California Press, 1980), esp. chap. 6; Nolan, *Visions of Modernity,* chaps. 2–4; Sasaki, "Tokyo bankoku kōgyō kaigi," 130–34.

[39] Nolan, *Visions of Modernity,* 42–50, 230; Merkle, *Management and Ideology,* 192–94; Thomas Hughes, *American Genesis* (New York: Penguin, 1989), chap. 6, "Taylorismus + Fordismus = Amerikanismus."

[40] Osaka furitsu sangyō nōritsu kenkyūjo, *Sangyō tōsei,* 88–89.

[41] Charles Maier, "Between Taylorism and Technocracy: European Ideologies and the Vision of Industrial Productivity in the 1920s," in *In Search of Stability: Explorations in Historical Political Economy* (Cambridge: Cambridge University Press, 1987; originally published 1970), 48; Nolan, *Visions of Modernity,* 39.

[42] Matsuoka, *Sangyō gōrika,* 94.

is only of secondary concern: the main problem is one of organization. In other words, the most important question is how we should plan for and organize the use of our plentiful supply of manpower."[43]

The importance of improving managerial techniques was felt acutely by the bureaucratic and business leaders of the rationalization movement and, from the start, the promotion of Scientific Management figured prominently in the goals of the state-led efforts. The first major statement on government rationalization policy, a 1929 report by the Commerce and Industry Deliberative Council (Shōkō Shingikai), emphasized "increasing the efficiency of enterprises" and underlined the need for "detailed investigations of management and business practices" in Japan.[44] This conclusion was echoed by Prime Minister Hamaguchi at the first meeting of the Emergency Industrial Deliberative Council (Rinji Sangyō Shingikai), a blue-ribbon study commission which laid the groundwork for the state's rationalization initiatives. Calling for a "fundamental reform of the industrial order," Hamaguchi cited "the application of the principles of Scientific Management" and "the standardization of manufactured goods" as essential components of rationalization.[45] The council itself affirmed the great importance of Scientific Management "under current industrial conditions in Japan" and stressed the extreme urgency of adopting "management approaches and techniques unburdened by the weight of traditional practices."[46] In short, by the time the Temporary Industrial Rationalization Bureau was established in 1930 as the main government organ for coordinating *sangyō gōrika,* the promotion of modern management techniques—that is to say, Scientific Management—was assumed to be a central concern of state policy in rationalization.

The nucleus of government efforts in managerial reform was the Production Management Committee (Seisankanri Iinkai), one of the five standing committees created within the Rationalization Bureau at its inception.[47] As it was widely recognized that management improvement could not be accomplished "under the coercion of legal force,"[48] the committee's functions were oriented toward research and promotion rather than control and direction. Specifically, the body was charged with making policy recommendations regarding factory management and disseminating information on the practical application of modern administrative methods in industry. The members of the committee

---

[43] Quoted in Nakamura, *Nihon seisansei,* 58.

[44] Tsūshō sangyō shō, ed., *Shōkō seisaku shi 9: Sangyō gōrika* (Tsūshō sangyō shō, 1961), 14.

[45] Ibid., 17.

[46] Ibid., 21.

[47] The other standing committees were Financial Management, Retail Management, Standardization, and "Buy Japanese." With the exception of the last, all the committees dealt to some extent with the modernization of management practices. As the most active of these committees, and as the one that dealt directly with factory management, the Production Management Committee will be emphasized here.

[48] Rinji sangyō gōrikyoku, "Seisankanri kaizen saku to chūō kikan setsuritsu an," *Tokyo kōjō konwakai kaihō* 55 (April 1931): 46.

came largely from the private sector (since the bureau was conceived as a public-private effort) and the majority were veterans of the Taishō efficiency movement. Not surprisingly, many prominent Taylorites became active proponents of rationalization in the late 1920s and were eager to cooperate with the government in spreading the good news of Scientific Management. Association with the Rationalization Bureau offered legitimation (as well as a pulpit) to Japan's first generation of management experts: as Leslie Hannah has perceptively commented, rationalization was readily embraced by "a new managerial class anxious to validate its position in the eyes of both the state and the workers."[49]

The roster of the Production Management Committee read like a "Who's Who" of the prewar Scientific Management movement. The chairman was Yamashita Okiie, the champion of time-and-motion study in the National Railways, who had imbibed the logic of rationalization as a delegate to the World Economic Conference in 1927. Among the committee members were Godō Takuo (father of the "limit gauge" at Kure Arsenal), Katō Takeo (Mitsubishi Electric's work study expert), Takeo Toshisuke (the Stevens Institute graduate at Karatsu Ironworks), Katō Shigeo (the Niigata Ironworks engineer), Araki Tōichirō (the Taylorite consultant), Teruoka Gitō (the labor scientist), Kanda Kōichi (of the Monopoly Bureau) and Noda Nobuo (of Mitsubishi Gōshi). Academic engineers and the business community were also represented on the committee, the latter by Nissan's Ayukawa Yoshisuke and Mimura Kiichi of the Besshi Copper Mine.[50]

The most striking omission from the membership roll of the Production Management Committee was Ueno Yōichi. The exclusion of the "father of the efficiency movement" has occasioned considerable scholarly discussion, although the most persuasive explanation has been offered by Noda Nobuo. Noda, who selected the members in consultation with his mentor Matsuoka Kinpei, points the finger at Yamashita, a "dyed-in-the-wool bureaucrat" who fervently believed in the professionalization of management and engineering. According to Noda, Yamashita refused to chair the body if "efficiency experts" —amateurish "popularizers" like Ueno—were offered membership.[51] In any case, the committee was stacked with the luminaries of the "practical" stream of the Taishō management movement, while Ueno and his colleagues were dismissed as unprofessional "efficiency peddlers" (nōritsu-ya) and denied the legitimacy of state recognition.

[49] Leslie Hannah, "Comments," in Government and Business, ed. Nakagawa Keiichirō, Proceedings of the Fifth International Conference on Business History (Tokyo: University of Tokyo Press, 1980), 101–5.

[50] An annotated listing of the committee members is given in Sasaki and Nonaka, "Kagakuteki kanrihō," 251.

[51] Noda, "Kagakuteki kanrihō kara," 7; see also Okuda, Hito to keiei, 188, n. 1. On Yamashita, see Tsuzaki Masanosuke, "Watakushi no nōritsudō (sono 1)," IE 11, no. 1 (January 1969): 116–20.

The main work of the committee was the writing and publication of position papers on a variety of issues concerning factory management. Over the course of the decade, the group produced more than thirty of these "pamphlets" (*panfuretto*), varying in length from a few pages to several hundred. The topics (selected by Noda in consultation with Matsuoka and Yamashita) encompassed a wide range of current concerns, running the gamut from the pedestrian ("Improving Fire Prevention Methods") to the controversial ("Profit Sharing with Employees"). The majority of the pamphlets focused on the implementation of the basic methodological elements of Scientific Management: aptitude testing, process control, wage systems, time-and-motion study.[52] The pamphlets themselves were generally quite technical in content and pragmatic in outlook, offering extensive case studies of how the recommended techniques had been successfully applied in Japanese firms. In most instances, committee members drew on their personal experience for these accounts: Yamashita's chairmanship (and the advanced state of railway management) ensured that a large portion of the case studies came from the files of the JNR.[53]

The publications of the Production Management Committee were clearly aimed not at the general public but at those specialists—professional managers and engineers—who were closest to the process of production in Japanese factories. Particular care appears to have been taken to target the reports at the managers of small- and medium-sized firms.[54] Proponents of rationalization agreed that the need for management reform was most acute in this sector of industry. Observers bemoaned the stagnant technology and unsystematic management practices of small-scale producers, especially as such enterprises employed the majority of Japan's industrial work force and accounted for a considerable share of Japanese exports.[55] Leaders of the Rationalization Bureau were adamant on the need to take positive steps to improve efficiency in small- and medium-sized firms. As Yoshino Shinji emphasized, in the context of the Depression these producers—and not the large firms that

---

[52] A listing of pamphlets is given in Tsūshō sangyō shō, *Shōkō seisaku shi 9*, 42–43.

[53] The dominance of practical examples from the JNR also reflects the reluctance of many private-sector firms to publicize widely their successes (or failures) in workshop management. After World War II, advocates of managerial reform soundly criticized this long-standing tendency in Japanese industry.

[54] Small- and medium-sized enterprises were defined as those manufacturers employing between 5 and 30 workers (small), and 30 and 100 (medium).

[55] For a fascinating perspective on small-scale industry in Japan which suggests why systematic management practices had difficulties taking root among small, labor-intensive producers, see Takeuchi Johzen, *The Role of Labour-Intensive Sectors in Japanese Industrialization* (Tokyo: United Nations University Press, 1991). Although, as Takeuchi details, labor specialization was often highly developed in the production of commodities like shell buttons and brushes, unstable markets and cheap labor militated against increased mechanization and rigorous managerial analysis of the work process in labor-intensive sectors.

had the wherewithal to help themselves—were most deserving of state assistance.[56] The Production Management Committee was, of course, a natural conduit for such technical guidance, and the body took great pains to make its message accessible to managers in small firms as well as large.[57] Most of the committee's pamphlets proclaimed in no uncertain terms that the methods of Scientific Management were applicable to firms of any size, and not simply to large-scale mass producers or those Japanese workshops which had already been partially Taylorized.

The committee's approach was forcefully stated in the first of its pamphlets, "The Basic Goals of the Proposed Production Management Committee."[58] "Our aim," the document announced, "is to correct what we believe to be the greatest defects in Japanese industry today." Rejecting "abstract theories" and the thoughtless mimicry of Western models, the committee sought to "identify those methods which have proven in actual practice to give the greatest results." In line with contemporary thinking on rationalization, the statement stressed the importance of lowering production costs and maintaining international competitiveness: "It is essential that we plan for economic growth based on the gains generated by processing imported raw materials and exporting the finished goods." At the same time, the committee harkened back to Taylorite ideals: "Production costs can be reduced if we endeavor to correct managerial faults, raise efficiency by eliminating wasted effort, and achieve the maximum production from the minimum input of labor. It will then be possible to pay relatively more for the same amount of work, and we can realize high wages and low production costs simultaneously. This is the hidden promise of production management." Cooperation was, of course, perceived as essential to the committee's (and the rationalization movement's) progress: "Reaching our ultimate objective depends on attaining the utmost effort and cooperation [kyōchō] from both labor and capital. It is no different from the crew of a ship at sea, who all—regardless of whether they are fighting the wind on deck or enduring the heat of the boiler room—struggle together for the single goal of reaching their destination." Needless to say, the payoff for cooperation and sacrifice, the endpoint of rationalization and management reform, was the hazy promise of "mutual gain": "increasing efficiency will, as a result of bringing prosperity to the entire economy, be of considerable benefit not only to capitalists and workers, but also to society as a whole."

Drawing on the Taylorite ideology and the cluster of ideas surrounding *sangyō gōrika,* the "Basic Goals" was a clear statement of both the Production

[56] Yoshino Shinji, "Waga sangyō gōrika no ni-daijūten," *Ekonomisuto,* 1 April 1930, 17–18.

[57] Rinji sangyō gōrikyoku, "Seisankanri kaizen saku," 49.

[58] Rinji sangyō gōrikyoku, Seisankanri iinkai, *Seisankanri iinkai teian no konpon shushi,* Pamphlet 0 (n.p., December 1930). All references in this paragraph come from this short document. For an incisive treatment of the recommendations of the Production Management Committee, see Tsunoda, "Rationalizing," chap. 2.

Management Committee's heritage in the efficiency movement and its endorsement of the agenda of rationalization. The themes developed in this first pamphlet ran through the entire series, which, taken as a whole, forms a snapshot of "best method" practice in Japanese factories during the 1930s. Not surprisingly, the committee's published recommendations were fully consistent ideologically, rhetorically, and methodologically with the notions of Taylorism which had taken shape during the Taishō period. The report on "Wage Systems," for example, affirmed the scientific managers' faith in incentive schemes but also stressed the importance of paying a living wage and fostering trust between employers and workers.[59] The recommendations on work study insisted on the necessity of standardized and simplified work regimens, yet also highlighted the findings of labor science on the physiological limitations of laborers.[60] Other pamphlets stressed the need for professional, neutral managers, the benefits of statistical methods and process control devices, and the importance of building cooperation on the shop floor and mobilizing the good will of workers. In a few respects, the pamphlets did depart from a strictly Taylorite model—notably in suggesting that workers be rotated through a number of different jobs so as to increase their skills and allow for more flexible staffing—yet such thoroughly pragmatic refinements hardly vitiated the dominant Taylorite thrust of the committee's work.[61]

Indeed, the Production Management Committee's pamphlets constitute what was, in many respects, the most coherent statement of the "revised" Taylorite approach articulated in prewar Japan. As these documents suggest, interwar Japanese managers did not conceive of Scientific Management as a rigid framework of shop-floor practice, a laundry list of specific techniques that became, in aggregate, the definitive "Taylor system." Rather, in Japan as in the West, Scientific Management was perceived by its advocates in terms of broad methodological imperatives and distinctive ideological proclivities. As expressed in a relatively distilled form in the pamphlets of the Production Management Committee—as well as in the more diffuse literature of the Taishō efficiency movement—the vision of a "revised" Taylorism was pivoted on

[59] Rinji sangyō gōrikyoku, Seisankanri iinkai, *Chingin seido,* Pamphlet 11 (Osaka: Nihon kōgyō kyōkai, 1935).

[60] Rinji sangyō gōrikyoku, Seisankanri iinkai, *Sagyō kenkyū,* Pamphlet 13 (Osaka: Nihon kōgyō kyōkai, 1936).

[61] Rinji sangyō gōrikyoku, Seisankanri iinkai, *Jugyōin tagaikawari seido,* Pamphlet 2 (Osaka: Nihon kōgyō kyōkai, 1930). Koike Kazuo has emphasized job rotation as a characteristic feature of skill formation among twentieth-century Japanese workers. Koike argues that the acquisition of wide-ranging skills through on-the-job training and internal transfers has led to the "white collarization" of shop-floor operatives and fundamentally shaped Japanese industrial relations. Koike Kazuo, *Understanding Industrial Relations in Modern Japan* (New York: St. Martin's Press, 1988); Koike Kazuo, *The Economics of Work in Japan* (Tokyo: LTCB International Library Foundation, 1995). See also Howard F. Gospel, ed., *Industrial Training and Technological Innovation* (London: Routledge, 1991).

a small number of central premises. Of critical importance, needless to say, was a commitment to the reorganization of the industrial workplace on a scientific basis, a process which included (but was not limited to) the specialization, simplification, and standardization of the production process. Closely allied with this was the conviction that complex systems—whether factories, companies, or even industries—only functioned optimally under the centralized control of a professional elite of management specialists and engineers. This cadre of experts was also to play a crucial role in the defusing of class tensions: as the neutral intermediaries in the "Mental Revolution," managers were to orchestrate capital-labor accommodation through the employment of scientific knowledge, an ethic of earnest cooperation, and the promise of plentiful rewards for all. Finally, due consideration was accorded the "human factor" in industry, as the mechanistic rigidity of rationalized production was to be tempered with systematic attention to the physiological, psychological, and spiritual needs of the factory work force.

But if the Production Management Committee's pamphlets thus presented a concise outline of the Taylorite approach as it was understood in interwar Japan, they also betrayed the difficulties Japanese advocates faced in forging a concrete and credible program of humanized, "revised" Scientific Management. For instance, the committee's adherence to the high-wage gospel, while clearly continuous with the Taylorite paradigm, seemed almost absurd—either icily cynical or hopelessly naive—in the context of the Great Depression.[62] Proposals for shop-floor discussion groups and profit sharing, not to mention the renewed calls for "harmonious cooperation," also rang a bit hollow under the prevailing circumstances. Even the comfortable symbiosis of Taylorism and paternalistic labor practices began to falter and fray during the early 1930s. The shine on corporate familialism was badly tarnished by the divisive Kanebō strike of 1930, waged by female workers who felt betrayed by their "warm" employers when wages—rather than dividends—were cut in a time of stringency.[63] Amidst widespread unemployment, industrial managers found the carrot expendable and the stick expedient in their dealings with labor. And while the Taylorites mobilized in the campaign for *sangyō gōrika* retained an almost dogmatic adherence to the Scientific Management gospel, they fell short of articulating a strategy of labor accommodation consistent with the economic realities of the 1930s. Thus the "Mental Revolution" remained an objective that was much esteemed rhetorically, but which was not adequately translated into a comprehensive (and viable) code of practice during Japan's rationalization movement.

Even in this light, the Production Management Committee's pamphlets furnished an impressive blueprint for the reform of Japanese workshops. Yet

[62] See Tsunoda, "Rationalizing," 88–90.

[63] Sheldon Garon, *The State and Labor in Modern Japan* (Berkeley: University of California Press, 1985), 172–73.

planning for change was inevitably much simpler than actually realizing it. Consequently, less than a year after its founding, the committee proposed that a central organ be established to distribute its pamphlets and actively promote the Rationalization Bureau's agenda of managerial modernization. Recognizing that the message of Scientific Management had to be sown at the grassroots level throughout the nation, the committee sought to mobilize an existing network of prefectural business associations called "Industry Roundtables" (Kōgyō Konwakai).[64] The Roundtables had originally been organized to diffuse information on the Factory Law, and their constituency was primarily the managers and owners of small- and medium-sized industrial concerns. Most of them were controlled by the police in their locality and all (with the exception of those in Tokyo and Osaka) had grown moribund after the Factory Law was fully implemented in 1929.[65] In April 1931, the Roundtables unanimously approved the Production Management Committee's proposal and agreed to federate under a new umbrella organization called the Japan Industrial Association (Nihon Kōgyō Kyōkai).

With the goals of "disseminating specific plans for industrial improvement" and fostering "mutual enlightenment" in the business community, the Industrial Association's operations began in earnest in 1932.[66] Start-up funding was provided by the Ministry of Commerce and Industry and a personal contribution from Nakajima Kumakichi. Operating expenses were covered by an annual subsidy channeled through the Rationalization Bureau and private donations solicited by Nakajima.[67] Nakajima's generosity did not go unrewarded: he was named chairman and, at his instigation, the new body was originally headquartered in Osaka.[68] The association's connections with the Production Management Committee were, of course, very strong, with Yamashita serving as an adviser (*komon*) to the organization and functioning as its main public spokesman. In addition to printing and distributing the committee's pamphlets, the association sponsored a wide range of activities: publishing a monthly journal, organizing conventions and research seminars, underwriting

---

[64] Rinji sangyō gōrikyoku, Seisankanri iinkai, *Seisankanri no kaizen o mokuteki to suru chūō kikan setsuritsu an,* Pamphlet 24 (Osaka: Nihon kōgyō kyōkai, 1931).

[65] Hazama Hiroshi, *Nihon no shiyōsha dantai to rōshi kankei* (Nihon rōdō kyōkai, 1981), 102–4.

[66] "Nihon kōgyō kyōkai no ninmu to sono jigyō," *Nihon kōgyō kyōkai kaihō* 4 (April 1933): 1–2.

[67] Nikaidō Shōji, "Nihon kōgyō kyōkai no koro o kataru," *IE* 9, no. 7 (July 1967): 703; Tsūshō sangyō shō, *Shōkō seisaku shi 9,* 154.

[68] Horime Ken'ichi, "Nihon kōgyō kyōkai no koro o kataru," *IE* 9, no. 6 (June 1967): 561. In 1936, the association's offices were moved to the Oji Paper Building in Tokyo. Nakajima was also given the honor of writing the calligraphy for the association newsletter's masthead. Much to the dismay of Yamashita (a strong proponent of the modernization of the Japanese language), Nakajima inscribed the characters in the traditional (right-to-left) order, rather than in the "rational" left-to-right style. Nikaidō, "Nihon kōgyō kyōkai," 702.

lecture tours for committee members, producing promotional films on management techniques, coordinating factory tours, and subsidizing exhibitions and essay contests. Drawing on the national network of Industry Roundtables (and the government's bankroll), the association quickly became a dynamic and high-profile vehicle for carrying the message of "rationalized" management to the unconverted.

Leaders of the Industrial Association recognized from the outset that publicity had to be bolstered by more active reform programs to deliver the desired level of results. The members of the Production Management Committee were aware that the typical small producer did not have the resources to hire managerial specialists, and they were convinced that unprofessional "efficiency experts" like Ueno did more harm than good.[69] As a result, the association resolved at its first convention to sponsor a consulting service, aimed primarily at small- and medium-sized firms, which would aid in the implementation of Scientific Management. Two young engineers who had worked under Yamashita at the JNR (Horime Ken'ichi and Ono Tsuneo) were hired in 1933 and dispatched into firms to adapt to their specific circumstances the techniques recommended by the Production Management Committee.[70] While progress was initially slow, consulting gained increasing prominence among the association's activities over the course of the 1930s.

With government financial aid and the support of Taylorite luminaries on the Production Management Committee, the Industrial Association was certainly the flagship organization of the modern management movement in early Shōwa Japan. It was not, however, the only such body promoting Scientific Management. A flurry of organization had taken place within the Japanese efficiency movement during the latter half of the 1920s, as the Taishō "boom" gave way to a more structured course of development. In 1925, the Osaka Industrial Efficiency Research Institute (Osaka Furitsu Sangyō Nōritsu Kenkyūjo) was founded by local authorities and regional business leaders to study administrative methods, train managerial experts, and promote "efficiency increase" in area industry.[71] Two years later, the nation's first organization of academic specialists in management, the Business Administration Association (Keiei Gakkai) was established with Ueda Teijirō as its chairman.[72] The year 1927 also saw the founding of the largest and most important of these new groups, the Japan Efficiency Federation (Nihon Nōritsu Rengōkai). An amal-

[69] Rinji sangyō gōrikyoku, "Seisankanri kaizen saku," 49; Nikaidō, "Nihon kōgyō kyōkai," 702–4.

[70] See Horime, "Nihon kōgyō kyōkai," 559–60; Ono Tsuneo, ed., *Mōshon-maindo: Horime Ken'ichi tsuitōroku* (Nihon nōritsu kyōkai, 1970), 27–28; "Nihon kōgyō kyōkai no nimmu to sono jigyō," 4.

[71] Osaka furitsu sangyō nōritsu kenkyūjo, *Nōken 50-nen shi* (Osaka: Sangyō nōritsu kenkyūjo, 1976), esp. 31–45.

[72] Yamamoto Yasujirō, *Nihon keieigaku 50-nen shi* (Keizai shinpōsha, 1977).

gamation of thirteen regional and specialist organizations, this was the only association for promoting modern management techniques that could rival the Industrial Association in scope during the 1930s.

The Efficiency Federation's official goals echoed the aims of the state-sponsored rationalization movement. "*Sangyō gōrika* is the only path for industry to take," one federation broadside maintained. "Our objective is to contribute to the mutual prosperity of labor and capital by eliminating all waste and irrationality from the various aspects of management."[73] Its activities clearly mirrored those of the Industrial Association: publishing a monthly journal, sponsoring conferences and exhibitions, holding lecture series and inspection tours. The federation did, however, have a distinct identity. While the Industrial Association became a headquarters for the "practical" wing of the modern management movement, the federation served as a haven for the "efficiency experts" who fell outside this new mainstream. The Efficiency Federation was, after all, created largely under the initiative of Ueno Yōichi, and his influence was evident throughout its early history. Predictably enough, the federation adopted a stubbornly populist tone (asserting, for example, that "we cannot hope to attain the goals of rationalization by depending solely on governmental organs")[74] and took a less technical view of management than did the Industrial Association. Concentrating more on the philosophy of management than on its methodology—on the mentality of "revised" Taylorism rather than on its specific application—the Efficiency Federation addressed a general audience and spoke more to retailers and small factory owners than to industrialists and professional managers.

Although the federation was active and claimed over sixteen hundred members in 1931, its finances were always shaky. Despite considerable gifts from Nakayama Taichi, who was a patron of Ueno ever since he had installed Scientific Management at Nakayama Taiyōdō, the federation was reluctantly forced to look to the state for financial support in the early 1930s. The economic bureaucracy was not averse to mobilizing "efficiency experts," and in 1933 Yoshino Shinji succeeded Ueno as the chairman of the federation. Ueno, already stinging from his exclusion from the Production Management Committee, became increasingly estranged from the management reform movement after this second slight and turned his attention more to spiritual and educational pursuits.[75] The coming of Yoshino did improve the federation's balance sheet—second-hand subsidies from the Industrial Association were arranged—yet not to the extent that the organization could greatly expand its activities. Elaborate schemes for regional efficiency bureaus (modeled on the Osaka Industrial Efficiency Research Institute), consultancy programs for

[73] *Nihon nōritsu rengōkai annai* (Nihon nōritsu rengōkai, 1931), preface.
[74] Ibid.
[75] Ueno Yōichi, *Ueno Yōichi den,* ed. Misawa Hitoshi (Sangyō nōritsu tanki daigaku, 1967), 147 ff.

small business, and management training courses were all stillborn or stunted due to lack of funds.[76] The Efficiency Federation continued its promotional activities through the 1930s, but it always played second fiddle in the Scientific Management movement to the wealthier, more prestigious, and more practically minded Industrial Association.

Surveying the Depression-era management movement as a whole, several points are worth noting. First, the movement was increasingly centralized and streamlined, due in no small part to the efforts of the state in mobilizing management experts under the umbrella of the Rationalization Bureau. At the same time, the split in the efficiency movement which appeared in the early 1920s was exacerbated and institutionalized during the early 1930s. Ueno and the other heirs of the Taishō "efficiency craze," branded "dilettantes" and "louts" by the self-styled professionals of the Production Management Committee, were progressively marginalized.[77] Despite the bureaucratic embrace of the Efficiency Federation, the "efficiency experts" were decidedly junior partners in the government's rationalization initiatives. The "technicians," meanwhile, were confirmed as the official vanguard in the state-sponsored effort to modernize Japanese factory management.

Second, despite the much-expanded government support for management reform in the early 1930s, the hand of the state lay surprisingly light on the orientation and functioning of the actual movement. More often than not, the bureaucracy's role was limited to funding, facilitating, and legitimizing the work of private-sector proponents of Scientific Management. Noda Nobuo, for example, has noted that the Ministry of Commerce and Industry had no input on the contents of the Production Management Committee pamphlets and took little interest in the subsequent efforts to promote them.[78] Several factors contributed to this arm's-length approach by the state: the widespread recognition that managerial reform was hard to coerce and impossible to legislate; the lack of government expertise in industrial management; the preoccupation of bureaucrats with the macro-level aspects of sangyō gōrika;[79] and, perhaps most importantly, the extent to which private-sector managerial experts and the government leadership of the rationalization movement were in accord on issues of management reform. As Perry Willson notes was the case in Fascist Italy, the government supported managerial modernization "less by actual intervention than by creating the conditions in which it could be implemented." In Japan as well, one might reasonably conclude that the state's

[76] "Dōchō-fuken-shi ni okeru sangyō gōrika shidō kikan shisetsu kanbi gutai an," Sangyō nōritsu 7, no. 4 (April 1934): 247–56.

[77] Noda Nobuo, "Ekonomisuto 50-nen o kaerimiru," IE 10, no. 10 (November 1968): 94; Ono, Mōshon-maindo, 37.

[78] Noda, "Kagakuteki kanrihō kara," 7–8.

[79] Ibid., 8. Noda noted coolly, "They were all amateurs in the Ministry of Commerce and Industry."

direct role in the Taylorization of industry was ultimately less significant than its indirect contributions.[80]

Third, the mainstream of the early Shōwa management movement was guided by what Yamashita Okiie characterized as "the absolute rejection of abstract, academic theories and the execution of the concrete proposals of the Production Management Committee."[81] With the objective of cutting costs and "rationalizing" factory management as quickly and thoroughly as possible, the state-sponsored movement did not expend much effort on experimentation or innovation. Rather, the program of the Industrial Association was based on transplanting the tried and true Scientific Management methods used in large, advanced firms (especially the JNR) to the unwashed masses of unsystematically managed smaller workshops. As Industrial Association engineer Horime Ken'ichi noted, the managerial technology of most prewar enterprises was thirty years behind the level attained in the National Railways (although the gap was closed during the Pacific War and reversed after it).[82] The management movement of the 1930s thus came to concentrate on a sort of remedial education, spreading the "best method" practice in Japanese industry to the vast majority of workshops that had not yet joined the Scientific Management "revolution."

Fourth, even though the mainstream of the modern management movement was increasingly concerned with technical expertise and professionalism, efforts to bring home the message of Scientific Management to factory workers and segments of the general public increased. In line with the rhetoric of mass mobilization which suffused *sangyō gōrika,* systematic attempts to rally broader-based support for managerial reform flourished in the late 1920s and early 1930s. Among the most important of these was the "Waste Elimination Week" (*muda nashi shūkan*), a national campaign sponsored by the Tokyo Industry Roundtable (Tokyo Kōjō Konwakai), which promoted factory-level activities—lectures, slogan and poster contests—to stimulate worker support for "efficiency increase."[83] The safety movement was another major undertaking on a similar pattern, and numerous smaller initiatives (such as "Orderly

---

[80] Willson asserts that "The role of the Fascists in creating an environment favourable to the introduction of Taylorism should not be underestimated. The destruction of free trade unions enabled employers to innovate in a manner they saw fit. This moulded not only the extent to which scientific management was introduced but also its particular form; in the union-free atmosphere of Fascist Italy it was easy for employers to introduce the American model selectively, ignoring innovations they considered too costly." Perry R. Willson, *The Clockwork Factory: Women and Work in Fascist Italy* (Oxford: Clarendon Press, 1993), 38–39. For a Brazilian perspective, see Barbara Weinstein, *For Social Peace in Brazil: Industrialists and the Remaking of the Working Class in São Paulo, 1920–1964* (Chapel Hill: University of North Carolina Press, 1996), 49–50.

[81] Yamashita Okiie, "10 nenkan no kaiko," *Kōgyō to keizai* 101 (May 1941): 2.

[82] Horime, "Nihon kōgyō kyōkai," 560.

[83] Tokyo kōjō konwakai, *Kōjō muda nashi shūkan jisshi gaiyō* (Tokyo kōjō konwakai, 1931).

Factory Week") were also born in the Depression years.[84] While the results of these programs are uncertain, their prevalence suggests a heightened interest on the part of managers and businessmen in gaining the active support (rather than just the passive cooperation) of labor in the effort to rationalize the shop floor.

Finally, it is important to recognize that there was no great break—ideologically or methodologically—between the Taishō efficiency movement and its early Shōwa successor. The informal consensus on "revised" Taylorism forged in industrial circles during the 1920s held firm and, as left-wing critics grew increasingly silent in the following decade, the once spirited debate over Scientific Management tapered off. Nevertheless, even though American managerial methods continued to dominate Japanese practice, a gradual shift seemed to be taking place over the course of the decade in the way Japanese management experts perceived Taylorism and foreign management models. With the ascendance of a more technical, "nuts and bolts" approach, Japanese Taylorites no longer sought legitimacy for Scientific Management in its American origins or its successes abroad, but rather in its proven effectiveness in Japanese workshops. For example, while the Industrial Association was busily pushing a profoundly Taylorite agenda of work study and incentive wages, a new set of translations of Taylor's works by Ueno Yōichi was a commercial flop.[85] In any case, after the Wall Street crash of 1929, the United States no longer seemed such a compelling model for emulation. During the Depression era, after the Taishō "boom" and its helter-skelter absorption of American models, Scientific Management was increasingly conceived as being grounded in the Japanese experience. The overseas origins of Taylorism seemed to fade in the popular consciousness as its methods were established in Japanese factories, as American techniques were accommodated to paternalism and the realities of Japanese industry, and as Japanese observers became more confident spokesmen for modern management, less and less dependent on "translated enlightenment." Scientific Management was, in short, progressively indigenized during the 1920s and 1930s. That is not to say that it was dramatically recast philosophically or overhauled methodologically by its Japanese practitioners; instead, Taylorite ways were gradually being internalized, and increasingly accepted as something intuitive and natural rather than imported and artificial. After two decades of experimentation, debate, and experience, Scientific Management had established firm roots in Japan. And although "revised" Taylorism was not yet embraced as "Japanese-style" management, this perceptual shift was clearly underway by the early 1930s.

[84] Tokyo kōjō konwakai, *Seiton shūkan jisshi gaiyō* (Tokyo kōjō konwakai, 1934); Tsūshō sangyō shō, *Shōkō seisaku shi 9*, 130–35.
[85] Okuda, *Hito to keiei*, 195.

Scientific Management's Depression

While the Scientific Management movement was increasingly centralized, focused, and active in the decade following the Shōwa financial crisis, it did not achieve the breakthrough—the "Second Industrial Revolution"—which it pursued. Indeed, participants and observers had to concede regretfully that the movement only enjoyed limited success in getting its message across during the early and mid-1930s. Noda Nobuo described the rationalization movement's record in improving factory management as "extremely disheartening."[86] Araki Tōichirō, a member of the Production Management Committee, later lamented, "We put out first-rate position papers [and] we spent a lot of time working on them. It's a shame that it was all for nothing."[87] The British economist G. C. Allen observed in 1940 that "Since the work of the [Rationalization Bureau standing] committees has been of a general and educational character, it is difficult to assess their achievements in the promotion of efficiency. Most Japanese manufacturers concur in the view that they have not been very successful."[88] Perhaps Yoshino Shinji summed it up best when he concluded that the accomplishments of the early Shōwa management movement were no more than "a drop in the bucket."[89]

To a certain extent, of course, such dire pronouncements should be taken with a grain of salt. The bemoaning of frustrated progress in managerial reform clearly reflected unrealistic goals and constantly rising expectations as well as—perhaps even as much as—objective circumstances. After the efficiency boom of the 1910s and 1920s, many Japanese Taylorites assumed that, with the added impetus provided by government patronage of *sangyō gōrika,* the techniques of Scientific Management would suffuse Japanese industry during the 1930s. From this perspective, the Depression years must surely have been a disappointment, even if the rationalization movement did not prove an utter exercise in futility.

As noted in chapter 1, quantifying the diffusion of Scientific Management is problematic and, as Allen recognized, statistically gauging the efficacy of rationalization movement initiatives is all but impossible. Aggregate figures on industrial productivity are ambiguous, yet do tend to support the observation that progress in "efficiency increase" decelerated after 1930. Statistics presented by Nishinarita Yutaka and Okuda Kenji suggest that labor productivity rose considerably over the 1920s, particularly in the latter half of the decade. Following the onset of the Depression, however, per-worker industrial pro-

---

[86] Noda, "Kagakuteki kanrihō kara," 8.

[87] Araki Tōichirō, *Nōritsu Ichidaiki* (Nihon nōritsu kyōkai, 1971), 51.

[88] G. C. Allen, "Japanese Industry," in *The Industrialization of Japan and Manchukuo, 1930–1940,* ed. E. B. Schumpeter (New York: Macmillan, 1940), 750.

[89] Yoshino, *Nihon,* 256.

ductivity leveled off and, in some sectors, actually declined. While it can be argued that even the modest gains realized are impressive considering the economic context of the early 1930s, the abiding impression is that the efficiency of Japanese industry increased only gradually during the most active years of the state-sponsored rationalization campaign.[90]

Looking at the span from 1927 to 1937, qualitative evidence indicates that rationalization on the firm level—especially so-called "technological" rationalization—did progress significantly in many Japanese industries.[91] Yet the record also suggests that much of this activity in factory mechanization and management reform was initiated before the onset of the Depression and thus did not derive directly from the official rationalization movement. In the spinning industry, for example, firms aggressively pursued managerial and technical improvements through the 1920s, anticipating the full enactment of the Factory Law in 1929 and a detrimental appreciation in the yen when Japan eventually returned to the gold standard. A trend toward corporate mergers and more integrated production was well underway in textiles prior to 1930, while mechanization (especially the introduction of automatic power looms) proceeded more briskly in the late 1920s than in the subsequent decade. As aggregate statistics for the industry suggest, such initiatives led to rapid increases in labor productivity between 1926 and 1931, but progress came to a virtual standstill thereafter.[92] A similar phenomenon was observed in other sectors as well. In the metals industry, for one, major technological and organizational reforms also seem to have preceded the establishment of the Rationalization Bureau.[93] Indeed, this pattern appears to have characterized all levels of Japanese manufacturing: as Minami Ryōshin reports, the indices of electrification and mechanization in small-scale factories (5–99 workers) rose steadily until 1930, then plateaued.[94]

[90] Nishinarita Yutaka, *Kindai Nihon rōshi kankeishi no kenkyū* (Tokyo daigaku shuppankai, 1988), 168–70; Okuda, *Hito to keiei,* 230–32. Figures supporting a more continuous rising trajectory of labor productivity in the 1920s and 1930s can be found in Christopher Howe, *The Origins of Japanese Trade Supremacy* (Chicago: University of Chicago Press, 1996), 248.

[91] G. C. Allen, *A Short Economic History of Modern Japan* (New York: St. Martin's Press, 1981), chap. 10.

[92] Howe, *Origins,* 205–16, 316–23. See also Yamazaki Toshio, *Gijutsushi* (Nihon gendaishi taikei. Tōyō keizai shinpōsha, 1961), 136–44. Among the reforms in one cotton mill was equipping female workers with roller skates so that they could move more quickly between the machines they tended.

[93] Takahashi Mamoru, "Shōwa shonen ni okeru sangyō gōrika seisaku dōnyū no keiki," *Seikei ronsō* (Hiroshima University) 24, no. 6 (January 1975): 98–101; Nakase Toshikazu, "The Introduction of Scientific Management in Japan and Its Characteristics," in *Labor and Management,* ed. Nakagawa Keiichirō, Proceedings of the Fourth International Conference on Business History (Tokyo: University of Tokyo Press, 1977), 187–88.

[94] Minami Ryōshin, *The Economic Development of Japan* (New York: St. Martin's Press, 1986), 126–27.

The reasons why the advance of Scientific Management practices appeared to stall during the early 1930s—and why the best efforts of the revamped management movement were of limited impact—are not as obvious as one might assume. The effects of the Depression on Taylorite proselytizing certainly should not be underestimated: as Horime Ken'ichi found, management reform—sometimes expensive, always something of a risk—was a hard sell under the straitened economic circumstances.[95] The situation of excess capacity which persisted in Japanese industry until 1936 certainly provided a strong disincentive for elaborate managerial improvement schemes. The lingering pool of unemployed workers (and the consequent stagnation in wage levels) had a similar effect, reinforcing the blasé attitude of many managers toward systematic administrative methods.[96] As Marxist critics claimed at the time, "normal" rationalization was premised on mechanization and increases in scale, but "Japanese-style rationalization" depended on the intensification of labor in "semifeudal" workshops.[97] Many Western observers lodged similar complaints, charging that Japan's export drive of the early 1930s was built on a policy of "social dumping" and the cynical exploitation of cheap labor.[98] Although the extent to which the "sweating" of workers increased during the Depression is unclear,[99] labor market conditions in Japan inevitably made this a more expedient and immediate antidote to sagging profit rates than substantive management reform. In this light, Mary Nolan's description of the Ger-

---

[95] Ono, *Mōshon-maindo,* 38.

[96] Nakamura Takafusa, *Economic Growth in Prewar Japan,* trans. Robert A. Feldman (New Haven, Conn.: Yale University Press, 1971), 216–17, 245, 267. Bank of Japan governor Fukai Eigo remarked in 1937 that "the days of easy increase of production by raising capacity utilization are gone. From now on, strenuous efforts should be expended to expand production, but at the same time we must endeavor to conserve material resources in all manner of ways, in the broadest sense."

[97] Takahashi Mamoru, *"Kagakuteki kanrihō" to Nihon kigyō* (Ochanomizu shobō, 1994), 15–16.

[98] In response to international allegations of "social dumping," Japanese spokesmen (and even some Western apologists) maintained that rapid increases in industrial efficiency and the spread of Scientific Management in the early 1930s were the secrets behind Japan's export drive. Yet in praising the accomplishments of Japan's rationalization movement, these spokesmen were generous with rhetoric and stingy with specifics. The fact that Japanese managerial experts made no claims of such success—but instead kept repeating their calls for greater diligence in implementing Scientific Management—only reinforces the foreign accusations of "sweated labor" and predatory trade practices. See Asahi Isoshi, *The Secret of Japan's Trade Expansion* (Tokyo: The International Association of Japan, 1934); James Scherer, *Japan's Advance* (Tokyo: Hokuseido Press, 1934), esp. chap. 10.

[99] The statistical evidence regarding the "sweating" of labor in the period of rationalization is ambiguous. Real wages, even calculated on a per-hour basis, only decreased slightly in the early 1930s and work hours actually declined on average. While the number of industrial accidents rose significantly, this may have been a side-effect of increased mechanization in the late 1920s as much as a result of redoubled "squeezing" of workers. See Nakamura, *Nihon seisansei,* 62–76; Nakamura, *Economic Growth in Prewar Japan,* 216–17.

man situation might as easily be applied to Japan: "Industry sought to gain the economic benefits of modern technology and factory organization without any of the leveling effects of Americanism. [It] wanted higher productivity without mass production; greater exports without mass consumption; and higher profits without higher wages. Efficiency was to be achieved without expensive technology by means of intensified labor and in a context of austerity."[100]

External economic conditions were not, however, the only factors which inhibited the advance of Scientific Management. Most veterans of the early Shōwa management movement put much of the blame for the impasse on their target audience, the owners and managers of Japan's small- and medium-sized industrial concerns. By the time the Production Management Committee was formed in 1931, most observers agreed that the vast majority of Japan's large, modern industrial enterprises had implemented at least the basics of systematic management and that some advanced firms had attained a level of managerial technology comparable to that in the United States. Bringing the not readily apparent benefits of Taylorism home to small businessmen was therefore the challenge, and it was one that the modern management movement was unable to master, at least during the 1930s. Management experts complained repeatedly of the conservatism of small-scale industrialists and the difficulty of weaning them from traditional, "irrational" approaches. According to Noda, "Small businessmen at the time all thought, 'That stuff [modern management] is for big factories and has nothing to do with my own company.'"[101] Whether or not such parochialism and timidity was the root cause of Scientific Management's slow progress—the dearth of capital, uncertain markets, and the economic disincentives noted above notwithstanding—it seems clear that the management movement did not enjoy the same receptive and precocious audience in the 1930s which it had a decade earlier.

An unresponsive clientele was not the modern management movement's only handicap. The shallowness of government interest in firm-level rationalization may have given the Production Management Committee a free hand in policy, yet it also meant that financial support and bureaucratic backup were not always solid. The Industrial Association, for instance, had to chip away at the tens of thousands of unreformed small-scale producers with only two full-time consultants during most of the 1930s. Furthermore, the modern management movement was increasingly constrained by its mission of spreading the Taylorite gospel to the least-advanced sectors of Japanese industry. Emphasizing generalized "best practice," the message of the movement's experts tended to stagnate and their techniques came to lag behind those in some progressive firms. This was especially the case from the mid-1930s, when large enterprises stepped up their investments in plant and equipment and the first Fordist

---

[100] Nolan, *Visions of Modernity*, 10.

[101] Noda, "Kagakuteki kanrihō kara," 9; "Dōchō-fuken-shi ni okeru sangyō gōrika shidō kikan," 249.

conveyor-belt assembly lines began to appear in Japan.[102] By the latter half of the decade, actual "best practice" had progressed beyond the nostrums of the management movement and a number of large firms felt they had little to learn from the management "experts."[103]

Looking at the Japanese rationalization movement more broadly, one cannot avoid the conclusion that the efforts of management reformers were also hampered by the internal contradictions of *sangyō gōrika*. On the conceptual level, decreased competition deriving from cartelization and combination may well have allowed for more efficient and cooperative operations, yet the promise of monopoly profits also reduced incentives for individual firms to modernize their management systems. Whether increased concentration under rationalization actually engendered this disincentive effect is unclear, although statistics suggest that cartelized industries were able to maintain monopoly price levels at least through 1934.[104] This was certainly not the only aspect of the streamlining of Japanese industry under rationalization which may have yielded unanticipated and undesirable results. In the wake of the "downsizing" of large industrial enterprises, for example, many of the discharged workers set up new small-scale workshops, producing goods for the export drive or subcontracting to their former factories. Thus, the process of making large-scale industry more efficient led ironically to the spawning of atomized, technologically primitive firms of the very sort hardest to reach with the message of Scientific Management.[105]

It should be noted that, as in the 1920s, labor resistance was not a serious impediment to the advance of Scientific Management under the rationalization movement. Although Yamashita's incentive wage schemes did meet opposition in some JNR shops, Horime Ken'ichi noted that, in most cases, workers in the factories where he consulted welcomed the predictability and impartiality of the Production Management Committee's Halsey premium system.[106] In Horime's view, workers did not seem to be any harder to convince of the benefits of Scientific Management than Depression-era managers and

[102] On Nissan, which established mass production of trucks by importing managerial and production technology from Detroit between 1933 and 1938, see Michael A. Cusumano, *The Japanese Automobile Industry: Technology and Management at Nissan and Toyota* (Cambridge, Mass.: Harvard University Press, 1985), 40–45. Nissan's imported assembly line was the state of the art in Japanese industry in the mid-1930s, and even established management experts sought to study its organization and operations. See Ueda Takehito, "Omoidasu mama ni—nōritsudō 50-nen," *IE* 10, no. 7 (July 1968): 92.

[103] See Noda, "Kagakuteki kanrihō kara," 8–9. The spinning and electrical machinery industries appear to have believed their managerial techniques were superior to those of the "experts" from relatively early in the decade.

[104] Nakamura, *Economic Growth in Prewar Japan,* 229.

[105] Nishinarita, *Rōshi kankeishi,* 322–23.

[106] Shōji Yukihiko, "Sangyō gōrika no sagyō shūdan to rōmu seisaku," *Keizaigaku kenkyū* 33, no. 3 (December 1983): 107–32; Okuda, *Hito to keiei,* 179.

factory owners were.[107] Indeed, labor's apparent tolerance of Taylorism in this period is far easier to account for than its muted compliance with the efficiency movement in the 1920s. With unemployment high and unions on the defensive, managers enjoyed more discretion over labor matters in the early 1930s than they had only a few years earlier. Moreover, in a time of mass dismissals, when *sangyō gōrika* more often meant slashed payrolls than managerial reform, labor organizations had little vitriol to spare for the continuing process of Taylorization. Indeed, as rationalization came to be synonymous with layoffs in industry, it was *sangyō gōrika* rather than Scientific Management that became the red flag for Japanese workers. As one observer noted, albeit in a rather ominous tone, "no objection is forthcoming from labour against the elimination of irrational processes in manufacturing or the installment of more efficient machines."[108]

In the final analysis, it is tempting to conclude, as Harold James has done in reference to Germany, that "it is almost impossible to detect what the alleged rationalization wave . . . actually consisted of."[109] Indeed, looking at the Japanese initiative, one cannot help being impressed by the volume of rhetoric produced, the energy expended on mobilization, and, ultimately, the paucity of results in rationalizing factory management. Although management experts were rallied to the cause and the efficiency movement was restructured, government sponsorship did not guarantee that managerial reform on the shop floor would proceed apace. Furthermore, while the "revised" Taylorite ideology was reaffirmed and Scientific Management increasingly indigenized during the 1930s, the advance of modern management techniques bogged down in the miasma of small business and was undermined by the conflicting incentives generated by the Depression and the process of rationalization itself. In the end, the deadlock in the early Shōwa management movement would only be shattered by the heating up of war production and the coming of a controlled economy at the decade's close.

[107] Ono, *Mōshon-maindo,* 38.

[108] Asahi, *Secret,* 32.

[109] Harold James, *The German Slump* (Oxford: Oxford University Press, 1986), 148–49. See also Nolan, *Visions of Modernity,* 132–33, 227.

3

The Wartime Economy and Scientific Management, 1937–1945

MOST OBSERVERS have anatomized Japanese industrial development during the China and Pacific Wars as a spiraling descent into collapse.[1] After heady growth during the late 1930s, the economic war machine appeared to sputter and stall even before Pearl Harbor. Although heavy industrialization progressed steadily (due in large part to the sacrifice of consumer production and small business), the economy's foundations were undermined by shortages of men and materiel, by an increasingly ponderous and irrational state control system, and, ultimately, by direct war damage.

Industrial management in wartime Japan has frequently been seen as tracing a similar trajectory of decline. Linking the economic debacle to the failings of Japan's overextended managerial structures, many observers have chronicled the wartime inadequacies of organizational methods and production technology.[2] Shortly after the defeat, one American engineer commented, with a victor's candor, that "[the Japanese] could not be called efficient managers. The waste of labor in Japan is appalling. Measured by any standards, the Japanese, technically, are far behind the Americans."[3] Few observers indeed—either at the time or in the decades since—would have disagreed with this modest but damning evaluation.

Nevertheless, the war years can hardly be seen as the nadir of Japan's efficiency movement. In fact, following the sluggish progress of the Depression years, the modern management movement was revitalized by an unprecedented, broad surge of interest in "efficiency increase." "War," one economic analyst noted, "is, after all, a question of efficiency."[4] Although the movement

---

[1] See, for example, Jerome Cohen, *Japan's Economy in War and Reconstruction* (Minneapolis: University of Minnesota Press, 1949); T. A. Bisson, *Japan's War Economy* (New York: Institute of Pacific Relations, 1945); Michael Barnhart, *Japan Prepares For Total War: The Search for Economic Security, 1919–1941* (Ithaca: Cornell University Press, 1987); Yamazaki Hiroaki, "Nihon sensō keizai no hōkai to sono tokushitsu," in Tokyo daigaku shakai kagaku kenkyūjo, *Fashizumu-ki no kokka to shakai 2: Senji Nihon keizai* (Tokyo daigaku shuppankai, 1979), 3–66.

[2] Among others, Cohen, *Japan's Economy,* chaps. 3–5; Okuda Kenji, *Hito to keiei: Nihon keiei kanrishi kenkyū* (Manejimento-sha, 1985), chaps. 11–12; Nakamura Seiji, *Nihon seisansei kōjō undō shi* (Keisō shobō, 1958), chap. 3.

[3] Quoted in Cohen, *Japan's Economy,* 352.

[4] Nagaoka Yasutarō, "'Senji seisanryoku kōyō tokushū' hakkan ni saishite," *Shakai seisaku jihō* 258 (March 1942): 1.

could boast few conspicuous triumphs, the war was a period of constructive growth, organizational development, and practical experience which would lay the foundations for the postwar "management boom." Rather than being discredited by defeat, Japanese proponents of Scientific Management emerged in 1945 more numerous, better connected, more seasoned, and with their knowledge more highly sought after than ever before. The war, in short, was no "dark valley" for the modern management movement.[5]

Wartime Economic Policy and the Efficiency Movement

By the time of the China Incident in July 1937, a major economic transition—marking the passage from recovery to mobilization—was well underway in Japan. Resurgence under the "quasi-wartime" economy was apparent by early in the year, as full employment and full utilization of industrial capacity were at last reattained. The widespread concern in business and government circles was that Japanese industry, after more than fifteen years of idling, would overheat in the sudden boom: inflation was already on the rise and the balance of payments deteriorating steadily. The administrative response was a realignment of planning and control organs—the Rationalization Bureau refurbished as the Control Bureau (Tōseikyoku), the Cabinet Planning Board (Kikakuin) established—with an eye to a more directed (and presumably smoother) course of mobilization. A holistic response to the labor problem also started to take shape in 1937: impelled by a new wave of unrest, bureaucrats and the Kyōchōkai began to fashion a wartime labor front, the Industrial Patriotic Movement (Sangyō Hōkoku Undō, hereafter Sanpō).[6]

The slogan popularized during 1937 that would guide the first years of mobilization was "the expansion of production capacity" (*seisanryoku kakujū*). Articulated as one of Finance Minister Kaya Okinori's and Commerce Minister Yoshino Shinji's celebrated "Three Principles," the approach was premised on state coordination of the private-sector economy in order to nurture industrial growth without inflation or payments crises. Improving the efficiency of Japanese producers was a natural corollary of this strategy. As

[5] An excellent overview of the wartime Scientific Management movement is Sasaki Satoshi's "The Rationalization of Production Management Systems in Japan during World War II," in *World War II and the Transformation of Business Systems,* ed. Sakudō Jun and Shiba Takao, Proceedings of the Twentieth International Conference on Business History (Tokyo: University of Tokyo Press, 1994), 30–54.

[6] On the transition from the "quasi-wartime" economy to mobilization, see Nakamura Takafusa, "Jun-senji kara senji keizai taisei e no ikō," in Kindai Nihon kenkyūkai, *Senji keizai,* Kindai Nihon kenkyūkai, *Senji keizai,* Kindai Nihon kenkyū nenpō, vol. 9 (Yamakawa shuppansha, 1987), 1–25; Chalmers Johnson, *MITI and the Japanese Miracle* (Stanford, Calif.: Stanford University Press, 1982), chap. 4.

Odaka Kunio later noted, Japan could not afford an American-style "waste be damned" mobilization, but had to expand production without increasing costs or squandering resources.[7] Efforts to increase productivity also had renewed appeal to the business community at the time: apprehensive that mobilization would lead to the creation of excess capacity (as had occurred in Japan during World War I), industrialists showed interest in raising production by managerial reform rather than by major investment in new plant and equipment.[8]

Although the campaign to expand production capacity rekindled public and private concern with management techniques, the state made no new efforts to mobilize the efficiency movement during the China War. Indeed, government subsidies to the Japan Industrial Association peaked in 1934 and continued to decline after 1937.[9] Nevertheless, the two national efficiency organizations responded eagerly to the national emergency and the opportunity it offered to extend their influence. An editorial in *Kōgyō to keizai* (Industry and Economy), the journal of the Industrial Association, enjoined its readers to put the managerial stalemate of the Depression behind them: "While there has been progress in some areas [since the beginning of the rationalization movement], the results have, regrettably, been incomplete so far. . . . With the resolve that there will never be so good a chance as now to carry through with what has not yet been attained, we must call up once again the energy we marshaled in 1929 and 1930. Then it was for breaking out of the Depression, now it is for seeing us through this national emergency!"[10] The Efficiency Federation was even more enthusiastic in its efforts to rally support for the wartime production program. A federation resolution called for "the eradication of waste" and "the complete dissemination of the ideas of efficiency," and bid Japan's managers to "push forward loyally, patriotically, and efficiently" in the current crisis.[11] Lists of rousing management slogans ("Don't Just Talk about Efficiency, Do It!") became a regular feature in the federation's journal. In both management reform bodies, publicity activities were expanded, shop-floor campaigns such as "Waste Elimination Week" were intensified, and barrages of policy recommendations were targeted at the government.

As the war on the continent dragged on, the industrial mobilization at home was yielding mixed results. Under a web of constantly increasing government controls, production in heavy industry jumped 75 percent between 1938 and 1941, although the balance of payments grew progressively shakier, bottlenecks began to appear, and labor productivity showed no signs of improve-

[7] Odaka Kunio, "Kōjō kanri no gōrisei ni kansuru jakkan no mondai," *Mita gakkai zasshi* 35, no. 8 (August 1942): 77.

[8] Nihon kōgyō kyōkai, *Senji ni okeru kōjō seisanryoku kakujū narabini sengo no taisaku,* Dai-13 kai kenkyūkai shiryō (1938), 7.

[9] "Nihon kōgyō kyōkai no jigyō hōkoku," *Kōgyō to keizai* 112 (April 1942): 24.

[10] "Seisanryoku no kakujū to sangyō nōritsu no zōshin," ibid., 61 (January 1938): 1.

[11] "Hijō jikyoku ni taisuru sengen," *Sangyō nōritsu* 11, no. 1 (January 1938).

ment.[12] The situation was particularly troubling to a number of military officers, bureaucrats and intellectuals, who looked to European fascist models for
inspiration and believed that greater progress could be achieved in Japan under a reformed political and economic structure. This group, which rallied
around Prince Konoe Fumimaro, sought "to ensure that industry fulfilled
'public' goals of the state, not private goals of capital,"[13] that ownership and
management were separated, and that production, rather than profit, was confirmed as the goal of business. With Konoe's assumption of the prime minis-
tership in 1940, this approach was elevated to state policy and the "New Order" (shin taisei) proclaimed.[14] As one Production Management Committee
pamphlet described it, "The true aims of the 'New Economic Order' are the
coordination of economic activity with national objectives, the planned expansion of production and advance of technology, and the realization of a high-
level 'National Defense State.'"[15]

Since the philosophy of the "New Order" was consistent with and, to a
certain degree, derived from the logic of Scientific Management,[16] it is hardly
surprising that the shin taisei stressed efficiency and rational management on
both the macro and micro levels. Especially with the start of the Pacific War
and the intensification of resource shortages, an increased emphasis was
placed on squeezing the utmost productivity from the inputs available. The
slogan "expansion of production capacity" gave way during 1942 to the catchphrase "stepped-up production" (seisan zōkyō), which implied the more desperate goal of "increasing output without adding to existing facilities."[17]
Within this straitened context, military production was to be maintained
through "prioritization" (jūtenshugi), the targeting of scarce resources to the
most essential and efficient sectors of the wartime economy. "New Order"
bureaucrats looked to a rational, streamlined, and thoroughly planned industrial structure—a "concentrated, organic, prioritized, high-efficiency, wartime
reformation of the domestic economy"[18]—that would allow Japan to rise
above its resource poverty and technical limitations.

[12] Nakamura, Nihon seisansei, 83.

[13] Andrew Gordon, Labor and Imperial Democracy in Prewar Japan (Berkeley: University of
California Press, 1991), 325.

[14] As T. A. Bisson noted, "As vague as it was richly suggestive, ["New Order"] had all the
requirements of the perfect Japanese slogan." Bisson, Japan's War Economy, 15; see also Sheldon
Garon, The State and Labor in Modern Japan (Berkeley: University of California Press, 1987),
220 ff.; Johnson, MITI, 150–54.

[15] Shōkōshō, Seisankanri iinkai, Shin keizai taisei ka ni okeru kikai kōgyō no shinkōsaku,
Pamphlet 36 (Nihon kōgyō kyōkai, 1941), 1.

[16] The influence of Taylorism on the evolution of economic planning and authoritarian thought
in wartime Japan will be discussed below, pp. 103–8.

[17] Hara Akira, "Taiheiyō sensō ki no seisan zōkyō seisaku," in Kindai Nihon kenkyūkai, Senji
keizai, 232; see also Johnson, MITI, 158–60.

[18] Kimura Kihachirō, "Seisan gōrika no shinkadai," Tōsei keizai 4, no. 5 (May 1942): 46.

Government efforts to stimulate management improvement on the firm level began soon after the proclamation of the "New Order." Many of the initiatives were connected with the so-called "New Scientific Order" (*kagaku shin taisei*), the campaign launched in 1941 to mobilize science and technology in the interests of wartime production.[19] The Japan Society for the Promotion of Science (Nihon Gakujutsu Shinkōkai), for example, sponsored research on production management and appointed standing committees to investigate urgent problems in business administration. The Ministry of Commerce, the Cabinet Planning Board, and the armed services cooperated to underwrite the Japan Cost Accounting Association (Nihon Genka Keisan Kyōkai) in 1941, with efficiency movement doyen Nakayama Taichi installed as chairman. Sanpō too was increasingly oriented toward the dissemination of management techniques and the Labor Science Research Institute was absorbed as its central research organ.[20]

Nonetheless, the government's mobilization of the management reform movement was, surprisingly, somewhat retarded. Proposals to create a single national organ to coordinate "efficiency increase" had long been on the table. From the late 1930s, the Efficiency Federation had repeatedly petitioned the government for a central body; in 1941, the influential Japan Economic Federation (Nihon Keizai Renmeikai) seconded the idea, calling for a unified public-private initiative to implement Scientific Management.[21] Only the Industrial Association appears to have balked, its members apparently unwilling to sully their self-styled professionalism by affiliation with the federation's "efficiency peddlers." Finally, under pressure from Commerce Minister Kishi Nobusuke (and with the Industrial Association approaching bankruptcy), the "rationalization" of the management movement was accomplished.[22] In the spring of 1942, the two existing organizations were dissolved and the Japan Efficiency Association (Nihon Nōritsu Kyōkai)[23] was established as the spearhead of state efforts to improve Japanese industrial management techniques.[24]

[19] On the *kagaku shin taisei,* see Hiroshige Tetsu, *Kagaku no shakaishi: Kindai Nihon no kagaku taisei* (Chūō kōron sha, 1973), chap. 6; Ben-Ami Shillony, *Politics and Culture in Wartime Japan* (Oxford: Clarendon Press, 1981), 134–41.

[20] Nihon keizai renmeikai chōsaka, *Sangyō nōritsu zōshin undō no genkyō* (1942).

[21] Kojima Seiichi, *Shin sangyō gōrika* (Chikura shobō, 1942), 307.

[22] Noda Nobuo, "Kagakuteki kanrihō kara seisansei undō e," *Keiei to rekishi* 9 (1986): 9. The animosity between the two efficiency organizations died hard: for decades after the merger, most Industrial Association alumni continued to speak disdainfully of "efficiency peddlers" and the dilution of professionalism that resulted from combination with the Efficiency Federation.

[23] The Nihon Nōritsu Kyōkai adopted "Japan Management Association" as the official English translation of its name after the war. The literal translation, which better captures the continuities with the prewar efficiency movement, is used here.

[24] Although the Japan Efficiency Association does not meet Gregory Kasza's definition of an "administered mass organization," much of his analysis is applicable to the establishment, goals, and operations of the association. Gregory Kasza, *The Conscription Society: Administered Mass Organizations* (New Haven, Conn.: Yale University Press, 1995).

This new headquarters for the efficiency movement was clearly intended to be a high-profile organization: its board boasted many of the luminaries of industry and the economic bureaucracy, while its finances were assured by generous grants from the army and navy.[25] At the founding ceremonies, the association's chairman, veteran Scientific Management proponent Godō Takuo, declared, "There have long been calls for increased industrial efficiency in Japan, but it has never been sought so insistently by the state nor been expressed with such newfound significance as it has of late."[26] Nevertheless, no major changes were planned in the scope or methods of the reorganized efficiency movement: as with the association's precursors, the spread of systematic management methods through publicity, consulting, and training was its primary charge.[27] In charting a course for the new body, Godō did, however, seek to create an ideological touchstone, articulating "three fundamental principles" for the Association: "(1) Devise and implement efficiency methods imbued with the Japanese spirit. (2) Emphasize practice over theory. (3) Dispense with equality [*heiretsushugi*] and trying to please everyone [*sōbanashugi*]; advance through true prioritization [*jūtenshugi*] and strict hierarchy [*jūretsushugi*]."[28] Under these banners, the Efficiency Association and its mission of managerial reform were comfortably integrated into the technocratic, authoritarian, and rhetorically nativistic mainstream of "New Order" mobilization.

The efficiency movement was unified just as wartime mobilization was pushed into high gear. As many analysts have concluded, however, the post-Guadalcanal drive to create a "National Defense State" was too little, too late. The various bottlenecks that had hindered early mobilization were increasingly overshadowed by chronic shortages of imported raw materials. Available resources were focused on progressively smaller numbers of key industries and firms until, in the final year of the war, all materiel, manpower, and managerial expertise were desperately thrown into aircraft production. As one observer noted, a centrally planned economy is like a net: a single hole can cause the entire system to be compromised.[29] Even in 1942, when the Japan Efficiency Association was chartered, the Japanese economic net was apparently tattered beyond the point where management reform alone could have repaired it. By the time American bombing delivered the death blow, Japanese industry and the "New Economic Order" had already been gutted by the exigencies of war.

---

[25] Subsidies to the Efficiency Association in 1942 were larger than the total government assistance given to the Industrial Association in its ten years of operation. Payment of the subsidies passed to the Munitions Ministry on its creation in 1943.

[26] "Kaichō aisatsu," *Nihon nōritsu* 1, no. 1 (June 1942): 5.

[27] "Nihon nōritsu kyōkai setsuritsu shuisho," *Kōgyō to keizai* 112 (April 1942).

[28] Morikawa Kakuzō, "Sōkan no ji," *Nihon nōritsu* 1, no. 1 (June 1942): 3.

[29] Nihon sangyō keizai seikeibu, *Seisan sen* (Itō shoten, 1943), 236.

Concluding the Debate over Taylorism

With the return of full employment and full utilization of capacity in the latter half of the 1930s, interest in management methods in general—and Scientific Management in particular—intensified. This reawakening was not due to an influx of new ideas from abroad: indeed, although Japanese experts continued to follow American developments, the flow of foreign management models into Japan slowed considerably over the course of the decade. Rather, the groundswell of interest appears to indicate that the message of the efficiency movement, so easily ignored during the gloom of the Depression, finally began to hit home with the stirrings of industrial mobilization. By the time of Pearl Harbor, the critical need for managerial improvement was almost universally appreciated in the business community and the economic bureaucracy, and the gospel of Scientific Management, which had languished for almost a decade, attracted a growing number of converts from their ranks.[30]

Once the necessity of Scientific Management had been recognized, the problem facing Japanese proponents was not simply one of implementation and methodology, but very much one of rhetoric and ideology as well. While efficiency engineers, "New Order" bureaucrats, and business leaders may have rationally, "scientifically" judged Taylorization to be essential, the challenge was impressing the need for management reform on the workers, the "unenlightened" in industry (notably small businessmen), and the general public. Especially as Taylorism was so closely associated with the United States and had long been branded exploitative and dehumanizing by its critics, making Scientific Management ideologically compatible with wartime intellectual trends and spiritual mobilization was an issue of some importance.

In an environment of mounting nationalistic fervor and nativistic introspection, Taylorism's all too apparent American origins were an immediate concern of those who hoped to naturalize Scientific Management. During the early 1930s, as Japanese efficiency experts grew more comfortable with modern management, they began to internalize it, gradually coming to perceive imported techniques as somehow less foreign. To many, however, Scientific Management retained a distinctly American flavor, even after more than twenty-five years of application and adaptation in Japan. This became particularly apparent as nativistic notions—part of a rich strain of Japanese management thought stretching back to the Meiji industrialists' litany of "beautiful customs"—gained new credibility and ideological appeal during the war. Amidst

---

[30] Early accounts of Taylorism in Japan and narratives of Frederick Taylor's life and career, surprisingly enough, attracted considerable interest in wartime Japan. During 1941 and 1942, for example, the Japan Efficiency Federation released three hefty volumes of essays on Taylorism originally published in the federation's journal in the 1920s. Although the material was well out of date (even by Japanese standards), the collections were well received. Nihon nōritsu rengōkai, *Nihon kōjō kanri no shomondai,* 3 vols. (Daiyamondo, 1941–42).

a swelling rhetoric of ethnic exceptionalism, many prominent commentators—
like Godō in his charge to the Japan Efficiency Association—called for the
injection of "Japanese character" into management thought. Outstanding in
this regard was the Efficiency Federation's 1942 call for an "Imperial Way of
Efficiency" (*kōdō nōritsu*). Noting that "up to now we have thoroughly researched Western efficiency issues," the federation maintained that Japan
could no longer rely on "translated enlightenment" but had to address its own
"unique problems in management." Bristling at the idea of being an intellectual dependency of the United States, the federation thus sounded the clarion
for an "autonomous, Japanese structure for efficiency increase."[31]

In actual fact, few management experts invested their time in trying to
define a "distinctively Japanese" management system, most concentrating instead on attempts to align Taylorism with nativist conceptions of a "Japanese"
management tradition. From the late 1930s, accompanying the surge in popular nationalism, efforts began in earnest to portray Scientific Management as
an indigenous species rather than as an imported transplant. A particularly
popular approach was to trace the origins of modern factory management back
to Ninomiya Sontoku, a mid-nineteenth-century peasant sage who preached
diligence and frugality. In 1936, for example, the management consultant
Sakamoto Shigeharu published a monograph entitled *Nōritsu gishi Ninomiya
Sontoku* (Ninomiya Sontoku, Efficiency Engineer). This study, underwritten
improbably enough by the Japan Society for the Promotion of Science, labeled
Ninomiya the "father of Japanese rationalization" and drew extensive paral-
lels between his teachings and the tenets of Scientific Management.[32] Similar
attempts to establish Ninomiya as Frederick Winslow Taylor's Japanese predecessor were made by highly respected management experts like Kanda
Kōichi and Inoue Yoshikazu.[33]

The vogue for Ninomiya was certainly not the only manifestation of efforts
to blend Scientific Management into Japanese history and traditional culture.
Office management expert Kaneko Rihachirō, for example, suggested that a
primitive form of the Gantt chart had actually been developed in the twelfth
century by Ōe no Hiromoto.[34] A manager at Hitachi posited that the age-old
routines of rice planting made Japanese workers more suited to the repetitive
motions of mass production than Western laborers, who lacked a "sense of

[31] "Kōdō nōritsu no kaitaku e," *Sangyō nōritsu* 15, no. 3 (March 1942): 1–2. Compare Shillony, *Politics and Culture,* 141–51; Thomas Havens, *Valley of Darkness* (New York: Norton,
1978), 30. For a fascinating overview of the German experience of aligning technological progress with "national character," see Jeffrey Herf, *Reactionary Modernism: Technology, Culture,
and Politics in Weimar and the Third Reich* (Cambridge: Cambridge University Press, 1984).

[32] Sakamoto Shigeharu, *Nōritsu gishi Ninomiya Sontoku* (Kenseisha, 1936).

[33] Kanda Kōichi, *Kōjō kanri kenkyū* (Dai Nihon kōgyō gakkai, 1938); Inoue Yoshikazu, "Nihon nōritsu shihō no genri to sono kōsei," *Sangyō nōritsu* 12, no. 4 (April 1939): 379–82.

[34] Kaneko Rihachirō, *Kōjō jimu kanriron* (Chikura shobō, 1937), 289–93.

rhythm."[35] One of the most interesting exegeses was given by Sugiyama Kō-ichi, the president of Amagasaki Seikō. Arguing that foreign methods had to be placed in a Japanese context rather than simply denigrated out of misplaced patriotism, Sugiyama bid his readers to consider the tea ceremony as an example of indigenous management techniques. Enumerating the characteristics of this uniquely Japanese custom—spare and routinized motions, highly adapted and specialized implements, a dedication to harmony, order, and simplicity—Sugiyama concluded that the principles of Taylor and work-study pioneer Frank Gilbreth were fully consistent with the traditional Japanese spirit.[36]

It should be noted that the wartime "Japanization" of Taylorism did not, in itself, seem to inspire any rethinking of modern management techniques, only of their origins. One need look no further than the writings of Andō Yaichi to dispel any doubts about the compatibility of Japanist rhetoric and the established methodologies of Scientific Management. Andō, a management consultant, sometime employee of Niigata Ironworks, and inventor of the "Andō-card" system of process control, was one of the most vocal advocates of "Japanized" management. Although he harshly criticized "literal translation" of Western methods, Andō chose to overlook the fact that his "invention" was an almost identical copy of American card systems from the turn of the century. Furthermore, in his 1940 book *Kōjō kaizen* (Factory Improvement), Andō rebuked Japanese writers for their dependence on Western models while devoting fifty pages to a microscopic retelling of Taylor's life and work.[37] With such a fluid divide between the foreign and the indigenous, it is hardly surprising that the ideological domestication of Taylorism could progress so effortlessly.

Establishing a Japanese ancestry for Taylorism proved easier than harmonizing Scientific Management with some aspects of the evolving wartime labor order and economic structure. The fundamental problem was reconciling modern management—frequently damned since its introduction into Japan as capitalistic, individualistic, and dehumanizing—with a wartime intellectual climate dominated by European fascist thought, communitarianism, and concerns with popular welfare. Taylorism, it seemed, required rehabilitation as well as indigenization. In order to meet the ideological demands of the war, Scientific Management had to be scrubbed of any lingering association with divisiveness and exploitation, and portrayed as a system which could deliver substantial economic benefits without unacceptable social consequences.

Renewed interest in Taylorism generated renewed criticism, yet the heat of the Taishō debate was not rekindled in wartime Japan. In particular, the un-

---

[35] Nihon sangyō keizai shinbunsha, *Zenkoku mohan kōjō shisatsuki* (Kasumigaseki shobō, 1943), 49–50.

[36] Sugiyama Kōichi, "Taryō seisan hōshiki to setsubi no nōritsuteki kaizen I" *Nihon nōritsu* 2, no. 4 (April 1943): 267.

[37] Andō Yaichi, *Kōjō kaizen—Nihon no kagakuteki kōjō kanri* (Daiyamondo, 1940).

equivocal opposition which Scientific Management had inspired in many observers was not revived during the war, when the urgency of industrial mobilization was broadly acknowledged. Rather, as Morito Tatsuo explained, the
issue was how to "maintain and develop those elements of capitalistic efficiency that promote production, while rectifying its unsound propensities."[38]
Like Morito, most commentators cautioned against throwing out the baby
with the bath water, and while excoriating capitalistic abuse of "scientific"
techniques, emphasized the salutary economic returns of Taylorization. Noda
Nobuo, for instance, argued that the ills of interwar industry and labor relations should not be blamed on Scientific Management (which catalyzed what
economic expansion there was), but on the free market and capitalism.[39] Kishi
Nobusuke, meanwhile, tempered his deep admiration for American management methods with the warning that "capitalistic efficiency" was synonymous
with exploitation and could not be tolerated in Japan.[40]

Such viewpoints were not, of course, entirely new. In the 1920s, many
Japanese and European Marxists argued that Taylorism per se was not dehumanizing or exploitative, but rather that its cynical appropriation by the capitalist class gave rise to abuses. Considering the extent to which "New Order"
ideology drew upon Marxist analyses,[41] the resuscitation of such a convenient
interpretation of Scientific Management is hardly surprising. Notwithstanding
the intellectual allure of this reasoning, the challenge was convincing workers
and their advocates that the legendary ills of Scientific Management could be
neutralized merely by taking Taylorism out of the hands of capitalists and
entrusting it to the state and managerial technocrats. Especially as wartime
experts emphasized the pressing need for those elements of Taylorism—
standardization, mechanization, motion study—which most reeked of dehumanization and deskilling, advocates of management reform recognized the
need to sell their agenda to labor. As a Japan Economic Federation report
explained, it was essential to "sweep away the prejudice that 'efficiency increase' is nothing more than the capitalist shorthand for the pursuit of
profits."[42]

Efforts to "sweep away" the political baggage of Scientific Management
took two main forms. The first was to redouble professions of concern for the
humanity and welfare of workers. In consonance with the ideology of the
wartime labor order, proponents of managerial improvement averred great
concern for the "human element" and respect for man over machine. Kanda

[38] Morito Tatsuo, "Shihonshugi to nōritsu mondai," *Shakai seisaku jihō* 258 (March 1942): 37.

[39] Noda Nobuo, *Kōgyō keizai shinron* (Daiyamondo, 1943), 312.

[40] Kishi Nobusuke, "Senji-ka no nōritsu zōshin," *Nihon nōritsu* 1, no. 1 (June 1942):19–21.

[41] On Marxism and the "New Order," see William Miles Fletcher III, *The Search for a New
Order: Intellectuals and Fascism in Prewar Japan* (Chapel Hill: University of North Carolina
Press, 1982).

[42] Nihon keizai renmeikai chōsaka, *Sangyō nōritsu to seishin shidō* (Sankaidō, 1943), 2.

Kōichi, for example, suggested that management should aim to increase welfare rather than profits, and that the "great capitalistic defects" of slighting worker health and the human spirit had to be exorcised from Scientific Management.[43] The Efficiency Federation was even more direct when it declared that the most important elements in winning the "industrial war" were "Number one, people; number two, people; number three, people."[44]

Hand in hand with this intensified "humanization" of management rhetoric went an attempt to redefine what "exploitation" by Scientific Management actually constituted. Glossing over the deskilling of labor and degradation of work associated with the Taylorization of the production process, wartime commentators pointed to incentive wage schemes as the most inhumane and extortionary aspects of modern management.[45] The corollary of this was that once "individualistic," "capitalistic" incentive schemes had been eliminated (or at least circumscribed), workers would have no cause to fear management reforms on the shop floor. With output-based wages thus installed as the litmus test of exploitation, "American-style Scientific Management" was judged to be fatally flawed, while Japanese management practices—which included living (*seikatsu*) wages—were hailed as fair, humane, and consistent with the common good.[46] The fact that Japanese experts continued to advocate the same techniques and approaches as their U.S. counterparts—and were thus equally open to charges of dehumanizing the work process—was conveniently (and no doubt consciously) left unspoken under the exigencies of industrial mobilization. In the end, wartime proponents of Scientific Management sought only a political denaturing of Taylorism's reputation and not a corresponding reform of its practice.

Viewed as a whole, the wartime discourse on management reform did not constitute a reprise of the Taishō debate over Taylorism so much as a coda to it. There was, at any rate, very little discord among wartime commentators: as Ueno Yōichi noted in 1939, "one no longer hears all those silly questions and complaints about the efficiency movement that one used to."[47] It is important to recall, however, that there had actually been very little intellectual debate surrounding Scientific Management since the late 1920s, when Japanese observers (like their counterparts in Europe and the United States) arrived at a loose consensus on the need for a "revised" Taylorism that could convincingly

[43] Kanda, *Kōjō kanri kenkyū*, 4, 42.

[44] "Rōmu to nōritsu," *Sangyō nōritsu* 15, no. 4 (April 1942): 319.

[45] See, for example, Fujibayashi Keizō, "Kōkoku kinrōkan to keiei rōdōsha seisaku," *Shakai seisaku jihō* 272 (May 1943).

[46] "Kotoshi ni oite wagakuni no ryoku o itasu kokusaku ni taiō suru nōritsu mondai," *Sangyō nōritsu* 12, no. 2 (February 1939): 145–47; "Chingin no Nihonshiki kazoku hon'i chingin e no hyōjunka," ibid., no. 3 (March 1939): 258–60; Neagari Kōichi, "Sangyō hōkoku undō to nōritsu zōshin mondai," *Shakai seisaku jihō* 258 (March 1942): 579–80.

[47] Ueno Yōichi, "Naigai ni okeru nōritsu undō no genjō," *Sangyō nōritsu* 12, no. 4 (April 1939): 357.

fuse mechanistic rationality and a "humanized" approach to labor. From this perspective, the wartime nondebate over Scientific Management seems less a redefinition than a reaffirmation of the existing consensus, albeit one fortified with considerable ideological window-dressing. Furthermore, as had been the case twenty years earlier, "classic," textbook Taylorism—now tagged "American-style" and "capitalistic"—was trotted out as the whipping boy. What had been the target of critics' ire during the Taishō debate was, in the changed wartime environment, manipulated as a convenient counterpoint to an allegedly "new," "Japanized," "nonexploitative" model of Scientific Management.

The assertion that the "revised Taylorite" consensus was confirmed and strengthened during the war is borne out by the wartime wrangle over a "Japanese-style" wage system. The debate pitted reformers from academia, the bureaucracy, and Sanpō who were touting a livelihood, family-wage structure against industrialists and managers more comfortable with output-based models. The eventual compromise was on a wage system that fused the "distinctively Japanese" living wage with the monetary incentives of Scientific Management.[48] Significantly, this "Japanese-style," "nonexploitative" compromise was similar in all essential respects to the "revised Taylorite" models propounded by the efficiency movement since the late 1920s. In seeking to guarantee a minimum income level, adjusted with a seniority element and supplemented by "scientific" incentives, the wartime structure was continuous with Noda and Katō's Mitsubishi Electric scheme, Araki's Yokohama Dock system, and the model recommended by the Production Management Committee in 1935.[49] Although the wartime wage debate generated much reformist sound and fury, it concluded with the endorsement and generalization of the existing "revised Taylorite" approach.

As the persistence of output-based wages suggests, some old ideas died hard during the war, even when they flew in the face of the dominant ideology and economic reality. This certainly was the case with the managerial dedication to shop-floor competition and monetary incentives. Despite the branding of such tools as "selfish" and "Western"—indeed, as the very yardstick of the exploitation of labor—Japanese management experts quietly maintained their faith in them. Sugiyama Kōichi, for instance, insisted on the necessity of incentive wages and Taylorite methods despite his revels in the tea ceremony and the Japanese spirit.[50] The Stakhanov movement—a Soviet plan to increase production by promoting interworker rivalries and glorifying "model"

[48] Andrew Gordon, *The Evolution of Labor Relations in Japan: Heavy Industry, 1853–1955* (Cambridge, Mass.: Harvard University Press, 1985), 276–79; Okuda, *Hito to keiei,* 524ff.

[49] Araki, at least, stressed this continuity and boasted of inventing the prototype of the wartime order. Araki Tōichirō, *Seisan kanri kaizen no chakuganten* (Keirishikai, 1942), 24–28.

[50] Sugiyama Kōichi, "Taryō seisan hōshiki to setsubi no nōritsuteki kaizen II," *Nihon nōritsu* 2, no. 5 (May 1943): 341–44.

laborers—attracted some wartime attention and emulation.[51] Surprisingly enough, even the high-wage/low-cost ideal continued to have its wartime adherents. Although maintaining even minimal living standards was problematic, and cost accounting was deteriorating under the controlled economy, some high-profile business spokesmen continued to trumpet the model of mutual gains. Foremost among them was Ōkōchi Masatoshi, the outspoken chairman of Riken Industries, whose Fordist vision of "scientific industry" (*kagaku-shugi kōgyō*) was premised on high-wage, high-productivity workers manufacturing low-cost, top-quality goods in technologically sophisticated workshops.[52] On a less dramatic scale, a few analysts hopefully concluded that the wartime provision of livelihood pay would constitute the "high-wage" part of the Fordist equation and that low production costs and low consumer prices would naturally follow.[53]

In general, the wartime "debate" over Scientific Management did not bring into question the methodologies or basic assumptions of Taylorism that had been accepted in Japan since the Taishō period. The war did inspire an ideological remolding of modern management, as proponents sought to extract Taylorism from its American roots, site it within an indigenous tradition of efficiency, and cleanse it of lingering overtones of capitalist exploitation. Nonetheless, the "revised Taylorite" consensus was affirmed and even more widely acknowledged, although now it was hailed as characteristically and inherently Japanese. Although management experts had begun to internalize Scientific Management during the early 1930s, only a decade later did the model of "humanized" Taylorism start to gain broad acceptance as "Japanese-style" management.

As Andrew Gordon has observed, "The fact that Japan's New Labor Order in the late 1930s could be persuasively presented as nativist, despite decisive outside influence, reveals the complex of common internal experience, international connections, and nationalistic fervor that contributed to the rise of fascist systems."[54] The wartime repackaging and reaffirmation of Taylorism

[51] See, for example, Arai Mitsuzō, "Soren no nōritsu shōkai," *Kōgyō to keizai* 99 (March 1941): 2–24. On the Soviet movement, Mark R. Beissinger, *Scientific Management, Socialist Discipline, and Soviet Power* (Cambridge, Mass.: Harvard University Press, 1988), 134–38; Arthur Bedeian and Carl Phillips, "Scientific Management and Stakhanovism in the Soviet Union: A Historical Perspective," *International Journal of Social Economics* 17, no. 10 (1990):31–34.

[52] Ōkōchi Masatoshi, *Tōsei keizai to keizai sen* (Kagakushugi kōgyōsha, 1940), 20; Michael Cusumano, " 'Scientific Industry': Strategy, Technology, and Entrepreneurship in Prewar Japan," in *Managing Industrial Enterprise: Cases from Japan's Prewar Experience,* ed. William Wray (Cambridge, Mass.: Council on East Asian Studies, Harvard University, 1989), 269–315; Tessa Morris-Suzuki, *The Technological Transformation of Japan* (Cambridge: Cambridge University Press, 1994), 126–29.

[53] Kobayashi Shigeyuki, "Nōritsu to chingin to no kanren ni tsuite," *Shakai seisaku jihō* 258 (March 1942): 491–519.

[54] Gordon, *Imperial Democracy,* 324.

bears this conclusion out in full, although it also demonstrates that the models being integrated and nativized in "New Order" Japan—the "decisive outside influence"—could be American as well as fascist in origin.

The Planned Economy and the Logic of Scientific Management

Scientific Management was more than just a tool in the hands of the Japanese wartime state. Indeed, Taylorism and the logic of efficiency which underlay it were among the intellectual building blocks of the entire wartime structure of economic and political control. The values of economic optimalization, technocratic neutrality, managerialism, and bureaucracy which characterized modern management also suffused the "New Order" and what has been labeled "Japanese fascism." To many observers at the time, the spread of economic planning and the broadening of state control seemed less a revolutionary break than an inevitable step, the logical end point of a process which stretched back to Taylorism by way of the rationalization movement. Ironically, while Scientific Management was being publicly indigenized in the cause of ideological conformity, its internal logic was already well assimilated into the intellectual core of the wartime Japanese state.

The impetus toward a controlled economy (and subsequently a planned one) derived in large part from the rationalization movement or, more precisely, from a widespread perception of its failures. By the late 1930s, most academic and bureaucratic observers agreed that *sangyō gōrika* had fallen well short of its potential. "Why didn't the rationalization movement of a decade ago make a greater splash?" one critic asked: "Because it was nothing more than rationalization to shore up company management, undertaken by firms in self-defense in a time of depression. Because it was not rationalization that aimed to increase the people's standard of living by assertively raising production. Because, in short, it was not a planned rationalization of all aspects of the national economy."[55] The problem, most seemed to conclude, was narrowness: in the early Shōwa rationalization movement, dominated as it was by business interests, the emphasis was on private gain, stabilization rather than expansion, and the containment of reform to the firm and industry level. Just as Taylorites had warned that internecine conflict between management and labor would impede progress on the shop floor, so analysts concluded that the pursuit of parochial interests had thwarted the complete rationalization of the Japanese economy during the Depression.

The way to break out of the straitjacket of "capitalistic" rationalization appeared obvious to many: the drive for efficiency had to be extended to the

---

[55] Nainen kikan henshūbu, *Sangyō nōritsu zōshin ni kansuru shomondai* (Sankaidō, 1943), 242.

level of the entire economy, placed under the guidance of centralized planning, and increasingly directed toward public rather than private gain. "Rationalization today," one Commerce Ministry bureaucrat declared in 1941, "takes as its starting point the correction of disequilibria throughout the national economy rather than the increase of efficiency in individual economic units."[56] Managerial reform on the firm level was certainly not to be ignored, yet the proponents of central planning conceived of it as only a single element in a coordinated effort to maximize the nation's economic production. "Organization is power," Kishimoto Seijirō keenly observed; "No matter what resources are available, if they are not fully organized, they will end up being wasted and efficiency will suffer."[57] Primary responsibility for the rationalization of economic life thus had to pass from individuals to the state, which (Kishimoto concluded) must look to "a structure for increasing industrial efficiency that considers all aspects of control (*tōsei*)."[58]

The fulcrum of this wartime economic revisionism was the idea of efficiency. Like many idealistic proponents of Scientific Management, the architects of the "New Order" considered efficiency itself a goal, rather than simply a way station on the road to corporate profits. Under a structure that valued public good over private gain, efficiency was to be installed as the standard by which economic success or failure was measured. According to Miles Fletcher, the Shōwa Research Association (Shōwa Kenkyūkai)—the brain trust of the "New Order" movement—promoted the enshrinement of efficiency, arguing the need "to replace the ethic of the free pursuit of profit with a commitment to serve national interests by seeking the most efficient methods of increasing production. . . ."[59] Inherent in this view was, of course, the belief that the state was to be not only the coordinator of industrial efficiency but also its prime beneficiary. As Tōjō Hideki, then army minister, advised the members of the Japan Efficiency Association at its inaugural meeting, the imperative of the day was "rationalization on the basis of the state" rather than "narrow" rationalization for private ends.[60]

Drawing direct lines of influence between the efficiency movement and the establishment of the "New Order" is difficult. Some prominent Japanese Taylorites did play supporting roles in the construction of the wartime control structure: Araki Tōichirō, for instance, chaired the National Economic Research Center (Kokka Keizai Kenkyūjo), a study group funded by aircraft industry pioneer Nakajima Chikuhei, which conducted some of the earliest

---

[56] General Affairs Section Chief Kanda quoted in Kojima, *Shin sangyō gōrika,* 20.

[57] Kishimoto Seijirō, "Tōsei keizai to sangyō nōritsu," *Shakai seisaku jihō* 258 (March 1942): 9.

[58] Ibid., 13.

[59] Fletcher, *Search,* 128.

[60] Tōjō Hideki, "Shukuji," *Nihon nōritsu* 1, no. 1 (June 1942): 9.

Japanese research on European economic planning.[61] Godō Takuo, mean-while, attained the highest bureaucratic advancement of any efficiency move-ment veteran, serving as commerce minister in the Hayashi and Abe cabinets. Although Scientific Management experts appear not to have penetrated the inner circle of economic policymaking, many of those who were influential in the conception and implementation of the "New Order" had extensive knowl-edge of Taylorism and the assumptions of modern management. This certainly was the case with bureaucrats like Yoshino Shinji and Kishi Nobusuke, who had cut their teeth on the rationalization movement, as well as government technocrats like Miyamoto Takenosuke and Matsumae Shigeyoshi, who had engineering training. Moreover, many of the intellectual patrons of the "New Order," especially those with backgrounds in Marxist analysis (like Takahashi Kamekichi, who chaired the Shōwa Research Association's economic sec-tion), approached the industrial and social dilemmas of the war with a firm grasp of the logic of Scientific Management.

The intellectual continuity between Taylorism and the wartime economic structure may have been best expressed by Morito Tatsuo in a 1942 essay in the journal *Shakai seisaku jihō*. Morito, the noted Marxist economist who had commented extensively on Taylorism during the Taishō debate, argued that the "efficiency problem" had traced a clear trajectory in both Japan and the West. Starting with Scientific Management on the shop floor and progressing through industrial rationalization, the focus of "efficiency increase" had fi-nally moved on to "the efficiency of the entire national economy, of society and the people in a broad sense." Not only had the scope of the efficiency movement been broadened, but so had its methods and goals: technical spe-cialization gave way to a more generalized approach, and dedication to "the nurturing of human beings" replaced the capitalistic preoccupation with profits.[62] Within this expansive wartime view, Morito suggested, the only suit-able coordinator of efficiency increase was the state. The responsibility could not be entrusted to "efficiency engineers, individual businessmen, industrial organizations, or the capitalist class," though each would have a role as part of greater efforts in economic and social reform. At a time when the efficiency problem had "gone beyond private interests and become a question of the very survival of the nation," Morito concluded that "the state will become our top efficiency manager."[63]

In Morito's analysis, efficiency was a concept with a life of its own in industrial society. Although the idea of "efficiency increase" had originally been spawned by capitalism to support the drive for profits, the logic inherent in Scientific Management ultimately turned in upon the system which created it. By its own standards of efficiency, Morito argued, free-market, individu-

---

[61] Araki Tōichirō, *Nōritsu ichidaiki* (Nihon nōritsu kyōkai, 1971), 80–92.

[62] Morito, "Shihonshugi to nōritsu mondai," 23–25, 36.

[63] Ibid., 25.

alistic capitalism had proven itself to be fatally inefficient. The only way to guarantee the maximization of society's resources was to shift to a planned economy, the "final version of the efficiency problem which had gestated in capitalism's own womb." In the construction of this thoroughly efficient, highly controlled, statist system, capitalism was, of course, to be eclipsed. In the end, Morito decided, the logic of efficiency was "both the greatest bulwark of the capitalist system and its deepest internal parasite."[64]

Thus, as Morito's essay suggests, the economic "New Order" was perceived as the final step in the extrapolation of Scientific Management from the factory to the economy, the ultimate manifestation of ideas of efficiency first elaborated in the Taishō period. Not surprisingly, then, the technocratic edge of Taylorism—emphasizing the unique ability of trained experts to manage economic life evenhandedly and optimally—was affirmed and elevated under the wartime structure. The "New Order" championed the "separation of ownership and management," the idea that industry should be administered by professional managers in the interest of maximum efficiency rather than by capitalists in the pursuit of maximum profits. The managerial stratum was to be given greater autonomy and responsibility: freed from the service of capital, managers were charged with giving a "fair return" to owners, guaranteeing the welfare of labor, and delivering the utmost production to society and the state.[65] This was, of course, consistent with the views of most Japanese scientific managers, who had long touted their neutrality and technical expertise as a justification for increased influence in the factory. A 1940 editorial in the Industrial Association journal, for example, declared that "today, the leaders of industry must be highly experienced. Management can't be left to novices like bank presidents and directors, but requires men with specialized knowledge." "It is only natural," the editorial concluded, "that the guiding spirit of management is undergoing great changes at this time."[66]

As Charles Maier has suggested was the case in interwar Europe, the ascendance of technocratic managerial thought and the evolution of authoritarian

---

[64] Ibid., 48–9.

[65] Noda, *Kōgyō keizai shinron,* 131 ff.; Hirao Hachisaburō, "Keieisha taru shikaku," *Kōgyō to keizai* 79 (July 1939): 1–2; Okazaki Tetsuji, "The Japanese Firm Under the Wartime Planned Economy," *Journal of the Japanese and International Economies* 7 (1993): 188–91, 195; Lonny Carlile, "Zaikai and the Politics of Production in Japan, 1940–1962" (Ph.D. diss., University of California, Berkeley, 1989), 128–29. A 1944 Army Ministry study stated that "it is necessary to transform stocks to interest-bearing securities, and the character of stockholders as recipients of such interest. The profits made by the firm should be distributed appropriately to all staffs and workers, to everybody who has generated such profits. In management, it is essential to consider first and foremost the people who work for the firm. In one way or another, management, technology, and labor depend on the overall manipulation of people. This aspect of management is invariably more important than capital itself." Okazaki, "The Japanese Firm," 199, n. 15.

[66] "Atarashii kōjō keiei e no kibō," *Kōgyō to keizai* 90 (June 1940): 1.

political systems were closely linked.[67] This confluence was apparent in Japan's "New Order" as well, with its emphasis on neutral, expert guidance of a centralized, hierarchical, highly controlled economic and political structure. For instance, as discussions of "prioritization" (*jūtenshugi*) demonstrated, proponents of the "New Order" looked to authoritarian solutions to wartime problems of industrial efficiency. "It would be optimal," Matsumae Shigeyoshi reasoned, "if we bolster those things that are necessary . . . and suppress those that are unnecessary and useless."[68] Economic Darwinism was, in other words, no longer to be a self-regulating process, but one tended and enforced by objective, "scientific" technocrats. Management did not, however, stop there: many observers stressed the state's responsibility to rationalize the fabric of everyday life, Andō Masakichi, for one, advising that "all aspects of the lives of workers must be thoroughly guided scientifically."[69] In the end, Ueno Yōichi may have summed it up best when he declared in 1939—just over a year before the proclamation of the "New Order"—that "it would be for the good if Scientific Management were applied to the political administration of our nation."[70]

In recent years, many analysts have stressed the influence of Nazism and Italian Fascism on the construction of Japan's wartime apparatus of political and economic control.[71] These European models have been portrayed as something of a deus ex machina, a ready-made structure transplanted (under the name "New Order") into the fertile soil of wartime Japan. The Japanese experience with Scientific Management, however, underlines the fact that Japan's path to economic planning and authoritarianism may have paralleled the European process as much as derived from it. While the inspiration of fascist models cannot be underestimated, the logic of efficiency inherent in modern management seems to have produced similar imperatives in Japan as it had in Europe. State planning, technocratic control, and authoritarian methods lay at the end of a trajectory that began with Taylorism and passed through the rationalization movement. Progressing on to the "New Order" seemed a logical and virtually inevitable step to Japanese intellectuals, bureaucrats, and managers. In short, beneath the nativistic rhetoric and fascist models which blanketed Japan's wartime economic and political structure, there lay a dy-

---

[67] Charles Maier, "Between Taylorism and Technocracy: European Ideologies and the Vision of Industrial Productivity in the 1920s," in *In Search of Stability: Explorations in Historical Political Economy* (Cambridge: Cambridge University Press, 1987; originally published 1970). Compare Sheldon Garon, "Rethinking Modernization and Modernity in Japanese History: A Focus on State-Society Relations," *Journal of Asian Studies* 53, no. 2 (May 1994): 346–66.

[68] Nihon sangyō keizai seikeibu, *Seisan sen,* 236–37.

[69] Andō Masakichi, "Kessenka ni okeru nōritsu-seikatsu-chingin," *Shakai seisaku jihō* 258 (March 1942): 468.

[70] Ueno, "Naigai ni okeru nōritsu undō no genjō," 360.

[71] Notably, Fletcher, *Search*; Garon, *The State and Labor*; Gordon, *Imperial Democracy*.

namic, pervasive stream of thought that stretched back to the Taishō efficiency movement and the principles of Scientific Management.

Scientific Management and the Dilemmas of Wartime Industry

If wartime developments revealed the intellectual depth and ideological durability of Scientific Management in Japan, they also revealed its weaknesses in actual practice. Wartime mobilization brought to the surface all of the fundamental problems in Japanese production management and proved that even basic tenets of Scientific Management had not yet spread fully through Japanese industry. "Since the Manchurian Incident," one observer concluded, "the necessity of raising efficiency through Scientific Management has increasingly come to be seen as the basis of a . . . rapid expansion of defense industries. [Nevertheless,] one certainly can't say that Scientific Management has permeated the industrial world or that the actual usage of its methods has progressed."[72] Paradoxically, the most managerially and technically advanced sector of the Japanese economy, textiles, was an early victim of the wartime buildup, while one of the least Taylorized, the machinery industry, became the focus of mobilization campaigns and "prioritized" planning from the start of the China War. As Murai Tsutomu, an Aichi Watch Company engineer, noted, "Rationalization in the form of Scientific Management penetrated all facets of company management in light industries (such as textiles). In heavy industry, particularly in machinery, however, . . . rationalization did not progress at all on the factory level. There is still great scope today for increasing efficiency on the shop floor in the machine industry."[73]

As Nakaoka Tetsurō has keenly argued, "the shortcomings of wartime production were due more to managerial problems than to technical ones."[74] Many observers at the time—including most Scientific Management proponents—would have reluctantly agreed. Miyamoto Takenosuke, the technocratic government engineer and ideologue of the New Scientific Order, gently chided the management movement: "Research on the efficiency problem is, I believe, quite retarded in Japanese industry today."[75] Kishi Nobusuke was more direct

[72] Neagari, "Sangyō hōkoku undō," 574.

[73] Murai Tsutomu, "Seisan gijutsu kōza 1: Sensō to seisan zōkyō ni tsuite," *Nihon nōritsu* 2, no. 6 (June 1943): 417–18; see also Cohen, *Japan's Economy,* 351.

[74] This is not to deny the importance of technological bottlenecks in wartime production. Nakaoka notes the distress caused by Japan's wartime lack of the technology necessary to produce specialty steels for die making and to manufacture high-precision die-cutting machines (both of which had previously been imported from the United States). Nakaoka Tetsurō, "Production Management in Japan Before the Period of High Economic Growth," *Osaka City University Economic Review* 17 (1981): 9–10.

[75] Miyamoto Takenosuke, "Sangyō nōritsu no zōshin ni tsuite," *Kōgyō to keizai* 102 (June 1941): 11.

in taking Japanese managers and management experts to task: in the flagship issue of the Efficiency Association's organ publication, Kishi concluded that the greater efficiency of American industry was due to "the gap between their factory management methods and ours." He proceeded to regale readers with tales of waste in Japanese workshops, including the story of one plant where a component was transported a total of 580 kilometers ("more than the distance between Tokyo and Osaka") from the time it left the stockroom to the time the finished product was rolled off the assembly line.[76]

Respect for the superiority of American management techniques was virtually universal in wartime Japan, as was the belief that Japan had to trace a similar path of industrial development in order to compete in the "industrial war." "Needless to say," Noda Nobuo declared in 1943, "the greatest concern in the Japanese efficiency world today is the conversion to mass production."[77] The problem was that while some firms and sectors had embraced advanced techniques, Japanese industry as a whole had not yet fully absorbed the basic elements of systematic management which were prerequisites for Fordist assembly-line production. Most notably, in each of the three key aspects of the Taylorization of the work process—standardization, specialization, and simplification—the Japanese record was, viewed as a whole, far from enviable. "The way goods are manufactured in Japan today," one engineer lamented, "is similar to the manner in which pictures are painted," lacking, in other words, rigid standards, division of labor, or firm managerial control.[78]

The problem of standardization had long been a concern of management reformers, but only during the war—when the absence of uniform and interchangeable components impeded the shift to mass production—were its implications widely acknowledged in the business community. Standardization had been a major initiative of the rationalization movement and, during the 1930s, a variety of government bodies had established hundreds of industrial standards. Business pressure assured, however, that these new specifications were no more than guidelines and that compliance by individual firms was voluntary.[79] Inevitably, there was no stampede to retool during the Depression, and with the exception of a few products (such as paper), standardization did not progress in actual practice. With the wartime drive for mass production, the inadequacies of Japanese standardization became clear: one manager noted that there were literally thousands of different varieties of ten-millimeter bolts on the market, when several dozen standard types would have

---

[76] Kishi, "Senji-ka no nōritsu zōshin," 17–19. On the travails of the wartime aircraft industry, see Richard J. Samuels, *Rich Nation Strong Army: National Security and the Technological Transformation of Japan* (Ithaca, N.Y.: Cornell University Press, 1994), 121–26.

[77] Noda Nobuo, "Zōsan kessen to taryō seisan," *Nihon nōritsu* 2, no. 5 (May 1943): 322.

[78] Nainen kikan henshūbu, *Sangyō nōritsu*, 234.

[79] Ibid., 259 ff.

sufficed. Victor Gartner, a Swiss engineer who worked as a consultant in wartime Japan, despaired of ever achieving mass production after visiting a small machine shop where thirteen different types of lathe, each calibrated to a different measurement standard, were in use.[80]

Beyond the lack of standardization, the transition to mass production in wartime Japan ran up against a continued dependence on skilled labor, betraying incomplete specialization and simplification of the production process. While the *oyakata* system had disappeared many decades earlier, the reliance of the machine industry on "old-fashioned, craftsman-style" workers apparently had not.[81] Skilled laborers, using multipurpose machine tools and working without benefit of scientific routines or uniform standards of accuracy, continued to be the norm in Japanese firms, even in many of the largest and most sophisticated enterprises. One Industrial Association report claimed, albeit with considerable hyperbole, that thorough specialization and simplification in Japanese machine shops could increase worker efficiency many tens of times over.[82]

The embryonic Taylorization of the work process presented a number of challenges to Japanese management experts and economic planners. In the first place, reliance on the experience of workers circumscribed managerial ability to reform the organization of production, even under wartime mobilization. As Morikawa Kakuzō suggested, "It has been said that there are no experts in production techniques in our country and, when you come to think of it . . . , in most cases the knowledge necessary for producing goods does lie entirely in the hands of the workers."[83] When attempting the wartime leap to mass production, many Japanese industrialists accordingly found, much to their dismay, that the "manager's brains" were still under the proverbial "workman's cap," and that craftsmen could be adamant in defending their autonomy on the shop floor. Furthermore, Japanese workers, irrespective of their skill level, were widely judged to be "unscientific," idiosyncratic, and inconsistent. Gartner declared that they had "a particularly retarded appreciation of exactness," while Godō Takuo bemoaned their lack of technical knowledge, their inadequate attention to planning, and their tendency to waste time chatting.[84]

---

[80] Ibid., 263; "Gaijin gishi o kakomu seisan gijutsu," *Nihon nōritsu* 1, no. 7 (December 1942): 14.

[81] Shinme Shinshichirō, *Kōjō kanri* (Kyōritsusha, 1941), 47. Nakaoka Tetsurō has suggested that Japanese machine shops in the 1940s looked much like those that Taylor and Ford had confronted half a century earlier. Nakaoka Tetsurō, "Senchū, sengo no kagakuteki kanri undō I," *Keizaigaku zasshi* 82, no. 1 (May 1981): 19.

[82] Nihon kōgyō kyōkai, *Senji ni okeru kōjō seisanryoku*, 6.

[83] Morikawa Kakuzō, "Nihon nōritsu kyōkai hossoku ni tsuite," *Nihon nōritsu* 1, no. 2 (July 1942): 84–85.

[84] "Gaijin gishi," 15; Nakaoka, "Production Management," 11.

Perhaps most importantly, the dependence on skilled workers seriously constrained government and business attempts to expand wartime production. While industrial mobilization increased the demand for experienced machinists, the military draft was simultaneously depressing the supply, giving rise to persistent labor bottlenecks. Despite much discussion during the war of a "labor famine," the problem was not really one of quantity, but of quality: in the end, no number of unskilled laborers could adequately replace a highly skilled worker in an un-Taylorized workshop. Double-shifting was rare in wartime Japan, not as a result of a general labor shortage or a Sanpō-induced concern for worker welfare, but due to the lack of enough skilled workers to make it viable.[85] As Okuda Kenji has persuasively argued, the "human wave" strategy of Japanese labor mobilization was a disaster because Japanese factories were not technologically or organizationally prepared to make good use of legions of unskilled employees.[86]

Two main approaches for responding to the wartime dilemmas in production management eventually emerged from the efficiency movement and Japanese industry. The first was to make the best of the existing conditions and seek to raise efficiency and production within the context of non-Taylorized workshops. Toward this goal, a variety of public and private bodies launched campaigns to train workers more effectively and encourage the use of jigs and gauges in machine shops. Yamashita Okiie even suggested that the army teach recruits to use lathes rather than rifles.[87] The second strategy was to redouble efforts to Taylorize the production process, placing ever greater emphasis on the munitions and machinery industries. Time-and-motion study to standardize work routines and simplify tasks was aggressively pursued by the Industrial Association and its successor, the Japan Efficiency Association. Many commentators, meanwhile, argued for the introduction of single-purpose ma-

[85] Cohen, *Japan's Economy,* 346–47.

[86] Okuda, *Hito to keiei,* 516 ff. The fact that the production process in wartime heavy industry was not highly Taylorized may help explain why the mobilization of female labor was not given greater priority by the Japanese state or business community. Compare Miyake Yoshiko, "Doubling Expectations: Motherhood and Women's Factory Work under State Management in Japan in the 1930s and 1940s," in *Recreating Japanese Women, 1600–1945,* ed. Gail Lee Bernstein (Berkeley: University of California Press, 1991), 267–95.

[87] Yamashita Okiie, "Senji seisanryoku no kakujū," in *Sensō to kōgyō,* ed. Nihon kōgyō kyōkai (Nihon hyōronsha, 1939), 116. According to proponents of jigs and gauges, their use would allow skilled machinists to produce items more accurately and unskilled workers to use multipurpose tools to mass-produce simple components. Many observers reported that these relatively basic devices were unknown in many Japanese machine-tool shops. Nakaoka, "Senchū, sengo I," 16; Cohen, *Japan's Economy,* 220–21; Tsuru Gorō, "Jigu oyobi kensagu no hyōjunka," *Nihon nōritsu* 1, no. 2 (July 1942): 117. The Japan Efficiency Association produced a one-thousand-page shop manual on the use of jigs but it was only published a few months prior to the end of the war. According to Okuda Kenji, the manual remained "highly useful" even in the 1970s. Okuda Kenji, "Managerial Evolution in Japan II," *Management Japan* 5, no. 4 (1972): 22.

chine tools which would permit the mass production of standard articles by unskilled labor.[88]

Despite the broad wartime appreciation of the need for managerial improvement, the various initiatives to increase efficiency, step up production, and create Fordist assembly lines did not appear to yield quick dividends. Training schemes collapsed as companies increasingly found they had no skilled workers to spare as instructors; jigs, gauges, work study, and dedicated machine tools remained the exception rather than the rule in many shops.[89] The situation was not entirely dismal: for example, a 1941 survey conducted by the Japan Society for the Promotion of Science revealed that over a third of the machine shops and chemical firms studied were using some form of assembly-line system.[90] A few managerial success stories became widely known: at Toyokawa Naval Arsenal, Efficiency Association consultants helped increase machine-gun production thirty-five-fold; a system of standardizing designs and streamlining production techniques dramatically boosted productivity at some shipyards; and, in the crucial aircraft industry, manufacturing techniques reached a level which Yamamoto Kiyoshi has described as "partial assembly-line production" (*han nagare sagyō*).[91] Nevertheless, while such achievements were encouraging, as one wartime report on management issues observed despondently, "When you really look into matters, there are actually very few shops using assembly-line production methods today."[92] The sober and disheartening reality of wartime industrial mobilization may have been captured best by one Tōshiba manager who noted simply that "despite government calls for motivation, and stimulants to production, the large wartime labor force became less and less efficient."[93]

The reasons why management reform and mass production did not appear to progress further in wartime Japan are numerous and overlapping. Moreover, different actors tended to emphasize different elements and, particularly in the desperate last years of the war, a rash of finger-pointing served to cloud the issue even more. All, however, could agree that the same factors which were

[88] See Yamashita Okiie, *Gijutsusha no kokoroe,* Sankaidō rikōgaku ronsō, vol. 24 (Sankaidō, 1942), 81 ff.; Ōkōchi, *Tōsei keizai,* 40–46; Nihon keizai renmeikai chōsaka, *Taryō seisan hōshiki jitsugen no gutaisaku* (Sankaidō, 1943), 7–32.

[89] Cohen, *Japan's Economy,* 274–75.

[90] Sasaki, "Rationalization of Production Management Systems," 42–43.

[91] Ibid., 33, 42–51; Shiba Takao, "Business Activities of Japanese Manufacturing Industries During World War II," in Sakudō and Shiba, *World War II and the Transformation of Business Systems,* 13; Yamamoto Kiyoshi, *Nihon ni okeru shokuba no gijutsu, rōdō shi* (Tokyo daigaku shuppankai, 1994), 225–73. On the automobile industry, which also achieved mass production levels during the war, see Michael A. Cusumano, *The Japanese Automobile Industry: Technology and Management at Nissan and Toyota* (Cambridge, Mass.: Harvard University Press, 1985), chap. 1.

[92] Fukushima Matsuo, "Rōmu kanri to seisan kanri," in Noda keizai kenkyūjo, *Shin kinrō kanri no jissai* (1943), 226.

[93] Quoted in Gordon, *Evolution,* 283.

hampering industrial mobilization in general were also putting the damper on attempts to streamline and mechanize shop-floor management. Bottlenecks in critical materials were certainly a major constraint, both to increasing efficiency and to realizing Fordist production. As many observers noted, shortages prevented extensive retooling as well as the running of existing plants at their full (and most efficient) capacity.[94] Most postwar analysts have concurred, noting the difficulties of attempting to revolutionize the production process in an environment of endemic resource shortages, instability in the workforce, and direct economic controls.[95]

The scarcity of trained management experts and the lack of suitable educational and research facilities were also widely acknowledged as barriers to the extensive reform of management. "The fundamental reason for Japan's industrial retardation," Araki Tōichirō declared in 1942, "is the lack of special university courses in Scientific Management such as they have in the United States."[96] Such sentiments were echoed by many, as were calls for more state-sponsored research on production technology, the addition of management training to the engineering curriculum, and the spread of science education in the schools.[97] Japan's dearth of technically trained managers and production engineers was felt particularly keenly in the Industrial Association, with its inclination toward practical expertise and professionalism. Claiming that Japan could boast only a handful of qualified process management engineers, the association sponsored intensive training courses in work study from 1937. Under the direction of Horime Ken'ichi (tagged the "Frank Gilbreth of Japan" by his students), over four hundred managers were trained during the course of the war in the basics of industrial engineering and the practical application of time-and-motion study.[98]

Business leaders were often the target of recriminations concerning efficiency, since they stood out as the group most directly accountable for the problems of industrial production. This was, of course, the view of "New Order" bureaucrats and intellectuals, who were dubious that the pursuit of profits was compatible with the maximization of productivity. The chairman of Sanpō, for example, declared in 1943 that managers seemed to be "taking it easy" by living off generous wartime credit arrangements, hoarding raw materials and labor, and showing little concern for efficiency or production.[99]

Needless to say, Japanese industrialists tended to trace the roots of the efficiency dilemma elsewhere, and they labored to shift as much of the blame as

[94] Nihon sangyō keizai seikeibu, *Seisan sen,* 232; Cohen, *Japan's Economy,* 201–3.

[95] Nakaoka, "Senchū, sengo I," 16; Yamamoto, *Nihon ni okeru shokuba,* 270–71.

[96] Araki, *Seisan kanri kaizen,* 1–2.

[97] See, among others, Nihon keizai renmeikai chōsaka, *Taryō seisan,* 34 ff.

[98] Ono Tsuneo, ed., *Mōshon-maindo: Horime Ken'ichi tsuitōroku* (Nihon nōritsu kyōkai, 1970), 60–70; Nihon nōritsu kyōkai, *Keiei to tomo ni* (1982), chap. 2.

[99] Okuda, *Hito to keiei,* 459.

they could onto the state and its economic control apparatus. As government regulation swelled, businessmen complained volubly of their loss of autonomy in the factory and its deleterious effect on production. One Kyōchōkai report on the aircraft industry observed that managers were being swamped by "guidance from a plethora of official control organs," the bulk of which ended up being inconsistent, time-consuming, and even counterproductive.[100] Some postwar analyses have supported the businessmen's claims against the state, arguing that the structure of controls offered managers no incentive to increase efficiency and actually promoted overstaffing and complacency rather than productivity and full mobilization.[101]

One of the most compelling arguments made by business critics of the state was the assertion that mass production was being stymied by the irrationality of military procurement plans. The wartime rivalry between the army and the navy was acutely manifested in the system of ordering munitions, especially aircraft, from the private sector. Rather than pooling their orders, which could have encouraged economies of scale, the services insisted on separate procurement procedures, separate designs, and even separate standards of measurement. Moreover, the military refused to recognize the nature of mass production and insisted on variations in specifications and frequent design changes which were incompatible with a Fordist manufacturing system.[102] A 1943 Japan Economic Federation study of productive efficiency identified unified state control over procurement as the single most important factor in the attainment of mass production.[103] The circumstances made many managers indignant: Noda Nobuo rebuked the state for daring to criticize private efforts in standardization when it couldn't even manage to coordinate public procurement.[104] Some observers even went so far as to say that there were no real shortages in the Japanese war economy, and that only the inefficiencies caused by interservice rivalries frustrated the "expansion of production capacity."[105]

Finally, it is worth noting that a more familiar affliction—opposition from skilled workers and reluctant managers—may have been as significant in limiting wartime managerial reform as the greed of capitalists, the shortage of technocrats, or the irrationalities of economic planning. While the demands of "industrial war" did generate an unprecedented recognition of the need for

[100] Tomizawa Kiichi, "Hikōki kōgyō no rōdō jijō to kinrō shisaku," *Shakai seisaku jihō* 272 (May 1943): 225.

[101] Okuda, *Hito to keiei*, 457–58.

[102] Cohen, *Japan's Economy*, 73–79, 212 ff.; Noda Nobuo recounted a visit to Mitsubishi's Nagoya aircraft factory near the end of the war. Both army and navy aircraft fuselages were being constructed in the same building, but on parallel assembly lines. The lines were separated by a high fence to prevent either side from spying on the production techniques of the other. Noda, "Kagakuteki kanrihō kara," 11.

[103] Nihon keizai renmeikai chōsaka, *Taryō seisan*, 1.

[104] Nainen kikan henshūbu, *Sangyō nōritsu*, 260–62.

[105] Johnson, *MITI*, 167. See also Samuels, *Rich Nation Strong Army*, chap. 4.

Scientific Management in Japan, not everyone seems to have jumped readily onto the bandwagon of Taylorization and mass production. This certainly was the impression of many of the graduates of Horime's work-study courses, who found resistance to their stopwatch and flow-chart techniques among entrenched, traditionally minded managers. Hoping that seeing would lead to believing, Horime (with the support of the Industrial Association), orchestrated the opening of the Shimamoto factory of the Niigata Ironworks as a "model plant" of advanced industrial engineering in 1940. Whether this succeeded in converting any of the doubters to Scientific Management is unclear, although it did attract considerable attention and a stream of curious visitors.[106] In any case, as late as 1943, when the final push of wartime mobilization was well underway, commentators still complained of "conservative attitudes" among managers regarding the need for managerial reform.[107]

The opposition of skilled workers to wartime efficiency initiatives is not so widely documented as the foot-dragging of unenlightened managers, yet would appear to have been significant as well. In 1941, Sanpō launched its "Movement to Increase the Usage Rate of Machines," a campaign aimed at boosting production and efficiency by the Taylorization of the work process in machine-tool shops.[108] Reporting on the movement's effectiveness a year later, the Tokyo bureau of Sanpō admitted that the program had floundered, due in large part to the reluctance of skilled laborers to cooperate in the simplification and specialization of production routines. Experienced machinists were, for instance, said to have rejected a plan to use unskilled workers as specialist tool sharpeners, insisting that the prerogative of sharpening one's own implements be retained.[109] The Tokyo branch also noted that some workers saw the movement's reforms as nothing more than a pretext for rate-cutting and a way for management to squeeze more effort out of labor.[110] Clearly, despite the calls for patriotism, unity, and harmony in the pursuit of a "national defense state," some workers seem to have recognized that wartime Taylorization was identical to peacetime Taylorization and that labor had to approach both with caution.

Labor, Spiritualism, and Management

The dilemmas of wartime industry not only revealed the weaknesses of production technology, but also brought home to Japanese managers and industrialists the importance of labor and labor management. While Japanese com-

[106] Ono, *Mōshon-maindo,* 61–63; "Risō kōjō no igi," *Kōgyō to keizai* 91 (July 1940): 1–2.

[107] Nainen kikan henshūbu, *Sangyō nōritsu,* 2.

[108] "Kikai jitsudōritsu zōshin undō yōkō," in *Shiryō Nihon gendai shi 7: Sangyō hōkoku undō,* ed. Kanda Fuhito (Ōtsuki shoten, 1981), 296–303.

[109] Dai Nihon sangyō hōkokukai, *Kikai jitsudōritsu zōshin undō: Dōfuken jisshi jōkyō hōkokushū* (1942), 1–4, 51–53.

[110] Ibid., 4, 57.

panies were frequently accused of a certain laxity in dealing with labor issues,[111] the wartime experience of shortages, absenteeism, and opposition convinced many managers of the need to take the administration and guidance of their employees more seriously. The Efficiency Association, for example, preached that "Labor power is the mother of efficiency, its very essence."[112] As one engineer at Tachikawa Aircraft put it, "Modern factory management methods like specialization, mass production, and work study are, of course, components of efficiency, but realizing their potential is in essence a human problem."[113]

The quandary facing managers was how to extract ever greater diligence from workers in an economic and ideological milieu that undermined traditional managerial strategies. Corporate familialism, which had already lost much of its shine during the Depression, was subsumed by wartime mobilization and dismissed as retrograde by "New Order" ideologues. As Keiō University professor Fujibayashi Keizō proclaimed in 1943, "Our native tradition of familialism has not taken root deeply in Japanese management. We have often heard businessmen speak of the 'beautiful customs' of industry . . . but these were simply emotional entreaties and morality tales told by employers."[114] Although many managers clung to the effectiveness of incentive wages, their use was increasingly frowned upon and their value was highly suspect in an environment of endemic shortages and the rationing of consumer goods. Speedups and other time-honored methods of squeezing greater output from labor proved problematic for similar reasons. Given the high demand for skilled workmen, the loosening of factory discipline, and the opposition to "sweating" from the authorities, heavy-handed techniques for driving labor were severely restricted. As one observer bemoaned, "These days, with the dearth of labor, it's impossible to stimulate efficiency increases through worker competition. However, under the current circumstances of raw material shortages, promoting the workers' will to produce is the most essential ingredient in boosting industrial output. One has to ask, how can we raise efficiency, production, and the desire to work of shop-floor employees?"[115]

The response to this rhetorical question was, most seemed to agree, to appeal spiritually to the workers. Chanting slogans like "Sweat instead of Blood" and "Spirit is the Nation's Motive Power," managers and Sanpō functionaries sought to fire enthusiasm for labor through nationalistic appeals.[116] Portraying toil as a patriotic duty and as service to the nation,

[111] Andō, "Kessenka ni okeru nōritsu-seikatsu-chingin," 466–67.

[112] "Nōritsu zōshin no shuppatsuten," *Nihon nōritsu* 2, no. 4 (April 1943): 241.

[113] Nihon sangyō keizai shinbunsha, *Zenkoku,* 17–18.

[114] Fujibayashi, "Kōkoku kinrōkan," 47–48.

[115] Kimura, "Seisan gōrika no shinkadai," 46.

[116] Nihon sangyō keizai shinbunsha, *Zenkoku,* 76; "Dai Nihon sangyō hōkokukai dai-nikai gijutsusha kaigi ketsugi," in Kanda, *Shiryō,* 376.

"management attempted to motivate workers by stressing an obligation to country, *not* company."[117] The novelty here was in the message rather than in the method: the wartime appeal to workers was more a reworking of paternalist rhetoric than a fresh awakening to the power of spiritualism. Whatever its origins, the spiritual, patriotic approach was increasingly acknowledged over the course of the war as the last possible salvation for Japanese industry. Even the staid and technocratic Efficiency Association signed on, declaring in 1942 that while Japan would never beat the West in the number or sophistication of its machines, the superior spirit of its people would ultimately bring victory.[118]

Notwithstanding such desperate optimism, the power of spiritual entreaties in wartime Japan seems to have been decidedly limited. This was nowhere more obvious than in the activities and accomplishments of Sanpō, which became something of a central clearinghouse for morale campaigns and nationalistic propaganda in industry. Although Sanpō was originally intended to reconcile labor and management, after the proclamation of the "New Order" in 1940, it focused increasingly on spiritualism and mobilization, its proponents becoming "cheerleaders calling for ever greater exertion and output."[119] Neither managers nor workers appear to have been particularly swayed by its appeals, however. Despite constant barrages of Sanpō patriotism, labor seems to have been lukewarm, mustering little excitement for the movement or its efforts to raise productivity.[120] Management was equally dismissive and regularly criticized Sanpō for its passivity and overreliance on empty rhetoric.[121] In the end, Sanpō's spiritualistic approach may have elicited more scorn than zeal on the factory floor.

Wartime managers may have discounted Sanpō's effectiveness, yet most came to recognize the significance of Sanpō's mission. In particular, managers gained a new appreciation for the potential benefits of attempting to motivate workers with methods other than wages and welfare facilities. Although the unsubtle and fervently patriotic appeals of Sanpō were hardly a persuasive model, the utility of spiritualism in extracting the maximum output from labor was impressed upon growing numbers of Japanese managers. As even the

---

[117] Gordon, *Evolution,* 306.

[118] "Shin sangyōdō," *Nihon nōritsu* 1, no. 4 (September 1942): 243.

[119] Gordon, *Evolution,* 300. On Sanpō and the limits of spiritualism, see Okuda, *Hito to keiei,* 538 ff.; Yasuda Hiroshi, "Kanryō to rōdōsha mondai," in Tokyo daigaku shakai kagaku kenkyūjo, *Gendai Nihon shakai 4: rekishiteki zentei* (Tokyo daigaku shuppankai, 1991), 317–62.

[120] Nishinarita Yutaka, *Kindai Nihon rōshi kankeishi no kenkyū* (Tokyo daigaku shuppankai, 1988), 395; Garon, *The State and Labor,* 226.

[121] In its report on the "Movement to Increase the Usage Rate of Machines," for instance, the Tokyo bureau of Sanpō conceded that its programs had been hamstrung by the prevalence of unenthusiastic managers who considered the Industrial Patriotic movement useless. Dai Nihon sangyō hōkokukai, *Kikai jitsudōritsu zōshin undō,* 53.

Industrial Association testified, "No matter how well equipment had been improved by work study, no matter how skillfully the production process is planned, and even if jigs are fully used, there will be no results if the workers are not motivated. We should not ignore the motivation of labor by focusing excessively on efficient technology."[122]

The clearest manifestation of this changing managerial attitude was the wartime surge of interest in "spiritual guidance" (*seishin shidō*). Combining an awareness of psychology with a continuing faith in the "humanization" of the workplace, this approach was premised on the notion that managers should not *make* their employees work but should *guide* them in their labor in a sympathetic, almost avuncular manner. In Noda Nobuo's words, "The fundamental goal of spiritual guidance is, quite simply, awakening in laborers joy in their work and devotion to it."[123] Commentators were vague on what concrete methods should be used for motivating workers, most only suggesting that appeals had to go beyond the trite homilies of traditional paternalism and Sanpō, utilize modern psychological knowledge, and address workers in small groups, rather than individually or en masse.[124] At any rate, proponents argued, the most essential concern was that "spiritual guidance and industrial efficiency be meshed together as completely as possible."[125]

As Andrew Gordon has concluded, "Much change . . . is found during the war itself only in the form of a blueprint for a potential future labor relationship."[126] This certainly was the case with the use of spiritualism as a managerial strategy, for although wartime efforts were largely abortive, foundations were laid for the postwar development of this approach to labor management. As Miyamoto Takenosuke saw it, the war brought home the realization that, "regarding the problem of efficiency increase, the spiritual element and the scientific element must be considered together, like the wings of a bird or the axles of a car."[127] By fully recognizing the significance of motivation and psychology to management, and by beginning to perceive that employers could well be leaders rather than dictators, wartime managers set the stage for the post-surrender entry of the American Human Relations school into Japan.

[122] "Nōritsu zōshin no igi," *Kōgyō to keizai* 111 (March 1942): 1.

[123] Noda, *Kōgyō keizai shinron,* 483.

[124] See, for example, Nihon keizai renmeikai chōsaka, *Seishin shidō*; Nihon keizai renmeikai chōsaka, *Taryō seisan,* 100.

[125] Nihon keizai renmeikai chōsaka, *Seishin shidō,* 3. Compare Joan Campbell, *Joy in Work, German Work* (Princeton, N.J.: Princeton University Press, 1989), esp. chap. 14; Anson Rabinbach, "The Aesthetics of Production in the Third Reich," in *International Fascism,* ed. George Mosse (London: Sage Publications, 1979), 189–222.

[126] Gordon, *Evolution,* 326.

[127] Miyamoto, "Sangyō nōritsu no zōshin ni tsuite," 9.

The Legacies of War

Painting the war as a time of triumph for the Japanese management movement would be an exaggeration, yet portraying it as a period of frustration,
dormancy, or collapse would be equally misleading and superficial. While
the war ended with chaos on the factory floor, the years from 1937 to 1945
witnessed important and unexpected progress for the gospel of Scientific
Management and its Japanese adherents. After the doldrums of the Depression, mobilization revitalized the efficiency movement, although this second
boom was one driven not by novelty but necessity, marked less by debate
than desperation. In the end, out of the intense wartime drive to indigenize
and apply the principles of modern management, the foundations were laid
for the spectacular development of managerial thought and practice in postwar Japan.

The confirmation of the "revised Taylorite" consensus as the essence of
"Japanese-style" management was undoubtedly the most significant outcome
of the wartime boom. In the buildup to a "national defense state," the paternalistic model was finally eclipsed, as the urgency of systematic reform of the
production process became apparent to industrialists, bureaucrats and intellectuals. Seeking an approach that would meet the ideological as well as the
economic dictates of mobilization, the ideal of a "humanized" Taylorism long
promoted by the efficiency movement gained widespread approval, though
wartime proponents hawked it under the label "Made in Japan." At the same
time, Japanese management reformers continued to struggle to find an integrated, workable strategy for "humanizing" the Taylorized workshop, as
Sanpō patriotism proved as unsystematic and unsatisfactory as paternalist
emotionalism had in the interwar decades. Thus, even as the need for a "revised Taylorite" regime was underscored by the experience of mobilization,
the specific means to such an end—a comprehensive methodological framework for attaining both technical efficiency and the "cooperative" compliance
of labor—remained elusive through the war.

The unprecedented surge of support for Taylorite reforms in wartime Japan
had considerable consequences for Japanese management experts, who had
generally been on the periphery of the industrial world. Now, however, the
sudden demand for their expertise increasingly brought scientific managers to
the center of business and government discussions of industrial development.
As a number of observers have noted, efficiency experts were able to expand
greatly their personal contacts with top management, the economic bureaucracy, and the scientific community, creating networks that would long outlast
the war. Not surprisingly, the status of Japanese management professionals
seems to have been enhanced as the importance of their work was more

broadly appreciated. Especially within the technocratic framework of the "New Order," the expertise and reputed objectivity of management specialists would appear to have gained them new respect in the industrial community.[128]

The number of managers and engineers familiar with the methods of Scientific Management also grew during the war. Not only did Horime's work-study course train hundreds of experts in production management, but the first academic programs in the field of industrial engineering also began to graduate specialist managerial personnel. Knowledge of Scientific Management passed far beyond these formally trained experts, however, as Taylorite techniques were aggressively publicized and implemented in Japanese workshops. Despite the generally dismal record of wartime industry, assembly-line methods were introduced in some key sectors, Taylorite fundamentals were diffused more widely than ever before, and, on the whole, the sound foundations of a mass production economy were laid. In any case, wartime mobilization spawned a strong cadre of experienced managers, conversant with and committed to modern techniques, who would eventually form the nucleus of postwar management reform efforts.[129]

While the quantity of scientific managers may have swelled during the war, the overall quality of Japanese management thought and practice was another matter. Indeed, the efficiency movement's wartime boom did not extend as far as methodological innovation and, with American contacts severed, the movement grew technically and conceptually stagnant. There had not, in any case, been a major inflow of new foreign methods since the start of the Depression. Through the 1930s, the movement had emphasized remedial reform and the spread of "best method" rather than the importation or development of more advanced approaches. Thus, as Okuda Kenji has argued, Japanese management experts, armed only with the teachings of Taylor and his disciples, found themselves woefully unprepared for the complex problems of the Fordist assembly line. The stopwatch and the Gantt chart, no matter how expertly wielded, could not alone solve the statistical and organizational conundrums of conveyor-belt mass production.[130]

Although methodological stagnation may have impeded wartime industrial expansion, the relative retardation of Japanese managerial thought set the stage for the prodigious influx of American models following the surrender. It is worth noting that, despite the great pains taken to "Japanize" Taylorism, management experts showed little hostility toward the United States and continued to declare their admiration for American administrative methods

[128] Nakaoka, "Production Management," 12–13.

[129] Nakamura Takafusa, *The Postwar Japanese Economy,* trans. Jacqueline Kaminski (Tokyo: University of Tokyo Press, 1981), 15; Nakaoka, "Senchū, sengo I," 24–27. As Tessa Morris-Suzuki concludes, "The most important legacy of war was a human rather than an organizational one." Morris-Suzuki, *Technological Transformation,* 155.

[130] Okuda, *Hito to keiei,* 516 ff.

throughout the war. If anything, the stature of American management was increased, as Japanese commentators hailed the triumphs of the U.S. war machine as nothing short of miraculous. While German science and spirituality were widely praised, it was American methods and American accomplishments that continued to define the "state of the art" to Japanese managers.[131] After nearly a decade of war, replete with progress as well as frustration, growth as well as stagnation, the Japanese efficiency movement was prepared to look once again to the United States for inspiration.

[131] The frontispiece to Noda Nobuo's 1943 textbook *Kōgyō keizai shinron* (New Perspectives on Industrial Economics), for example, was a woodcut of Springfield, Massachusetts. The city was presented as a model to Japan because of its famous machine shops, which attained high precision and high efficiency despite their small scale.

4

Management and Ideology, 1945–1960

SURVEYING the worldwide devastation of World War II, Henry Ford II mused that "it is not only *things* which have been destroyed. The landscape is littered with wrecked ideas and faiths. Political and economic systems have been torn up and lie twisted and broken like a great railroad yard after a bombing raid."[1] This certainly was the case in Japan, where defeat pushed the fragile domestic economy close to collapse and fatally undermined the intricate ideological structures of wartime mobilization. Nevertheless, while Japan's "national defense state" and "New Order" may have been "twisted and broken," the approaches and assumptions of the wartime program of industrial production were consumed neither by fire-bombing nor by defeat. Despite an altered social, political, and economic context, the Japanese legacy of modern management thought—the "revised Taylorite" ideology and its accreted intellectual baggage—found renewed relevance after 1945. Supported by the American creed of productivity, Taylor's "Mental Revolution" and the Taylorite view of technocratic rationality were regenerated as the foundations for a new social consensus on labor relations and industrial growth in postwar Japan.

The Crisis of Capitalism and the Keizai Dōyūkai

Japan's industrial elite initially confronted defeat and occupation with composure and a certain optimism. The business leader Fujiyama Aiichirō later recalled the jubilation of managers who anticipated an end to bureaucratic control and a rapid resumption of foreign trade under American stewardship: "At the time of the surrender, I heard there were a good many in Karuizawa who broke out the champagne and toasted that 'The age of the industrialists is here!'"[2] At an emergency board meeting of a major business federation, one director begged for calm in the face of U.S. occupation, reputedly assuring his colleagues (in English, no less) that "Our friends are coming."[3]

---

[1] Quoted in Howell Harris, *The Right to Manage: Industrial Relations Policies of American Business in the 1940s* (Madison: University of Wisconsin Press, 1982), 95.

[2] Quoted in Nakase Jūichi, *Sengo Nihon no keiei rinen shi* (Kyōto: Hōritsu bunka sha, 1967), 10; see also Joe Moore, *Japanese Workers and the Struggle for Power, 1945–1947* (Madison: University of Wisconsin Press, 1983), 25.

[3] Yabe Yōzō, "Keizai dōyūkai no kessei jijō ni tsuite," *Keizai shūshi* (Nihon University) 48, nos. 3, 4 (October 1978): 93.

Yet the vision of Japan as a businessman's paradise patrolled by benevolent American proconsuls was, at the very least, premature. Arriving with the assumption that monopoly had gone hand in hand with militarism in Imperial Japan, the occupation reformers were no champions of big business in their initial plans for "demilitarization" and "democratization." To the horror of the financial old guard, the Americans took aim at the zaibatsu, seeking to dismantle their industrial holdings while blithely purging the upper echelons of business along with the military top brass. To many, the occupation looked less like the savior of Japan's capitalist order than the agent for its demolition.

Nevertheless, it was the postwar groundswell of union activism and the rapid politicization of labor that dealt the most sobering blow to Japanese industrialists. With the collapse of Sanpō, the discrediting of paternalist and Japanist rhetoric, and the loosening of controls over union organization and political expression, the Japanese labor movement was reborn, with unprecedented energy and ambitions. Driven by mounting resentments and the specter of hunger, the unions attracted almost five million members by the end of 1946, fully ten times their prewar peak. From the management perspective, the most threatening manifestation of this surge in unionism was the wave of "production control" (*seisan kanri*) strikes which began in the fall of 1945. This innovative tactic—in which workers seized a factory and operated it without a managerial presence—brought into question not only the necessity of shop-floor supervision but, more importantly, the legitimacy of the entire capitalist order.[4]

In the end, however, the direct challenges of defeat, militant unionism, and occupation reformism weighed most heavily only on the upper reaches of the business elite. The bulk of the large managerial class which had emerged during the 1930s and 1940s evaded the taint of war responsibility, the full force of American "democratization," and the recriminations of labor. The purge, for example, took only a light toll among professional managers and technocratic civil servants, while the ranks of Japanese Taylorites and modern management proponents were barely touched, with Godō Takuo the only notable loss.[5] The plutocrats of the old guard became the lightning rod for political retaliation and punitive action, and the managerial class remained largely intact, with the opportunity to adapt to—and shape—the evolving political order.

---

[4] Moore, *Japanese Workers,* chap. 2; Andrew Gordon, *The Evolution of Labor Relations in Japan: Heavy Industry, 1853–1955* (Cambridge, Mass.: Harvard University Press, 1985), 343–44; Solomon B. Levine, *Industrial Relations in Postwar Japan* (Urbana: University of Illinois Press, 1958), chap. 3; Theodore Cohen, *Remaking Japan: The American Occupation as New Deal* (New York: Free Press, 1987), part 4.

[5] Chalmers Johnson, *MITI and the Japanese Miracle* (Stanford, Calif.: Stanford University Press, 1982), 173; Godō was incarcerated until March 1952 as a war criminal. Nihon nōritsu kyōkai, *Keiei to tomo ni* (Nihon nōritsu kyōkai, 1982), 50, 57.

The most assertive attempt by industrial managers to come to terms with their environment during the early postwar years was the forming of the Keizai Dōyūkai (Economic Friends' Association). Styling itself "a progressive organization of midlevel economic actors,"[6] the Dōyūkai aimed to take the initiative in stabilizing and preserving the capitalist system, albeit in a form consistent with Occupation democratization and labor activism. As a "child of crisis,"[7] the Dōyūkai believed that the realistic acceptance of change was the only basis for stability, and endorsed cooperation with organized labor and the legitimacy of workers' demands for participation in management. At the same time, the leaders of the association realized the possibility of reaching an accord with labor on terms that would ultimately benefit the managerial technicians of industry as much as, if not more than, the unions or the workers on the shop floor. In the vision of the Keizai Dōyūkai, the pacification of labor relations was compatible with (and indeed dependent on) the enhanced autonomy and authority of a professional, "neutral" and ascendant managerial class.

The impetus for organizing the Dōyūkai came from a small circle of businessmen and management experts, most of whom had been associated with the wartime Jūyō Sangyō Tōsei Dantai Kyōgikai (Conference of Major Industries Control Associations—Jūsankyō), a group founded to promote the "New Order" in the business world.[8] The leader of these efforts was Gōshi Kōhei, a former managing director of the conference. Although trained in theology (including an abortive stint in a New York seminary), Gōshi was an economist and long-time associate of Marxist critic (and Shōwa Research Association member) Takahashi Kamekichi.[9] Also prominent in the establishment of the Dōyūkai was Noda Nobuo, the general factotum of the prewar efficiency movement and one of the most respected and well-connected proponents of Scientific Management in Japan.

Founded on April 30, 1946, the Dōyūkai was marked from the start as an assembly of young, forward-thinking, middle-ranking managers. The majority of the charter members were in their forties and were employed in the wartime growth sectors of heavy industry and manufacturing. Few, with the notable exception of Noda, were affiliated with the "Big Four" zaibatsu interests, but most worked in firms associated with relatively advanced managerial practices.[10] With an image of youth and what would quickly emerge as a reflective and independent intellectual bent, the supporters of the Dōyūkai were aptly labeled the "Hamlets of the business world."[11]

[6] Keizai dōyūkai, *Keizai dōyūkai jūnen shi* (Keizai dōyūkai, 1956), 22.

[7] Ibid., 3.

[8] Ibid., 20; Lonny Carlile, "Zaikai and the Politics of Production in Japan, 1940–1962" (Ph.D. diss., University of California, Berkeley, 1989), 132–45.

[9] Carlile, "Zaikai," 340.

[10] See Yabe Yōzō, "Kesseiji ni okeru keizai dōyūkai no seisan kōzō," *Keizai shūshi* (Nihon University) 51, no. 3 (October 1981): 85–108.

[11] "Dōyūkai 20-nen no rinen to genjitsu," *Gendai no me* 7, no. 9 (September 1966): 101.

The starting point for Dōyūkai thought was the assumption that Japan was undergoing a crisis of capitalism, a crisis in which old guard industrialists were being revealed to be ineffective and outmoded while the labor movement was growing to become the most dynamic element in society. Stating the obvious in 1946, one Dōyūkai member warned that "From now on, there's no separating industrial management from the labor problem."[12] Accordingly, the Dōyūkai leaders argued, the most pressing need was to transcend the bigotry of prewar, "feudal" capitalism, recognize the legitimacy of organized labor, and seek a constructive, cooperative relationship between managers and the unions.[13] The key to this reconciliation—and by extension to Japan's economic revival and social stabilization—was the affirmation of a new, reformed capitalist order, one (not surprisingly) which pivoted on the professional managerial class which the Dōyūkai represented.

In the Keizai Dōyūkai analysis, the experience of war and occupation was catalyzing fundamental structural changes in Japanese capitalism. The most important of these was the so-called "separation of management and capital," a phenomenon which was said to have derived from the expansion of the modern corporation, with its increasingly diffused pattern of ownership and its bureaucratic superstructure of expert managers. The result of this process, the Dōyūkai maintained, was a transformation of authority relations within industry, as ownership no longer connoted control and as the capital-labor divide was blurred by the appearance of management technicians as an independent interest group. Not subservient to capital (as the zaibatsu *bantō* had been) but likewise differentiated from labor (in that they possessed the ability to lead modern industry and comprehend modern technology), the managers of this intermediate stratum were touted as the agents of a new political and economic equilibrium.[14]

Management, the Dōyūkai argued, was evolving as a politically neutral and technically elite middle force, standing between labor and capital, balancing their respective interests with the economic and technological dictates of modern industry.[15] These "new managers," the business economist Furukawa Eiichi noted, "emphasize benefits to state, society, and the people rather than individual profits. They esteem jobs and labor more than money."[16] Moreover, as one speaker at the Dōyūkai inaugural meeting proclaimed, managers had the practical skills necessary to take a more assertive position: "Calling on our individual knowledge, ideas and enthusiasm, we in our different fields of industry must contribute positively to the reconstruction of the Japanese econ-

[12] Quoted in Yabe, "Keizai dōyūkai no kessei jijō ni tsuite," 104.
[13] Ibid., 102; Moore, *Japanese Workers,* 144 ff.; Keizai dōyūkai, *Jūnen shi,* 18 ff.
[14] Moore, *Japanese Workers,* 144 ff.; Ōtake Hideo, "The *Zaikai* Under the Occupation," in *Democratizing Japan: The Allied Occupation,* ed. Robert Ward and Sakamoto Yoshikazu (Honolulu: University of Hawaii Press, 1987), 370–71.
[15] Ibe Masakazu, "Shūsei shihonshugi e no michi," *Keizai* 1, no. 10 (December 1947): 9–11.
[16] Furukawa Eiichi, *Shin keieisha* (Moriyama shoten, 1948), 116.

omy. . . . With our sound, first-hand knowledge and expertise of the workplace today, we aspire to a major role in the setting of the national policy
agenda."[17] At a time of endemic finger-pointing and apportioning of blame,
the Dōyūkai recognized the political advantages of stepping forward and
claiming new responsibility for the professional managerial class.

The foremost exposition of Keizai Dōyūkai thought in the early years of the
Occupation was the 1947 *Kigyō minshūka shian* (Proposal for the Democratization of Enterprises).[18] Written under the direction of Japan Specialty
Steel's Ōtsuka Banjō, the document recommended a sweeping revision of
power relations in the firm, with capital's influence circumscribed, labor
granted legitimacy and a voice, and management laying claim to unprecedented autonomy and authority. In the first place, the enterprise and its profits
were no longer to be considered the sole property of the shareholders; rather,
the firm was to be constituted as a "community" (*kyōdōtai*) of capital, management, and labor, each of which had the right to a "fair distribution" of gains
and a say in corporate administration.[19] Accordingly, the annual stockholders'
meeting was to be replaced as the ultimate policymaking organ by a new
"general meeting" (*kigyō sōkai*) in which each of the three interest groups
would have equal representation.[20] The "democratic" operation of the firm
would thus be negotiated by a delicate process of checks and balances:

> If labor's demands grow excessive or degenerate into class interests and threaten the
> foundations of the firm, then capital and management can come together and block
> them. On the other hand, if capital abuses its powers and seeks to make the enter-
> prise simply a tool for making profits, then management and labor can cooperate to
> stop it. Moreover, if management complacently ignores the welfare of the workers
> and slights the interests of the shareholders, or managers seek to use the firm as a
> tool for increasing the power of the managerial class, then labor and capital can work
> together to prevent such action.[21]

Although the Ōtsuka proposal promised a "fair," "democratic" resolution of
class tensions in industry, there clearly were winners and losers under the
plan. Capitalists, already on the defensive after the defeat, were to be stripped
of their formal authority over the enterprise and its management, and were to
lose sole claim to corporate profits. The legitimacy of unions, meanwhile, was
to be affirmed, although the Dōyūkai obviously hoped to focus labor activity
on bread-and-butter issues within the firm rather than on broader political

[17] Keizai dōyūkai, *Jūnen shi*, 22.

[18] The proposal was never endorsed as official association policy, as some aspects seemed too
radical even for the self-styled reformers of the Dōyūkai.

[19] Keizai dōyūkai kigyō minshūka kenkyūkai, *Kigyō minshūka shian* (Dōyūsha, 1947), 70–
88; see also Ōtake, "*Zaikai*," 370–72; Carlile, "*Zaikai*," 223–28; John Price, *Japan Works: Power
and Paradox in Postwar Industrial Relations* (Ithaca, N.Y.: ILR Press, 1997), 64–65.

[20] Keizai dōyūkai kigyō minshūka kenkyūkai, *Shian*, 110–25.

[21] Ibid., 60–61.

demands.[22] Management, needless to say, stood to gain the most: freedom from subservience to stockholders, recognition as an independent interest group, paramount authority as experts and intermediaries. In Ōtsuka's conception of the new equilibrium,

> On the one hand monopoly capital has already been dissolved and on the other the right of labor unions to strike has been publicly recognized. We therefore believe that if managers were to be legally guaranteed an autonomous position, then, as the central axis of enterprise operations, they could effectively perform the function of a medium linking capital and labor. . . . It is impossible to hope for the democratization of enterprise management unless the status of capital is lowered by one step and the status of labor is simultaneously raised one step—thereby giving the two parallel standing—by making managers independent in this manner.[23]

The Ōtsuka proposal may have posited a radical change in the structure of the firm, yet the Dōyūkai approach to harmonizing labor relations—seeking cooperation through consultative labor-management bodies—had roots stretching well back into the prewar period. Since 1946, union leaders, especially those of the more moderate Sōdōmei (Japan General Federation of Labor), had promoted the establishment of firm-level "management councils" (*keiei kyōgikai*) as a forum for substantive discussion and policy making.[24] The Dōyūkai endorsed these councils—suggesting that the "separation of management and capital" allowed for meaningful and constructive labor-management dialogue[25]—and drew on them as a model when distilling the idea of the general meeting of the firm. Nevertheless, although the Dōyūkai was progressive in the context of the Japanese business community, it fell short of the more sweeping reforms envisioned by some unionists, and its view of the managerial councils' role stressed consultation more than the diffusion of power within the company. Participation, the Ōtsuka report carefully noted, meant the right to speak and be heard, and to participate in representative organs, but did not imply any specific delegation of authority.[26] Indeed, while the Dōyūkai showed respect for organized labor and would even admit a legitimate role for strikes, the protection of managerial authority—framed as "the rights of the firm" (*kigyō ken*)—was of prime concern.[27]

Despite frequent protestations of novelty and fundamental reform, one of the most striking aspects of the early Keizai Dōyūkai philosophy was its reliance on prewar and wartime models. The concept of the "separation of management and capital," for example, had long been discussed in Japanese aca-

---

[22] Ibid., 167; Ōtake, *"Zaikai,"* 371.
[23] Quoted in Carlile, *"Zaikai,"* 226.
[24] Ibid., 189–91; Moore, *Japanese Workers,* 140–42.
[25] Keizai dōyūkai kigyō minshūka kenkyūkai, *Shian,* 52.
[26] Ibid., 12.
[27] Carlile, *"Zaikai,"* 235–36.

demic circles and amongst management experts. As early as 1929, Mukai Shikamatsu proclaimed the appearance of a rising class of "new managers" (*shin keieisha*) that was poised to transform the industrial landscape.[28] The assertion of such a "separation" was, of course, a central component of "New Order" reformism as well, but whereas the wartime technocracy stressed the enhanced efficiency of managerialism, the Dōyūkai's immediate postwar repackaging emphasized the equity, democracy, and stability which independent, "neutral" managers could deliver. A similar continuity with "New Order" thought was evident in the Dōyūkai's championing of "modified capitalism" (*shūsei shihonshugi*), an epithet which became all but synonymous with the association. In positing a "middle road" between socialism and laissez-faire capitalism based on technocratic management and comprehensive planning, the Dōyūkai model mirrored the "New Order" dream, albeit with private-sector (rather than bureaucratic) leadership.[29]

As noted earlier, the Dōyūkai approach to reconciliation with labor was also derivative, although the continuities seemed to run more to the progressive strategies of business in the 1920s than to the statist settlement of the war years. The logic of acknowledging the legitimacy of unionization and the workers' desire for participation, while simultaneously incorporating labor into a managerially dominated order through consultative councils, had been persuasively elaborated more than two decades before the Dōyūkai was founded. The postwar progressives were thus the heirs to the Kyōchōkai philosophy of the 1920s as well as to the thought of "revised Taylorite" proponents like Noda Nobuo (who, significantly, chaired the Dōyūkai "labor problems" study group). Indeed, in conceptualizing the postwar system of management councils and the abortive national "Economic Recovery Conference" (Keizai Fukkō Kaigi), the leaders of the Dōyūkai looked to the same models— Whitley councils, Weimar works committees, American labor-management cooperation—that they and their predecessors had embraced during the 1920s.[30]

Beyond these linkages with prewar and wartime thought, the Dōyūkai line exhibited considerable resonances with contemporary American managerial ideologies. There was, to a certain extent, direct intellectual influence: Dōyūkai planners, for example, carefully studied James Burnham's *Managerial Revolution* and discovered there ample theoretical justification for an ambitious political and economic program.[31] More pervasive, however, were the similarities which the Japanese "Hamlets" shared with the advocates of corporate liberalism in the United States: a dedication to managerial values and technical expertise, a cooperative and confident approach to labor, inclinations

---

[28] Mukai Shikamatsu, *Shin keieisha gaku* (Nihon hyōronsha, 1929).

[29] Keizai dōyūkai kigyō minshūka kenkyūkai, *Shian,* 71–72.

[30] Noda Nobuo, *Kindaiteki keiei ni okeru ningen mondai* (Daiyamondo, 1953), 404–49.

[31] Yabe, "Keizai dōyūkai no kessei jijō ni tsuite," 105.

toward economic planning and internationalism.[32] This affinity would, over the course of the Occupation, grow increasingly strong and formalized, as the Dōyūkai became a conduit for American business thought and the ideology of productivity, the export model of corporate liberalism marketed by the Committee for Economic Development. With mutual roots in the advanced management thought of the 1920s—and, in particular, in the logic of "revised" Taylorism—the mingling of the Dōyūkai and corporate liberal approaches was natural under the postwar American stewardship of Japan. Not surprisingly, the Keizai Dōyūkai would later adopt "Japan Committee for Economic Development" as the official English version of its name—a loose translation to be sure, but one which made explicit its links with the progressive vanguard of American management.

Management Autonomy and Rationalization Redux

By 1947, Moroi Kan'ichi, managing director of Chichibu Cement and one of the founders of the Dōyūkai, could confidently declare that "the status of us managers is, at long last, greatly improving."[33] This was surely the case, though the gains made by the professional managerial class had apparently come at the expense of capital, weakened as it was by trust-busting, hyperinflation and the purge. As one Dōyūkai observer saw it, "the retreat of capital" meant "the advance of management."[34] Yet while the position of managers vis-à-vis the stockholders had improved, no lasting reconciliation between employers and workers had been achieved by 1947, despite the best efforts of the Dōyūkai to begin a dialogue with labor. Although the management councils enjoyed some success, the Economic Recovery Conference was undone by political bickering, and the Ōtsuka proposal failed to inspire large numbers of either managers or workers. Only after 1947, as the unions were increasingly thrown on the defensive, did the outlines of a durable settlement between management and labor begin to take shape.

The rollback of militant unionism, which would pave the way for the stabilization of labor relations on terms favorable to management, was a mutual effort of occupiers and occupied. Even the most ardent American reformers had a low tolerance for union radicalism—reflecting the prevalence of depoliticized, "business" unions in the United States—and the Occupation's permissive attitudes toward organized labor soon wore thin. Concluding that the Japanese labor movement had to be "housebroken," the Occupation supported

---

[32] On the corporate liberal approach in the United States during the 1940s, see Harris, *The Right to Manage,* 135–39.

[33] Keizai dōyūkai, *Jūnen shi,* 74.

[34] Ibid., 76.

a series of policies to channel, circumscribe, and neutralize union activism. Beginning with MacArthur's scuttling of the general strike in February 1947 and running through the ideological cleansing of unions in the "Red Purge" of 1950, the Americans endeavored to reconstitute the legal and political framework which had spawned the supposed excesses of Japanese labor.[35]

The apparent rightward swing of Occupation labor policy was heartening to the beleaguered conservative mainstream in Japanese industry. Although the Dōyūkai's self-styled reformism had dominated debate during the confused early years after the war, the muted majority of the business community grew increasingly assertive after 1947. With the founding of Nikkeiren (the Japan Federation of Employers' Associations) in April 1948, momentum seemed to pass from the Dōyūkai and its strategy of conciliation and partnership to a more hard-edged approach to labor-management accord. Under the slogan, "Managers! Be righteous, be strong!," Nikkeiren quickly took the offensive, launching a movement to reassert "management authority" (*keiei ken*) on the shop floor.[36] Rejecting the concessions of the Ōtsuka proposal as too extreme, Nikkeiren spurred businessmen to take a firm line against union demands and reclaim ground lost since the defeat. "Managers," one document declared, "steadfastly believe that there is no alternative but to exercise resolutely those management rights which they should properly possess, and to pursue the rapid establishment of managerial authority."[37]

The accomplishments of the Nikkeiren initiative ultimately depended less on the strength and righteousness of managers (and perhaps even less on the reorientation of Occupation labor programs) than on the major shifts in economic policy which began in late 1948. The inflationary approach to recovery of the first three years of occupation had a salutary effect on the labor movement, as expansionary monetary and fiscal policies provided the financial support for management concessions over wages and job security.[38] American concerns over Japan's economic reconstruction and the squandering of U.S. aid funds led, however, to a reconsideration of economic strategy and an abrupt shift from inflationary to rigidly deflationary policies. Business balked at the loss of subsidies and easy money, but soon discovered the convenience of using the stringency as a pretext for wage cuts, contract renegotiations, and layoffs. Faced with mass unemployment and a loss of political support, the unions found themselves increasingly unable to resist the reassertion of management authority.

[35] Gordon, *Evolution,* 332–33; Cohen, *Remaking Japan,* chaps. 15–16, 24.

[36] Carlile, "Zaikai," chap. 6, presents a full analysis of the Nikkeiren battle for "authority." See also Gordon, *Evolution,* 368–69; Nikkeiren sōritsu jūshūnen kinen kigyō iinkai, *Jūnen no ayumi* (Nikkeiren, 1958), 9–11, 84, 100.

[37] "Keieiken kakuho ni kansuru ikensho" (1958), ibid., 100; Carlile, "Zaikai," 289.

[38] Gordon, *Evolution,* 335–36.

While deflation thus provided a suitable environment for managerial re-surgence in labor relations, it also furnished Japanese bureaucrats with a conve-nient opportunity to resurrect the moribund rationalization movement. Al-though the early years of the Occupation have been described as a "bureaucratic promised land"[39]—and although the dramatis personae of the economic bu-reaucracy remained virtually unscathed by defeat—the interlude of industrial dislocation and inflationary recovery policies had not been conducive to a renewed government offensive on industrial rationalization. Only in 1949, as questions of labor efficiency and international competitiveness again came to the fore, did rationalization reenter the national agenda. Arguing that "Rational-ization is essential . . . in rebuilding a stable national economy in equilibrium with the world economic order," the Ministry of International Trade and Indus-try (successor to the Ministry of Commerce) proposed a postwar rationalization movement, gaining cabinet endorsement in September 1949.[40] With the subse-quent formation of a blue-ribbon "Rationalization Deliberative Council" (San-gyō Gōrika Shingikai) and the passage of the Enterprise Rationalization Promo-tion Law in 1952, the movement was launched with ambition and authority surpassing that of its interwar predecessor.

Despite the apparent continuities, a number of scholars have concluded that the postwar version of rationalization bore little trace of its Depression-era paternity. Laura Hein, for instance, has argued that "Industrial rationalization in postwar Japan far surpassed any prewar project in both scale and content," even deeming it a "new approach."[41] Certainly proponents at the time, seek-ing to defuse labor opposition, endeavored to deny any links with the prewar movement. Most, echoing wartime advocates of the "new rationalization," argued that early Shōwa efforts had been narrow, capitalistic, and exploitative, while the postwar incarnation, rooted in the "separation of management and capital" and aimed at thorough economic reform, promised benefits to all strata of society. The economist Takamiya Susumu, for example, contended that Japan had progressed beyond "negative" rationalization by layoffs to a more "positive" approach, "eliminating the most waste and spurring the entire economy on to the highest level of efficiency."[42] Yamashiro Akira went even further, suggesting that rationalization was metamorphosing into a new, pro-foundly unhierarchical movement, one in which all the members of a firm,

---

[39] Johnson, *MITI,* 173.

[40] "Kigyō kosei no shin tenkai ni tsuite" (August 1949) in Tsūshō sangyō shō, *Shōkō seisaku shi 10: Sangyō gōrika II,* (Shōkō seisaku shi kankōkai, 1972), 37.

[41] Laura E. Hein, *Fueling Growth: The Energy Revolution and Economic Policy in Postwar Japan* (Cambridge, Mass.: Harvard University Press, 1990), 148, 160. See also Takahashi Mamoru, "Shōwa 20-nendai no sangyō gōrika seisaku" in Sangyō seisaku shi kenkyūjo, *Sangyō seisaku shi no kadai to hōhō,* (1978), 41–44.

[42] Takamiya Susumu, "Keiei gōrika to shitsugyō mondai," *Jitsumu techō* 3, no. 11 (September 1949): 30.

from the shop floor to the board room, participated equally in realizing the greatest economic potential.[43]

The postwar advocates of rationalization, however, all seemed oblivious to the fact that, in emphasizing the novelty of the rejuvenated movement, they were actually repeating (almost ritualistically) the wartime attempt to cleanse "capitalistic" rationalization ideologically. One leftist critic, after disparaging *sangyō gōrika* as "exploitation camouflaged by science," noted acutely that "The term 'rationalization' can be used in so many ways. It's a completely convenient word."[44] Despite the elasticity of the concept of rationalization in the hands of its intellectual defenders, the aims, methods, and even the rhetoric of the postwar movement were broadly continuous with those of the early Shōwa and wartime initiatives. With the overriding goal of reducing costs to bolster Japanese industrial competitiveness, postwar rationalization—along with its predecessors—looked to macro-level strategies (such as state planning to ensure overall coordination and optimalization) as well as micro-level policies (like the introduction of new technology and the improvement of managerial methods).[45] Moreover, like its Depression-era counterpart, the postwar rationalization movement took a rather blasé view of mass layoffs, although, as before, all was cloaked in compassionate rhetoric and assurances of the limited and temporary nature of such infelicitous side effects.[46]

Management reform and labor efficiency figured highly in the concerns of the rationalization movement, yet in both prewar and postwar incarnations, the bureaucrats who set the agenda had only vague notions of how to realize these specialized goals. Noda Nobuo, who headed the Rationalization Deliberative Council's management section, observed that MITI bureaucrats were as inexperienced (and uninterested) in firm-level management issues as the "amateurish" Commerce Ministry bureaucrats had been during the 1930s.[47] Furthermore, even though the council had a labor policy section (which the prewar Rationalization Bureau lacked), the economic bureaucrats appeared uncomfortable addressing issues of labor relations and did not articulate a convincing framework for labor-management accommodation in their plans for *sangyō gōrika*. Thus, while the government rationalization movement provided a blueprint for bureaucratic efforts to strengthen export production, promote technological development, and create a domestic environment for in-

---

[43] Yamashiro Akira, "Keiei gōrika no kako, genzai, shōrai," ibid., 2–8.

[44] Kitagawa Yoshikazu, "Sangyō gōrika to wa nani ka," *Kagaku to gijutsu* 9 (August 1948): 16.

[45] On the content of the movement, see Hein, *Fueling Growth,* 163 ff.; Sangyō gōrika shingikai sōgōbukai, *Wagakuni sangyō gōrika ni tsuite* (Tsūshō sangyō shō, tsūshō kigyō kyoku, 1951), 1–5; Tsūshō sangyō shō, *Shōkō seisaku shi 10,* chaps. 3–5.

[46] Hein, *Fueling Growth,* 169; Sangyō gōrika shingikai, *Wagakuni,* 10.

[47] Noda, "Kagakuteki kanrihō kara seisansei undō e," *Keiei to rekishi* 9 (1986): 13; Nakaoka Tetsurō, "Production Management in Japan before the Period of High Economic Growth," *Osaka City University Economic Review* 17 (1981): 23.

dustrial growth, it did not offer a model for management reform, a solution for labor-management frictions, or an ideological basis for the evolving postwar managerial order.

Discovering the Ideology of Productivity

As Japan entered the 1950s, with the Korean War buoying business and the return of sovereignty in sight, the management community looked to the future with a certain optimism, albeit tempered by a lingering sense of insecurity. In 1951, Nikkeiren could boast that "shop-floor order has been conspicuously improved," bringing "an epochal and favorable impact on production increases."[48] But while deflation and Nikkeiren offensives may have restored tolerable discipline to Japanese factories, layoffs, rationalization, and management authoritarianism seemed a shaky foundation for a long-term accord between employers and workers. It was apparent after 1947 that any lasting accommodation was to take place on terms favorable to management, yet labor relations remained tense, as Nikkeiren had achieved compliance—not cooperation—with management's demands for authority. As Lonny Carlile has observed, even though managerial prerogatives were reasserted in the late 1940s, no political consensus or broad public support for a final, pro-management resolution of shop-floor antagonisms had emerged by the start of the new decade.[49]

The inability of Nikkeiren's hard-line approach to provide a guiding ethos for the postwar managerial order furnished a new opportunity for the Keizai Dōyūkai, whose fortunes had been on the wane since 1947. By the early 1950s, the leaders of the Dōyūkai clearly perceived the need to revitalize their organization and reclaim ideological leadership of the business community. Although rallying under the slogan "Let's return to our founding spirit!,"[50] the Dōyūkai recognized that the nostrums of the past—"modified capitalism," democratization of the firm, etc.—were much less compelling to businessmen in the new climate of enhanced managerial autonomy.

The rethinking of the organization's approach was formalized in the 1953 resolution "Wareware no kakugo," a document which affirmed support for the goals of early Dōyūkai philosophy, yet which viewed reform more cynically, with an eye to consolidating rather than revolutionizing the position of managers in society. Declaring that "Economic recovery is the keystone to Japan's independence and the well-being of its people," the resolution argued that "managers are the foremost agents of this reconstruction."[51] Taking as given

---

[48] Quoted in Carlile, "Zaikai," 309.
[49] Ibid., 323–24.
[50] Keizai dōyūkai, *Jūnen shi*, 333–37.
[51] Ibid., 515.

the neutrality and expertise of managers, the Dōyūkai maintained that responsibility for eliminating waste, improving efficiency, and harmonizing labor relations lay with them, not with bureaucrats, politicians, or intellectuals. While endorsing fully the goals of rationalization, the resolution also stressed the urgent need for ideological accord between labor and management, implicitly acknowledging the limitations of Nikkeiren dogmatism. "Workers," the document proclaimed, "are partners in production. Without their cooperation, attempts to reduce costs will just end up in disaster."[52]

Although "Wareware no kakugo" indicated the Dōyūkai's groping for an ideological approach that could fuse rationalization, management autonomy, and a cooperative view of labor relations, the "trump card" (as Nakamura Seiji would later describe it) eventually had to be imported.[53] The dilemmas which Japanese business faced were not unique and, like their counterparts in Western Europe, the management vanguard of the Dōyūkai looked to the United States for the intellectual and technical apparatus of a political settlement in industry. During the first postwar decade, the key to this settlement seemed to lie in the ideology of productivity (*seisansei* in Japanese). According to Charles Maier, the concept had a "venerable" history in the United States: from the Progressive Era, "recurrent ideas all stressed that by enhancing productive efficiency, whether through scientific management, business planning, industrial cooperation, or corporatist grouping, American society could transcend the class conflicts that arose from scarcity."[54] After the Second World War, these ideas—systematized by American proponents of corporate liberalism and institutionalized under the Marshall Plan—were diffused across the Atlantic. In the impoverished and politically volatile conditions of early Cold War Europe, the United States promoted the "apolitical" solution of productivity, arguing that "The true dialectic was not one of class against class, but waste versus abundance."[55] Put more bluntly, the movement was "first and last, a strategy for defeating Communism and exporting the American way of life."[56] In any case, the ideology of productivity seemed to offer accord with labor, reconstruction through new management methods and technology, and a planned, managerial approach to industrial development to the battered economies and polities of the postwar world.

News of the productivity movement in Europe started filtering to Japan in the late 1940s, although American-sponsored publicity in a productivist vein

[52] Ibid., 356–65, 514.

[53] Nakamura Seiji, *Nihon seisansei kōjō undō shi* (Keisō shobō, 1958), 173.

[54] Charles Maier, "The Politics of Productivity: Foundations of American International Economic Policy After World War II," in *In Search of Stability: Explorations in Historical Political Economy* (Cambridge: Cambridge University Press, 1987; originally published 1978), 128. See also Mark Rupert, *Producing Hegemony: The Politics of Mass Production and American Global Power* (Cambridge: Cambridge University Press, 1995).

[55] Maier, "The Politics of Productivity," 130.

[56] Anthony Carew, *Labour Under the Marshall Plan: The Politics of Productivity and the Marketing of Management Science* (Detroit: Wayne State University Press, 1987), 156.

had been evident from quite early in the Occupation.[57] The Labor Ministry took an active role in disseminating materials, as did the Ministry of International Trade and Industry, whose Rationalization Deliberative Council had proposed a "Japan Productivity Center" in 1951.[58] Of particular importance to the evolution of the Japanese movement was Dōyūkai director Gōshi Kōhei's 1953 visit to Europe. Gōshi returned highly impressed by the Anglo-American Productivity Council and moved by Graham Hutton's propagandistic *We Too Can Prosper*. To Gōshi, the greatest successes of the European efforts were not tangibly technical or institutional but rather ideological: in promoting a cooperative spirit among workers and an apolitical "economism" among unions, the concept of productivity seemed to have much to offer Japanese managers.[59]

In late 1953, U.S. officials approached Gōshi and the Dōyūkai, offering to sponsor a productivity program in Japan similar to that in place in Western Europe. The association was receptive, as the productivity ideology meshed well with the Dōyūkai agenda, and Gōshi gained the endorsement of the other three major business organizations, Nikkeiren, Keidanren (the Federation of Economic Organizations), and the Japan Chamber of Commerce (Nihon Shōkō Kaigisho). The conservatives in these bodies originally envisioned the movement in Japan as a management-only affair, without official labor participation, yet ultimately acceded to the more inclusive (and ideologically potent) approach of Gōshi and the program's American backers.[60] In any case, the Japanese business community was favorably disposed to the establishment of a new productivity organization, especially one that would further the goals of rationalization but would not be dominated by the economic bureaucracy.[61] With industry in a post–Korean War slump, the trade balance dismal, and labor beginning to chafe at management authority, jumping onto the American productivity bandwagon seemed sensible from an economic as well as an ideological perspective.[62]

---

[57] In 1947, for example, the journal *Keizai* published a U.S. Information Service report entitled "Labor and Management Solve Problems Together"; *Keizai* 1, no. 9 (November 1947): 26–27. In 1949, a report of Britain's Trades Union Congress called "Greater Industrial Productivity" was run in the journal *Seisan*; *Seisan* 4, no. 8 (November 1949): 5.

[58] Nihon seisansei honbu, *Seisansei undō 30-nen shi* (1985), 26–27.

[59] Keizai dōyūkai, *Jūnen shi*, 348; Gōshi Kōhei, "Seisansei kōjō undō," in Ekonomisuto henshūbu, *Shōgen: Kōdo seicho ki no Nihon*, vol. 2 (Mainichi shinbunsha, 1984), 233; Carlile, "Zaikai," 347–48.

[60] Carlile, "Zaikai," 353–54; Nihon seisansei honbu, *Seisansei undō 30-nen shi*, 94–104.

[61] On the response of the business community to postwar rationalization efforts, see Hein, *Fueling Growth*, 165–66; Takase Shōtarō, ed., *Sangyō gōrika to keiei seisaku* (Moriyama shoten, 1950), preface; Okamoto Hideaki, "Management and Their Organizations," in *Workers and Employers in Japan*, ed. Ōkōchi Kazuo, Bernard Karsh, and Solomon Levine (Princeton, N.J.: Princeton University Press, 1974), 163–215.

[62] Nakase, *Sengo Nihon*, 42; Yamabe Takashi, *Seisansei kōjō no rironteki shomondai* (Nihon seisansei honbu, 1957), 65–68.

The Japan Productivity Center (JPC, Nihon Seisansei Honbu) was founded on February 14, 1955, as the "nucleus of an evenhanded movement to boost productivity," and as "the cornerstone of Japan's economic progress."[63] Start-up funding was provided by the U.S. International Cooperation Administration ($500,000), business contributors (¥100 million) and the Japanese government (¥40 million), although the center was styled a "national movement" of "managers, workers, and academic experts."[64] Gōshi Kōhei was named managing director and the board was crowded with business leaders and prominent economists. Premised on the notion that Japan had to accept the "trend of the times" and get in shape to compete in the "productivity Olympics,"[65] the center was charged with importing, studying, and publicizing all aspects of productivity thought and practice. The movement's ultimate goal, the JPC founding statement concluded, was "to advance the mutual interests of managers, workers and consumers, striving to . . . improve real wages and the standard of living through a reduction of costs achieved by the more effective and scientific employment of resources, manpower, and equipment."[66]

From the start, the Productivity Center was invested with two basic functions. The first was to act as a conduit for introducing advanced management methods into Japan, stimulating interest in new techniques, educating managers in modern approaches, and coordinating programs of research and reform. The government's postwar rationalization plans had stressed the importance of such efforts and it was the JPC that eventually took them on, performing a role analogous in many ways to that of the Production Management Committee during the 1930s. The second function of the center was to hone and disseminate the ideology of productivity, that aspect of the movement which Gōshi and the Americans took to be the most significant. While management reform constituted the technical basis for industrial growth, the conditioning of a suitable environment for recovery—one based on harmonious labor relations, a compliant working class, and a social consensus that legitimized a managerial, technocratic order—was the primary task of the productivity ideology.

At the intellectual core of productivity thought, in Japan as in Europe, was the so-called "pie theory." Although dismissed by some as the "mythic idyll of American workers and management jointly striving to create a bigger pie and then amicably sitting down to divide it,"[67] the concept exhibited considerable

---

[63] Quoted from the JPC's founding statement of principles in Nihon seisansei honbu, *Seisansei undō 30-nen shi,* 107.

[64] Kurokawa Toshio and Satake Gosaku, *Nihon seisansei honbu* (Aoki shoten, 1970), 18; Nihon seisansei honbu, *Seisansei undō 30-nen shi,* 106–7. Using the official exchange rate of ¥360 = $1, the total Japanese contribution (¥140,000,000 = $390,000) was significantly smaller than the American donation.

[65] Quoted from "Seisansei kōjō undō no shiori" (1956) in Yamabe, *Seisansei kōjō,* 65.

[66] Nihon seisansei honbu, *Seisansei undō 30-nen shi,* 107; see also Carlile, "Zaikai," 355.

[67] Carew, *Labour,* 166.

appeal across the political spectrum and across national boundaries. In brief, the theory suggested that managers and workers would do better cooperating to increase the size of the pie of industrial production than forever bickering over how best to divide it. If management and labor recognized their mutuality of interests, worked together to apply the "neutral" principles of modern management, and submitted to the "unpoliticized" dictates of technological rationality, productivity could be raised, costs lowered, and returns increased. By "fairly" apportioning the gains (in the form of higher profits, better wages, and lower consumer costs), the demands of management and labor could be satisfied, and the interests of society at large could be served.[68] But the benefits of productivism did not come without responsibilities:

> Upon management it imposes the obligation to keep its product prices as low as possible . . . and to share equitably with labor, in the form of higher real wages and improved conditions of work, the fruits of increased production. Upon labor, it imposes the obligation to keep production at high levels and to recognize the need for adequate earnings by management to maintain and improve its equipment, technology, and general competitive strength. Upon the general public, it imposes the responsibility for providing . . . the economic and social institutions favorable to improved productivity. . . .[69]

If these obligations were fulfilled, the pie theory promised an escape from zero sum industrial relations: in a newfound "paradise of production," the abundance bestowed by the apolitical beneficence of science would yield such wealth to all as to make class conflict unthinkable. "Marxist theory," Noda Nobuo would somewhat prematurely declare, "is a thing of the past."[70]

The fanfare with which the productivity ideology was introduced, along with the unfamiliarity of the word *seisansei* itself, tended to obscure the fact that the pie theory and the JPC model of industrial accord were actually not very novel at all. Indeed, the propaganda of the productivity movement resonated with echoes of the Taylorite "Mental Revolution." While only a few observers stressed direct continuities between the ideologies of Scientific Management and productivity, the prewar vocabulary of the "Mental Revolution"— "brotherly love," "mutual gains," and so on—was reprised to describe the potential of the JPC program.[71] The connections should hardly be surprising: the American idea of productivity derived in no small part from the philosophy

[68] See, for example, Noda Nobuo, *Seisansei dokuhon* (Nihon seisansei honbu, 1957); Japan Productivity Center, *The Productivity Program in Japan* (Tokyo: Japan–U.S. Operations Mission to Japan, 1960), 5–6.

[69] Japan Productivity Center, *Productivity Program*, 6.

[70] Noda Nobuo, "Amerika ni okeru seisansei no kongen," *Seisansei no riron to jissai* 2 (February 1956): 218.

[71] See, for example, Takamiya Susumu, "Seisansei kōjō to keiei kanri," in *Wagakuni kigyō to seisansei kōjō*, vol. 1, ed. Yamanaka Tokutarō et al. (Tōyō keizai shinpōsha, 1958), 28; Yamabe, *Seisansei kōjō*, 57, 215.

of Scientific Management, as the corporate liberals who supported the international productivity movement drew heavily on the intellectual legacy of Taylorism and the progressive business thought of the 1920s. In Japan, this linkage between the prewar management vanguard and the advocates of productivism was no less strong, as the busy Noda Nobuo, head of the Productivity Research Institute (Seisansei Kenkyūjo), was the movement's chief ideologue and as the JPC counted efficiency movement veterans Godō Takuo, Ueno Yōichi, and Ota Tetsuzō among its advisors.[72]

At the core of the pie theory and the ideology of abundance that underlay productivity thought was the old nostrum of a "high-wage/low-cost" economy. Japanese Taylorites in the 1920s took as their major selling point the idea that increased industrial efficiency could accrue benefits to both capital and labor. While this ideological approach went underground in the patriotic fervor of mobilization—reeking as it did of narrow and separate class interests—it returned to favor in the management community immediately after the war. Prominent advocates of Scientific Management were quick to resuscitate the high-wage/low-cost model, arguing that managerial and technological improvements could restore Japan's competitive position and diffuse social tensions.[73] Scientific Management and its ideals were reasserted as economic common sense and, even more compellingly, as a vehicle for social rapprochement. "Realizing high wages and low costs," management expert Shingō Shigeo averred, "is attainable only through high efficiency."[74] As one Fuji Electric engineer wrote in 1946, foreshadowing the ideological pitch of the JPC, "I am convinced that the key to solving the problems between workers and employers lies in the development of production technology, in the promotion of industrial recovery, and in the creation of a vital community which fuses the mutual interests of labor and capital by shortening work hours, increasing income, decreasing production costs, and stimulating demand. I feel that Japanese production management should strive idealistically for this goal."[75]

The continuities between prewar Taylorite approaches and postwar strategies for industrial regeneration and social harmonization were demonstrated clearly in the writings of Katō Takeo, a Scientific Management pioneer and active participant in the Keizai Dōyūkai and the JPC. Musing on America's economic triumphs, Katō concluded that the same factors which had made the United States successful in the 1920s had also conferred its postwar prosperity. As a guide to the American way, Katō recommended a book written by two Britons, Bertram Austin and W. Francis Lloyd, which had been translated

[72] Noda Kazuo, *Sengo keieishi* (Nihon seisansei honbu, 1965), 1006–7. Among the JPC "consultants" were Morikawa Kakuzō, Katō Takeo, and Araki Tōichirō.

[73] See, for example, Noda Nobuo, "Nihon no gijutsu," *Seisan* 1, no. 1 (November 1946): 2.

[74] Shingō Shigeo, *Seisan kanri no kaizen* (Nihon keizaisha, 1951), introd., 2.

[75] Kojima Kenji, "Gijutsusha no risō," *Seisan* 1, no. 1 (November 1946): 30.

and had attracted considerable interest in Japan before the war. The book, which was in many ways a prewar analogue to Hutton's *We Too Can Prosper,* was simply and directly titled *The Secret of High Wages*.[76]

Some observers have concluded that the high-wage/high-value-added/low-cost model was a distinctively postwar approach in Japan. Laura Hein, for example, points to an influential 1946 report issued by the Ministry of Foreign Affairs as the genesis of the high-wage/high-efficiency strategy, what she terms "a major break from the past."[77] Although the report may have stimulated government interest in this model (and thus contributed to the intellectual foundations of productivism), the championing of high wages and low costs was hardly so revolutionary ideologically. As the history of the Japanese efficiency movement suggests, this "mutually beneficial" vision was endorsed—although never actually put to the test—by forward-looking managers well before World War II. Nonetheless, even if the reaffirmation of a high-wage/low-cost strategy did not mark a "major break," the fact that the productivist ideal would eventually gain widespread legitimacy—and be realized to a significant extent in actual practice—did constitute a genuine watershed in postwar Japan.

As the "Mental Revolution" and the philosophy of mutual gains were reiterated in the ideology of the productivity movement, so too were the assertions of scientific neutrality, managerial expertise, and technocratic leadership which had long characterized modern management thought. The logic of *seisansei* was premised on the idea that productivity could be raised (and mutual benefits attained) only if the technical dictates of the production process—which were presumed to be scientific and hence politically neutral—were scrupulously followed. As Lonny Carlile has described the JPC's "objective" resolution of class tensions, "While the respective interests of [employers and employees] are certainly involved, the technical requirements of the production process—not the relative power or influence of the respective parties per se—must structure problem solving. . . . Resolutions of conflicting interests must be arrived at that are technically efficient so as not to endanger the shared interest in maximizing the expansion of the pie."[78] In Noda Nobuo's words, "Both labor and management must show respect for the neutral, scientific viewpoint."[79] Implicit in this statement, however, was the assertion of managerial autonomy in directing the firm, as only managers were assumed to have the technical expertise and freedom from narrow class inter-

[76] Katō Takeo, *Keiei no hanashi, keiei kaizen no kyūsho* (Manejimento kyōkai, 1950).

[77] Hein, *Fueling Growth,* 111 ff.; the Ministry of Foreign Affairs report, "Nihon keizai saiken no konpon mondai," prepared by a blue-ribbon commission of civil servants and leftist economists, has been translated as Okita Saburo, ed., *The Postwar Reconstruction of the Japanese Economy* (Tokyo: University of Tokyo Press, 1992).

[78] Carlile, "Zaikai," 374–75.

[79] Noda Nobuo et al., *Seisansei kōjō no hōhō* (Daiyamondo, 1955), 17.

ests necessary to be "neutral" and "scientific." Noda argued in 1953, prefiguring the JPC approach, that there was no reason why stockholders should have more say in the running of a firm than its employees, yet, in the end, both labor and capital had to yield to the "unconditional" autonomy of professional managers.[80] As one Productivity Center document put it, "respect for managerial authority is an indispensable element in the healthy progress of business."[81] Although such a declaration sounded as much like Nikkeiren dogmatism as "revised Taylorism," productivity advocates clearly drew on the rich intellectual seam running from Scientific Management through "New Order" technocracy and Dōyūkai revisionism in touting an order based on the primacy of science, the denial of politics, and the dominance of professional managers.

The concept of productivity thus lay at the end of almost half a century of evolution in Japan's modern management movement. Marketed to business, labor, and the public under the new name *seisansei,* the concept sounded like a more original and inventive departure than it actually was. Indeed, the very fact of giving an established approach a new name—one that lacked the intellectual baggage and shopworn familiarity of the old one—was itself a well-established pattern in Japanese management reform. In other words, the ideology of productivity absorbed the assumptions, strategies, and rhetorical tactics of "revised Taylorism" and the efficiency movement, but without inheriting the politically loaded catchphrases *kagakuteki kanrihō* (Scientific Management), *sangyō gōrika* (rationalization), or *nōritsu zōshin* (efficiency increase). Yet the postwar repackaging of the "Mental Revolution" was not simply cosmetic, for although the ideology of productivity was not new, the social and economic environment in which it appeared was. Before the Occupation, mass production, a powerful labor movement, and a high-wage consumer economy seemed distant and alien in Japan; by the 1950s, however, the approaches long endorsed by Japanese Taylorites—mutual gains, managerialism, the scientific management of industry—were all conceivable (and even seemed attainable) under the rubric of productivity.

Spreading the Good News of Productivity

Although the Productivity Center was intended as a tripartite organ of business, labor, and academic experts, workers were not present at its creation. The reluctance of organized labor to sign on too readily is hardly surprising. The productivity program was, after all, devised primarily by management reformers, business representatives, and bureaucrats: the JPC consequently reflected the assumptions and strategies of these groups more than the con-

---

[80] Noda, *Kindaiteki keiei,* 449.

[81] Nihon seisansei honbu, *Seisansei undō 10-nen no ayumi* (1965), 151.

cerns of Japanese unionists. As Gōshi, Noda, and their supporters anticipated, however, the productivity ideology offered a palatable vision of labor-management accord to "realistic" labor leaders and "sound" trade unions.[82] The cooperation of the moderate, economistic and less politicized wing of the labor movement—led by the Sōdōmei federation—was thus gained by the JPC in good order. Converting the large left wing of organized labor remained more of a challenge, although after several years of vitriol and invective, it too came around, tacitly accepting—if not officially endorsing—the productivity agenda.

From the start, the "realistic" unions on the right wing of the labor movement viewed the JPC settlement with cautious optimism. Sōdōmei, which both before and after the war showed considerable intellectual congruence with business progressives, was the first to signal its approval of the productivity program. Less than six months after the founding of the JPC, the federation released a list of eight principles which summarized its conditions for participating in the center's activities. Insisting that productivity "must be different from the various rationalization and efficiency movements" of the past, Sōdōmei looked for *seisansei* to bring "increased living standards and economic independence," not further unemployment, accelerated industrial concentration, or "the increase of corporate profits through the squeezing of labor." In endorsing the establishment of substantive organs of industrial democracy and formal labor-management agreements on the division of economic gains from productivity, the Sōdōmei principles did go somewhat beyond the cautious parameters delineated by the JPC's founders.[83] For the most part, however, the Sōdōmei document confirmed the essential compatibility between the productivity ideology and the approach of "realistic" unionism.[84]

The large and vocal left wing of organized labor took a far less sanguine view of the productivity program and its implications for the fate of industrial relations in Japan. Sōhyō (the General Council of Japanese Trade Unions), which claimed nearly half of all union members in the nation, greeted the inauguration of the JPC with both alarm and derision. From Sōhyō's perspective, the productivity movement was a manifestation of American economic imperialism, "a series of measures which allow the United States to control Japan" and, in the end, a device "for safeguarding capitalism and exploiting the workers."[85] According to left-wing critics, the JPC aimed to focus worker

[82] On the "realistic" unions, see Garon, *The State and Labor,* 231–48.

[83] Nihon seisansei honbu, *Seisansei undō 30-nen shi,* 155–56.

[84] This also came through in the attitude of the avowedly anti-Communist All-Japan Labor Union Congress (Zenrō Kaigi), which along with Sōdōmei (its largest member) seemed the natural constituency for the productivity agenda in the Japanese union movement. Carlile, "Zaikai," 363–68; Nihon seisansei honbu, *Seisansei undō 30-nen shi,* 163–68. See also Sheldon Garon and Mike Mochizuki, "Negotiating Social Contracts," in *Postwar Japan as History,* ed. Andrew Gordon, (Berkeley: University of California Press, 1993), 158–59.

[85] Quoted from a Sōhyō statement at its 1956 annual meeting in Yamabe, *Seisansei kōjō,* 151.

attention on personal, capitalistic gain, diverting labor's energy away from broader political concerns and onto the methodologies of increasing production. In this respect, the movement appeared nothing more than an insidious "class harmonization campaign" designed to "subjugate labor unions and paralyze the workers' class consciousness."[86] Sōhyō's official response to the launch of the productivity program was unambiguous: "America has provided the funding for the JPC and, using the smokescreen of labor-capital harmonization [rōshi kyōchō], has tried to draw workers and their unions into the productivity movement. The movement, however, is nothing more than a means to enforce layoffs, wage cuts, and exploitation, to extract excess profits from each worker and each workshop, and to suppress the unions. Aiming to Sanpō-ize organized labor, the JPC looks to split the unions by driving a wedge into the labor movement."[87]

As this Sōhyō critique indicates, the left was aware of the extent to which the "new" ideology of productivity echoed established approaches to labor relations and industrial management. In addition to recognizing that the Sanpō-like integration of unions into a business-dominated order was conceivable under the banner of seisansei, Sōhyō was particularly concerned that productivity "had much in common with the rationalization movement."[88] Indeed, the assertion that the productivity program was nothing more than a souped-up and more elaborately camouflaged version of prewar and wartime rationalization efforts became a major theme in left-wing attacks on the JPC. The most famous exposition of this view was given in a series of articles written by the Marxist journalist Horie Masanori which appeared during 1955 and 1956 in the magazine Chūō kōron.[89] Maintaining that productivity was just the latest attempt to cloak capitalist exploitation in the mantle of objectivity and science, Horie argued that the movement aimed to fragment and neutralize the working class, thus paving the way for the unchallenged introduction of Scientific Management into all Japanese workshops. Enjoining his readers not to be taken in by the recycled and repackaged postwar versions of old managerial strategies, Horie blasted the advocates of the productivity movement as "the Taylorites of today."[90]

The proponents of seisansei appreciated the difficulties of winning over their detractors and, like the Taylorites of days past, recognized that theirs

---

[86] Ibid., 101. Plentiful critiques of the productivity movement are provided in Kurokawa and Satake, Nihon seisansei honbu, a study sponsored by Sōhyō.

[87] Quoted in Nakamura, Nihon seisansei, 204.

[88] Yamabe, Seisansei kōjō, 101.

[89] The series took the form of a dialogue between Horie and Nakayama Ichirō, the chairman of the Central Labor Relations Board (Chūō Rōdō Iinkai) and one of the most active academic proponents of productivity.

[90] Horie Masanori, "Seisansei kōjō undō hihan," Chūō kōron 70, no. 10 (October 1955): 151–55.

would have to be a proselytizing mission. Tokunaga Hisatsugu, head of MITI's Enterprises Bureau (Kigyō Kyoku), framed the challenge as follows: "In order to permeate all parts of the Japanese economy with the gospel of the JPC, a great many years and a dedication like that shown by Jesus will be necessary. Although there are some fervent apostles and adherents—and a great many people who seek after a miracle—there are also countless unbelieving Jews whose souls are firmly shut. Only when the hearts of these doubters are softened and a sense of hope restored can the Japanese economy be redeemed. One has to say that the apostles' mission is a weighty one indeed."[91] Even beyond portraying their efforts in such terms of religious enlightenment and conversion—metaphors much favored by Japanese Taylorites since the 1920s—the supporters of the JPC followed closely the established discursive strategies of the efficiency and rationalization movements. Thus, in preaching to the labor movement and addressing the doubts of the left wing, the advocates of productivity not only embraced the gospel of "revised Taylorism"—science, high wages/low costs, managerial neutrality— but many of its evangelical methods and rhetorical flourishes as well.

When critics denounced the productivity movement as a clone of rationalization, for example, spokesmen for the JPC followed the familiar pattern of denying their ideology's heritage and promoting it as a bold new formulation. "The postwar productivity movement," Yamabe Takashi declared, "has historical ties with the rationalization movements of the past . . . yet is entirely different in form and substance."[92] Gōshi Kōhei was especially sensitive to aspersions cast on productivity's paternity and endeavored to dispel the notion that the movement was merely a throwback. "Unfortunately," Gōshi stated, "the prewar rationalization movement was unable to solve many social irrationalities like unemployment and wage reductions. Consequently, I don't intend to defend that effort strongly or attempt to cover up its negative aspects. Rather, I believe that by honestly and humbly reconsidering such former experiences, our initiatives today can better move forward."[93] Productivity was thus portrayed as a reaction to rationalization, more a reasoned departure from prewar approaches than a repackaged revival of past practice.

The defenders of productivity stressed that the fundamental difference between the new movement and its alleged predecessors lay in the ability of the concept of *seisansei* to transcend narrow class imperatives. Productivity, it was claimed, looked beyond the selfish, capitalistic interests taken to be the motive force of prewar rationalization and addressed the development of the economy as a whole. According to a widely distributed JPC pamphlet, "Pre-

---

[91] Tokunaga Hisatsugu, "Seisansei kōjō undō no fukyū hōhō o kangaete hoshii," *Seisansei no riron to jissai* 1 (February 1956): 6.

[92] Yamabe, *Seisansei kōjō,* 120; see also Nakamura, *Nihon seisansei,* 264–65.

[93] Gōshi Kōhei, "Seisansei to kindaiteki keiei," *Seisansei no riron to jissai* 1 (February 1956): 15.

vious rationalization efforts have centered on capitalists and have offered nothing but a subordinate role to the workers. . . . The brand-new productivity movement takes a broader viewpoint, however, drawing on the participation of management, labor, and society as a whole. With an acute sensitivity to improving the living standards of all citizens, the movement takes as its objective the prosperity of the entire national economy."[94] The transformation which allowed for this "broader viewpoint" was, productivity advocates claimed, the emergence of the "modified," managerial capitalist order following the war. Borrowing the logic of the Dōyūkai, the supporters of the JPC assured workers that exploitation was impossible under the productivity program, since capitalists had been supplanted by professional managers and the profit motive subordinated to welfare concerns. As Yamabe Takashi put it, while the rationalization movement had been conceived in class-based terms, *seisansei* was premised on the politically neutral approach of the new managerial capitalism, and thus allowed for equity, cooperation, and broadly based economic advance.[95]

While most boosters were content to portray *seisansei* as a politically denatured reformulation of rationalization, some went even further, touting it as the fundamental force propelling economic development and social progress in the modern world. In a rebuttal of Horie Masanori's *Chūō kōron* essays, for example, Nakayama Ichirō took Marxist critics of the JPC to task for confusing the medium with the message, condemning the gospel of productivity simply because its prophets were managers and industrialists. Dismissing left-wing complaints as superficial, Nakayama maintained that the logic of *seisansei* had been confirmed theoretically and historically, and that there could be no argument that the progress of industrial society was inseparable from the progress of productivity.[96] This interpretation was most fully elaborated in *Gijutsu kakushin to Nihon keizai* (The Technological Revolution and the Japanese Economy), a commemorative volume published by the JPC on its fifth anniversary. Rewriting Japanese history since the Meiji Restoration as the inexorable march of productivity, the book articulated an ideology of growth which equated economic expansion and societal advancement with productivity increases.[97] *Seisansei,* like science, was thus portrayed as com-

[94] Quoted from "Seisansei kōjō undō no shiori" (1956) in Nihon seisansei honbu, *Seisansei undō 30-nen shi,* 130. Such arguments have apparently had lasting appeal: a 1986 center publication declared that the "Productivity Revolution" was neither capitalist nor socialist, but was rather a "spiritual revolution" premised on progress, humanity, and economic growth. Murakami Motohiko, *Seisansei to wa nani ka* (Nihon seisansei honbu, 1986), 24–28.

[95] Yamabe, *Seisansei kōjō,* 120–21, 216.

[96] Nakayama Ichirō, "Seisansei kōjō undō hihan o hanhihan suru," *Chūō kōron* 71, no. 1 (January 1956): 46–52, and "Seisansei mondai no shozai," ibid., no. 13 (December 1956): 96–101.

[97] Nihon seisansei honbu, *Gijutsu kakushin to Nihon keizai* (1960) in *Nihon keiei shiryō taikei, 3: Soshiki, gōrika,* ed. Katō Takabumi (San-ichi shobō, 1989), 319–41.

mon sense rather than as political construct, and was naturalized by its proponents as the neutral and unalterable motive force of progress in the industrial
age.

Organized labor did agree, to a large extent, with such appraisals of productivity's potential, much as prewar critics had endorsed the theory, if not the
practice, of rationalization and Scientific Management. Ever since the defeat,
labor leaders across the political spectrum had supported the expansion of
production as the paramount goal of postwar enterprise management. "Recovery of production is the workers' slogan," one Communist Party publication
trumpeted in 1948.[98] Although influenced to some degree by the experience of
wartime exhortation, Japanese unionists surely recognized the value of a moderate, production-minded approach in putting pressure on business and on
winning broad support for labor's economic demands. This rhetoric had
proved successful early in the Occupation—when inflation had dampened industry's eagerness to actually produce—yet organized labor found itself
trumped by the management initiative on *seisansei*. Even Sōhyō had to acknowledge the powerful logic of productivity: "Increasing the productivity of
labor is what we desire above all. Raising efficiency, increasing production,
and assuring its abundance, sending out inexpensive commodities in large
quantities, and pulling up the standard of living are the joys of labor."[99] Thus
finding themselves in rough theoretical accord with the JPC, union leaders fell
back on the strategy Nakayama Ichirō decried, focusing their attacks on the
movement rather than on the ideology of productivity. The opponents of
seisansei (like its advocates) turned to established discursive patterns in the
debate over productivity, following in the path of the many Marxist critics
who had denounced the prewar efficiency movement while still endorsing
Taylorite approaches. As one labor leader characterized Sōhyō's stand, "We're
not opposed to productivity per se . . . but we are against it if, as at present, it
is based on monopoly capitalism."[100]

In the end, despite the continued influence of "monopoly capitalism" in
the JPC, much of the early labor opposition to the productivity movement was
dulled and diffused. The "realistic" unions offered only token resistance and
enrolled in the movement readily. Sōhyō was harder to win over and never
formally signed on as a partner in the Productivity Center. Nevertheless,
the federation's determination to oppose the JPC appeared to recede over the
1950s, as the vitriol of left-wing criticism was seemingly washed away by the
tidal wave of productivist propaganda. Whether persuaded by JPC rhetoric,
swayed by the mounting evidence of economic success, or ultimately cowed
by union busting, Sōhyō gradually softened its hard-line position and, as early

[98] Kitagawa, "Sangyō gōrika to wa nani ka," 21.

[99] Carlile, "Zaikai," 357.

[100] Takita Minoru, "Seisansei o meguru shin nendo no kadai," *Seisansei no riron to jissai* 7
(April 1958): 96.

as 1956, member unions were participating in Productivity Center programs.[101] By the end of the movement's first decade, the once dogmatic opposition of organized labor's politicized left had been transformed into tacit approval and active (if not particularly enthusiastic) cooperation.[102]

The neutralization of labor antipathy and the integration of "realistic" unions into the Japanese productivity movement paralleled the experience in Europe, and especially that in Great Britain. Although initially critical of productivity, the British Trades Union Congress (TUC) was soon converted to the productivist gospel, accepting that increased living standards could only be attained by cooperating in the technological and managerial renovation of industry. As one union leader reasoned, "Can we, under a capitalist system, obtain a higher standard of life for . . . workers by being modern Luddites?"[103] Thus committed to bread-and-butter issues, and convinced by the supposed scientific neutrality of productivism, the TUC strongly supported the agenda of the Anglo-American Council on Productivity.[104] In Britain then, as in Japan, the unions—which many feared would be the greatest impediments to the productivity program—actually ended up among the movement's most dedicated participants, embracing business unionism and the technocratic, materialist appeal of productivity in an environment where the scope for political activism was increasingly constrained. In seeking to create "rational," "modern" unions, that is to say, organizations which acknowledged managerial values and emphasized economic interests over political ones,[105] the productivity movement—in Japan as in Britain—seems to have achieved considerable success.[106]

---

[101] Representatives of Sōhyō affiliates participated, for example, in the second JPC labor union mission to the United States, dispatched in August 1956. See Nihon seisansei honbu, *Rōshi kyōei e no michi,* Productivity Report 28 (Nihon seisansei honbu, 1957).

[102] See Carlile, "Zaikai," 417–19, 424. As Andrew Gordon has observed, "At the enterprise level it appears that labor accepted the movement from the start almost regardless of national affiliation; already in 1957 the Labor Ministry hailed 'the birth of a practical, rather than an abstract, response to the productivity movement' at major manufacturers." Andrew Gordon, "Contests for the Workplace," in *Postwar Japan as History,* ed. Andrew Gordon (Berkeley: University of California Press, 1993), 377.

[103] Quoted in Carew, *Labour,* 203.

[104] Ibid., 133–39; Jim Tomlinson, "The Failure of the Anglo-American Council on Productivity," *Business History* 33, no. 1 (1991): 88–89.

[105] See Nihon seisansei honbu, *Seisansei undō 10-nen no ayumi,* 163 ff.; Japan Productivity Center, *Productivity Program,* 35–37.

[106] On postwar Japanese unionism, see Garon, *The State and Labor,* 242–48. On the legacies of productivism in Europe, see Carew, *Labour,* 240–50; Federico Romero, *The United States and the European Trade Union Movement,* trans. Harvey Fergusson II (Chapel Hill: University of North Carolina Press, 1992), 218–19. For a fascinating cultural perspective on productivism in France, see Richard F. Kuisel, *Seducing the French: The Dilemma of Americanization* (Berkeley: University of California Press, 1993), esp. chap. 4, "The Missionaries of the Marshall Plan."

Completing the Consensus on Productivity

As Taylor had cautioned in *The Principles of Scientific Management,* the "Mental Revolution" required not only the cooperation of labor, but the full understanding and commitment of management as well. This was an imperative well appreciated by the advocates of productivity, who discovered that their ideological message was often a harder sell to employees and managers than it was to workers and unionists. Although all the major business federations endorsed the founding of the JPC, the progressive corporate-liberal approach to integrating organized labor did not sit well with business conservatives. Nikkeiren's embrace of productivity, at least at the start, was consequently a rather cool one.[107] Yet even managers of a less dogmatic bent found that the assumptions and implications of productivism could seem uncomfortably threatening to the status quo on the shop floor and in the board room.

The productivity movement was, after all, premised on the need for managerial reform and the implicit notion that managers, and not just workers, had to bear their share of the responsibility for Japan's industrial problems. In some instances, JPC criticism of existing management practices was explicit: a much-hyped 1956 report prepared for the center by William Landes, an American business consultant, concluded that Japanese managers were "illogical" and that the major failing of Japanese industry was the lack of managerial expertise.[108] It is hardly surprising that, faced with such frank evaluations, many managers greeted the productivity movement and its implied challenge to "business as usual" with only muted enthusiasm.[109]

A similar dynamic also developed in Europe, where the productivity movement and its relentless promotion of advanced American methods alienated a considerable portion of the business community. In France, Italy, and Great Britain, many employers bristled at the glorification of modern administrative practices and the cooperative approach to labor relations which characterized the productivity agenda.[110] In Britain, where the unions were particularly active in supporting the Anglo-American Productivity Council, industrial

---

[107] Nikkeiren, *Jūnen no ayumi,* 97–98; Carlile, "Zaikai," 384; Yamabe, *Seisansei kōjō,* 152.

[108] William S. Landes, *Nihon no keiei o shindan suru* (Nihon seisansei honbu, 1956), 15. Similar condemnations of Japanese management methods appeared regularly in JPC publications.

[109] The 1953 Dōyūkai declaration "Wareware no kakugo" foreshadowed this disinclination to reform, stating, "The current situation is that the upper ranks of management are relatively indifferent to innovation in managerial methods. . . ." Keizai dōyūkai, *Jūnen shi,* 513–14; see also Carlile, "Zaikai," 339–43; Kurosawa Kazukiyo, "Some Considerations on Productivity Schemes," *Keizai shūshi* (Nihon University) 48, no. 2 (July 1978): 106.

[110] Carew, *Labour,* 211–17; Tomlinson, "Failure"; Romero, *United States,* 202–3; Luc Boltanski, "Visions of American Management in Post-War France," *Theory and Society* 12, no. 3 (May 1983): 378.

leaders were annoyed by the constant pressure for managerial reform and seem to have resented the movement's implicit questioning of their competence. As Jim Tomlinson notes, "[Most scholars believe] that scientific management was essentially a technique for subordinating labour, assumed to be always a congenial objective to management. But in the British case, management did not see the issue quite in that way. The rhetoric of scientific management threatened their traditional way of doing things as much as it threatened labour's traditional prerogatives."[111]

In Japan, the JPC may well have anticipated a lukewarm managerial response to its message, and the center expended at least as much effort convincing the business community of productivity's value as it spent on wooing labor. The lion's share of the JPC publicity blitz—books, journals, lectures, short courses, training sessions, and so on—was aimed specifically at management rather than at the unions or the general public.[112] The delegations of Japanese sent to investigate American industrial life—the well-known "productivity missions"—were also carefully designed so as to maximize their publicity value within the business world. Whereas in Europe most such study missions to the United States included shop-floor workers as mission representatives,[113] in Japan the teams were generally composed entirely of managerial personnel and government representatives. Moreover, the JPC sought to choose as delegation members only high-profile figures in the business community and those in a good position to influence managerial opinion on the movement.[114] The center even established a club in its headquarters building for the private use of productivity mission veterans.[115]

The ambivalence of many in industry toward productivism and its emphasis on systemic managerial reform was manifested in the reports written by the various JPC study teams. Although uniformly fulsome in their praise for American management methods and philosophies, most of the mission reports stopped short of endorsing extensive, immediate reform based on U.S. models. Even those teams which concluded that Japanese business *should* move closer to an American ideal were dubious that Japanese firms *could* adopt the same practices as their trans-Pacific counterparts, at least in the foreseeable future. Stressing the great differences between Japan and the

---

[111] Tomlinson, "Failure," 85. See also Barbara Weinstein, *For Social Peace in Brazil: Industrialists and the Remaking of the Working Class in São Paulo, 1920–1964* (Chapel Hill: University of North Carolina Press, 1996), 48.

[112] The tenth anniversary history of the JPC declared that "The movement and its publicity activities are two sides of the same coin." See Nihon seisansei honbu, *Seisansei undō 10-nen no ayumi*, 88–121, 213–37.

[113] Carew, *Labour*, 159. Carew further asserts that the propaganda of British missions was aimed more at a labor audience than at business managers; 139 ff.

[114] Nihon seisansei honbu, *Seisansei undō 10-nen no ayumi*, 39–42; Japan Productivity Center, *Productivity Program*, 16, 31.

[115] Nihon seisansei honbu, *Seisansei undō 10-nen no ayumi*, 248.

United States—differences conceived more often as technological and financial rather than as social and cultural—a number of the missions cautioned against the hasty importation of American organizational practices, labor relations practices, and production management routines. The tone of the mission reports suggests that many of Japan's business leaders looked suspiciously at the reformist thrust of productivism and were not inclined to go too fast in altering the familiar landscape of management philosophy and practice.[116]

Yet businessmen and managers—and even the hard-liners of Nikkeiren— eventually accepted and internalized the logic of productivity. By the early 1960s, Nikkeiren rhetoric on labor relations and management reform closely paralleled the positions associated with the productivity movement.[117] The goals and strategy of the JPC were, after all, broadly supportive of business values and managerial interests, despite the movement's implicit criticisms of existing arrangements. The productivity program held out the promise of a depoliticized and "rationalized" labor movement, increased productive efficiency (and presumably profits), as well as a more autonomous and responsible role for the professional managerial stratum. Perhaps most appealing to the business world was the fact that the productivity ideology offered detente with labor under the pie theory but remained notoriously vague on the critical question of distribution. Despite union pressure to formalize the apportionment of the ever-growing pie, the JPC and its business supporters evaded such broad contractual commitments and promoted distributive solutions (like Rucker and Scanlon bonus plans) at the level of the individual firm.[118]

Acceptance of the productivity agenda in the business community was also furthered by a renewed ideological offensive from the Keizai Dōyūkai. At its 1956 annual meeting, the association articulated a broadened philosophical conception of the mission of corporate management in Japan, endorsing a new ideology of the "social responsibility of managers" (*keieisha no shakaiteki sekinin*). Drawing heavily on contemporary American ideas—although clearly consistent with the Dōyūkai vision of "modified capitalism"—this new formulation sought to claim for management a social and economic role

---

[116] See the following mission reports (all edited and published by the Nihon seisansei honbu): *Han'ei keizai to keiei: Toppu manejimento shisetsudan hōkokusho*, Productivity Report 1 (1956); *Hyūman rireeshon*, Productivity Report 12 (1957); *Amerika ni okeru indasutoriaru rireeshonzu*, Productivity Report 50 (1958).

[117] As Carlile notes, Nikkeiren's symbolically potent fifteenth anniversary declaration at its 1963 annual meeting closely echoed JPC approaches; Carlile, "Zaikai," 420–25.

[118] The "Spring Labor Offensive" (*shuntō*), which began in 1955, must be considered a significant means by which labor was able to maintain and even increase its share of the pie. Tokunaga Shigeyoshi, "A Marxist Interpretation of Japanese Industrial Relations, with Special Reference to Large Private Enterprises," in *Contemporary Industrial Relations in Japan,* ed. Shirai Taishirō (Madison: University of Wisconsin Press, 1983), 317–21; Shirai Taishirō, "Collective Bargaining," in Ōkōchi, Karsh and Levine, *Workers and Employers,* 305.

that transcended the firm and suffused the body politic.[119] "Today's managers," the Dōyūkai declaration stated, "cannot simply pursue the interests of their own enterprises, either in theory or in practice. Rather, through the harmonization of the economic and the social, they must strive to combine the factors of production as efficiently as possible, to manufacture inexpensive and high-quality goods, and to offer their services to society."[120]

Going beyond Taylorite technocracy, the state managerialism of the "New Order," and early Dōyūkai concepts of professionalism, the ideology of "social responsibility" implied that managers were not simply mediators between labor and capital, but were entitled to be independent brokers of diverging political and economic interests. In short, the Dōyūkai posited that the managers of industry had the qualifications, the influence, and indeed the duty, to be the impartial "fixers" of society under a productivist political settlement. To postwar Japanese managers, who had already attained ascendancy within the enterprise, *seisansei* and the notion of "social responsibility" offered the prospect of enhanced autonomy and authority in society at large.[121]

Yet management was not won over to the JPC cause simply by the appealing logic and ideological implications of productivism. Certainly the intellectual legacy of Scientific Management, rationalization, and the wartime efficiency drive made the ideology of productivity seem familiar and ensured, at the very least, that many managers were comfortable with the basic assumptions of the productivity program. But the ideology of *seisansei* eventually gained levels of public exposure and an acceptance in the business community which the movement's prewar ancestors—and specifically the Taylorite "Mental Revolution" and its vision of labor-management accord—had never attained. Perhaps more than anything else, the receptiveness of postwar Japanese managers to the reprised "Mental Revolution" testifies to the extent to which the experience of war, defeat, and occupation had transformed the social and economic context of industrial management and labor relations in Japan. In comprehending the ascendance of productivism, due accord must be

[119] The impetus for this new ideological initiative appears to have come from the Keizai Dōyūkai members who had participated in the early JPC missions to the United States and were highly impressed with the American ideology of the social responsibility of business. See Nihon seisansei honbu, *Han'ei keizai to keiei,* 20–23. Even at the time, some observers felt uncomfortable with the new ideology because it sounded so American. Some suggested that the Dōyūkai resolution on "social responsibility" read much like a direct translation from English. "Dōyūkai 20-nen no rinen to genjitsu," 105; see also Nakamura, *Nihon seisansei,* 186–88.

[120] Keizai dōyūkai, *Keizai dōyūkai 15-nen shi* (Keizai dōyūkai, 1962), 119–20, 391–92.

[121] In claiming "social responsibility," the Keizai Dōyūkai apparently hoped to trump the state and its efforts to expand bureaucratic influence over business and industry. The 1956 Dōyūkai declaration noted, "If managers do not fulfill their responsibilities, we must be concerned that the autonomy of firms will be compromised by the intervention of state power and that economic advancement will thus become impossible." Ibid., 120. Compare Weinstein, *For Social Peace in Brazil,* 2–3.

given to "environmental" factors: the rise of a confrontational (though ultimately defanged) labor movement, shifts in the scale of production and the structure of industry, advances in technology, the transformation of the international economy, and the emergence of a professional managerial class steeped in the technocratic values and methodological approaches of Scientific Management.[122] Given such developments, it is hardly surprising that a "revised Taylorite" settlement—promising both rigorous technical efficiency and a "humanized" integration of labor—was even more attractive to Japanese managers in 1955 than it had been three decades earlier.

As was shown by the increasing receptiveness of business, the thawing of labor resistance, and the public enthusiasm for Prime Minister Ikeda's productivist "Income Doubling Plan" of 1960, a broad consensus on the ideology of productivity was attained by the tenth anniversary of the JPC. But the forging of this ideological compact was only half of the story of managerial reform in postwar Japan. As Mori Gorō and Matsushima Shizuo have noted, while management all but cracked the problem of organized labor by 1960—thanks to the carrot of productivism and the stick of union busting—managers still had to face the long-standing dilemma of how best to organize the production process and supervise workers on the shop floor.[123] The logic of *seisansei* established the ideological parameters for the reform of managerial practice and promised the mutual commitment of labor and management to a cooperative, growth-oriented strategy. Yet while the success of the movement hinged on the provision of an ever-growing pie, the productivity program was remarkably nebulous on the question of how industrial management was actually to achieve such growth. Significantly, in the productivist approach, the authority of managers—as experts, as "neutral" intermediaries between capital and labor, and as the self-appointed fixers of modern society—was paramount. Now that Japanese managers had been accorded professional respect and social responsibility, the onus was clearly placed on them to deliver the much-anticipated fruits of *seisansei*. In the search for the improved management methods which would ensure a growing pie—as in the postwar search for ideological accord with labor—Japanese managers would look both to the United States and to their own past practice of Taylorism.

---

[122] See, for example, Johnson, *MITI,* 313; Sumiya Mikio, "Contemporary Arrangements: An Overview," in Ōkōchi, Karsh and Levine, *Workers and Employers,* 49–87; Gordon, *Evolution,* chaps. 9–10; Murakami, *Seisansei,* 114–15; Elizabeth P. Tsunoda, "Rationalizing Japan's Political Economy: The Business Initiative 1920–1955" (Ph.D. diss., Columbia University, 1993), 549–50.

[123] Mori Gorō and Matsushima Shizuo, *Nihon rōmu kanri no gendaika* (Tokyo daigaku shuppankai, 1977), chap. 2.

5

The Long Shadow of Taylorism

LABOR RELATIONS AND "LEAN PRODUCTION," 1945–1973

DESPITE THE EXPERIENCE of industrial collapse and economic prostration, Japanese faith in the methods of modern production management remained unshaken through war and defeat. Indeed, the very triumph of the United States—that birthplace of Taylorism and the assembly line—seemed to confirm to Japanese managers that production technology and managerial skills were the only sure foundations of national power. The abiding lesson of the economic catastrophe of World War II was not that modern management methods had failed Japan, but rather that Japan had failed to make the most out of imported techniques and approaches. Thus, in production management, as in managerial ideology, defeat and occupation did not precipitate a rupture with existing "best practice" so much as a renewed attentiveness to Scientific Management and American models of industrial administration.

Nevertheless, in their postwar homecoming to American management methods, Japanese businessmen and engineers discovered that much had changed in the landscape of U.S. management since the prewar heyday of the efficiency movement. In the 1930s, and especially during the Second World War—a period of remarkable development in American management thought—Japan was almost entirely isolated from the technical and philosophical transformations across the Pacific. Hence Japanese industry, which had at best an uncertain grasp of Scientific Management at the end of the war, was faced with a sometimes dizzying array of post-Taylorite refinements, non-Taylorite innovations, and anti-Taylorite invectives. How these imported approaches were received and digested—as well as how they intersected with (and ultimately reaffirmed) the existing "revised Taylorite" consensus—constituted a central dynamic in the evolution of Japanese production management in the quarter century after 1945.

The Old and the New in Occupied Japan

As was the case with many institutions of Japan's wartime mobilization, the management reform movement made the transition to peace with striking continuities in personnel and organization. A few management-related organs—

notably the Labor Science Research Institute—did become targets of Occupation demilitarization,[1] yet the vast majority of associations and individual specialists concerned with managerial issues escaped any official taint of war responsibility. Unlike the business world, where economic crisis and the purge opened the way for a younger generation of "new managers," the modern management movement underwent no major changes in leadership in the wake of defeat. Not surprisingly, the reformers' approach changed little during war and occupation: Scientific Management techniques continued as the methodological backbone—and "revised Taylorite" thought as the intellectual core—of the immediate postwar efficiency movement.

The Japan Efficiency Association, the vanguard organization of the movement, weathered the dislocations of defeat but floundered in the postwar industrial doldrums. Cut off from government subsidies—which had sustained the association's wartime activities—the organization shriveled to a fraction of its former size. In 1946, its staff was slashed to just seventeen full-time workers, and cash had to be raised through black market sales of raw materials donated by sympathetic companies.[2] The association aimed to support itself through management consulting, yet conditions at the time were hardly auspicious for such an undertaking. Hyperinflation, endemic shortages, and mass unemployment made managerial reform and productive efficiency very low priorities in corporate boardrooms during the first years of the Occupation.[3]

Through persistence, the judicious use of wartime contacts, and the assistance of the state bureaucracy, however, the Efficiency Association was able to make a remarkable recovery in spite of the harsh industrial environment. The association's first consultancy assignment was with Hitachi Rolling Stock, a contractor to the JNR (a long-time proponent of Scientific Management), and other much-needed business was provided through the Ministries of Commerce and Transportation. The consulting service was recommended to firms involved in the government's "Priority Production Program" (Keisha Seisan Hōshiki), and the organization carried out extensive training and work

---

[1] The institute was dissolved in 1945 due to its connections with Sanpō, yet was later allowed to reorganize by the Occupation authorities. Miura Toyohiko, *Rōdō to kenkō no rekishi,* vol. 6 (Kawasaki: Rōdō kagaku kenkyūjo, 1990), 135, 147–48.

[2] Nakaoka Tetsurō, "Senchū, sengo no kagakuteki kanri undō II," *Keizaigaku zasshi* 82, no. 3 (September 1981): 43.

[3] Onitsuka Mitsumasa, "Sengo Nihon ni okeru seisan kanri no hatten," in *Sengo Nihon no kigyō keiei,* ed. Sengo Nihon keiei kenkyūkai (Bunshindō, 1991), 216–17. The poverty and pessimism of early postwar Japan was revealed in a roundtable discussion by business leaders published in the magazine *Enjinia kurabu* (Engineers' Club) in 1948. The industrialists agreed that Japan should have an automobile industry, but earnestly debated whether it should produce vehicles powered by charcoal or by coalite. "Keizai fukkō keikaku to yūso, seisan, gijutsu," *Enjinia kurabu* 5 (3 October 1948): 2; Nakaoka Tetsurō, "QC Nihon no shūhon de," in *Sengo Nihon o kangaeru,* ed. Hidaka Rokurō (Chikuma shobō, 1986), 62.

redesign programs in the coal industry.[4] A major boost was provided by the Dodge deflation of 1949 and the subsequent Korean War boom. Although association president Morikawa Kakuzō described 1949 as "Japan's most painful year,"[5] consulting contracts increased 20 percent as industry was rudely awakened to the need for "management rationalization." By the end of the Occupation, the Efficiency Association had achieved stability and independence in its finances, sponsored considerable educational and promotional activities, and could boast a staff of more than fifty consultants.[6]

The Efficiency Association's training and consulting was almost entirely Taylorite in content and, at least until the early 1950s, was virtually indistinguishable from the organization's wartime work. Most of the association's projects centered on the standard methods of Scientific Management long used in Japan: time-and-motion study, plant layout, waste elimination, jig design, and so on.[7] In fact, the Efficiency Association went as far as declaring that "the goal of this organization is widely disseminating the principles of Scientific Management derived from the work of Taylor."[8] In 1950, the association's journal *Nihon nōritsu* (Japan Efficiency) even published a special edition solemnly commemorating the thirty-fifth anniversary of Frederick Winslow Taylor's death.[9]

The revival of interest in Scientific Management and its American pioneers was accompanied by the unexpected return to prominence of several luminaries of the interwar efficiency movement. The most notable of these was Ueno Yōichi, who had sunk into obscurity during the war, scorned by the bureaucracy and the military as an unprofessional "popularizer."[10] His reputation was restored, however, when Occupation reformers, impressed by Ueno's

[4] Nihon nōritsu kyōkai, *10 nenkan no sokuseki* (1952), 56 ff.; Nakaoka, "Senchū, sengo II," 46; "Tankō gōrika undō no tenbō," *Seisan nōritsu* 4, no. 4 (July 1949): 1; Tsūshō sangyō shō, *Shōkō seisaku shi 10: Sangyō gōrika II* (Shōkō seisaku shi kankōkai, 1972), 276.

[5] Morikawa Kakuzō, *Keiei gōrika no soshiki* (Daiyamondo, 1950), 2.

[6] Nihon nōritsu kyōkai, *10 nenkan,* 62. Contracts jumped a further 30 percent in 1951 as a result of the Korean War expansion; Nakaoka Tetsurō, "Production Management in Japan before the Period of High Economic Growth," *Osaka City University Economic Review* 17 (1981): 14.

[7] Nihon nōritsu kyōkai, *10 nenkan,* 67; Nakaoka, "Senchū, sengo II," 46–48.

[8] Nihon nōritsu kyōkai, *10 nenkan,* 113.

[9] *Nihon nōritsu* 9, no. 4 (May 1950). The issue included essays by such veterans of the Japanese Scientific Management movement as Hoshino Yukinori, Teruoka Gitō, Andō Yaichi, Katō Shigeo, and Inoue Yoshikazu. One writer contributed a fictionalized tearoom conversation between Ueno Yōichi and a resurrected Frederick Winslow Taylor.

[10] Like fellow Taylorite Araki Tōichirō, Ueno was a bitter and open critic of the war in its latter stages. Due to his professional marginalization, however, Ueno never incurred official rebuke. Ueno Yōichi, *Ueno Yōichi den,* ed. Misawa Hitoshi (Sangyō nōritsu tanki daigaku, 1967), 223; Andrew Gordon, "Araki Tōichirō and the Shaping of Labor Management," in *Japanese Management in Historical Perspective,* ed. Yui Tsunehiko and Nakagawa Keiichirō, Proceedings of the Fifteenth International Conference on Business History (Tokyo: University of Tokyo Press, 1989), 179.

presidency of the Japan branch of the Taylor Society, selected him as one of the original commissioners of the National Personnel Agency (Jinjiin).[11] Ueno's narrow devotion to the gospel of efficiency had only been confirmed by the war, and although he emerged as a somewhat curious museum piece in the postwar management movement, the Taylorite approach he espoused remained broadly relevant in Occupation-era Japan.

Despite the long-standing (and lasting) consensus among managers that reform on a Taylorite model would be beneficial for Japanese industry, the impression remained strong that Scientific Management (at least as practiced in Japan) was far from perfect. On the one hand, the sense that Taylorite approaches required further "humanizing" to be effective continued to worry Japanese management experts. Especially in the turbulent context of postwar industrial relations, the need for "revised Taylorite" strategies that could boost efficiency without unduly alienating labor seemed more pressing than ever to many observers.[12] On the other hand, there was considerable concern that Japanese Taylorism was stagnant and that even "best practice" methods were ineffective and outdated. Emerging from the isolation and economic chaos of the war, many experts sought new scientific techniques and imported managerial tools that would revive and promote modern management in Japan.[13]

Not surprisingly, many of the shortcomings of Taylorism which worried Japan's scientific managers had also troubled their American counterparts. Since the Great Depression, management theory and practice had moved in two general directions in the United States. First, in reaction to Taylorite dehumanization and the challenge of New Deal industrial unionism, a systematic, scientific approach to the "human element" in factory management (the Human Relations school) was articulated and widely adopted. Second, renewed efforts to perfect Taylorite management through empirical refinement and scientific innovation (such as industrial engineering and operations research) flourished during the mass production mobilization for World War II.[14] In the latter half of the Occupation, both of these streams of management thought attracted Japanese attention. Both were greeted by an enthusiastic audience, one intellectually

---

[11] Yamashita Okiie, a longtime critic of Ueno's "unscientific" approach to Scientific Management, was ironically enough another one of the three original commissioners of the Jinjiin. Ueno, *Ueno Yōichi den,* 223.

[12] See, for example, Awaji Enjirō, "Keiei kanri jō no hyūman rireeshonzu," *Hyūman rireeshonzu,* ed. Odaka Kunio et al. (Daiyamondo, 1952), 30 ff.; Kobayashi Yasuo, *Kagakuteki kanri to rōdō* (Osaka: Nunoi shobō, 1953), 231–32; Noda Nobuo and Mori Gorō, ed., *Rōmu kanri kindaika no jitsurei* (Daiyamondo, 1954), 423–28.

[13] Kiribuchi Kanzō, *Kōjō keiei no jissai* (Iwasaki shoten, 1951), preface.

[14] See Stephen P. Waring, *Taylorism Transformed: Scientific Management Theory since 1945* (Chapel Hill: University of North Carolina Press, 1991), 9–19; Richard Gillespie, *Manufacturing Knowledge: A History of the Hawthorne Experiments* (Cambridge: Cambridge University Press, 1992), chaps. 7–9.

prepared by thirty years' experience with Taylorism and highly receptive to the latest American reformulations of Scientific Management.

Information on the Human Relations (HR) approach entered Japan soon after the end of the war and spread rapidly. Tokyo University professor Baba Keiji is usually credited with introducing HR thought to Japan in 1949.[15] Other academics followed Baba's lead, and reports on Elton Mayo, industrial sociology, and the seminal Hawthorne experiments soon appeared in profusion in management journals. The impression that Human Relations represented the state of the art in U.S. management—as well as the apparent intellectual linkages between HR and "democratization"—promoted considerable curiosity about the new import. By the early 1950s, an active and sophisticated dialogue on Human Relations thought emerged in academic and business circles, and HR techniques (such as suggestion systems and attitude surveys) began to appear in practice in Japanese industry.[16] Interest in HR was not limited to the management elite: public awareness was greatly increased when, in 1950, the Japanese edition of *Readers' Digest* published an article on Human Relations which maintained that "happy feelings" made for efficient workers.[17]

The simplicity and commonsensical appeal of the HR message clearly struck a chord with Japanese managers. As one noted after visiting the United States, Human Relations practitioners appreciated the obvious fact that time and muscle power could be bought, but that the enthusiasm of workers could not.[18] "Economic measures alone will not suffice in management rationalization," a 1952 study declared; "Out of necessity, broader social, psychological, and moral needs must also be considered and addressed."[19] Many Japanese commentators called for modern, American-style Human Relations in place of the "predemocratic," "feudal" heritage of Japanese labor management practice, and as a necessary corrective to the dehumanizing "overrationality" of Taylorite mass production.[20] One analyst argued that managerial insensitivity to the social and psychological requirements of workers was the fundamental flaw of prewar rationalization. Another suggested that the evolutionary trajectory of modern management ran from Taylorism through labor science to

[15] Mizutani Masaichi, "Wagakuni ningen kankei kanri no genjō to mondaiten," in Nikkeiren, *Hyūman rireeshonzu,* (Nikkeiren, 1957), 120; "Teidan: Amerika-shiki keiei kanri no juyō to fukyū," *Keiei to rekishi* 10 (July 1987): 13–14.

[16] Noda Kazuo, ed., *Sengo Keieishi* (Nihon seisansei honbu, 1965), 669–72; Mori Gorō, *Sengo Nihon no rōmu kanri* (Daiyamondo, 1961), 85–86. A 1950 study by the Kantō Managers Association (Kantō Keieisha Kyōkai) showed that over 30 percent of the 365 companies surveyed used some sort of HR-inspired management technique.

[17] "Rōmusha ni wa tekishita shigoto o ataeyo!" *Seisan nōritsu* 5, no. 5 (May 1950): 10.

[18] Nakase Jūichi, *Sengo Nihon no keiei rinen shi* (Kyōto: Hōritsu bunka sha, 1967), 118–19.

[19] Odaka Kunio et al., *Hyūman rireeshonzu* (Daiyamondo, 1952), 1–2.

[20] Takamiya Susumu, "Jinji kanri no hatten," *Keizai* 1, no. 3 (April 1947): 9–11; Odaka Kunio, "Keiei ni okeru ningen no mondai," *Rōmu kenkyū* 2, no. 5 (May 1949): 7–11.

Human Relations, and that Japanese industry would eventually have to trace this path.[21]

Underlying the "Human Relations boom" and all of the various arguments in favor of industrial sociology was the sense that this newfound approach was particularly timely and germane in occupied Japan. In the context of an assertive labor movement's demands for "respect as human beings" and "full membership" in the firm for workers, HR offered management a coherent (and not particularly threatening) framework for discussing the humanization and democratization of industry. As an "objective," managerial (and thus presumably apolitical) solution to the problem of worker dissatisfaction, Human Relations—like the productivity ideology—promised the pacification of labor relations, but without the loss of management authority. Moreover, at a time when union power made companies wary of incentive wages schemes and when the spiritualistic, nationalistic rhetoric of the past had been discredited, Japanese industrialists welcomed a new, social-scientific basis for stimulating worker morale and productivity.[22]

HR was not embraced with blind enthusiasm by all, however. A number of detractors argued persistently that Japanese industry had no need for the Hawthorne experiments or American teachings on "communications" and "teamwork." Japanese business, these critics maintained, traditionally favored warm human relations and the psychological well-being of its workers over Western-style technological rationality.[23] While this reprise of the language of "beautiful customs" may well have seemed reassuring to many beleaguered postwar managers, the proponents of HR emphasized that it was more than familial rhetoric and the provision of welfare facilities. HR, management reformers constantly stressed, was not *noblesse oblige* or warm emotionalism, but a systematic, scientific approach to the "human problem" in modern industry.[24] As one specialist put it,

It has long been appreciated, especially in traditional Japanese labor management . . . , that human relations are a significant factor in increasing productivity and boosting efficiency in industry. What we now call HR is, however, quite different

[21] Eto Saburō, "Rōmu kanri no kindaika ni tsuite," in Noda and Mori, *Rōmu kanri,* 15–27; Kaneko Hiroshi, "Shokuba moraaru no bunseki," *Rōmu kenkyū* 2, no. 5 (May 1949): 18–20.

[22] See "Teidan: Amerika-shiki keiei kanri," 14; "Kōjō mo mata hitotsu no shakai," *Seisan nōritsu* 4, no. 5 (August 1949): 1; "Ibara no michi ni manabu kanri gijutsu no shimei," ibid., no. 6 (September 1949): 1.

[23] JUSE TWI kenkyūkai, *Kaisha, kōjō ni okeru TWI jisshi no keikaku to kōka no hakki* (Nihon kagaku gijutsu renmeikai, 1951), 130; "Hyūman rireeshonzu no Nihonteki genjitsu," *Seisansei* (June 1959): 14; Mori, *Sengo Nihon,* 117–22; Kaneko, "Shokuba moraaru," 18. On the persistence of this view, see Takezawa Shin'ichi, "Nihon ni okeru keiei kyōiku," *Sangyō kunren* 31, no. 363 (November–December 1985): 45; Tsuda Masumi, "Study of Japanese Management Development Practices II," *Hitotsubashi Journal of Arts and Sciences* 18, no. 1 (September 1977): 6.

[24] Eto, "Rōmu kanri," 22; Nihon seisansei honbu, *Hyūman rireeshon,* Productivity Report 12 (1957), 5; Odaka Kunio, *Sangyō ni okeru ningen kankei no kagaku* (Yūhikaku, 1953).

from the time-honored Japanese practice of relying on feudal relationships bolstered by spiritualism. What is known as HR in the U.S. and Europe is not premised on totalitarian methods or control from above. Rather, it attempts to deal with human relations in the workplace through a scientific approach to mental attitudes and spiritual desires. . . .[25]

Despite the doubts of traditionalists (and the dismissal of HR as "scientific paternalism" by some on the political left),[26] a tentative consensus on the value of Human Relations had emerged in Japanese management circles by the early 1950s. The mainstream of management thinking affirmed the HR approach as a useful, even necessary, component of factory administration, and agreed that Japanese industry had long appreciated the importance of the "human element," albeit not in a scientific, modern form. Nevertheless, as virtually all observers seemed to agree, Human Relations was not considered a replacement for Scientific Management in Japan, but rather a complement to it. Many experts noted that, in light of Japan's technological and managerial backwardness, industry could not afford to focus solely on humanization but had to pursue wide-scale Taylorite rationalization at the same time. As engineer Shingō Shigeo explained in 1951, there were two fundamental elements to manufacturing: the methods of work (as determined through Scientific Management) and the will to work (as addressed by HR).[27] In short, Japanese managers came to assume that growth depended on the rationalization and modernization of both the human aspect of management and the economic, technical components of industrial production.[28]

What is striking about this Japanese conception of Human Relations is its deviation from the philosophical assumptions (if not the actual practice) of the American HR movement. In the United States, HR was understood on a theoretical level as the antithesis of Taylorism, as an approach to factory organization fundamentally at odds with Scientific Management and its starkly efficient imperatives. The Japanese view of Human Relations apparently accorded more with American reality than with American theory. In application, HR techniques and rhetoric proved remarkably compatible with mass production and Taylorite methods in the United States as well as in Japan. As business historians have increasingly recognized, the two approaches were far closer intellectually, politically, and methodologically than their respective

---

[25] Kiribuchi Kanzō, "Hito no katsudō kara mita keiei," in *Keiei no sōgō kanri,* ed. Kiribuchi Kanzō, Kōjō keiei jitsumu kōza, vol. 1 (Nihon keizaisha, 1952), 105.

[26] Nihon seisansei honbu, *Hyūman rireeshon,* 91; Nakase, *Sengo Nihon,* 32 ff.

[27] Shingō Shigeo, *Seisan kanri no kaizen* (Nihon keizaisha, 1951), 2.

[28] Eto, "Rōmu kanri," 18–21; Noda Nobuo, "Rōmu kanri no genjō to shōrai no arikata," in Noda and Mori, *Rōmu kanri,* 6. The Efficiency Association presented a somewhat more sanguine view of the new emphasis on Human Relations: "The management of people is one face of management, but the elimination of people by mechanization and automation is rationalization's other side." Nihon nōritsu kyōkai, *10 nenkan,* 125.

proponents in America ever cared to acknowledge.[29] Certainly in Japan, philosophical incompatibility was never a stumbling block to the assimilation of the Human Relations school. HR was accepted within the rubric of the existing "revised Taylorite" consensus and, as with prewar paternalism and the wartime concern with "spiritual guidance," it was not considered a barrier to the rationalization of the production process.[30]

The easy accommodation of the seemingly contradictory Human Relations and Taylorite approaches was revealed almost comically in the publication program of the Japan Efficiency Association. In a single year, the association released both a Japanese version of Mayo's HR classic *The Human Problems of an Industrial Civilization* and a new Ueno Yōichi translation of *Cheaper by the Dozen,* the romanticized account of Frank Gilbreth and his family that defined the efficiency movement in the American popular imagination.[31] In the end, as the unselfconscious reconciliation of Mayo and Gilbreth suggests, Human Relations did not undermine Japanese faith in Scientific Management, but buttressed the "revised Taylorite" emphasis on "the human element" with new scientific evidence and fresh American affirmation.

Reconnecting with American Management

Although the apparent ease with which HR was integrated into Japanese management thinking was noteworthy, it was not the only Occupation-era import to be so readily embraced. Of particular significance were several high-profile, American-sponsored initiatives that aimed to elevate and reform Japanese management practices through infusions of advanced U.S. methods. While the techniques and philosophies transferred may have fallen short of being revolutionary in their impact, the American efforts did play a major role in stimulating the progress of modern management in postwar Japan. In outlining new empirical refinements to Scientific Management, in publicizing Human Relations (under the banner of democratization), and especially in promoting management training programs, the Occupation's accomplishments were considerable.

The main U.S. initiative in managerial reform grew out of Occupation frustrations with efficiency and quality in the Japanese electronics industry. The occupiers—who looked to develop a modern communications network and encourage local suppliers of telephones and radios—soon found that the prewar reputation of Japanese manufactures as "cheap and shoddy" was still well

[29] Waring, *Taylorism Transformed,* 18–19; Daniel A. Wren, *The Evolution of Management Thought,* 4th ed. (New York: Wiley, 1994), 250–51, 373–75.

[30] On the continuities between paternalism and HR, see Mori Gorō and Matsushima Shizuo, *Nihon rōmu kanri no gendaika* (Tokyo daigaku shuppankai, 1977), 20–25, 233; Mori, *Sengo Nihon,* 210–18.

[31] Nihon nōritsu kyōkai, *10 nenkan,* 17.

deserved. Responsibility for improving the production of much-needed tele-communications equipment fell to the Industrial Division of the Civil Communications Section (CCS) of the American headquarters, and particularly to three members of the unit: Homer Sarasohn, Charles Protzman, and Frank Polkinghorn. These officers—all engineers with experience in major U.S. corporations—worked closely with Japanese firms, inspecting, advising, and often berating owners and managers. Although electronics was one of the more managerially advanced sectors in prewar Japan, the Occupation engineers despaired of Japan's crude production techniques and lax administrative standards. Unable to overcome persistent defect rates of 50 to almost 100 percent in communications hardware, Sarasohn and his colleagues concluded that fundamental retraining was the only option for strengthening Japanese management and salvaging Japanese industry.[32]

The program that emerged from this dissatisfaction in the Civil Communications Section was an intensive eight-week seminar—known simply as the "CCS course"—that was offered to top executives of Japanese electronics firms during 1949 and 1950. The seminar, designed and presented by Sarasohn and Protzman, was structured as a comprehensive introduction to "best practice" methods of production management and corporate organization in the United States. The content of the course was eclectic, running the gamut from the mundane (shop cleanliness and safety) to the philosophical (the goals of industry, the character of managers, and so forth). The bulk of material presented was in a Taylorite vein and stressed the importance of scientific, empirical approaches to planning, organization, cost management, and quality. At the same time, Human Relations thought also figured prominently: the CCS textbook implored Japanese managers to seek cooperation, communications, and teamwork. "Workers must be given more than just wages," the seminar emphasized, "even employees must be treated as people."[33] Above all, however, the course stressed the tremendous responsibilities of corporate management and the need for firm, proficient, and humane leadership in industry. "A country's fate," Sarasohn warned his Japanese students, "rests on the shoulders of its business leaders."[34]

Despite the breadth of its message, the CCS course was, in practice, a rather limited effort: offered just twice under American sponsorship, it directly reached only a small fraction of Japan's managerial elite. Nevertheless, as one

---

[32] On the CCS activities in management reform, see the detailed studies by Kenneth Hopper: "Creating Japan's New Industrial Management: The Americans as Teachers," *Human Resource Management* (Summer 1982): 13–34, and "Quality, Japan and the U.S.: The First Chapter," *Quality Progress* (September 1985): 34–41. See also Robert Chapman Wood, "A Lesson Learned and a Lesson Forgotten," *Forbes,* 6 February 1989, 70–78.

[33] Nihon denki tsūshin kōgyō rengōkai, Keiei kanri kenkyūkai, *CCS keiei kōza,* 2 vols. (Daiyamondo, 1952), 2:207.

[34] Ibid., 1:15.

of the first postwar conduits for up-to-date American management thinking, the course's teachings did prove influential in the business world.[35] Other management training initiatives sponsored by the Occupation were considerably more ambitious in scope from their inceptions. Training Within Industry (TWI) was a program originally developed to provide leadership skills to new foremen in America's wartime workshops. With the aim of "spreading the scientific spirit and democracy" to first-line supervisors,[36] TWI was introduced in Japan in 1950 with the cooperation of the Labor Ministry. A similar scheme for furnishing middle managers with basic administrative theory—the Management Training Program (MTP)—was also promoted by the Occupation authorities in association with the Ministry of International Trade and Industry (and later, Nikkeiren). Both training courses were accepted enthusiastically and rapidly by industry, and soon assumed mass movement dimensions: by 1954, 46,000 managers had taken MTP, while over 300,000 had completed the TWI program.[37] The systematic diffusion of modern management thought on such a scale (and to such an audience) was unprecedented in Japan.

In spite of the achievements of CCS, TWI, and MTP, observers of Japan's postwar management history have tended to discount the importance of the Occupation's education programs. The CCS course, one Japanese commentator noted, left "no great legacy" and American-style supervisory and middle management training enjoyed only faddish successes.[38] Other historians have argued that the Occupation efforts, while ambitious, actually offered "nothing that new" to Japanese managers.[39] Nevertheless, while the training programs may not have reshaped Japanese conceptions of business administration, their importance in creating a broader consciousness of modern management should not be overlooked. The conclusion of one executive that, after CCS, "the scales had fallen from my eyes" is surely hyperbolic,[40] but the courses were significant in reconnecting Japanese managers with current trends in

[35] A crucial factor in this spreading influence was the translation of the seminar text (by efficiency movement veteran Katō Takeo) and the reoffering of the course with Japanese instructors. Tsuda Masumi, "Study of Japanese Management Development Practices I," *Hitotsubashi Journal of Social Studies* 9, no. 1 (May 1977): 10.

[36] Ōuchi Tsuneo, "Wagakuni ni okeru TWI undō ni tsuite," *Rōmu kenkyū* 3, no. 7 (July 1950): 3.

[37] Tsuda, "Study of Japanese Management Development Practices I," 11–12; see also Lola Okazaki-Ward, *Management Education and Training in Japan* (London: Graham and Trotman, 1993), 29–31.

[38] "Teidan: Amerika-shiki keiei kanri," 14–15; see also Mori and Matsushima, *Nihon rōmu kanri,* 25.

[39] Sasaki Satoshi and Nonaka Izumi, "Nihon ni okeru kagakuteki kanrihō no dōnyū to tenkai," in *Kagakuteki kanrihō no dōnyū to tenkai—sono rekishiteki kokusai hikaku,* ed. Hara Terushi (Kyōto: Shōwadō, 1990), 266.

[40] Hopper, "New Industrial Management," 21.

American managerial thought. As many observers have conceded, the Occupation initiatives were a powerful catalyst, "enlightening" participants and stirring postwar curiosity in imported management techniques.[41] Moreover, as would become apparent in the days of the "management boom," the various courses performed the crucial function of giving managers at all levels of the firm a "common language" of management, something that had been lacking in prewar Japanese industry.[42]

Although both Human Relations and American training schemes were novel concepts in postwar Japan, their appeal is easy to understand in the context of Occupation-era industrial management. On the one hand, the new imports appeared to address two widely perceived lessons of the managerial debacle of World War II: first, that Japanese management required more science and less empty spiritualism; and second, that systematic education of managers was necessary to transcend the laxity, arbitrariness, and irrationality of past practice.[43] As Japanese managers appreciated, the highly structured Occupation initiatives and the scientific (yet humane) HR philosophy spoke to both these concerns. At the same time, training and Human Relations also offered companies some hope of relief and support in the politically charged climate of postwar labor relations. Management training—particularly TWI—promised better managerial discipline and consistency, and armed supervisors with new, HR-based strategies for subduing labor resistance.[44] Training, of course, also reinforced the postwar emphasis on professionalized, "neutral" managerialism, providing a concrete expression of managers' ideological justification for their status in the firm.

More fundamental, however, in making Human Relations and U.S. management training so accessible to a Japanese audience was their congruence with existing modes of management thought. By the end of the Occupation, HR was comfortably integrated into the "revised Taylorite" assumptions of Japanese management experts. The content of the American education programs also proved a good fit with established approaches. The engineers who designed the CCS course, for example, considered their thinking authentically Taylorite, although leavened with a touch of HR humanism.[45] TWI

[41] Onitsuka, "Sengo Nihon," 220; Nihon nōritsu kyōkai, *Keiei to tomo ni* (1982), 68; Noda Nobuo, "How Japan Absorbed American Management Methods," in *Modern Japanese Management* (London: Management Publications, Ltd./The British Institute of Management, 1970), 53.

[42] "Teidan: Amerika-shiki keiei kanri," 15.

[43] Shingō, *Seisan kanri,* 1–3; Nihon nōritsu kyōkai, *10 nenkan,* 3; Tanaka Kunio, "Watakushi wa hinshitsu kanri o kō kangaeru," *Hinshitsu kanri* 3, no. 8 (August 1952): 2; Katō Takeo, *Keiei no hanashi, keiei kaizen no kyūsho* (Manejimento kyōkai, 1950), 204.

[44] Gillespie, *Manufacturing Knowledge,* 234–39; Tsuda, "Study of Japanese Management Development Practices I," 11.

[45] Hopper, "New Industrial Management," 28. As Robert Chapman Wood observed, "Like many of America's best engineers at the time—and like many Japanese managers today—

was a hybrid construction as well: while heavy on Human Relations and "democratizing" rhetoric, it was grounded in Taylorite strategies and the rationalization of the work process.[46] One Japanese trainee remarked with some surprise that "TWI is the combination of things which aren't really new at all."[47] Indeed, although there was great change in American management during the Depression and war, much of it was evolutionary rather than revolutionary at core, thus making the postwar reintegration of American practice with Japanese thinking remarkably smooth. In other words, with an extensive prewar background of familiarity with the ideas (if not always the application) of Scientific Management, Japanese managers could readily comprehend postwar U.S. approaches. While Tsuda Masumi has called the Occupation-era introduction of American management methods "transplanting," it seems that "grafting" would be a more apt metaphor for the first wave of postwar importation.[48]

The "Miracle Economy" and Management Reform

Reconnecting with American "best practice" may have replenished the technical arsenal of Japanese management reformers, yet it was profound postwar shifts in the economic, political, and social context of Japanese industry that gave rise to an environment highly conducive to sweeping managerial change. The basic foundations of a modern mass production system were laid in Japan's long wartime mobilization: the transition to heavy industry, the growing ranks of skilled managerial and production personnel, and the trial-and-error experience of wartime assembly-line manufacturing formed the crucial bedrock for postwar developments. The fertile conditions were also shaped significantly by Occupation reformism, which (even after a conservative swing in midcourse) greatly increased levels of intercorporate competition, injected new blood into managerial hierarchies, and enhanced the bargaining power of industrial labor. Perhaps most importantly, in Japan's post-Occupation "era of high-speed growth," the major impediments which had stood in the way of widespread Taylorization and the attainment of mass production in prewar

---

Sarasohn and Protzman saw no conflict between 'scientific' management that carefully measured and analyzed everything about a company, and 'democratic' management that fully respected employees." Wood, "A Lesson Learned," 75.

[46] As Ōuchi Tsuneo described it, TWI harmonized rationality and humanity, avoiding the "sentimentalism" and "favoritism" of past labor management, as well as the "heartless techniques" of "so-called efficiency experts." Ōuchi Tsuneo, "TWI to kantokusha kyōiku," in Noda Nobuo et al., *Amerika no keiei gijutsu* (Daiyamondo, 1951), 118.

[47] Yokouchi Tatsuo, "TWI jukō oyobi kunren jisshi no kansō," *Rōmu kenkyū*, 3, no. 7 (July 1950): 33.

[48] Tsuda, "Study of Japanese Management Development Practices I," 10.

Japan were finally overcome. While the productivist consensus of the late 1950s formed the ideological infrastructure for the diffusion of Scientific Management, a constellation of related economic and political developments—the attainment of mass markets for Japanese goods, the provision of adequate investment capital, the rewards of a pervasive "technological revolution," and the snowballing effects of industrial growth itself—would prove essential catalysts in the postwar transformation of Japanese factory management.

Japanese industrialists had long considered the lack of large, dependable markets as a fundamental barrier to the introduction of mass production techniques in Japan. Prior to World War II, when the business strategy of low-wage, labor-intensive production suppressed the growth of consumer markets at home, only export-oriented sectors (like textiles) and armaments makers could achieve sophisticated, high-volume standards of manufacturing. In the rubble of Japan's defeat, however, bureaucratic and corporate leaders grudgingly came to acknowledge that the establishment of a dynamic domestic base of mass consumption was essential to economic regeneration and the attainment of critical economies of scale in industrial production.[49] The commitment to a high-wage/low-cost developmental model was institutionalized in the Japan Productivity Center and enshrined in public policy (as well as in the popular imagination) by Prime Minister Ikeda Hayato's "Income Doubling Plan" of 1960.[50] Yet the importance of domestic demand as a motor of economic growth and as a stimulant to mass production methods in industry had already been established in practice by the early 1950s. Japan's first "consumption boom" followed the economic windfall of the Korean War, and through the 1950s and 1960s unprecedented levels of domestic consumption provided Japanese manufacturers with the markets necessary to justify sweeping programs of technological improvement and managerial reform.[51]

At the same time, a large postwar expansion in export markets furnished another ready outlet for the products of Japan's new assembly lines. With the American-sponsored establishment of an open world trade structure and a stable global monetary system, the volume of international commerce grew steadily, tripling in the short span between 1955 and 1970.[52] U.S. patronage

[49] See Laura Hein's *Fueling Growth: The Energy Revolution and Economic Policy in Postwar Japan* (Cambridge, Mass.: Harvard University Press, 1990), and her article "In Search of Peace and Democracy: Postwar Japanese Economic Debate in Political Context," *Journal of Asian Studies* 53, no. 3 (August 1994): 752–78.

[50] On the "Income Doubling Plan," see Uchino Tatsurō, *Japan's Postwar Economy,* trans. Mark A. Harbison (Tokyo: Kodansha, 1978), 113–15; Kosai Yutaka, *The Era of High-Speed Growth,* trans. Jacqueline Kaminski (Tokyo: University of Tokyo Press, 1986), 130–33.

[51] Kosai, *The Era of High-Speed Growth,* 74–76, 99–100; Uchino, *Japan's Postwar Economy,* 73–75, 104–8; Laura Hein, "Growth Versus Success: Japan's Economic Policy in Historical Perspective," in *Postwar Japan as History,* ed. Andrew Gordon (Berkeley: University of California Press, 1993), 112–15; Charles Yuji Horioka, "Consuming and Saving," ibid., 259–92.

[52] Nakamura Takafusa, *The Postwar Japanese Economy,* trans. Jacqueline Kaminski (Tokyo: University of Tokyo Press, 1981), 54–63.

was crucial in the postwar revival of Japanese trade: impelled by Cold War geopolitics, American policymakers endeavored to reintegrate Japan into the international economy as a vigorous "workshop of Asia."[53] Japanese exporters made the most out of this singular historical moment, expanding aggressively into overseas markets. Yet the reasons for Japan's trade successes went beyond mere opportunism. For example, a new bureaucratic apparatus for the promotion of exports, centered on the Ministry of International Trade and Industry, provided firms with critical financial assistance, information, and technical guidance in the pursuit of foreign markets.[54] In addition, and even more significantly, cost reductions achieved by technological rationalization and the accomplishment of mass production made Japanese manufacturers increasingly competitive on an international basis.

If insufficient markets were one major stumbling block on the path to thorough Taylorization in prewar Japan, the dearth of capital was another conspicuous obstacle to the wholesale modernization of Japanese factories. Although investment funds remained scarce even well after World War II, Japanese business and the state devised a variety of institutional arrangements for squeezing the utmost capital out of the domestic financial system and focusing it on industrial development. Government rationalization programs provided direct aid to firms, giving subsidies and tax breaks (such as accelerated depreciation allowances and outright exemptions) for new investments in plant and machinery. A number of specialized government financial institutions, most notably the Export-Import Bank and the Japan Development Bank, were established in the early 1950s as conduits for channeling funds to large private-sector producers. Most ingeniously, a system of bank "overloan" and corporate "overborrowing"—in which financial institutions made advances and firms assumed debt at levels far above conservative Western norms— made the most of Japan's limited supply of capital.[55] Moreover, as the citizens of "miracle economy" Japan became prodigious savers (as well as eager consumers), a steadily increasing flow of investment funds made possible the expansion and retooling of Japan's industrial workshops.[56]

The final crucial ingredient in the transition to a mass production system was technology. Compared to the prewar period, access to foreign (and particularly American) technological know-how was extraordinarily easy and inexpensive during the 1950s and 1960s. As a Cold War ally and, at least at the

[53] William S. Borden, *The Pacific Alliance: United States Foreign Economic Policy and Japanese Trade Recovery, 1947–1955* (Madison: University of Wisconsin Press, 1984).

[54] Chalmers Johnson, *MITI and the Japanese Miracle* (Stanford, Calif.: Stanford University Press, 1982), chap. 6.

[55] Kosai, *The Era of High-Speed Growth*, 88–90; Johnson, *MITI*, 203, 217–18; Yonekura Seiichirō, *The Japanese Iron and Steel Industry, 1850–1990* (New York: St. Martin's Press, 1994), 209, 224–26.

[56] Horioka, "Consuming and Saving."

time, an unthreatening economic rival, Japan was able to transfer state-of-the-art manufacturing techniques from the United States with few restrictions. Furthermore, because of the "technological gap" which had opened up between Japan and the industrial West during World War II, Japanese firms could draw on a wide range of overseas innovations and could judiciously pick and choose among various technological alternatives.[57] The transfer process was facilitated and encouraged by the Japanese state, yet the postwar "technological revolution" was driven primarily by private-sector competition, as Japanese enterprises vied with each other (and with their foreign counterparts) to reduce costs and secure new markets through technical advances in production.[58] As the 1956 Economic White Paper soberly declared, "technological innovations are the driving force behind investment activities; these in turn have wide repercussions through the whole economy, and propel modernization."[59]

Despite managerial faith that new machinery and methods would "propel modernization" in postwar industry, the reform of the production process hinged to a considerable extent on the existence of a favorable system of shop-floor labor relations. Labor's prominence within the firm increased substantially following World War II, yet by the end of the 1950s, the Occupation-era surge in the power of organized labor had largely been contained by corporate management. In the employment system that emerged from the labor turmoil of the first postwar decade, workers gained a new sense of membership in the enterprise as well as implicit guarantees of job security, but the preeminent authority of managers in the workplace was confirmed.[60] Managerial discretion over the structure and conditions of work was also bolstered by the general economic environment of the time: in a setting of rising incomes and consistent economic growth—which assured that even technological rationalization seldom meant job losses—labor was generally tolerant of creeping mechanization and shifting management norms.[61] Although managers did not enjoy a completely free hand—Chalmers Johnson's description of postwar labor as "a workforce made docile" is overstated[62]—Japanese firms did have considerable leeway in modify-

---

[57] Tessa Morris-Suzuki, *The Technological Transformation of Japan* (Cambridge: Cambridge University Press, 1994), 166–72.

[58] Yonekura, *The Japanese Iron and Steel Industry,* 212, 278–82; Kosai, *The Era of High-Speed Growth,* 86–87.

[59] Quoted in Johannes Hirschmeier and Yui Tsunehiko, *The Development of Japanese Business,* 2d ed. (London: Allen and Unwin, 1981), 292.

[60] Andrew Gordon, *The Evolution of Labor Relations in Japan: Heavy Industry, 1853–1955* (Cambridge, Mass.: Harvard University Press, 1985), chap. 10.

[61] Hein, *Fueling Growth,* 14–15, 240–42; Sumiya Mikio, "Contemporary Arrangements: An Overview," in *Workers and Employers in Japan,* ed. Ōkōchi Kazuo, Bernard Karsh, and Solomon Levine (Princeton, N.J.: Princeton University Press, 1974), 74–75.

[62] Johnson, *MITI,* 240.

ing production routines and introducing new manufacturing technology during the "miracle economy" decades.

In the late 1950s, as the mechanisms of high-speed growth began to mesh, a congenial chain reaction of consumption, investment, and technological progress was ignited in Japan. As predicted by the ideologues of the JPC (as well as by prewar Taylorites), an elaborate sequence of economic stimuli and managerial responses set Japan on the course of realizing a sustainable high-wage, high-productivity, low-cost industrial order. As economic growth surged, employment rose and, especially in the tight labor market of the 1960s, real wages increased briskly. The thicker wallets of Japanese workers fueled the postwar "consumption booms" while, at the same time, escalating labor costs created new incentives for mechanization and improved management practices in Japanese factories. Rising domestic demand and the pressure to control expenses sparked business investment in plant and equipment, increasing the scale and speed of manufacturing, and leading, in turn, to higher efficiency and reduced production costs. As new waves of investment and mounting productivity spurred further economic expansion, the cycle of growth, improved living standards and industrial advance—the "ever-growing pie" of the productivist vision—was set into motion once again.[63]

Thus, in the heady days of the "miracle economy," Japanese Taylorites seemed poised on the threshold of the managerial promised land. Half a century of goals appeared within reach as the economic pitfalls, institutional barriers, and conceptual hurdles of the past were swept away by the snowballing effects of growth, wealth, and innovation. Yet as the nitty-gritty process of "modernizing" labor management practices and introducing technological changes on the shop floor would demonstrate, even in an extremely favorable environment, the path to mass production and the Taylorized workshop was far from smooth. Moreover, as in the past, despite the durability of the "revised Taylorite" ideal, the trajectory of managerial change was not always predictable and Japan's scientific managers had to be adaptable and inventive in their ongoing endeavor of reform.

The Wage Conundrum

The wage system was one aspect of labor management where the course of postwar change was particularly rocky and convoluted. Wage determination procedures were, of course, a perennial source of friction in Japanese indus-

[63] Harry T. Oshima, "Reinterpreting Japan's Postwar Growth," *Economic Development and Cultural Change* 31, no. 1 (October 1982): 37–38; Morris-Suzuki, *Technological Transformation,* 164. For interesting statistics on the motivating factors in plant and equipment investment during the 1960s (which show the roughly equal weight Japanese managers placed on reducing labor costs and meeting new surges of demand), see Nakamura, *The Postwar Japanese Economy,* 181.

trial relations, yet seldom was the wage issue more charged than in the quarter century following World War II. As the employers of Nikkeiren declared in 1953, "The rational solution of the wage problem is the most important element in stabilizing labor relations, increasing labor efficiency, and, in turn, bringing industrial peace."[64] But as many observers (both at the time and in the decades since) have lamented, no "rational solution" was attained, with "modern" wage systems imported from the West consistently failing to supplant "traditional," "feudal" patterns of wage determination in Japan.[65] Nevertheless, as close scrutiny reveals, despite the sound and fury of postwar debates, the long-standing "revised Taylorite" approach was eventually reconfirmed and generalized as the basis for an enduring settlement of Japan's thorny wage tangle.

Wages were an incendiary issue in the immediate aftermath of the war, and Japan's energized labor movement was initially able to put its stamp on revised wage determination formulae in industry. Workers looked to institutionalize a need-based, livelihood wage system, termed the "labor version" by Andrew Gordon, that would be founded on "the logic of labor more than of capital."[66] Rejecting output-based efficiency schemes and wage structures set unilaterally (and seemingly capriciously) by management, labor sought pay packets responsive to fluctuations in the cost of living and tailored to the "objective" characteristics of individual workers (such as age, seniority, and family size).[67] A critical labor victory was the "Densan system," a livelihood wage formula wrung from management by the electric power workers in 1946. Under this plan, employees were guaranteed a minimum standard of living (pegged to changes in the price level) and base wages were set according to age and personal circumstances.[68] In a time of labor strength and corporate infirmity, the Densan arrangement became an important precedent for union demands and a much-copied prototype for wage settlements throughout Japanese industry.

Needless to say, the "labor version" of wages codified in the Densan system was extremely unpopular with managers. Livelihood provisions and cost-of-living guarantees diminished managerial discretion over wages and under-

---

[64] "Kihonteki rōdō taisaku ni kansuru iken" (June 4, 1953), in Nikkeiren sōritsu jūshūnen kinen kigyō iinkai, *Jūnen no ayumi* (1958), 201.

[65] See, for example, Noda Nobuo, "Nenkō chingin," *Seisansei* 2, no. 5 (May 1960): 58–59; Sakamoto Fujiyoshi, *Keieigaku nyūmon* (Kōbunsha, 1958), 114 ff.; Funahashi Naomichi, "The Industrial Reward System: Wages and Benefits," in Ōkōchi, Karsh, and Levine, *Workers and Employers in Japan,* 373–75.

[66] Gordon, *Evolution,* 355.

[67] Ibid., 349–62.

[68] "Densan" was the contracted form of Nihon denki sangyō rōdō kumiai, the name of the electrical workers' union. Ibid., 351–55; Hein, *Fueling Growth,* 98–106. According to Hein, 68.2 percent of the average wage packet was based on age and family size, 3.7 percent on seniority, 19.4 percent on skill level, and 8.7 percent on regional and seasonal differentials.

mined employers' long-standing reliance on monetary incentives. Managers continued to profess their faith in efficiency wages, but the use of output-based schemes declined precipitously in a climate of intense union hostility.[69] Even Japan's American occupiers, the original sponsors of the unions' post-war efflorescence, were none too comfortable with labor's livelihood wage concept. Invariably predisposed toward solutions "Made in the U.S.A.," Occupation officials promoted job wages—the state of the art in American industrial relations thought—as the most appropriate model for reform in Japan. The job wage system had roots stretching back to the turn of the century but was only institutionalized in the course of America's mobilization for World War II. Premised on the notion of "equal pay for equal work," job wages were based on the nature of the task being performed rather than on the personal attributes of the individual doing the work. Factors such as age and family situation were irrelevant in a job wage regime, and only systematic, scientifically framed measures of work content were used in classifying jobs and calculating standard pay rates.[70] Thus, in theory at least, American "best practice" stood fundamentally at odds with the "labor version" of wages ascendant in early postwar Japan.

The job wage concept was first introduced into Japan through the National Personnel Agency. Under Occupation pressure, and with the support of agency commissioners Ueno Yōichi and Yamashita Okiie, a job classification system and a new American-style wage structure were imposed on the civil service beginning in 1948.[71] Although this first experiment was not a conspicuous success, Japan's beleaguered employers soon embraced the imported job

[69] Gordon, *Evolution,* 358–60, 382; Ishida Mitsuo, "Chingin taikei to rōshi kankei I," *Nihon rōdō kyōkai zasshi* 27, no. 8 (August 1985): 6–7. See also Samada Mutsuo, "Seikatsukyū taikei kara nōritsukyū taikei e," *Nihon nōritsu* 8, no. 2 (February 1949): 10–12; Nikkeiren, *Jūnen no ayumi,* 106, 120. For statistical information on the long-term decline of efficiency wage use in postwar Japan, see Nikkeiren, *Wagakuni rōmu kanri no gensei,* Dai 3-kai rōmu kanri shoseido chōsa (Nikkeiren, 1971), 18.

[70] John Price, *Japan Works: Power and Paradox in Postwar Industrial Relations* (Ithaca, N.Y.: ILR Press, 1997), 69–71; Tsuda Masumi, "Study of Japanese Management Development Practices II," *Hitotsubashi Journal of Arts and Sciences* 18, no. 1 (September 1977): 2–3; Funahashi, "The Industrial Reward System," 368–69. On the job wage system in the United States, see Sanford Jacoby, *Employing Bureaucracy: Managers, Unions and the Transformation of Work in American Industry, 1900–1945* (New York: Columbia University Press, 1985); Katherine Stone, "The Origins of Job Structures in the Steel Industry," in *Labor Market Segmentation,* ed. Richard Edwards, Michael Reich, and David Gordon (Lexington, Mass.: Lexington Books, 1975), 24–84; Robert E. Cole, *Work, Mobility, and Participation* (Berkeley: University of California Press, 1979), 103–7.

[71] Price, *Japan Works,* 69–71, 104–7; Jinjiin, *Jinji gyōsei 20-nen no ayumi* (Ōkurashō insatsukyoku, 1968), chaps. 2 and 6. On the Occupation role, see also Theodore Cohen, *Remaking Japan: The American Occupation as New Deal* (New York: Free Press, 1987), chap. 20; T. J. Pempel, "The Tar Baby Target: 'Reform' of the Japanese Bureaucracy," in *Democratizing Japan: The Allied Occupation,* ed. Robert E. Ward and Sakamoto Yoshikazu (Honolulu: University of Hawaii Press, 1987), 157–87.

wage strategy. Job wages (*shokumu kyū* in Japanese) lacked the incentive component cherished most dearly by managers, yet the system promised to restore at least partial autonomy to management in the process of wage determination. Moreover, as the U.S. benchmark—and thus as the presumed standard for rationality and sophistication—job wages were accepted almost instinctively by Japanese managers intent on following the American path of economic and social progress.[72] As Ishida Mitsuo derisively describes it, the employers who clutched at this latest managerial import were fired by an "extreme modernism," pursuing "modernity in the footsteps of the West."[73] In any case, Nikkeiren formally endorsed job wages in 1949, resolving to "establish job classifications," "rationalize wage systems," and "increase labor productivity by clarifying work duties on the basis of job analysis."[74] As a 1955 Nikkeiren study more resolutely (and eloquently) put it, "There is no mistaking that job wages are the Pole Star [*hokkyokusei*] of wage rationalization, and one cannot deny that the quest for job wages lies on the righteous path [*ōdō*] of wage modernization."[75]

In the 1950s rollback of labor's power, Japanese employers made some significant gains on the wage front. Although the basic contours of the Densan system remained intact, seniority—which managers found a far more palatable standard than age or family size—was installed as the key component in setting base wages.[76] Yet despite this revival in managerial authority, the job wage alternative championed by Nikkeiren made only slight headway in private-sector workshops. Job wages were touted as rational, scientific, objective, and even democratic[77]—a desirable and obligatory step toward modern industrial relations on the American model—but the system saw only limited application due to labor opposition and managerial diffidence. Unions, which viewed classification systems as a capitalist attempt to revive the despised status hierarchies of the past, balked at reform. Managers, meanwhile, reluctant to push workers too far and daunted by the complexities of scientific job analysis, were lukewarm in their commitment to Nikkeiren's ambitious program of change.[78]

---

[72] Ishida, "Chingin taikei I," 6–10; Okuda Kenji, *Rōmu kanri no Nihonteki tenkai* (Nihon seisansei honbu, 1972), 75.

[73] Ishida, "Chingin taikei I," 8.

[74] "Rōso-hō kanzen jisshi ni kansuru ketsugi" (September 30, 1949), in Nikkeiren, *Jūnen no ayumi*, 87.

[75] Quoted from the report *Shokumu kyū no kenkyū* in Ishida, "Chingin taikei I," 10.

[76] Gordon, *Evolution*, 374–86.

[77] See, for example, the Nikkeiren report "Kigyō gōrika ni tomonau chingin seido to nōritsu kyū" (1949), in Nikkeiren, *Jūnen no ayumi*, 131–32; Ishida, "Chingin taikei I," 6–10.

[78] Tsuda, "Study of Japanese Management Development Practices II," 3; "Shin rōdō kanri ni kansuru kenkai" (1950), in Nikkeiren, *Jūnen no ayumi*, 148; Fujibayashi Keizō, "Rōdō mondai," in *Rōdō mondai*, ed. Keizai dōyūkai, Keiei kiso kōza, vol. 5 (Daiyamondo, 1953), 19–21; Ishida Mitsuo, "Chingin taikei to rōshi kankei II," *Nihon rōdō kyōkai zasshi* 27, no. 9 (September 1985): 43–47.

Although the sluggish spread of job wages was widely lamented in business circles, there were a few outstanding success stories—like the much-publicized case of Jūjō Paper[79]—and statistics showed that a considerable number of firms had instituted some form of American-style wage structure. JPC consultant William Landes chided Japanese managers for their ignorance of job analysis techniques in 1955,[80] yet Nikkeiren surveys showed that almost 15 percent of all manufacturers (and over 20 percent of very large concerns) were using job wage systems by 1963.[81] Nevertheless, many commentators concluded that job wages, even where conscientiously applied in Japan, led to few substantive changes in workers' pay packets, and frequently seemed little more than a crypto-seniority system. In most cases, job wage programs either meshed with existing seniority schemes or functioned as mere supplements to them. Thus, even in Japanese firms equipped with intricate, up-to-date job classification practices, the "irrational," "prescientific" yardstick of seniority remained the implicit basis of wage determination mechanisms.[82] As Ronald Dore observed,

> The introduction of "western-style" job-related wages has been hailed as a great advance, the final breakthrough out of a transitional adolescent stage of repressive feudalism into a state of full maturity in which workers are paid "properly"—as economists would say, according to market principles, or as sociologists would say, according to achievement rather than ascriptive norms.
>
> To say the least this is an exaggeration. . . .

[79] "Shin keiei gijutsu no shippai rei to seikō rei," *Kindai keiei* 4, no. 5 (April 1959): 12–13; Takahashi Kō, *Gendai Nihon no chingin kanri* (Nihon hyōronsha, 1989), 124.

[80] William S. Landes, *Nihon no keiei o shindan suru* (Nihon seisansei honbu, 1956), 22.

[81] 14.8 percent of all firms and 22 percent of firms with more than five thousand employees reported using job wages. Nikkeiren, *Wagakuni rōmu kanri no gensei,* Dai 2-kai rōmu kanri shoseido chōsa (Nikkeiren, 1965), 46–47. In a 1967 survey, 14.1 percent of companies reported using job analysis (*shokumu bunseki*) across the board, while a further 20.7 percent reported using it selectively. Nikkeiren and Kantō keieisha kyōkai, *Nōryokushugi kanri ni kansuru kigyō no jittai chōsa,* Rōmu shiryō, vol. 89 (Nikkeiren, 1968), 6.

[82] Noda Kazuo, "Shin keiei gijutsu wa Nihon ni sodatsu ka?" *Kindai keiei* 4, no. 5 (April 1959): 6–9; Fujibayashi, "Rōdō mondai," 24–25; Robert Ballon, "Lifelong Remuneration System," in *The Japanese Employee,* ed. Robert Ballon (Tokyo: Sophia University, 1969), 154; Takahashi, *Gendai Nihon no chingin kanri,* 125–26; Funahashi, "The Industrial Reward System: Wages and Benefits," in Ōkōchi, Karsh, and Levine, *Workers and Employers in Japan,* 367–68; Noda and Mori, *Rōmu kanri,* 14–15; Mori, *Sengo Nihon,* 87–93, 210–18.

Some firms were able to introduce output-based productivity standards into their wage formulae in the 1950s, yet these standards tended to be based on large work units (such as departments or entire factories) rather than on individual workers. As a consequence, such measures seldom had a meaningful incentive effect on employees. James Abegglen, *The Japanese Factory: Aspects of Its Social Organization* (Glencoe, Ill.: Free Press, 1958), 50; Gordon, *Evolution,* 359–60; Ronald Dore, *British Factory—Japanese Factory: The Origins of National Diversity in Industrial Relations* (Berkeley: University of California Press, 1973), 107–8.

[T]he so-called job-evaluation exercise turned out to be not an evaluation of jobs, but an evaluation of chaps.[83]

In 1960, the annual Labor White Paper concluded that the prospects of establishing a job wage system in Japan were poor, and even the most ardent business supporters of American-style industrial relations were reluctantly inclined to agree.[84] As the failings of the Nikkeiren job wage initiative became apparent, employees increasingly emphasized "ability" as a central component in wage determination. Rather than basing pay on an intricate calculus of job requirements, managers looked to evaluate individual workers using broadly defined standards of merit, "hard work, loyalty, quickness at learning new skills."[85] Much of the enthusiasm for this shift in strategy came from a resurgence of managers' abiding faith in monetary incentives and wage systems that fostered competition on the shop floor.[86] At the same time, however, Japanese employers were also strongly influenced by changing conditions in the labor market and in production technology. As companies rapidly expanded their work forces in the late 1950s and early 1960s, both seniority systems and rigid job wage schemes became the source of considerable rank-and-file discontent, especially among the growing numbers of young (and ambitious) factory operatives. Moreover, in a time of rising mechanization and organizational development, the job wage program—despite its impeccable American credentials—seemed too inflexible to meet the ever-changing demands of Japan's technological revolution.[87] Out of this environment would emerge Nikkeiren's concept of *nōryokushugi kanri*—"ability-based management"—and its revised blueprint for a lasting settlement of the wage question in Japan.

Nikkeiren began investigating the potential usefulness of "ability" as a labor management tool in the mid-1960s. Only in 1969, however, with the publication of a special report on *nōryokushugi kanri*, was Nikkeiren's vision fully articulated and a systematic program of reform outlined. As this report, compiled by top personnel managers from twenty-one leading firms, declared,

[83] Dore, *British Factory—Japanese Factory,* 104–5.

[84] Ono Tsuneo, "Postwar Changes in the Japanese Wage System," in *The Labor Market in Japan: Selected Readings,* ed. Nishikawa Shunsaku, trans. Ross Mouer (Tokyo: University of Tokyo Press, 1980), 161.

[85] Andrew Gordon, "Contests for the Workplace," in *Postwar Japan as History,* ed. Andrew Gordon (Berkeley: University of California Press, 1993), 386; Ishida, "Chingin taikei I," 10–14.

[86] See, for example, Nikkeiren, *Nōritsu kyū no gendaiteki kōsatsu: nōritsu kyū no kindaika no tame ni* (Nikkeiren, 1956).

[87] Nikkeiren nōryokushugi kanri kenkyūkai, *Nōryokushugi kanri* (Nikkeiren, 1969), 19–20; Y. Kaneko, "Employment and Wages," *The Developing Economies* 8 no. 4 (December 1970): 471–72; Tsuda, "Study of Japanese Management Development Practices II," 6; Ishida, "Chingin taikei I," 13; Takahashi, *Gendai Nihon no chingin kanri,* 127–28.

What with labor shortages, capital liberalization, and so forth, the conditions facing corporate management today are growing increasingly severe. As a result, managers are under great pressure to step up the revision of personnel administration practices.

With this in mind, the industrial community has resolved . . . to establish a system of labor management which relies upon small numbers of proficient individuals [*shōsū seiei shugi*], a system which develops and utilizes the abilities of each worker to the fullest, a system which seeks to motivate labor through impartial treatment in the true sense of the term, allowing for the demonstration of individual talents without being shackled by standards of academic experience, age, or seniority. We have christened this system of labor management "ability-based" [*nōryokushugi*].[88]

Nikkeiren stressed the novelty of the new approach and, seeking to set it apart from the abortive job wage campaign, emphasized that "ability-based management" was distinctively Japanese and not simply another direct import from the United States. *Nōryokushugi kanri,* the 1969 report concluded, was fundamentally different from the "ability concepts of the West based on rights and obligations," and marked a clear departure from the Western Taylorite tradition.[89] Nevertheless, the premises of Nikkeiren's "ability" strategy clearly resonated with longtime Taylorite preoccupations and productivist doctrines: "The goal of *nōryokushugi kanri* is, above all, achieving the largest outcomes with the least personnel . . . , simultaneously attaining high efficiency, high wages, low costs, and high profits."[90] Nikkeiren sold its new scheme as equitable, scientific, and objective, boasted that it could fuse "the pursuit of economic rationality with respect for human beings," and even promoted it as a "revolution in consciousness" (*ishiki kakumei*).[91] Furthermore, Nikkeiren claimed that in an age of "political democracy and social meritocracy," wages should be based on assessments of individual capabilities and concrete standards of performance, on the actual, demonstrated abilities of workers (that is, results) rather than on measures of "potential ability" (such as seniority or education).[92] Competition and monetary stimuli would thus drive workers on to new levels of productivity: "If wage determination is based upon ability, the desire for higher wages will merge with the desire to

[88] Nikkeiren nōryokushugi kanri kenkyūkai, *Nōryokushugi kanri,* 1. See also Ishida, "Chingin taikei II," 39–42; Tsuda Masumi, "Study of Japanese Management Development Practices III," *Hitotsubashi Journal of Social Studies* 10, no. 1 (April 1978): 19–20.

[89] Nikkeiren nōryokushugi kanri kenkyūkai, ed., *Nōryokushugi kanri,* 21, 26.

[90] Ibid., 5.

[91] Ibid., 20–28. See also Kumazawa Makoto, *Portraits of the Japanese Workplace: Labor Movements, Workers, and Managers,* ed. Andrew Gordon, trans. Andrew Gordon and Mikiso Hane (Boulder, Colo.: Westview Press, 1996), 133–34.

[92] Nikkeiren nōryokushugi kanri kenkyūkai, *Nōryokushugi kanri,* 1, 43–46, 48–49.

improve one's skills, the incentive effect will flourish, and an overall rise in ability will naturally follow."[93]

In practical terms, Nikkeiren recommended that wages be determined by supervisor ratings of worker performance in specific jobs, using substantive evidence and explicit standards of ability.[94] Yet *nōryokushugi kanri* was not portrayed as being altogether incompatible with labor's livelihood concerns and the seniority system. The employers of Nikkeiren recognized the value of existing arrangements in sustaining worker morale and, in the proposed injection of "ability" into wage calculations, managers hoped to remedy the shortcomings of the seniority regime rather than supplant it entirely.[95] Indeed, what eventually emerged from the *nōryokushugi kanri* initiative was a hybrid wage structure which combined seniority elements with a prominent ability-based component. As Tsuda Masumi described it, "Into the traditional concept emphasizing the whole personality was woven the concept of competence. The present system represents a mix of the two."[96] Statistics suggest that by the early 1970s, a clear majority of firms were using this synthetic approach, while about one-third of all employers relied on pure merit or job classification systems, and just over 10 percent continued to base wages solely on personal characteristics.[97] Despite a continuing process of experimentation and variation, the fusion of seniority and Nikkeiren's ability principle appears to have formed the cornerstone of a durable new wage determination structure during the 1970s and beyond.[98]

From the start, critics faulted *nōryokushugi kanri* for being too vague and too derivative, some even dismissing it as a tired rehash of the American job wage concept.[99] Many commentators—especially Westerners and academics in the field of labor relations—were equally disparaging of the mixed wage system which ultimately came to predominate. Through the 1970s, analysts continued to deplore the "premodern" nature and "disreputable backwardness" of Japanese wage determination procedures.[100] The hybrid structure of

[93] Ibid., 95.

[94] Ibid., 55–63; Murata Kazuhiko, "Personnel Management in Japanese Business Enterprises," *Hitotsubashi Journal of Commerce and Management* 25, no. 1 (December 1990): 39–41.

[95] Nikkeiren nōryokushugi kanri kenkyūkai, *Nōryokushugi kanri,* 89, 555, 558–59.

[96] Tsuda, "Study of Japanese Management Development Practices II," 7.

[97] Ono, "Postwar Changes," 167–68. Compare Nikkeiren and Kantō keieisha kyōkai, *Nōryokushugi kanri ni kansuru kigyō no jittai chōsa,* 11, on use of combined ability and seniority standards in determining promotions.

[98] Takahashi, *Gendai Nihon no chingin kanri,* 129–32; Murata, "Personnel Management." For case studies of hybrid systems in actual use, see Robert M. Marsh and Mannari Hiroshi, *Modernization and the Japanese Factory* (Princeton, N.J.: Princeton University Press, 1976), chap. 6.

[99] Mori and Matsushima, *Nihon rōmu kanri,* 60–61; Tsuda, "Study of Japanese Management Development Practices III," 20.

[100] Funahashi, "The Industrial Reward System," 373; Odaka Kunio, *Toward Industrial Democracy: Management and Workers in Modern Japan* (Cambridge, Mass.: Harvard University Press, 1975), 2. See also Dore, *British Factory—Japanese Factory,* 104–8.

the new arrangements was also troubling: Mori Gorō and Matsushima Shizuo, for example, described "traditional" labor management practices as a saucer into which imported U.S. methods had been ungraciously poured after World War II.[101] But while the *nōryokushugi kanri* wage settlement was assailed on an abstract level, in practice it proved agreeable to both labor and management. In the end, employers gained considerable discretion over wages, a reaffirmation of monetary incentives, and a heightened atmosphere of competition in the workplace.[102] Labor, meanwhile, was mollified by the continued managerial commitment to seniority, and the rank and file proved remarkably receptive to the new merit system. As Ishida Mitsuo has argued, Japanese workers considered "ability" a fair basis for wage differentials and were predisposed to support Nikkeiren's vision of *nōryokushugi kanri*.[103] Survey data from the 1970s confirm that a sizeable majority of workers—as well as managers—endorsed the ability principle and rated merit a more appropriate basis for wage determination than seniority, education level, or family size.[104]

Significantly, the hybrid wage structure born of the seniority system and *nōryokushugi kanri* was broadly continuous with the "revised Taylorite" strategy first articulated in the 1920s. In combining livelihood elements with individual incentives determined by management, the mixed system generalized in the 1970s lay in an evolutionary trajectory stretching back through wartime experiments, the Production Management Committee scheme, and Araki Tōichirō's Yokohama Dock plan, to the 1925 Mitsubishi Electric program and Godō Takuo's Kure Arsenal formula.[105] In this light, as Andrew Gordon has acutely observed, there is a certain irony to the postwar lamentations of Japan's "disreputable backwardness" in wage determination. While the seniority principle denounced by many analysts as "traditional" was, in fact, a largely postwar phenomenon, the "modern" systems said to have floundered in postwar Japan actually had roots running all the way to the Taishō Scientific Management movement. As Gordon concludes, "Tradition and modernity are slippery notions. . . . The modern concern with efficiency and output was always manifest in the wage policy of managers."[106] One might justifiably (if somewhat perversely) conclude that with the ability-based wage settlement of the

[101] Mori and Matsushima, *Nihon rōmu kanri,* 233.

[102] Gordon, "Contests," 386.

[103] Ishida, "Chingin taikei I," "Chingin taikei II." See also Kumazawa, *Portraits of the Japanese Workplace,* 146.

[104] Sakuma Ken, "Changes in Japanese-Style Labor-Management Relations," *Japanese Economic Studies* 16, no. 4 (Summer 1988): 33–37; Marsh and Mannari, *Modernization and the Japanese Factory,* 147–54; Nikkeiren nōryokushugi kanri kenkyūkai, *Nōryokushugi kanri,* 554–58.

[105] For an explicit (but derogatory) discussion of continuities between the Production Management Committee program and postwar wage compromises, see Fujibayashi, "Rōdō mondai," 24–25.

[106] Gordon, *Evolution,* 386.

1970s, a tradition of modern wage practices—the heritage of the "revised Taylorite" approach—was reaffirmed in postwar Japan.

Some observers have suggested that the failure of American-style job wages and the evolution of a "distinctively Japanese" mixed wage package are symptomatic of the rejection of Taylorism in contemporary Japan.[107] Yet such a view distorts not only the nature of the ability-based management concept, but also the implications and the origins of the job wage system. Although the job wage plans promoted in Japan during the 1950s were consistent with Taylorite ideas of specialization, their American roots lay in post-Taylorite structures of "bureaucratic control" and labor strategies for ensuring equitable treatment and union authority on the shop floor.[108] Thus the presumption that job wages were coincident with Scientific Management is mistaken and, in turn, the implication that Japanese coolness toward job classification schemes amounted to a disavowal of Taylorism is ultimately untenable.[109] Clearly, U.S. "best practice"—in the form of job wages—was repudiated in postwar Japan. At the same time, however, in the hybrid system that would eventually prevail, the longstanding assumptions of Japanese Taylorites were confirmed and generalized.

The Origins of "Lean Production"

Like the hybrid wage settlement, postwar Japan's distinctive constellation of workshop management practices—branded "lean production" by Western scholars in the early 1990s—is widely assumed to be a telling rejection of American managerial traditions. Japan's "lean" factories are now celebrated, by Western and Japanese observers alike, as symbols of Japan's transcendence of the outdated nostrums of Taylor and Ford. Against a background of Japanese industrial ascendance, such assertions have proven convincing empirically as well as ideologically: the "lean" paradigm, which evolved in the shops

[107] See, for instance, Aoki Masahiko, *Information, Incentives, and Bargaining in the Japanese Economy* (Cambridge: Cambridge University Press, 1988), 11–20; Ishikawa Kaoru, *What is Total Quality Control? The Japanese Way,* trans. David Lu (Englewood Cliffs, N.J.: Prentice-Hall, 1985), 25–28. Even Andrew Gordon appears to make this implication; "Contests," 387. Compare Cole, *Work, Mobility and Participation,* 101–13; Price, *Japan Works,* 290–91.

[108] Stone, "The Origins of Job Structures"; Jacoby, *Employing Bureaucracy,* 150–54, 250–53; Richard Edwards, *Contested Terrain: The Transformation of the Workplace in the Twentieth Century* (New York: Basic Books, 1979), chap. 8; Michael Piore and Charles Sabel, *The Second Industrial Divide: Possibilities for Prosperity* (New York: Basic Books, 1984), 111–32.

[109] A contemporary account which explicitly differentiates between job wages and Taylorite strategies is Ōike Hisato, "Shokumu hyōka to jinji kōka," *Rōmu kenkyū* 3, no. 7 (July 1950): 15–19.

of the Toyota Motor Company in the thirty years after World War II, certainly appears a significant methodological departure from the now-demonized Fordist assembly line. As described by Michael Cusumano, the model pioneered by Toyota is "an integrated system characterized by a flow of processing information backward from final assembly, 'flexible' machinery and workers, tightly rationalized job routines, low lead and setup times, and small lots for manufacturing, in-house conveyance, and deliveries from subcontractors."[110] Yet in hailing these arrangements as a revolutionary advance in production management—in framing the system as a flexible, decentralized, and humane alternative to Fordism—most observers have overlooked the extent to which the Toyota system was built upon Taylorite assumptions and fabricated from Taylorite techniques. Perfected within the specific economic and political environment of postwar Japan, the "lean" manufacturing order emerged as an innovative strategy of mass production, distinct from the idealized Fordist prototype but premised firmly on the rigorous application of Taylorite ideology and shop-floor methods.

From the start of automobile production at Toyota in the mid-1930s, the company's managers and engineers looked to the assembly lines of Detroit for inspiration. Like the vast majority of prewar Japanese observers, however, the Toyota personnel—while awed by the Fordist achievement—were dubious that the American model of mass production could be replicated in Japan. Toyoda Kiichirō, Toyota's founder, traveled extensively in the United States and found much to emulate in Detroit, yet as he and his subordinates designed the firm's first modern factory in 1937, they explored means of adapting the Ford system to Japanese conditions of scarce resources, expensive capital, and limited markets. Toyota could not afford a full conveyor-belt system, but Kiichirō sought to establish a highly coordinated "flow" process of production, using flexible, multipurpose machine tools to make a wide range of components. In particular, by creating an even stream of parts from production and processing through final assembly, Toyota engineers tried to slash inventories and stocks of work in process, aiming ultimately to realize considerable economies in material requirements, warehouse space, and overhead costs.[111] As

---

[110] Michael A. Cusumano, *The Japanese Automobile Industry: Technology and Management at Nissan and Toyota* (Cambridge, Mass.: Harvard University Press, 1985), 291. Compare James Womack, Daniel Jones, and Daniel Roos, *The Machine that Changed the World* (New York: Rawson Associates, 1990), 12–13; Monden Yasuhiro, *Toyota Production System: An Integrated Approach to Just-In-Time,* 2d ed. (Norcross, Ga.: Industrial Engineering and Management Press, 1993), 1, 13–14.

[111] Wada Kazuo, "The Emergence of the 'Flow Production' Method in Japan," in *Fordism Transformed: The Development of Production Methods in the Automobile Industry,* ed. Shiomi Haruhito and Wada Kazuo (Oxford: Oxford University Press, 1995), 12–21; Toyota Motor Corporation, *Toyota: A History of the First 50 Years* (Toyota City: Toyota Motor Corporation, 1988), 66–73. According to Ōno Taiichi, Kiichirō reputedly remarked in 1933 that "We shall learn production techniques from the American method of mass production. But we will not copy it as

Kiichirō's son later recounted, "What [my father] had in mind was to produce the needed quantity of the required parts each day. To make this a reality, every single step of the operation, like it or not, had to be converted over to his flow production system. Kiichirō referred to this as the 'just-in-time' concept. By this he meant: 'Just make what is needed in time, but don't make too much. . . .' That marked the beginning of the Toyota production system."[112]

Despite Kiichirō's best efforts, even by the end of World War II Toyota factories had made only slight progress toward the ambitious goal of "just-in-time" production. As one contemporary observer noted, in the wartime assembly plants, "Process flows were often disturbed, work-in-process inventories piled up, and there was a lack of balance in machine utilization."[113] In any case, under government mobilization plans that stressed quantity over efficiency, a thoroughly synchronized and streamlined flow system was clearly premature. Indeed, the full elaboration of the Toyota system only took place after Japan's surrender and, more specifically, only after the engineer Ōno Taiichi began a sweeping program of managerial experimentation and reform in Toyota workshops. Ōno was a graduate of the Nagoya Higher Industrial School and worked for over a decade at Toyoda Spinning and Weaving, a corporate predecessor of Toyota Motors. Ōno rose steadily up the corporate hierarchy—moving from manager of Toyota's main machine shop in 1947, to general manager of the Motomachi factory in 1959, to executive vice president in 1975—and under his guidance what is now known as the Toyota production system was developed, systematized, and installed throughout Toyota's manufacturing operations.[114]

Ōno's efforts to reform the production process began in the immediate wake of the war, when Toyota (like all of corporate Japan) was under intense pressure to cut costs, conserve resources, and boost efficiency. Ōno's first goal was to extract greater productivity from labor. By altering workshop layouts, imposing more rigorous job routines, and installing new jigs and automatic devices to simplify procedures, Ōno sought to "eliminate all unnecessary movements and allow no idle time, for machines or workers."[115] Under Ōno's

---

is. We shall use our own research and creativity to develop a production method that suits our own country's situation." Ohno Taiichi, *Toyota Production System: Beyond Large-Scale Production* (Cambridge, Mass.: Productivity Press, 1988), 91. See also Toyota jidōsha kōgyō kabushiki kaisha, Shashi henshū iinkai, *Toyota jidōsha 20-nen shi* (Koromo, Aichi-ken: Toyota jidōsha kabushiki kaisha, 1958), 41.

[112] Toyoda Eiji, *Toyota: Fifty Years in Motion* (Tokyo: Kodansha International, 1987), 57–58.

[113] Wada, "The Emergence of the 'Flow Production' Method in Japan," 20. On wartime management at Toyota, see Toyota jidōsha, *20-nen shi,* 112–30.

[114] Cusumano, *The Japanese Automobile Industry,* 267–69; Ohno, *Toyota Production System*; Noguchi Hisashi, *Toyota seisan hōshiki o tsukutta otoko: Ōno Taiichi no tatakai* (TBS Buritanika, 1988).

[115] Cusumano, *The Japanese Automobile Industry,* 272. See also Japan Management Association, *Kanban: Just-in-Time at Toyota,* rev. ed., trans. David Lu (Cambridge, Mass.: Productivity Press, 1989), 120–24.

scheme, an employee who had formerly tended a single machine was able to operate a number of units simultaneously. By 1955, the seven hundred workers at one Toyota factory were using three thousand five hundred machine tools, with some operators running as many as seventeen different pieces of equipment at once.[116] This system of "multimachine handling" led to substantial labor savings: thanks in part to Ōno's innovations, during the 1950s Toyota increased automobile production tenfold while expanding its work force only a parsimonious 10 percent.[117]

Having thus transformed work standards and labor productivity, Ōno next turned his attention to Kiichirō's notion of "just-in-time" manufacturing. The logic of Kiichirō's plan was appealing but the Fordist example (and the wartime failures at Toyota) suggested that such a level of coordination and such a radical reduction of inventories were unattainable. Nevertheless, inspired by the model of the American supermarket, Ōno eventually devised an elegant mechanism for attaining a smooth flow on the assembly line: just as supermarket shoppers could purchase the products they wanted, when they wanted, so (Ōno reasoned) production stations in the factory should be able to obtain components at the precise time and in the precise quantities required. Only when components were actually used—withdrawn from the stock of the factory's imagined supermarket—would replacements be manufactured. Thus, instead of production being "pushed" by mounting stocks of parts—as it was in the typical Fordist operation—automobiles would be "pulled" through the Toyota system, with components and subassemblies being fabricated only as they were needed and utilized. To maintain overall coordination between the supply and demand of parts within the factory, Ōno instituted the now-famous system of *kanban*—tags attached to component lots and work in process—as a self-regulating means of ordering materials, synchronizing production streams, and channeling information among workshops.[118] With *kanban* functioning as the "automatic nerve of the production line,"[119] and Ōno's adroit recasting of "just-in-time" applied to subcontractors as well as to main assembly plants, Toyota was able to slash inventories and realize a virtually seamless flow system by the end of the 1950s.

The final key ingredient in the Toyota management strategy was the system of small-lot production. In the context of limited and rapidly shifting markets, Toyota could not mass produce on the Fordist blueprint, but had to use its factories flexibly to manufacture a variety of automobile models in relatively

[116] Shingō Shigeo, *A Study of the Toyota Production System from an Industrial Engineering Viewpoint*, rev. ed., trans. Andrew P. Dillon (Cambridge, Mass.: Productivity Press, 1989), 72; Cusumano, *The Japanese Automobile Industry*, 274. See also Wada, "The Emergence of the 'Flow Production' Method in Japan," 21–24; Toyota jidōsha, *20-nen shi*, 381–83.

[117] Cusumano, *The Japanese Automobile Industry*, 396.

[118] On the evolution of "just-in-time," the supermarket system, and *kanban*, see ibid., 275–84, 287–98; Shingō, *A Study of the Toyota Production System*, chap. 9; Ohno, *Toyota Production System*, 25–44.

[119] Ohno, *Toyota Production System*, 29.

small quantities. Ōno, however, recognized that the American system—with automakers churning out standard products in large volumes using specialized equipment—had its limitations and that manufacturing a wide array of products in low volumes with multipurpose machine tools, when allied with the "clockwork-like meshings of just-in-time,"[120] could be even more efficient than traditional Fordist arrangements. Crucial to Ōno's vision was the perfection of a system for drastically reducing machinery setup times, allowing for the sequential production of small lots without long, unproductive periods of retooling and recalibration. Under the guidance of Shingō Shigeo, an industrial engineer and consultant to Toyota, a number of creative means for rapidly changing dies in machine tools were developed. By the end of the 1960s, Shingō had so simplified setup procedures for stamping presses—a complex operation which required hours or even days in Western factories—that Toyota could complete a full changeover in less than ten minutes.[121] With such techniques in place, Toyota's "lean" production paradigm was complete, and the mature system was diffused throughout the company's workshops by the early 1970s.

For all the declarations of the Toyota production system's distinctiveness—one observer judged it "completely independent from conventional expertise," others have proclaimed it "unique and unparalleled"[122]—"lean production" was constructed from classic Taylorite assumptions and the time-tested methodologies of Scientific Management. The ideological backbone of "Toyotism" was patently Taylorite: at the core of the "lean" model lay a compulsive urge to eradicate all waste within the manufacturing process, reduce costs, and boost the efficiency of labor. "The most important objective of the Toyota system has been to increase production efficiency by constantly and thoroughly eliminating waste," Ōno Taiichi maintained. "Unless all sources of waste are detected and crushed, success will always be just a dream."[123] In fighting managerial fat, science and empirical rationality were to be the weapons of choice. The Toyota approach, one study concluded, was "a system of production, based on the philosophy of total elimination of waste, that seeks the utmost in rationality in the way we make things."[124] "Lean production" was premised on a "scientific attitude emphasizing facts" or, as Ōno put it, on a "scientific and rational nature."[125] In stressing the evils of waste and the potential of science, the ideologues of "lean production" echoed the spare

[120] W. Mark Fruin, *The Japanese Enterprise System: Competitive Strategies and Cooperative Structures* (Oxford: Clarendon Press, 1992), 256.

[121] Cusumano, *The Japanese Automobile Industry*, 284–87; Shingō, *A Study of the Toyota Production System*, 43–57.

[122] Ogawa Eiji, *Modern Production Management: A Japanese Experience* (Tokyo: Asian Productivity Organization, 1984), 119; Japan Management Association, *Kanban*, 23.

[123] Ohno, *Toyota Production System*, xiii, 59.

[124] Japan Management Association, *Kanban*, 23.

[125] Ibid., 27; Ohno, *Toyota Production System*, 80; Noguchi, *Toyota seisan hōshiki*, 26–28.

homilies of the Taishō efficiency movement and the economizing prescriptions of generations of Japanese scientific managers.

Another Taylorite preoccupation reaffirmed in the Toyota system was a passion for the setting of explicit work standards and the enforcement of strict labor regimens. Even in the early days of automobile production, Toyoda Kiichirō was an advocate of the rigorous standardization of procedures. As Kiichirō's son described the establishment of mass production in the 1930s, "We were bringing in a radically new system. To get our people to accept it, we had to rid them entirely of their notions of the old way of doing things. It was, in a sense, a brainwashing operation. Kiichirō's manual was impressive. A full four inches thick, it described in meticulous detail the flow production system we were to set up. This is the text that I and the other instructors used to teach the new system to the workers."[126] Such practices were continued— and, in fact, intensified—by Ōno Taiichi, whose intricate system of multi-machine handling was premised on exacting work instructions. Ōno was a stickler for details: as Toyota's official history states, "A system was implemented for making Standardized Work Charts at the production site and for ensuring that each floor employee precisely carried out assigned tasks. Since these Standardized Work Charts clearly stated the procedure for making the needed items at fixed times, the standard duration for every job and the standard in-process stock for every machine, each person knew exactly what work was to be done at all times. With these Standardized Work Charts hanging in front of them, it was possible for every employee to perform the assigned job with precision. . . ."[127] Using words that would have pleased Frederick Winslow Taylor himself, one overview of "lean" manufacturing declared that "standard operations are the mother of improvement" and that, "under the Toyota system, everything is standardized."[128]

Moreover, "lean production" techniques were fully consistent with traditional Taylorite notions of simplification and specialization. The architects of the Toyota system were sanguine—and surprisingly overt—in seeking to extract skills and information from shop-floor workers and invest any such commandeered knowledge in new machinery or standard work routines. Automation was a crucial aspect of the Toyota strategy, as engineers endeavored "to transfer the work of human hands to machines, and . . . to transfer the work of the human brain to machines."[129] As Ōno Taiichi declared, "The key is to give human intelligence to the machine and, at the same time, to adapt the simple

[126] Toyoda, *Toyota: Fifty Years in Motion,* 58.

[127] Toyota Motor Corporation, *Toyota,* 114. See also Ohno, *Toyota Production System,* 20–23; Kamata Satoshi, *Japan in the Passing Lane,* trans. Akimoto Tatsuru (New York: Pantheon, 1982), 42.

[128] Japan Management Association, *Kanban,* 118, 155.

[129] Shingō, *A Study of the Toyota Production System,* 149. See also Cole, *Work, Mobility and Participation,* 198–99.

movement of the human operator to the autonomous machines."[130] Indeed, "lean production," like the textbook application of Scientific Management, appeared "human centered" only to the extent that tapping the skills and defining the duties of individual workers would allow for the further ascent of labor productivity.

Although champions of the Toyota system have praised its job rotation and multimachine handling schemes for creating "multiskilled" or "polyvalent" workers,[131] the benefits of "lean production" in enriching the experience of industrial work are far from certain. As many critics have argued, the Toyota regime endows employees not with new skills, but with new responsibilities. The ability to perform a number of simplified and standardized tasks, skeptics note, is (at best) only marginally more rewarding to workers than the repetitive execution of a single task. As Naruse Tatsuo has explained, "Making a line worker multifunctional in the Toyota system means only training him in improved work methods. In other words, his work itself is essentially unskilled or semiskilled, not multiskilled, but he is required to be multifunctional. . . ."[132] Some scholars have been even more damning: according to Katō Tetsurō and Rob Steven, for example, "a multiplicity of simple skills acquired over a lifetime offers workers less protection from layoffs than does the power that comes with being needed for a particular job. The real meaning of being multi-skilled is being willing to be pushed about for the entirety of one's working life."[133] Even the supporters of the Toyota approach implicitly acknowledge that the system has the objective, as well as the effect, of diluting worker skills. In a statement that undermines assertions of "polyvalent" skill creation under the "lean" paradigm—and reverberates with the maxims of Taylor and Ford—Ōno Taiichi pronounced that "it should only take three days to train new workers in proper work procedures."[134]

Despite the currently widespread preconception that the Toyota system is uniquely humane, flexible, and participative, Taylorite ideals of control, discipline, and expertism appeared paramount in the "lean" approach to workplace

---

[130] Ohno, *Toyota Production System,* 7. See also Noguchi, *Toyota seisan hōshiki,* 21.

[131] See, for example, Martin Kenney and Richard Florida, *Beyond Mass Production: The Japanese System and Its Transfer to the U.S.* (New York: Oxford University Press, 1993), 38–39; Womack, Jones and Roos, *The Machine that Changed the World,* 101–2. Although not focused on Toyota or the automobile industry, an influential (and generally rosy) appraisal of the Japanese job rotation system is Koike Kazuo, *Understanding Industrial Relations in Modern Japan* (New York: St. Martin's Press, 1988).

[132] Naruse Tatsuo, "Taylorism and Fordism in Japan," *International Journal of Political Economy* 21, no. 3 (Fall 1991): 46.

[133] Katō Tetsurō and Rob Steven, *Is Japanese Capitalism Post-Fordist?* Papers of the Japanese Studies Centre, Monash University, no. 16 (Melbourne, 1991), 14. See also Kumazawa, *Portraits of the Japanese Workplace,* 4.

[134] Ohno, *Toyota Production System,* 22. See also Wada, "The Emergence of the 'Flow Production' Method in Japan," 21.

labor relations. Rigid obedience, rather than nurturing inclusion, seemed to define Toyota's shop-floor strategy. As one observer advised, echoing many "lean production" experts, "Supervisors must drill into the minds of workers that they must strictly abide by standard operations."[135] Although generous with the leveling rhetoric of teamwork and "people building," the creators of the Toyota system retained a technocratic faith in "top-down" management: using a familiar metaphor, Ōno Taiichi stressed that "the production control or engineering departments . . . correspond to the brain in the human body."[136] "Unless there is complete control," Toyoda Kiichirō declared, "it is impossible to make a single automobile."[137]

Thus markedly consistent with Scientific Management in general approach, the Toyota production system was also continuous methodologically with the Japanese practice of Taylorism. In remaking the Japanese workshop, the pioneers of "lean production" drew upon the arsenal of techniques first arrayed by the interwar and wartime efficiency movements. Most notably, Ōno Taiichi's conspicuous success in boosting labor productivity was based on the rigorous application of the two Taylorite methodologies most highly developed in Japan, time-and-motion study and layout design. These basic techniques—used in a thoroughly orthodox manner by Ōno and his associates—were crucial to the establishment of multimachine handling, the intricately coordinated flow system, and the meticulous standardization of work at Toyota. Other aspects of the "lean" strategy—like rapid die-change procedures—were attained using the familiar methods of incremental improvement, work study, and trial production.[138]

In some respects, the architects of the Toyota system inherited the frustrations as well as the technical repertoires of their Taylorite predecessors in managerial reform. For example, in describing his sweeping work reorganization of the late 1940s, Ōno observed that

> It is never easy to break the machine-shop tradition in which operators are fixed to jobs, for example, lathe operators to lathe work and welders to welding work. It worked in Japan only because we were willing to do it. The Toyota production system began when I challenged the old system. . . .

[135] Japan Management Association, *Kanban,* 117.

[136] Ohno, *Toyota Production System,* 45.

[137] Quoted in Toyota Motor Corporation, *Toyota,* 67.

[138] For broad considerations of "Toyotism's" methodological roots in Scientific Management, see Mauro Guillen, *Models of Management: Work, Authority, and Organization in a Comparative Perspective* (Chicago: University of Chicago Press, 1994), 292; Knuth Dohse, Ulrich Jurgens and Thomas Malsch, "From 'Fordism' to 'Toyotism'? The Social Organization of the Labor Process in the Japanese Automobile Industry," *Politics and Society* 14, no. 2 (1985): 141. For more specific treatments, see Cusumano, *The Japanese Automobile Industry,* 272, 285; Wada, "The Emergence of the 'Flow Production' Method in Japan," 21–24; Shingō, *A Study of the Toyota Production System,* 150–56; Yamamoto Kiyoshi, *Nihon ni okeru shokuba no gijutsu, rōdō shi* (Tokyo daigaku shuppankai, 1994), 306–12.

In 1947, we arranged machines in parallel lines . . . and tried having one worker operate three or four machines along the processing route. We encountered strong resistance among the production workers, however, even though there was no increase in work or hours. Our craftsmen did not like the new arrangement requiring them to function as multi-skilled operators. They did not like changing from "one operator, one machine" to a system of "one operator, many machines in different processes."[139]

Ōno encountered similar opposition when he sought to strip machinists of the responsibility for sharpening their tools. As Wada Kazuo explained, "Foremen-type workers prided themselves on grinding their own jigs. Therefore, when the company proposed that the company should have responsibility for controlling and grinding the jigs, workers stiffly resisted the proposal. They thought the company's proposal was denying them their inherent right as craftsmen."[140] Scientific managers in the wartime Industrial Patriotic Movement had attempted similar reforms in Japanese machine shops only a few years earlier, yet had been stymied by the defiance of skilled laborers. Ōno persevered, however, and with a torrent of operating manuals, explicit job standards, and firm managerial pressure, successfully imposed his rationalized, Taylorite scheme on the Toyota craftsmen with only limited direct resistance.

That "lean production" was an heir to the Taylorite agenda should hardly be surprising, considering the background of the engineers who created it and the history of the corporation in which it first appeared. The Japanese automobile industry—and specifically Toyota—was closely linked to those sectors of prewar and wartime industry with the most advanced regimes of production management. Toyota Motors was a corporate offshoot of Toyoda Automatic Loom, a pioneer in textile equipment and one of prewar Japan's most innovative and technically proficient machinery manufacturers.[141] The aircraft industry, which was the focus of wartime efforts at managerial reform, also had a major impact on Toyota. Following Japan's defeat, many experienced engineers from aeronautical firms found employment at the automaker, and the origins of numerous aspects of the Toyota system—most notably, flow

---

[139] Ohno, *Toyota Production System,* 10–11. See also Kenney and Florida, *Beyond Mass Production,* 38.

[140] Wada, "The Emergence of the 'Flow Production' Method in Japan," 23; Toyota jidōsha, *20-nen shi,* 282.

[141] The idea of multimachine handling at Toyota was inspired by Toyoda's G-type loom, perfected in 1925. Thanks to the provision of automatic mechanisms to change used spools and detect irregularities, one mill worker could operate twenty-five G-type looms. See Toyota Motor Corporation, *Toyota,* 34–35; Toyota jidōsha, *20-nen shi,* 24–25; Ohno, *Toyota Production System,* chap. 4; Ohno Taiichi, *Workplace Management,* trans. Andrew P. Dillon (Cambridge, Mass.: Productivity Press, 1988), 72.

production—can be traced to wartime airplane factories.[142] Moreover, with the exception of the Pacific War years, Toyota managers had considerable opportunity to evaluate American managerial practices firsthand: from Kiichirō's tours of the United States in the 1920s to JPC missions in the 1950s and 1960s, a steady stream of Toyota executives was able to observe the fabled assembly lines of Detroit.[143]

Among those most influenced by the American example were the primary architects of the Toyota system, Toyoda Kiichirō, Ōno Taiichi, and Shingō Shigeo. Both Toyoda and Ōno were impressed and inspired by the work of Henry Ford, and were attracted by the gospel of high productivity, low costs, and high wages. Ōno—who one author described as having a "penchant for Taylorism"[144]—was first exposed to the methods of Scientific Management in the late 1930s and became an experienced practitioner of work study and job standardization during the war.[145] Shingō, who would perfect rapid setup procedures for Toyota, was even more steeped in Japan's Taylorite heritage. Inspired in high school by the works of Ikeda Tōshirō, Shingō read *The Principles of Scientific Management* in 1931, graduated from Horime Ken'ichi's wartime course on time-and-motion study, and was a prominent spokesman for management reform in the early postwar period. Up until his death, Shingō was adamant in expressing his intellectual debt to the American giants of Scientific Management: proudly declaring himself a "steadfast believer" in the methods of work-study pioneer Frank Gilbreth, Shingō avowed that "my thinking is based on Frederick Taylor's analytical philosophy."[146]

Taken as a whole, the Toyota system can be seen as an innovative model of mass production achieved by mobilizing Taylorite approaches and adapting them to the specific demands of postwar Japanese automobile manufacturing. As most scholars agree, the "lean" strategy is a production regime distinct from the classic Fordist prototype.[147] Whether or not one sees the Toyota

[142] Wada, "The Emergence of the 'Flow Production' Method in Japan"; Fujimoto Takahiro, "A Note on the Origins of the 'Black Box Parts' Practice in the Japanese Motor Vehicle Industry," in Shiomi and Wada, *Fordism Transformed,* 194; Cusumano, *The Japanese Automobile Industry,* 120.

[143] In 1934, for example, prior to the construction of the Koromo facility, one Toyota executive (Kan Takatoshi) visited 130 U.S. factories, 7 research institutes, and 52 universities. Toyota jidōsha, *20-nen shi,* 33.

[144] Price, *Japan Works,* 288.

[145] Ohno, *Toyota Production System,* 20–22, 93–109; Toyota Motor Corporation, *Toyota,* 42; Cusumano, *The Japanese Automobile Industry,* 268. See also Shingō Shigeo, *The Shingō Production Management System: Improving Process Functions,* trans. Andrew P. Dillon (Cambridge, Mass.: Productivity Press, 1992), 58–59.

[146] Shingō Shigeo, *The Sayings of Shigeo Shingō: Key Strategies for Plant Improvement,* trans. Andrew P. Dillon (Cambridge, Mass.: Productivity Press, 1987), xv–xvii; Shingō, *The Shingō Production Management System,* 29–31, 68, 188.

[147] See, for example, Kenney and Florida, *Beyond Mass Production,* 25; Laurie Graham, *On*

arrangements as a more humane, inclusive alternative, the techniques of multimachine handling, "pull" production, and flexible, small-lot operations clearly set the "lean" system apart from the traditional mechanisms of the assembly line. Furthermore, for all its emphasis on automation, equipment layout, and "flow," the Toyota model departs significantly from the Fordist reliance on technological solutions to managerial problems. Instead of depending on the conveyor belt as a mechanical means of ensuring worker discipline and productivity, Toyota engineers sought to optimize the efficiency of each individual step in the production process and use the Taylorite reform of work—rather than capital investment in manufacturing technology—as the primary means of cutting costs and extracting the most from shop-floor labor.[148]

As Michael Cusumano has argued, "lean production" may have revolutionary implications, "yet, to a large degree, the changes Toyota made were 'evolutionary' adaptations to the circumstances surrounding the company and its domestic market needs."[149] Faced with a complex landscape of restrictions and opportunities—rapid growth in demand, low production volumes, highly diversified product lines, competitive pressure to reduce costs and improve quality, limited capital, and increasingly scarce labor—the creators of the Toyota system subtly modified Taylorite methods and mind-sets to address urgent needs. Some have maintained that the critical environmental factor in the evolution of "lean production" was the lack of sustained labor opposition: according to Dohse, Jurgens, and Malsch, for example, " 'Toyotism' is simply the practice of the organizational principles of Fordism under conditions in which management prerogatives are largely unlimited."[150] Even Ōno Taiichi conceded that his reforms might have been impossible in an environment of powerful craft unions and hostile workers.[151] However appealing, the assertion that "lean production" was premised on the managerial evisceration of labor resistance is not entirely convincing. Such a view underestimates the informal influence of worker sentiment on management decision making (as revealed in the forging of the postwar wage compromise), and it ignores the fact that Japanese workers historically accepted Taylorization much more

---

the Line at Subaru-Isuzu: The Japanese Model and the American Worker (Ithaca, N.Y.: ILR Press, 1995), 131; Stephen Wood, "The Japanization of Fordism," *Economic and Industrial Democracy* 14 (1993): 535–55. Compare Onitsuka, "Sengo Nihon," 246.

[148] Ohno, *Toyota Production System,* 130; Cusumano, *The Japanese Automobile Industry,* 209; Wood, "The Japanization of Fordism," 540.

[149] Cusumano, *The Japanese Automobile Industry,* 266. See also Price, *Japan Works,* 187–88.

[150] Dohse, Jurgens, and Malsch, "From 'Fordism' to 'Toyotism'?" 141. See also Price, *Japan Works,* 13–14. Burawoy notes that "the Japanese [case] most closely approximates the despotic order of early capitalism"; Michael Burawoy, *The Politics of Production* (London: Verso, 1985), 143–45. See also Kumazawa, *Portraits of the Japanese Workplace,* 4, 11.

[151] Cusumano, *The Japanese Automobile Industry,* 306–7; Kenney and Florida, *Beyond Mass Production,* 38.

readily than their American counterparts did. Moreover, under the prevailing productivist consensus in postwar Japan, workers may well have accepted extensive job redesign—and even tolerated work intensification—as a fair price for rising wages and improving lifestyles.[152]

In some ways, however, the Toyota system did constitute an application of Taylorite principles more rigorous than even what American managers were accustomed to. Pursuing waste elimination with a thoroughness bordering on obsession, Ōno and his colleagues were able, in the words of one Western analyst, to "out-Taylor us all."[153] In his attempts to slash "non-value-added work," for instance, Ōno applied job routines far stricter than the standards recommended by American Taylorites or the experts of Japan's efficiency movement. Under the Toyota regime, standard times for workshop tasks were based on the abilities of the most skilled workers, rather than being pegged at an average level or set in accordance with scientifically determined optimal times. As Ōno explained, "If you are going to run the operation 10 times, take the shortest time as the standard. Some people say this makes the standard too stringent, but what is stringent about it? Whatever method takes the shortest time is the easiest." What's more, Ōno warned, "When you establish standard times, leave no breaks at all for workers to attend to personal hygiene."[154] Indeed, Ōno seemed to believe that even the slightest wasted motion or idle time on the part of workers was a form of soldiering and had to be eradicated. Going beyond the most rigid Taylorite notions, Toyota ordered that employees with time to spare stand at attention by their machines or report to a designated area so that managers could see that they were underutilized and could assign them additional duties.[155]

For all the Toyota system's elaborations on Scientific Management, its rhetorical emphasis remained rooted in the vocabulary of "revised Taylorism." "Lean production"—which Ōno Taiichi tagged a "revolution in consciousness"[156] —was portrayed by its advocates as a distinctive fusion of rationalization and respect for humanity. In the estimation of Monden Yasuhiro, "The Toyota production system attempts to increase productivity and reduce manufacturing

[152] Compare Wood, "The Japanization of Fordism," 551 n. 2: "There seems no reason why we should refer to unfettered managerial prerogatives as a specific hallmark of a Japanese Fordism. Was not this precisely what Taylor and Ford urged, and in the latter case fought bitterly to maintain, albeit unsuccessfully?"

[153] Richard J. Schonberger, *Japanese Management Techniques: Nine Hidden Lessons in Simplicity* (New York: Free Press, 1982), 193. See also Graham Sewell and Barry Wilkinson, "'Someone to Watch Over Me': Surveillance, Discipline, and the Just-In-Time Labour Process," *Sociology* 26, no. 2 (May 1992): 271–89; Frank Webster and Kevin Robins, "'I'll be Watching You': Comment on Sewell and Wilkinson," *Sociology* 27, no. 2 (May 1993): 243–52.

[154] Ohno, *Workplace Management,* 151–52.

[155] Ogawa, *Modern Production Management,* 120; Japan Management Association, *Kanban,* 76, 139.

[156] Ohno, *Toyota Production System,* 15.

costs. Unlike other such systems, however, it reaches its goal without a loss in the human dignity of the worker."[157] As another observer proclaimed, "Production management encompasses both technological and human elements. The Toyota system suggests an entirely new method of analyzing these two elements simultaneously under one scheme. . . . In this sense, the Toyota system is a monument in the history of production management."[158]

Nevertheless, as with previous Japanese initiatives in managerial reform, "Toyotism's" definition of "human dignity" was vague, the managerial commitment to change was weak, and humanization remained peripheral to the larger project of Taylorization. Most champions of the "lean" system paid only lip service to humanization: as Shingō Shigeo advised, "However great its rewards may be, total employee involvement still remains a seasoning. We must not allow its benefits to distract us from basic flaws in production management functions."[159] Some proponents, on the other hand, endeavored—earnestly, and with a remarkable ability to ignore glaring contradictions—to align Toyota's mode of Taylorite rationalization with a spirit of humanity. According to one Japanese observer,

> Respect for human dignity, as Toyota understands it, means "to eliminate from the work force worthless, parasitical persons who should not be there and to awaken in all the awareness that they can improve the work place through their own efforts and to foster a feeling of belongingness. . . ."
>
> Usually progress in standardization results in repetitious work and leads to alienation from the job. On the other hand, a strict standardization makes it easier to understand a job, leads to the discovery of questionable or deficient points, and makes it easier to identify parasitical persons.[160]

In the end, therefore, like prior efforts at reform in the "revised Taylorite" vein, the "lean" paradigm offered a rich rhetoric of humanization, but articulated neither a consistent vision nor an explicit blueprint for change.

Despite such limitations, the Toyota system represented an important achievement. "Lean manufacturing" was an ingenious and practical rearrangement of the Taylorite building blocks of the Fordist order, resulting in a new—and seemingly non-Fordist—model of industrial production. As such, the Toyota accomplishment undermined the conviction, so long cherished on both

---

[157] Monden, *Toyota Production System,* 177. See also Kosuge Toshitaka, *Tashu shōryō seisan no tankyū* (Osaka: Seikōsha, 1988), part 1.

[158] Ogawa, *Modern Production Management,* 133. Ogawa also maintained that "the Toyota system is a means of nurturing people" while remarking blithely that "on the other hand, workers having value gaps, ill health and weak minds become dropouts" (130).

[159] Shingō, *The Shingō Production Management System,* 81.

[160] Quoted in Dohse, Jurgens, and Malsch, "From 'Fordism' to 'Toyotism'?" 127. Ōno claimed that "Carrying out the standard work methods in the cycle time helps worker harmony grow"; Ohno, *Toyota Production System,* 22. Monden declared that rapid die changes can lead to a "morale boost" among employees; Monden, *Toyota Production System,* 121.

sides of the Pacific, that there was a single evolutionary trajectory of production management running from the Taylorized workshop to the Fordist assembly line. Like the postwar "ability wage" compromise, the Toyota system constituted a rejection of contemporary American "best practice" yet represented an unmistakable reaffirmation of longstanding Taylorite mind-sets and methods. Despite postwar changes in Japan's political economy that appeared to favor the Fordist transformation of industry, the logic of Taylorite solutions—most basically, the drive to wring the utmost efficiency out of existing facilities and personnel through incremental change—remained firmly ingrained in the consciousness of Japanese managers.

Considering the volume of new and updated techniques that flooded into Japan from the United States during the 1950s and 1960s, such continuity is particularly striking. Although confronted by an often overwhelming barrage of imported innovations, Japanese managers used the "revised Taylorite" consensus as a consistent standard for appraising alternative models of reform. Measured by this yardstick, some of the postwar introductions (like Human Relations) were embraced and readily integrated into established practice, others (like job wages) were tested and modified to accord with existing assumptions, while a few (like the dictates of classic Fordism) were scrutinized, evaluated, and ultimately passed over in favor of more familiar Taylorite approaches. As this pattern suggests, not only was the landscape of managerial reform increasingly complex and diverse in the decades following World War II, but Japanese managers were growing increasingly discriminating and self-assured as they picked and chose, adapting and rejecting even "state-of-the-art" American techniques. Yet more significantly, as the course of shop-floor managerial reform during the Occupation and the "miracle" economy revealed, the methods of Scientific Management and the "revised Taylorite" ideology remained a durable touchstone for Japanese managers through the postwar experience of dislocation, sweeping systemic change, and unprecedented industrial growth.

6

Taylorism Transformed?

SCIENTIFIC MANAGEMENT AND QUALITY CONTROL, 1945–1973

ALTHOUGH "lean production" is now celebrated as the decisive managerial breakthrough of postwar Japan, neither just-in-time nor the kanban system—indeed, none of the shop-floor innovations that made up the Toyota model—could provide the final element vital to completing the "revised Taylorite" transformation of Japanese industry. For all its sophistication and dynamism, the Toyota program was not able to surmount the two major obstacles that had dogged Japan's scientific managers since the days of the Taishō efficiency movement: first, the lack of a reformist agenda that could credibly fuse respect for humanity with economic rationality, and second, the absence of an organizational structure and strategy that could effectively disseminate new management models throughout Japanese industry. Like previous Taylorite initiatives, the Toyota system failed to address the issue of "humanization" in a meaningful way, relying on rhetorical flourishes rather than a concrete program of reform. Moreover, "lean production" remained a prototype with limited application outside the factories of Toyota, at least until the mid-1970s. As a virtually proprietary invention, the "lean" paradigm could not become an effective engine of innovation and stood in the background, rather than the vanguard, of Japanese efforts at managerial modernization. In the end, it would be Japan's postwar quality control movement—and not the vaunted "lean production" regime—that would define an explicit mechanism for "humanization," establish an organizational apparatus for diffusing change, and deliver at last on the Taylorite ideals long embraced by Japanese management reformers.

What would prove ironic, and yet well in keeping with the history of Scientific Management in Japan, was that quality control would be hailed almost universally as the essence of a singular "Japanese-style management," a potent symbol of the departure of Japanese ways from a discredited American managerial heritage. But those who celebrated the techniques of Japanese quality control as distinctive innovations which transcended the classic tenets of Taylorism were not entirely off target. As in the making of the Toyota production system, in the postwar forging of the quality control movement Japanese managers and engineers appear to have realized the promise of Taylorism and yet, simultaneously, recast the practice of traditional Scientific

Management. Thus, in the thirty years after World War II, quality control would emerge both as the definitive manifestation of what makes "Japanese-style management" unique and as the long-awaited innovation which would finally render the "revised Taylorite" vision into shop-floor reality.

The Discovery of Quality

The quality of manufactured goods was historically a sore point for Japanese industry. Through the interwar period, pallid efforts at standardization, a limited spread of Taylorized mass production, and the prevalence of unsystematic, rule-of-thumb techniques (even in nominally "modern" workshops) translated into a poor record of product precision, reliability, and uniformity. The "cheap and shoddy" character of Japanese manufactures reached its nadir during the Pacific War, when mobilization emphasized quantity to the virtually complete sacrifice of quality. After the war, as industrialists and economic planners began to think anew of reentry into world trade, the abysmal international reputation of Japanese goods haunted those who put their faith in export-led growth.[1]

Developed in the United States and Britain in the 1920s, modern quality control (QC) is usually understood as the use of statistical analysis in the production process to ensure conformity to standards. The concept was formally introduced into Japan by Scientific Management proponent Kiribuchi Kanzō in a 1934 monograph, although a few firms with foreign technical tie-ups had begun experimenting with managerial statistics well before this time.[2] For example, starting in 1931, QC pioneer Ishida Yasushi (a Tokyo Shibaura engineer and member of Ikeda Tōshirō's Efficiency Society) studied the latest American techniques and developed a distinctive "scroll" (*makimono*) system of control charts.[3] During the war, there was a surge of interest in modern QC among academic statisticians and managers in the military industries. In 1942, Ishida and Kyūshū University professor Kitagawa Toshio published a translation of the classic E. S. Pearson work *The Application of Statistical Methods to Industrial Standardization and Quality Control.* The following year, a public-private "research group" (*kenkyū tonarigumi*) of engineers and statisticians was formed under the auspices of the Technology Agency (Gijutsu-in)

---

[1] See, for example, Tsūshō sangyō shō, *Nenpō 1949* (Tsūshō sangyō shō, 1949), 171; Higashi Hidehiko, "Wagakuni ni okeru hinshitsu kanri," *Hinshitsu kanri* 1, no. 2 (April 1950): 5.

[2] Kiribuchi's book, *Kōgyō kanri yōran* (Yoshida kōmujō shuppanbu, 1934), only included three pages on what he called *hinshitsu tōsei.* Sasaki Satoshi and Nonaka Izumi, "Nihon ni okeru kagakuteki kanrihō no dōnyū to tenkai," in *Kagakuteki kanrihō no dōnyū to tenkai—sono rekishiteki kokusai hikaku,* ed. Hara Terushi (Kyōtō: Shōwadō, 1990), 261.

[3] "Zadankai: Nihon no hinshitsu kanri no ayumi o kaerimiru," *Hinshitsu kanri* 9, no. 6 (June 1958): 34–37; Sasaki and Nonaka, "Kagakuteki kanrihō," 262.

to study mathematical approaches to mass production.[4] Nevertheless, such wartime initiatives remained more theoretical than practical in outlook. Although traditional Taylorite techniques for assuring quality (particularly inspections) were widely used, modern statistical QC was not systematically applied in any Japanese workshops before 1945.[5]

In the years immediately following the war, quality remained a major industrial problem, yet one which attracted minimal practical attention. The first significant effort to address the issue of product quality and increase awareness of modern QC was the work of the Civil Communications Section of the American Occupation bureaucracy. As noted earlier, much of the consulting and training conducted by the CCS engineers was devoted to introducing fundamental methods for improving precision and conformity to standards in the Japanese electronics industry.[6] Moreover, even though only a small part of the "CCS course" was dedicated to QC, many observers credit the seminar series with kindling top-management interest in quality and laying the groundwork for the postwar QC movement.[7] But notwithstanding the catalytic effects of the American initiatives, it was not CCS consulting or the legacy of Occupation engineers that ultimately powered the "QC revolution" in Japan. Rather, it was the efforts of Japanese activists, and primarily the exertions of one organization—the Union of Japanese Scientists and Engineers (Nihon Kagaku Gijutsu Renmeikai, usually abbreviated JUSE)—that would play the pivotal role in the postwar drive for quality.

JUSE was formally established in May 1946, but it had roots stretching back well into the war years. JUSE was the successor to the Dai-Nihon Gijutsu-kai (Greater Japanese Technological Association), an umbrella organization formed in 1944 from the merger of three prominent groups of scientific personnel.[8] The members of these wartime organizations were primarily discontented government engineers and technical officers, specialists who were barred by tradition from top bureaucratic posts. Emphasizing the value of scientific expertise to modern industry and warfare, the associations aimed,

---

[4] Ibid., 263–64.

[5] Fujita Tadashi, "Hinshitsu kanri hatten no rekishiteki kōsatsu," *Hinshitsu kanri* 5, no. 11 (November 1954): 69.

[6] On CCS consulting, see Nonaka Izumi, "SQC no dōnyū (2)," Ibid., 41, no. 3 (March 1990): 56–60.

[7] Discussion of QC constituted about 60 pages of the 350-page CCS course textbook. Kogure Masao, *Nihon no TQC* (JUSE, 1988), 18–20; Watanabe Eizō and Miura Shin, "SQC no dōnyū (1)," *Hinshitsu kanri* 41, no. 2 (February 1990): 68. Homer Sarasohn's contributions were particularly appreciated and he was later tagged a "benefactor" (*onjin*) of Japanese quality control. Koyanagi Ken'ichi, "Joshiki no sekai o kaerimiru," *Hinshitsu kanri* 2, no. 1 (January 1951): 29; "Zadankai: Nihon no hinshitsu kanri," 39–40.

[8] The groups were the Industrial Policy Association (Kōseikai, founded 1918), the Japan Technological Association (Nihon Gijutsu Kyōkai, 1935), and the All-Japan Federation of Science and Technology (Zen-Nihon Kagaku Gijutsu Tōdōkai, 1940). The organizational ancestry of JUSE is described in Sasaki and Nonaka, "Kagakuteki kanrihō," 269–70.

through collective action, to increase the social status and professional opportunities of engineers and scientists.[9] JUSE, therefore, was the postwar heir to a
rich tradition of "New Order" technocracy and reformism. While some have
asserted that the group adopted the title "union" just to satisfy Occupation
authorities, JUSE clearly had a politicized heritage and an activist edge. The
inaugural issue of the organization's newsletter was headed with the slogan,
"Scientists and Engineers! Join Hands for the Sake of Our Native Land!" and
called for a "united front in science and technology."[10]

Nevertheless, as Nakaoka Tetsurō has remarked, JUSE was hardly "an engineers' trade union."[11] Rather, in the first years after the war, JUSE had more
of the air of a social club. Offering members "chic" and "comfortable" sitting
rooms and a snack bar in the Osaka Shōsen building near Tokyo Station, the
"Engineers' Club" was a forum for informal contacts among government
technicians and, increasingly, private-sector engineers and executives.[12]
Styled an "oasis," the club was a haven of sorts for technical personnel whose
factories were bombed out or who were underemployed in the postwar hyperinflation.[13] In a broader sense, the JUSE "Engineers' Club" had significance
as a venue for debating the scientific aspects of economic reconstruction, and
as a place where managers and bureaucrats could transcend the "feudal" proclivities of the past and freely discuss their visions of the future.[14]

From the start, JUSE was keenly aware of its members' potential importance to Japan's economic recovery. As managing director Koyanagi Ken'ichi
observed in 1948, Japanese industry lacked many essential inputs—capital,
raw materials, and so forth—but what it needed most desperately was modern
scientific knowledge.[15] "Industrial rationalization is in your hands!" the
group's chairman declared; "The technical level of our workshops can sky-
rocket as a result of your stimulus and exertions."[16] Such an approach, of
course, promised not only industrial prosperity, but also enhanced status for
engineers and scientists: "The Mission of Technologists Is Growing Ever
More Weighty," one association slogan averred.[17]

[9] Nakaoka Tetsurō, "Senchū, sengo no kagakuteki kanri undō II," *Keizaigaku zasshi* 82, no. 3
(September 1981): 52; see also Mizuno Shigeru, *Zensha sōgō hinshitsu kanri* (JUSE, 1984), 364;
Ikezawa Tokio, "SQC no reimeiki," *Hinshitsu kanri* 41, no. 1 (January 1990): 74–75.

[10] *Nihon kagaku gijutsu renmei nyūsu,* 25 July 1946, 1; "Zadankai: Nihon no hinshitsu kanri,"
41.

[11] Nakaoka Tetsurō, "Production Management in Japan before the Period of High Economic
Growth," *Osaka City University Economic Review* 17 (1981): 16.

[12] *Enjinia kurabu* 1 (June 1948): 1.

[13] Ibid., 3 (August 1948): 2; Miura Shin, "Hinshitsu kanri sōgyō jidai no kaiko," *Hinshitsu
kanri* 31, no. 3 (March 1980): 28.

[14] See Ishikawa Ichirō, "Gijutsusha no shinboku to renraku," *Enjinia kurabu* 1 (June 1948): 1.

[15] Koyanagi Ken'ichi, "Atarashii minshū sekai o gijutsusha no nichijō," ibid., 2.

[16] Ishikawa Ichirō, "Fukkō e no michi . . . ," ibid., 12 (May 1949): 1.

[17] Ibid., 14 (July 1949): 1.

On a more mundane level, however, the JUSE leadership was aware that contributing to the nation's industrial recovery could provide the organization with a sharper sense of purpose and a means for raising much-needed funds. Like the Efficiency Association, JUSE flirted with bankruptcy after losing its wartime subsidies, but in 1949 was granted a generous contract from the Economic Stabilization Board (Keizai Antei Honbu) to produce a report on wartime technological advancements abroad.[18] The project not only ensured solvency, but it also allowed the organization's staff to investigate the relevance of new scientific discoveries to Japan's economic reconstruction. JUSE apparently recognized the opportunity to identify—and then appropriate—promising foreign technologies for introduction into Japan. After combing the Occupation's American library at Hibiya and evaluating subjects like atomic energy, heat-resistant alloys, and ultra high-frequency communications, JUSE's leaders finally settled on a topic which could serve as the fulcrum of the organization's research, educational, and promotional activities.[19] The new technology judged most relevant and promising for JUSE-sponsored introduction was statistical quality control.

The selection of modern QC—and, more generally, the field of industrial management—was well considered and well timed. In the wake of the war, management experts began to recognize the importance of statistical methods in American mass production, and their almost total absence in Japanese industry.[20] As JUSE officer Niki Shōichirō argued in 1949,

> We were deeply impressed by our recent finding that in Britain and the United States statistical quality control developed enormously during the war. . . . Why can we not have such refined techniques? . . . Every Japanese will remember the fact that during the war our industry produced innumerable planes which couldn't keep aloft long enough to meet any enemy plane to fight with. Many promising youths were doomed to die in the Pacific Ocean because our production control, so formidably imposed, lacked the least bit of scientific spirit. It is even more regrettable, however, to find that many company managers still believe that such refined techniques are not suitable to the methods of "backward Japan." This is a terrible complex which will keep Japan permanently an underdeveloped country. . . . We must realize that cheap, intensive labor and old-fashioned craftsmanship are of no use for modern industry now. . . . If our manufacturers want to keep up the competitiveness of their products in overseas markets, the only solution is to adopt scientific techniques right now.[21]

[18] "Zadankai: Nihon no hinshitsu kanri," 41; Nakaoka, "Senchū, sengo II," 53; Watanabe and Miura, "SQC no dōnyū (1)," 68–69.

[19] Nakaoka, "Senchū, sengo II," 53; Miura, "Hinshitsu kanri sōgyō," 29; "Zadankai: Nihon no hinshitsu kanri," 41.

[20] Nakayama Takasachi, *Shin nōritsu soshiki no tatekata* (Sangyō keiri kyōkai, 1947), 2; Noda Nobuo, "Amerika-shiki kagakuteki keiei," in *Amerika no keiei gijutsu,* ed. Noda Nobuo et al. (Daiyamondo, 1951), 6.

[21] Nakaoka, "Production Management," 17.

Striking a less strident note, the chairman of JUSE explained in 1950 that Japan needed a "positive" approach to rationalization that avoided the "negative," job-slashing strategies of the past. At the same time, he warned, industry was too strapped financially to undertake the massive investments in new technology prescribed by government economic planners. The way out of the dilemma seemed obvious: the quality control expertise of JUSE offered companies a cheap technological shortcut in reducing costs and boosting competitiveness.[22]

By 1950, then, quality control was firmly installed as the focus of JUSE efforts to support economic recovery by "reviving science and perfecting technology."[23] It is significant to note that, even at this early point, several broad tendencies and characteristics that would mark the Japanese QC movement had already become apparent. First, although there were a number of organizations promoting quality methods in the latter half of the Occupation —the Efficiency Association, the Japan Standards Association (Nihon Kikaku Kyōkai), the Ministry of International Trade and Industry—modern QC was regarded with virtually proprietary interest by JUSE. There was (and would continue to be) considerable unspoken competition among the various management reform groups. Each sought to define its turf in such a way as to ensure almost monopolistic methodological autonomy and, presumably as a result, financial stability. JUSE never became a consultancy firm like the Efficiency Association, yet QC-related programs and publishing income were the organization's economic lifeblood. JUSE thus seized upon the concept of modern quality control much as the Efficiency Association had long claimed a somewhat broader approach to Taylorism as its rightful province.

Second, the leadership of the postwar quality movement was remarkably well defined even before the end of the Occupation. The breeding ground for this relatively small core of leaders was the "Quality Control Research Group," the JUSE committee that "discovered" QC and set up the organization's first quality training courses in 1949 and 1950. Among the group members were later QC luminaries Koyanagi Ken'ichi, Gotō Masao, Miura Shin, Mizuno Shigeru, Watanabe Eizō, Kogure Masao, and Nishibori Eizaburō.[24] A noteworthy participant was Ishikawa Kaoru, who would emerge as the intellectual rudder of the quality movement, but was then a newly appointed professor of engineering at Tokyo University. Ishikawa was recommended to the

---

[22] Ishikawa Ichirō, "Sōkan no kotoba," *Hinshitsu kanri* 1, no. 1 (March 1950): 2; see also "Kagaku gijutsu undō no tōitsu sensen no kyūmu," *Nihon kagaku gijutsu renmei nyūsu*, 25 July 1946, 2.

[23] "Kagaku no fukkō, gijutsu no jūjitsu," *Enjinia kurabu* 20 (January 1950): 1.

[24] The original members of the Research Group were Koyanagi, Gotō, Miura, Mizuno, Watanabe and Baba Shigenori. Koyanagi Ken'ichi, *The Deming Prize*, rev. ed. (Tokyo: JUSE, 1960), 2–3; *Enjinia kurabu* 16 (September 1949): 1; Mizuno, *Zensha sōgō*, 364–65; Ikezawa Tokio, "SQC no reimeiki," 75.

group by his father, the founding chairman of JUSE, Ishikawa Ichirō.[25] Beyond bequeathing his son to the quality cause, Ishikawa senior had a profound influence on the early QC movement: as a wartime leader of the chemical industry control association, the postwar president of corporate giant Shōwa Denkō, and the first chairman of the powerful industrial federation Keidanren, he established strong, lasting links between the big business community and JUSE.[26] Thus, modern quality control was propelled in Japan by a dynamic alliance of top managers, engineering staff from the major industries, and prominent scientific scholars.[27]

Third and finally, it should be noted that although the direct ties between JUSE and Japanese Taylorism were not particularly strong, the indirect ties and the philosophical overlap were extensive. Among the early activists in JUSE, only Katō Takeo (who was involved in QC training programs) was a prominent veteran of the prewar efficiency movement. Some JUSE quality experts did have prior experience with the Efficiency Association: Kogure Masao, for instance, was a graduate of Horime's wartime work-study course and Nishibori Eizaburō was an association advisor. Yet like Ishikawa Kaoru, most of the leaders were either too young or too professionally distant from management (as academic engineers or statisticians) to have been efficiency movement adherents.[28] Nevertheless, all of the early QC advocates were apparently conversant with Scientific Management and some, such as Gotō Masao, conceded being deeply influenced by Taylorite thought.[29]

Moreover, the objectives and assumptions of the JUSE leadership were steeped in Taylorism. In celebrating the power and objectivity of science, in seeking to introduce scientific analysis into management, in promoting the status of technologists, and in embracing technocratic managerialism, the fundamental tenets of JUSE were clearly consistent with Scientific Management. Even if quality control engineers remained somewhat scornful of unprofessional "efficiency experts," and the Efficiency Association occasionally bris-

[25] Ishikawa Kaoru, "Koyanagi-san no omoide," *Hinshitsu kanri* 16, no. 2 (February 1965); Ishikawa Kaoru, "Taidan: Nihonteki hinshitsu kanri no tenkai," *Keiei to rekishi* 9 (September 1986): 18–20.

[26] Since Ishikawa Ichirō, every chairman of JUSE had been a serving or past president of Keidanren. Robert E. Cole, *Strategies for Learning* (Berkeley: University of California Press, 1989), 276; Michael A. Cusumano, *The Japanese Automobile Industry: Technology and Management at Nissan and Toyota* (Cambridge, Mass.: Harvard University Press, 1985), 323–24.

[27] Many of the academic participants in the QC effort had records of antiestablishment activism, and thus made strange bedfellows for some of the corporate functionaries associated with JUSE. Nakaoka, "Senchū, sengo II," 54–55; Nakaoka Tetsurō, "QC Nihon no shūhon de," in *Sengo Nihon o kangaeru,* ed. Hidaka Rokurō (Chikura shobō, 1986), 68.

[28] Ishikawa, "Taidan," 28; Kogure, *Nihon no TQC,* 494.

[29] Gotō Masao, "Hinshitsu kanri shi shodai henshū kanjichō no koro," *Hinshitsu kanri* 16, no. 3 (March 1965): 2; Hara Yasusaburō, "Keiei no seishin," ibid., 15, no. 1 (January 1964): 13.

tled at JUSE scholasticism and snobbery, the two organizations and their members stood on the same philosophical bedrock.[30]

W. Edwards Deming and Japanese Quality Control

The genesis of quality control in Japan is almost universally associated with the name W. Edwards Deming. A statistician and management consultant, Deming was involved in the Japanese quality movement from its inception, advising, teaching, and working with JUSE from 1950 until his death in 1993. Through most of his long career, Deming labored in obscurity, virtually unknown in American academic and business circles. In the early 1980s, however, Deming and his role in Japanese QC were "discovered" by the American media, and he was hailed as "the American who taught the Japanese about quality."[31] The irascible, opinionated octogenarian soon became a media darling and much sought-after lecturer, invariably stressing the message of American decline and Japanese managerial triumph. Constructed by his admirers as a statistical superman, a "capitalist revolutionary," a Jeremiah in the industrial wilderness, the Commodore Perry of management, Deming and his work in Japan soon assumed legendary proportions.[32]

In American business schools and boardrooms, W. Edwards Deming was credited with almost single-handedly revolutionizing Japanese management practice, and thus indirectly spawning the postwar Japanese economic "miracle." One tidy exposition of this flourishing mythology stated that "During the early 1950s, Deming was invited to Japan to advise business leaders on quality. What he told them sparked the Japanese industrial revolution. . . ."[33] Dubbed "the genius who revitalized Japanese industry,"[34] Deming feigned no

[30] Statement by Morikawa Kakuzō, "Hinshitsu kanri shi: 100-gō kinen ni yosete," ibid., 9, no. 6 (June 1958): 5.

[31] Rafael Aguayo, *Dr. Deming: The American Who Taught the Japanese About Quality* (New York: Lyle Stuart, 1990); see also W. Edwards Deming, *Out of the Crisis* (Cambridge: Cambridge University Press, 1982); Lloyd Dobyns and Claire Crawford-Mason, *Quality or Else: The Revolution in World Business* (Boston: Houghton Mifflin, 1991); Andrea Gabor, *The Man Who Discovered Quality* (New York: Penguin, 1990); Cecelia S. Kilian, *The World of W. Edwards Deming,* 2d ed. (Knoxville, Tenn.: SPC Press, 1992); Mary Walton, *The Deming Management Method* (New York: Perigee Books, 1986). For a kid-gloved effort to demystify Deming's role in Japan, see Robert Cole, "What was Deming's Real Influence?" *Across the Board* 24, no. 2 (February 1987): 49–51. For a more complete evaluation of Deming's contributions, see William M. Tsutsui, "W. Edwards Deming and the Origins of Quality Control in Japan," *Journal of Japanese Studies* 22, no. 2 (Summer 1996): 295–325.

[32] Lloyd Dobyns, "Ed Deming Wants Big Changes, and He Wants Them Fast," *Smithsonian* 21, no. 5 (August 1990): 82.

[33] Aguayo, *Dr. Deming,* jacket copy.

[34] Walton, *Deming Management Method,* jacket copy.

modesty regarding his contributions to Japanese QC. "I exported to Japan what had never been done before," he declared, "I took to them a new theory, a theory of a system. They learned it. . . . I taught them."[35] As he noted elsewhere, "The whole world is familiar with the miracle of Japan, and knows that the miracle started off with a concussion in 1950."[36] In the context of such vigorous self-promotion and widespread lionization in the popular press, Deming became a hero to American business thinkers, his legend offering the therapeutic message that Japan's management successes were really "Made in America."

Whether or not one sees Deming as the progenitor of the "miracle" economy or the father of Japanese quality control, he undeniably had a high profile in Japan's early QC movement.[37] Deming first visited Japan in 1947, as part of an Occupation team assisting in the preparation of a postwar census. Based on this experience, and his reputation as a pioneer in statistics and QC, he was invited by JUSE in 1950 to return to Japan and deliver a series of lectures on quality techniques. Deming subsequently visited Japan on an almost annual basis, developing a close relationship with JUSE and many of its leaders, and teaching QC courses to a large number of engineers, middle managers, and top-brass industrialists. A Japanese translation of one set of Deming's lectures was published and Deming donated the royalties to JUSE. Deming's generosity was more symbolic than financial: at the exchange rate of the time, the gift was only a small sum in U.S. dollars.[38] Nonetheless, the leaders of JUSE used these funds to create an award, named for its American benefactor, which they hoped would draw attention to the fledgling quality movement. In this, of course, the Deming Prize exceeded all expectations. Within a decade of its inception in 1951, the prize was acknowledged as the premier accolade in corporate Japan and had become a source of considerable publicity for JUSE. For Deming, a modest donation ended up yielding huge returns in prestige: the success of the prize cemented Deming's reputation as a pathbreaker in Japanese management and guaranteed that his name would become inextricably linked with Japanese advances in quality control.

Deming's first lectures in the summer of 1950 were well received, especially in the business community, and certainly stimulated broader interest in quality control at a crucial juncture for the nascent movement. Nevertheless,

---

[35] Quoted in Dobyns and Crawford-Mason, *Quality or Else,* 94.

[36] Deming, *Out of the Crisis,* 486.

[37] On Deming's activities in Japan, see Kilian, *World,* chaps. 1–7, 15; for a Japanese account, see Watanabe and Miura, "SQC no dōnyū (1)," 70; Ishikawa Kaoru, *What Is Total Quality Control? The Japanese Way,* trans. David Lu (Englewood Cliffs, N.J.: Prentice-Hall, 1985), 17–18.

[38] As of 1960, the total royalties that had accrued to JUSE from the Deming donation were ¥261,764. At the ¥360 = $1 exchange rate, this amounted to only $727. Koyanagi Ken'ichi, *The Deming Prize,* rev. ed. (Tokyo: JUSE, 1960), 21.

Deming's offerings did not have an incendiary intellectual impact among the growing ranks of QC advocates associated with JUSE. To these young engineers and managers, Deming was an august teacher who explained statistical concepts clearly and engagingly, not a visionary innovator who proffered novel approaches and methods.[39] Indeed, Deming's wisdom (which centered on statistical sampling models) appeared rather prosaic to the vanguard of quality experts in JUSE who had exhaustively studied the prewar and wartime American literature on QC. Even by the time of Deming's second lecture tour in 1951, thinly veiled expressions of disappointment and disillusionment were common in JUSE publications. Expecting to be dazzled with new statistical advances from the United States, many Japanese observers were discouraged to find that Deming had no new tricks to pull from his statistical hat.[40] Deming did continue to inspire some of his Japanese audience—a few responding with almost religious zeal[41]—but the sense that the Japanese students had already outstripped their American teacher was unspoken but widespread.

In short, Deming was only fleetingly the intellectual beacon of the Japanese quality movement. Although the QC enthusiasts at JUSE fully embraced the statistical approach to quality Deming advocated, they arrived at their understanding independently of Deming's teachings and prior to his fabled 1950 lectures. Thus, rather than enlightening the unenlightened Japanese—providing the "spark that lighted the way" as he once put it[42]—Deming's work in Japan served more to reinforce and confirm the existing inclinations of JUSE's precocious QC activists. Deming was, in other words, preaching to the converted, and the gospel was already familiar and cherished by his earnest congregation. Not surprisingly, then, Deming never assumed the same exalted status in the Japanese annals of quality control which he attained in American retellings of the 1980s and 1990s. Most Japanese chroniclers have dismissed Deming as a curious footnote to the story of Japanese QC, often damning his contributions with faint praise or enveloping him in saccharine, sentimental hyperbole.[43]

Even if it is apparent that W. Edwards Deming did not single-handedly revolutionize Japanese manufacturing or directly sow the seeds of the economic "miracle," he did perform significant functions within the early QC movement. Contrary to the popular mythology, Deming's lasting importance

[39] Ishikawa, "Taidan," 22.

[40] "Zadankai: Deming hakase no shidō ni manabu," *Hinshitsu kanri* 2, no. 9 (September 1951): 9–14; Mizuno Shigeru, "Deming hakase no sokuseki," ibid., no. 10 (October 1951): 7–8.

[41] Ina Masao, "Deming hakase no erementarii kōsu o jukō shite," ibid., no. 9 (September 1951): 9–11.

[42] "Statistical Techniques as a Natural Resource: A Message from W. Edwards Deming to the Ceremony for the Annual Award of the Deming Prize," ibid., 6, no. 12 (December 1955): 2.

[43] Tsutsui, "W. Edwards Deming," 321–23.

was as an instrument, rather than as an instigator, in the promotion of quality control in postwar Japan. Almost from the start, Deming's value lay not in his knowledge (which could as easily be acquired from books) but in his very presence in Japan. As a status symbol, as a source of authority, and as a kind of living talisman for quality control, Deming was a boon for JUSE and the quality movement. As an American expert who could lay claim to a certain professional standing, Deming added cachet to JUSE's QC initiatives and provided a drawing card that improved the organization's financial standing and its profile in the business world.[44] Prior to the founding of the JPC, Western management specialists were infrequent visitors to Japan and JUSE's exclusive association with Deming was a prestigious and highly visible feather in its institutional cap. JUSE was by no means averse to making the most of this special relationship. For example, the Deming Prize medal, designed by professors at the Tokyo University of Fine Arts and depicting the donor in full profile, was used prominently in JUSE publications and was for many years something of an unofficial logo for the organization. Thus the image of Deming—as well as his name—was appropriated as a tool in marketing quality control to the Japanese public.

Beyond this symbolic role, Deming also provided invaluable psychological support to the first generation of leaders in the quality movement. The relationship between Deming and JUSE sometimes seemed little more than a sugarcoated mutual admiration society.[45] Deming was treated with deference, respect, and even indulgence in his visits to Japan, and he reciprocated by showering hyperbolic praise on his Japanese students. Fulsome with compliments, encouragement, and expressions of faith, Deming told the Japanese QC pioneers exactly what they wanted to hear. If industry adopted QC, he assured his audiences, Japan could be a great exporter in a matter of years, leaving its international competitors begging for protection.[46] Over and over again, he stressed that Japanese quality control was in the hands of exceptionally skilled specialists, and that he had great confidence in their prospects of success.[47] "Statistical talent is Japan's natural resource," he repeatedly announced, to the great satisfaction of his hosts.[48] Such phrases made good copy for JUSE publicity—and they were readily used as such—but his words also confirmed and encouraged the ambitions of the Japanese QC vanguard.

---

[44] On Deming's financial and status benefits to JUSE, see Kilian, *World,* 20–21.

[45] On his visits to Japan, Deming was treated virtually as a god on earth. Deming took to the role well. He was constantly indulged by his Japanese hosts who recorded his every sentence and tried to read significance into his every action. Koyanagi Ken'ichi, "Dr. Deming to tomo ni," *Hinshitsu kanri* 2, no. 9 (September 1951): 5–7; Nishibori Eizaburō, "Deming-san to Ete-san," ibid., 9, no. 6 (June 1958): 25.

[46] Kilian, *World,* 10.

[47] See, for example, ibid., 8; Koyanagi, "Dr. Deming," 6.

[48] Mizuno, "Deming hakase," 7.

Ultimately, Deming's contributions in Japan—his contagious confidence, his talismanic authority, his media appeal—were only catalysts in propelling the quality movement forward. As he would later boast, Deming may well have been present at the "birth of the New Japan,"[49] yet he was neither the father nor the midwife in this momentous nativity. In the end, it was the efforts of the indefatigable JUSE faithful—and the opportune contributions of other American management experts—that had the more profound influence on the evolution of quality control in postwar Japan.

Breaking the Logjam in Quality Control

The first postwar decade has frequently been characterized as Japan's "Age of Statistical Quality Control." Strongly influenced by the traditional mainstream of American QC thought and confirmed by the teachings of Deming, the early advocates of quality in Japan concentrated on narrow, mathematically rigorous approaches to management reform. Stressing statistical sampling methods and the use of elaborate control charts in the production process, the initial JUSE efforts were highly specialized, technical, and arid. Some quick successes (as at Furukawa Electric and the chemical maker Shōwa Denkō) provided good publicity and, by the early 1950s, statistical techniques made solid headway in the advanced sectors of Japanese manufacturing. Although a 1954 survey showed that only 13 percent of some 46,000 factories used modern quality control techniques, the figures suggested that QC was relatively well diffused through larger firms and in those industries where production was already highly Taylorized. Thus, 34 percent of electronics companies reported using QC, as did 25 percent of chemical producers and about three-quarters of the firms surveyed with more than two hundred employees.[50]

Nevertheless, there was a nagging sense that despite a growing quality movement, and considerable advances in publicizing QC and understanding it theoretically, progress on the shop floor was not living up to expectations. By the end of the Occupation—indeed even by the time of Deming's second JUSE lecture tour in 1951—the QC vanguard was beginning to show its dissatisfaction with the sophisticated but abstract principles endorsed by Deming. A growing concern of the JUSE leaders was that Japanese experts, by scrupulously following their American mentors, had become excessively theoretical in their conception of quality control. The general impression was that,

---

[49] Kilian, *World,* 23.

[50] Statistics from Ishikawa Kaoru, "Nihon no hinshitsu kanri (2): QC team hōkoku," *Hinshitsu kanri* 9, no. 9 (September 1958): 89–95. The figures showed that only 5 percent of spinning firms and 16 percent of machinery firms were using modern QC. Only 8 percent of small enterprises (4–29 employees) and 26 percent of medium-sized enterprises (30–200) reported using quality control. See also Nakaoka, "Production Management," 19.

fired by a precocious zeal to learn from the United States, Japanese students of QC had fixated on the statistical paraphernalia of quality control while ignoring the question of how to apply their textbook knowledge to actual workshop situations.[51] Despite this realization, bridging the gap between abstraction and application was a constant challenge to the first generation of Japanese quality control activists. As Kogure Masao reflected on the early days of the movement (with the limited hindsight available in 1954), "Statistical methods themselves occupied the seat of honor in QC. One might say it was a time when tools used people, when it was thought that statistics were the same thing as quality control."[52]

Looking back on the early travails of quality control in Japan, many recent observers have concluded that QC made lackluster progress in industry because the methods first presented by JUSE were too complicated for shop-floor employees to comprehend. "Japanese consultants and academics had no problem understanding American statistical techniques," Michael Cusumano tells us, "although middle managers and workers who lacked specialized training in engineering and mathematics found them to be too difficult."[53] At Nissan auto plants, for example, early postwar initiatives in quality control were said to have languished because employees "found the statistical methods too difficult for anyone 'except scholars.'"[54] As Onitsuka Mitsumasa explains it, the overly theoretical presumptions of QC experts confused and alienated workshop personnel, leading to a deadlock in the advance of quality methods.[55] Thus, from the perspective of the 1980s and 1990s—when Japanese quality control has been considered synonymous with a participative approach toward labor—the statistical complexity of early postwar QC (and the Taylorite assumptions which presumably underlay it) have seemed explanation enough for the movement's first growing pains.[56]

Yet more is required to explain the logjam in the nascent quality movement than casually dismissing JUSE QC methods as too ethereal technically for shop-floor workers. Certainly, complexity was a relevant factor: even at the

[51] Nihon seisansei honbu, *Amerika no hinshitsu kanri,* Productivity Report 65 (Nihon seisansei honbu, 1959), 204–5; William S. Landes, *Nihon no keiei o shindan suru* (Nihon seisansei honbu, 1956), 40–41; Gotō Masao, "Gijutsusha no yakuwari," *Hinshitsu kanri* 2, no. 4 (April 1951): 4.

[52] Kogure Masao, "Nihon ni okeru QC shisō no hensen," ibid., 5, no. 10 (October 1954): 6. The idea that Japanese management specialists were too theoretical was, of course, a long-standing concern of the Scientific Management movement. Both during the war and after, Efficiency Association rhetoric emphasized the need to transform textbook comprehension into practical results.

[53] Cusumano, *The Japanese Automobile Industry,* 325.

[54] Ibid., 343.

[55] Onitsuka Mitsumasa, "Sengo Nihon ni okeru seisan kanri no hatten," in Sengo Nihon keiei kenkyūkai, *Sengo Nihon no kigyō keiei* (Bunshindō, 1991), 223.

[56] See Ishikawa, "Taidan," 21–24.

time, a number of experts worried about the practical difficulties of using advanced statistics in Japanese factories.[57] But the issue so accentuated by later observers—that statistical quality techniques were too challenging for production-line operatives—was apparently not a prime source of anxiety for the movement's leadership. Indeed, complexity was only one of many impediments to the progress of quality control and was, in many ways, more a symptom of deeper dynamics than a malady in its own right. At most, the impression that modern QC (as imported from the United States) seemed too sophisticated and theoretical reflected the fact that, in a majority of Japanese firms, neither the organizational structure nor the production process had yet been thoroughly Taylorized. As QC's frustrated pioneers were relatively quick to realize, breaking the logjam in quality control hinged on the accomplishment of broader management reforms, and not only on the simplification or popularization of JUSE's statistical message.

As anatomized at the time by the intellectual leaders of the QC movement, the cultivation of quality control in Japanese industry faced obstacles on three separate levels during the early 1950s. The first dilemma was that, despite JUSE's considerable institutional ties with big business, it was difficult to convince firms to follow through with quality control programs. In light of Japan's short experience with QC and the movement's teething pains, top and middle management were, understandably enough, not entirely enthusiastic about quality control at first. As JUSE came to appreciate, executives had to be persuaded that QC was viable and valuable, and that the corporate top brass should sponsor and support shop-floor quality initiatives.[58] "Naturally," one JUSE report observed, "in order to develop a program of QC where the quality responsibilities and duties of each part of the organization are well defined, . . . top management's clear understanding and consciousness are necessary."[59] The JPC quality mission of 1958 was struck by the folksy but acute wisdom of one American engineer: "All QC programs grow from the bottom. But they have to be watered and given sunlight from the top."[60] In short, the JUSE vanguard recognized in the early 1950s that a more active approach to cultivating management support was indispensable to the progress of QC and the survival of the quality movement.

The second underlying problem identified by quality experts was that, even if QC techniques were aggressively introduced into a firm, gaining the compli-

[57] See, for example, Kogure Masao et al., "Juran hakase ni yoru hinshitsu kanri kōshōkai ni sanka shite," *Hinshitsu kanri* 5, no. 8 (August 1954): 19–20; Ishikawa, "Taidan," 21.

[58] Ishikawa Kaoru, "Juran hakase wa shachō, jūyaku ni nani o hanasareta ka," *Hinshitsu kanri* 5, no. 8 (August 1954): 5; Nishibori Eizaburō, "Nihon kōgyō no chōsho to tansho," ibid., no. 10 (October 1954): 7–8; "Zadankai: Nihon no hinshitsu kanri," 47; Ishikawa, "Taidan," 24.

[59] Hinshitsu kanri shi henshū iinkai, *TQC kōza: Minna de yaru hinshitsu kanri* (JUSE, 1962), 19. Hereafter, *Minna de yaru hinshitsu kanri.*

[60] Nihon seisansei honbu, *Amerika no hinshitsu kanri,* 179.

ance of assembly-line workers with staff directives on quality was by no means assured. In Japanese companies—including those using advanced managerial and production technologies—specialist staff traditionally held only limited sway over the line, reflecting the incomplete Taylorization of factory administration. Finding the shop floor a virtual kingdom unto itself, early proponents of QC were distressed to discover that intricate staff plans for quality improvement could be scuttled by workers and supervisors who ignored or distorted them.[61] The stumbling block was not that workers thought statistics too complex—or even that they opposed management reform for expressly political reasons[62]—but instead that work groups (and particularly their foremen) resented "expert" interference and external pressure for change.[63] QC specialists and QC reforms thus ran up against the powerful inertia of the shop floor, often spawning mutual distrust and hostility. Staff engineers bristled at the intractability of the line: "The shop floor is insolent," many early reformers agreed.[64] Workers and foremen, meanwhile, could grow cranky and obstinate in the face of staff meddling. "For a long time we haven't been doing those things the QC expert told us about and we've gotten by," one laborer maintained; "Bothering with that kind of stuff is useless."[65] In short, the nascent quality movement keenly felt the challenge of penetrating the shop floor, of finding a way to compel, cajole, or convince the workers actually to use the new techniques provided for them.

The QC pioneers were well aware, however, that even if top management was won over and the shop floor could be trusted, the accomplishment of meaningful, lasting change remained uncertain. The fundamental predicament faced by early postwar quality experts was, quite simply, that many of the techniques greedily imported to Japan were too advanced to be put into practice at the time. As both Japanese and American observers were quick to admit, even a decade after the end of the war, Japanese industry as a whole had yet to reach a Taylorite level of factory organization, let alone a highly coordinated Fordist system.[66] Whereas modern quality control was premised on the existence of a fully Taylorized mass production order (as realized in many American industries), a majority of Japanese firms had not subjected their work routines to systematic administration. The fundamental components of Scientific Management, and the very elements prerequisite to the effective use of statistical QC—

[61] Ibid., 80.

[62] Ishikawa, "Taidan," 24.

[63] *Minna de yaru hinshitsu kanri,* 14–15.

[64] "Zadankai: Nihon no hinshitsu kanri," 36.

[65] *Minna de yaru hinshitsu kanri,* 14.

[66] Nihon seisansei honbu, *Amerika no hinshitsu kanri,* 106 ff.; Takase Shōtarō, ed., *Sangyō gōrika to keiei seisaku* (Moriyama shoten, 1950), 20ff.; Noda Nobuo, "Nihon no gijutsu," *Seisan* 1, no. 1 (November 1946): 2; Ono Tsuneo, "Seisan gijutsu ni okeru kihon bunsekihō to seisan kanri no shohōshiki to no kankei ni tsuite," ibid., 3; Noda Nobuo and Mori Gorō, eds., *Rōmu kanri kindaika no jitsurei* (Daiyamondo, 1954), 423–28.

standardization, specialization, and simplification—were acknowledged to be primitive in much of Japanese manufacturing.[67] In those sectors prepared managerially and technologically to accept and profit from QC, progress in the first postwar decade was significant.[68] Yet elsewhere, QC experts faced a challenge analogous to fitting jet engines on wooden biplanes.

Thus Japan's quality leadership groped for a way out of the impasse of the early 1950s. Although Japanese practitioners were moving uncertainly toward solutions, it was the intervention of yet another American expert, Joseph Juran, who would spark the reconceptualization of the Japanese quality movement. Juran, like Deming, was a prominent QC consultant yet, unlike his predecessor in Japan, he was not a professional statistician and took a considerably less technical view of quality control. Invited to Japan in 1954 by JUSE, Juran inspected factories, conducted training courses, and evaluated the QC movement. Based on his observations, Juran pronounced that Japanese experts (like most American corporations) had made the mistake of defining quality control in too narrowly mathematical a fashion. Criticizing the "mania" for statistics on both sides of the Pacific, Juran decried the construction of QC as an arcane code for engineers divorced from normal managerial functions, the fabric of the workshop, and the organization as a whole.[69] Effective QC, Juran stressed, depended more on pragmatism than theoretical competence, on the appreciation of economics as well as science, and on the mobilization of the entire company.[70] Juran advised the Japanese to reframe their vision of quality control, to consider QC an integral part of the production process, a "tool of management" rather than a statistical veneer.[71]

Juran's critiques accorded closely with the perceptions of the JUSE vanguard, and his suggestions for a reconceptualization of QC were almost immediately hailed as the movement's salvation.[72] Indeed, the general thinking of Japanese quality experts had been moving gradually toward the idea of a broadened QC since the early 1950s, and Juran's intervention finally provided the impetus and direction for a major reevaluation.[73] Juran's central message—that quality control had to go beyond statistics and diffuse outward

[67] Ishikawa Kaoru, "Nihon no hinshitsu kanri (1): QC team hōkoku," *Hinshitsu kanri* 9, no. 8 (August 1958): 9–10; Kogure, "Nihon ni okeru QC shisō," 6; Nihon seisansei honbu, *Amerika no hinshitsu kanri*, 26–28.

[68] Nakaoka, "Production Management," 19.

[69] J. M. Juran, "Nihon ni okeru hinshitsu kanri ni taisuru inshō," trans. Koyanagi Ken'ichi, *Hinshitsu kanri* 5, no. 9 (September 1954): 1–4.

[70] Ibid., 4; Kogure, "Nihon ni okeru QC shisō," 4–6; Nishibori Eizaburō, "Juran hakase ni manabu mono," *Hinshitsu kanri* 5, no. 8 (August 1954): 1–4.

[71] Ishikawa, *What is Total Quality Control?* 19.

[72] Nishibori, "Juran hakase"; Kogure et al., "Juran hakase," 19; Morioka Shirō and Kumasaka Hiroshi, "QC to hoka no kanri to no kanren oyobi chōsei," *Hinshitsu kanri* 8, no. 5 (May 1957): 16.

[73] Kogure Masao, "TQC e no taidō to tanjō," ibid., 41, no. 7 (July 1990): 61–62.

from the specialist staff—seemed a holistic prescription for the ills afflicting the Japanese movement. "QC's sphere of activities must be extremely broad," one convinced listener reported: "The measures which QC addresses should include everything."[74] For some, Juran's wisdom was a virtual epiphany: "QC by all employees, by the whole firm, is the true QC," one Japanese convert affirmed.[75] Above all, though, Juran preached pragmatism, shifting the movement's focus from the perfection of mathematical techniques to the attainment of the actual objectives of management reform. Herein, it seemed, lay the blueprint for cracking the deadlock in quality control in Japan.[76]

As is apparent from the subsequent trajectory of the quality movement, Joseph Juran's teachings had a more profound impact on Japanese QC thought than Deming's earlier and more celebrated contributions. But while Juran's 1954 tour galvanized the Japanese to chart a new strategy in quality control, making the break from the old conceptions was not entirely painless. Since the evolving approach was premised on the rejection of much of Deming's bureaucratic, statistics-heavy methodology, JUSE was in the difficult position of having to repudiate its patron saint, as well as its own past practice. The spokesmen of Japanese QC were thus forced into agonizing rhetorical contortions to promote the new conceptions without overtly disparaging the old orthodoxies. In what would become a refrain in the quality literature of the mid-1950s, Mizuno Shigeru explained that one should not simply conclude that Juran is right and Deming is wrong, "but it is clearly an error to contend that if you just understand statistical methods, you'll be able to do QC."[77] Another commentator offered a horticultural metaphor: "Deming planted a seedling which has grown into a big tree with a large trunk and many branches. Now Juran has given this tree a fabulous pruning."[78]

The Japanese QC vanguard was quick to conclude that Juran's visit marked a watershed in the history of the movement. Within weeks of Juran's tour, observers were proclaiming the start of a new era in Japanese QC.[79] Juran's teachings gave the Japanese the confidence and the external approval that they needed to rethink—even to abandon—an approach which they had embraced for a decade, yet had long been critical of. As Nishibori Eizaburō remarked at the time, Juran's inspiration was like "welcome rain" to the parched and wilting quality control movement.[80]

[74] Suzuki Takeshi, "Juran hakase no kanri shisō to wagasha no soshiki," ibid., 5, no. 10 (October 1954): 34.

[75] "Juran hakase raichō," ibid., no. 8 (August 1954): 18.

[76] Nishibori, "Juran hakase."

[77] Mizuno Shigeru, "Nihon ni okeru hinshitsu kanri shisō no hensen," *Hinshitsu kanri* 5, no. 10 (October 1954): 3; see also Nishibori, "Juran hakase," 1.

[78] "Juran hakase raichō," 18.

[79] See, for example, Kogure, "Nihon ni okeru QC shisō," 4–6.

[80] Nishibori, "Juran hakase," 1. For an alternative view of Juran's role in Japan, which stresses the instrumental use of Juran and his reputation by JUSE activists, see Nonaka Izumi, "The

TQC: Creating Consciousness

In the decade following Juran's visit, the Japanese quality movement reassessed, retooled, and refashioned itself. By the early 1960s, JUSE had sweepingly redefined its methodologies, promotional techniques, and strategies for diffusing QC into industry. The impasse of the mid-1950s was broken and soon forgotten, as the reborn movement grew to be the most dynamic element of management reform efforts in "miracle economy" Japan. At the root of this renaissance was a profound broadening of the Japanese approach to quality control, a process which can be traced along two principal axes. First, consciousness and technical knowledge of QC were extended from the specialist staff into the line, spreading from statisticians and engineers upwards to top executives, across to middle managers, and downwards to shop-floor supervisors (and eventually, to the workers themselves). Second, the domain of quality thought was enlarged beyond mathematical analysis to a more expansive view of management reform, one which could embrace techniques both old and new, from Taylorite standbys to Human Relations innovations. In short, between 1955 and 1965, Japanese quality control was transformed from a narrow specialty, the obscure sorcery of progressive engineers, into a far-reaching, comprehensive framework for making Japanese factory management more systematic and scientific.[81]

One lesson of the QC logjam—and a point stressed by Juran—was that the movement had to do a better job of impressing the importance of quality on those directly responsible for the production process. Given the organizational impotence of the staff in many Japanese firms, specialists had to induce, rather than dictate, programs of reform. The onus was thus on quality advocates to spread understanding of QC through the managerial hierarchy and inspire the willing cooperation of those individuals with line authority. As visitors to foreign factories noted, even in the fully Taylorized United States, companies with highly trained and quality-conscious managers tended to be the most successful in QC.[82] JUSE had long appreciated the importance of winning over the business elite, but from the mid-1950s, intensified efforts were made to educate all levels of corporate management about the goals, methods, and potential benefits of quality control. In the wake of Juran's visit, a new series

---

Development of Company-wide Quality Control and Quality Circles at Toyota Motor Corporation and Nissan Motor Co. Ltd.," in *Fordism Transformed: The Development of Production Methods in the Automobile Industry,* ed. Shiomi Haruhito and Wada Kazuo (Oxford: Oxford University Press, 1995), 146.

[81] On QC as an almost utopian approach to introducing science into industry, see Nakaoka, "QC Nihon no shūhon de," 64–65, 69–70; *Minna de yaru hinshitsu kanri,* 119.

[82] The members of the 1958 JPC mission on quality control stressed the importance of extending QC education to all members of the management structure. Nihon seisansei honbu, *Amerika no hinshitsu kanri,* 41, 69.

of top-management seminars was initiated and an innovative program of quality education for middle managers (*buchō* and *kachō*) was designed.[83] Soon
thereafter, the first systematic attempts to extend QC training to first-line supervisors, a group long recognized as crucial to quality progress, were also
inaugurated by JUSE.[84]

By the late 1950s, the various educational efforts aimed at developing a
managerial audience for QC began to be consolidated into a broader, unified
strategy for promoting quality reforms in industry. Extrapolating from Juran's
teachings—and inspired by the writings of General Electric quality guru Armand Feigenbaum—Japanese proponents increasingly argued that QC required the cooperation and understanding of all the members of an organization, and not simply its managers. Feigenbaum's name for this new conception
—total quality control (TQC)—was appropriated, as were many of his ideas
for diffusing quality responsibilities within a firm.[85] Yet from the start, the
rhetoric of Japanese TQC was somewhat more expansive, and its appeal to
labor more immediate, than was the case in most quality programs in the
United States.[86] TQC, one JUSE report stated, was "quality control from the
president at the top to the janitor at the bottom."[87] The new notion of quality
was to be company-wide and comprehensive, and looked toward complete
mobilization for management reform: "All employees must think, 'What
should I myself be doing about QC?'"[88] In short, the expansive and embracing message of TQC stressed that "in quality control, there is nothing more
crucial than the cooperation of all."[89]

[83] On the middle management course, Kogure, "TQC e no taidō," 63–64; Kogure, *Nihon no
TQC*, 33–34; Mizuno, *Zensha sōgō*, 368. Ishikawa Kaoru has remarked that convincing top
managers of the value of QC was difficult because of the generation gap between the elderly
executives and the young quality engineers. Ishikawa, "Taidan," 24. At the "Directors' Special
Course" (Jūyaku tokubetsu kōsu), held from 1957 at Karuizawa, golf (rather than QC) seems to
have been what bridged this gap. "Karuizawa no hinshitsu kanri seminaa: Jūyaku tokubetsu kōsu
no tanjō to omoide," *Hinshitsu kanri* 41, no. 10 (October 1990): 49–56.

[84] Suzuki Takeshi, "Shokuchō kyōiku kōsu: Shokuchō no rikai shita hinshitsu kanri,"
Hinshitsu kanri 6, no. 10 (October 1955): 1–3; Ishikawa, "Taidan," 26; *Minna de yaru hinshitsu
kanri,* 116.

[85] Armand V. Feigenbaum, *Total Quality Control: Engineering and Management* (New York:
McGraw-Hill, 1961). Feigenbaum first used the name "total quality control" in 1957, although the
Japanese had been following his work at GE since the early 1950s. On the extent to which
Japanese QC thought was an extension beyond Juran's vision, see Nishibori, "Juran hakase," 4.

[86] An exception was the program at General Electric, Feigenbaum's guinea pig. The 1958 JPC
quality mission was deeply impressed by QC organization at GE and the extent to which it
stressed the commitment of all workers to a quality effort. Particular praise was accorded the two
QC slogans at GE: "Quality Is Everybody's Job" and "Because Quality Is Everybody's Job, It
May Become Nobody's Job." Nihon seisansei honbu, *Amerika no hinshitsu kanri,* 56–58.

[87] *Minna de yaru hinshitsu kanri,* 14.

[88] Ibid., 118.

[89] "Aru kikai kōjō no 4-nin no kumichō no taikendan," *Hinshitsu kanri* 11, no. 3 (March
1960): 28.

As many observers have recognized, by the end of the 1950s, the increasingly confident Japanese QC movement was beginning to stray from slavish devotion to imported quality teachings.[90] Nonetheless, early Japanese constructions of a "total" approach to quality were profoundly conditioned by American models. Moreover, the broad rhetoric and participative entreaties of the TQC approach were fully consistent in language and in tone with the other major managerial ideologies in Japan. The TQC emphasis on unity and cooperation echoed productivity thought, as well as the older nostrums of paternalism. Calls for "teamwork" and "all-employee participation" (*zen'in sanka*) resonated with Human Relations dogma. Perhaps most noticeably, however, the vocabulary and imagery of Scientific Management, and particularly the "revised Taylorite" message, suffused many of the new TQC appeals. As Ishikawa Kaoru wrote, in words often repeated in JUSE publicity, "Since the new QC is a kind of mental revolution [*shisō kakumei*] in management, a change in the thinking of all employees—from the president down to the last worker—is essential for its accomplishment."[91]

Some scholars have described the evolution of the quality movement after 1955 as a "trickle-down" process, wherein the methodology of QC (once the monopoly of specialist staff) was progressively disseminated through the organizational hierarchies of Japanese firms.[92] Yet the TQC initiative was focused more on exhortation and guidance than on the empowerment of managers and workers by the sharing of technical knowledge. Neither "democratization" (that Occupation-era catchphrase) nor "participation" (the management motto of the 1970s) entered into the discourse on quality during the 1950s and early 1960s. One JUSE offering from 1960, for example, described thirteen ways in which factory operatives could manifest their cooperation with TQC efforts. All that seems to have "trickled down" were new calls for diligence and deference:

1. No matter what your position in the firm, understand management goals and your quality responsibilities. Fulfill these, and don't be grudging with your cooperation.

2. Understand the principles of scientific management. Respect their rationality and objectivity. . . .

3. Study and understand QC techniques and statistics. . . . If you do not, you will be left behind the times.

4. Always strive to add new technical capabilities to existing production methods. Endeavor to increase efficiency. . . .

---

[90] TQC "was built on the ideas of American QC experts, although Japanese firms experimented with these concepts and Japanese consultants made several important modifications." Cusumano, *The Japanese Automobile Industry,* 326; see also Kogure, "TQC e no taidō."

[91] Ishikawa Kaoru, *Hinshitsu kanri nyūmon,* QC Series, vol. 1 (JUSE, 1964), 35.

[92] Sasaki and Nonaka, "Kagakuteki kanrihō," 274 ff.; Ishikawa, "Taidan," 26.

9. Don't be ashamed to admit your own shortcomings; instead, take pride in teamwork. . . .

13. In addition to quality, be careful not to add to costs, and strive to boost productive efficiency and improve conditions.[93]

As TQC proponents readily acknowledged, however, their objective was not the full-scale transfer of quality expertise and jurisdiction to the line, but rather the building of a pervasive corporate "consciousness" of QC. JUSE spokesmen encouraged the cultivation of a "quality mind," a "quality philosophy," and a "statistical way of thinking" among workers and managers.[94] According to one commentator, the goal of the broadened QC was the creation of a "rich, beautiful atmosphere of quality-mindedness."[95] The contours of this new mindset were left ambiguous, but its intention—to gain the compliance of unconverted production personnel with the QC agenda—was apparent. Unable to achieve unilateral advances in the introduction of QC, quality specialists sought to use education and the familiar rhetoric of cooperation to induce a receptive consensus in boardrooms and workshops. In the words of one seminal JUSE report, "As each component of the firm—the employees on the shop floor, the foremen, the staff and the top managers—focused their respective energies on the simple goal of TQC, harmony prevailed and great results followed from the heightened quality consciousness of all."[96]

An increasingly important part of the JUSE strategy for raising awareness and equipping more Japanese with a "quality mind" were initiatives to publicize and popularize QC on a nationwide, mass basis. From the mid-1950s, the idea of taking the broadened conception of QC to a popular audience was discussed among the JUSE leadership. Beginning in 1956, JUSE sponsored a series of introductory QC courses broadcast on NHK radio. The early response was encouraging, as sales of the accompanying texts exceeded 100,000 copies.[97] In 1958, on the occasion of the hundredth issue of the journal *Hinshitsu kanri* (Quality Control), Ishikawa Kaoru proclaimed that "I believe it is possible QC can progress as a national popular movement."[98] Based on the premise that "QC is not a problem limited to one firm, but is a problem

---

[93] Tomizawa Hiroshi, "Hinshitsu kanri to wa," *Hinshitsu kanri* 11, no. 3 (March 1960): 13.

[94] "TQC tōronkai (2)," ibid., no. 12 (December 1960): 8; Cusumano, *The Japanese Automobile Industry,* 342.

[95] Yamaki Naomoto, *Hinshitsu kanri,* Seisan kōgaku kōza, vol. 15 (Nikkan kōgyō shinbunsha, 1960), 127.

[96] *Minna de yaru hinshitsu kanri,* 18.

[97] Nonaka Izumi, "QC saakuru no tanjō," *Hinshitsu kanri* 41, no. 9 (September 1990): 77–78; Ishikawa, "Taidan," 26. At the time, the average educational radio course sold approximately 20–30,000 copies of the accompanying text. Only English language courses regularly exceeded 100,000 in sales.

[98] Ishikawa Kaoru, "Kongo no QC to hinshitsu kanri shi," *Hinshitsu kanri* 9, no. 6 (June 1958): 23.

of society's welfare, of the national economy," plans for a national "Quality Month" were outlined in 1960.[99] Emulating the successful tactics of the safety movement and the Ministry of International Trade and Industry's "standardization month," JUSE earmarked November for an annual publicity blitz. Mass-marketing the concept of TQC with (it was claimed) "the spirit of the QC pioneers," JUSE endeavored to infect the general public with a "quality control mood."[100]

While training programs and Quality Month aimed to build a consensus on quality from the roots up in Japanese industry, JUSE also aspired to stimulate QC from the outside in. Corporate employees may have been the prime target of TQC hype, but by the early 1960s, the movement saw potential in developing a new and untapped audience. As quality became a popular movement, the contagion of QC consciousness was introduced into Japanese homes and extended to the front-line rank and file of the consumer economy, the housewives of Japan. JUSE reasoned that by informing and mobilizing this economically potent segment of society—by making the price-conscious Japanese consumer more quality conscious—external leverage then could be applied to those manufacturers dragging their heels on QC reform. The consuming public was thus swept in as an active participant in total quality control: "We will not attain our goals without the cooperation of consumers, [since] the consumer is king."[101] As Ishikawa Kaoru was fond of saying, "Japanese quality control lies in the hands of the fairer sex."[102]

Underlying the various educational and promotional campaigns of the late 1950s and early 1960s was the recognition that QC had to be "sold," both within the firm and to society at large. The implicit assumption of the JUSE TQC offensive was that engineers and technologists could only effect managerial reform by working through the line hierarchy and winning over the uncommitted majority to a "QC way of thinking." This strategy of broadening the audience for quality was conditioned by the relatively low Taylorization of Japanese corporate organizations, but was not inherently anti-Taylorite (or even non-Taylorite) in conception. QC proponents did not reject the Taylorite emphasis on the specialist, but acknowledged (after the failures of the young movement) that the narrowly elitist approach of Scientific Management had

[99] "Sagyōin-hen ni tsuite," ibid., 11, no. 3 (March 1960): 3.

[100] Ishikawa Kaoru, "Dai-ikkai hinshitsu gekkan ni tsuite," ibid., 12, no. 7 (July 1961): 1; see also Nakaoka Tetsurō, *Kōjō no tetsugaku: Soshiki to ningen* (Heibonsha, 1971), 214–16.

[101] Ishikawa Kaoru, "Shōhisha no minasama e no onegai," *Hinshitsu kanri* 11, no. 3 (March 1960): 69–70; see also Ishikawa Kaoru, "10 shūnen o mukaete," ibid., 1; "Zadankai: Shufu no mita shin seihin," ibid., 10, no. 5 (May 1959): 56–65; Mitsumaki Akiko, "QC to korekara no shōhisha undō," ibid., 16, no. 11 (November 1965): 1–3.

[102] Ishikawa, "Shōhisha," 69. The 1960s JUSE appeal to housewives was consistent with prewar efforts by the state and private-sector women's groups to "rationalize" consumption patterns. See Sheldon Garon, *Molding Japanese Minds: The State in Everyday Life* (Princeton, N.J.: Princeton University Press, 1997), 136.

been impractical in the early postwar context of Japanese industry.[103] The emphasis, then, was on education, or perhaps better yet, indoctrination: awakening the uninformed to the value of QC experts' expertise, creating a market for the specialists' specialty, marshaling ideology to bring down the walls of shop-floor "kingdoms."[104]

Considering JUSE's original mission to improve the status of engineers, it is hardly surprising that the TQC approach, while geared toward a general audience, remained broadly consistent with Taylorite ideas of elite expertism. Indeed, JUSE's fundamental concern with the prestige and influence of technologists in industry seemed little altered in the expansion of QC rhetoric during the 1950s and 1960s. In TQC, a central role was reserved for the engineers: "QC consciousness" was to be shared with all, but not so staff authority or expertise. Indeed, under TQC, the relative standing of the staff was to be enhanced. As one JUSE analysis recommended, top management was to set broad goals, and workers were to be well trained and "burning with the quality spirit," while QC engineers took charge of designing and guiding the actual management reforms.[105] Moreover, one of the explicit aims of TQC was releasing staff experts from the drudgery of supervising routine production, and allowing them to make the most constructive use of their valuable technical skills. "Engineers [should] be employed in the true meaning of engineers," Ishikawa Kaoru declared; "Engineers are the individuals who skillfully make science economical, who develop new products and new technological advances. At present, there are many scientists and technicians in Japan who are called engineers, but there are few [real] engineers and this is hindering our country's true progress."[106] Under a successful QC regime, however, engineers would be freed to perform their true roles, to "devote their time to proper jobs": "As the floor workers begin solving day-to-day problems and as the workshop is kept well under control, engineers can become more flexible and direct their efforts to more constructive jobs, overall coordination, and the development of new products and technology."[107] Thus, beneath its populist message, TQC promised the liberation of Japanese engineers, a liberation which still appeared fundamentally elitist and recognizably Taylorite in outline.

[103] Ishikawa, *Hinshitsu kanri nyūmon,* 20.

[104] See, for example, "TQC tōronkai (1)," *Hinshitsu kanri* 11, no. 10 (October 1960): 4; Ishikawa, *Hinshitsu kanri nyūmon,* 54 ff.; Yamaki, *Hinshitsu kanri,* 64; Nihon seisansei honbu, *Amerika no hinshitsu kanri,* 80.

[105] Hinshitsu kanri shi henshū iinkai, *Hinshitsu kanri to hito no mondai* (JUSE, 1966), 74–75. Hereafter, *Hinshitsu kanri to hito no mondai.* See also Ishikawa, "Nihon no hinshitsu kanri (1)," 6.

[106] Ishikawa, *Hinshitsu kanri nyūmon,* 14, 53.

[107] *QC Circle Koryo: General Principles of the QC Circle* (Tokyo: QC Circle Headquarters, JUSE, 1980; original Japanese edition, 1970), 34–35.

TQC: Redefining the Message

During the years from 1955 to 1965, the Japanese quality movement underwent what could best be called a renaissance. Transcending the sterile and
stagnant efforts of the first postwar decade, quality control became more vital,
more widely known, and more widely applied after the adoption of the expansive TQC approach. Yet the broadening of the quality appeal was not the only
factor contributing to the surge of interest in QC and the acceleration of its
progress through Japanese industry. On a more fundamental level, the course
of economic growth, the "technological revolution," and the consequent expansion of mass production methods created a more hospitable environment
for implementing modern QC.[108] The rising specter of a labor shortage put a
premium on managerial techniques (like quality control) that promised cost
reductions.[109] Moreover, the maturing of the domestic mass consumption
economy provided new incentives for the production of quality goods.[110] Finally, though perhaps most importantly, the nagging threat of foreign
competition—a familiar bogeyman in "miracle economy" Japan—seemed a
powerful force impelling businessmen and workers alike to reconsider the
potential benefits of QC. As JUSE spokesmen argued with vehemence
through the 1960s, "Shouldn't we consider a positive, aggressive approach to
the trade liberalization problem, rather than a conservative, defensive strategy
relying on the protection of governments and nations, exchange rates and
duties? [Shouldn't we] undertake the structural reform of firms through quality control, under the slogan 'Trade liberalization through QC!'?"[111]

The renaissance of quality control was not, however, an isolated incident in
the industrial world, but was part of a larger phenomenon known as the "management boom" (*keiei būmu*). In the late 1950s, popular interest in business
management surged, fostered by economic expansion, JPC publicity, and the
rapid postwar growth of white-collar employment.[112] Ignited by two 1958
bestsellers—James Abegglen's *The Japanese Factory* and Sakamoto Fu-

---

[108] Onitsuka, "Sengo Nihon," 226 ff.; Noda Kazuo, ed., *Gendai keieishi* (Nihon seisansei
honbu, 1969), 180–82.

[109] Miura Shin, "Shinnen ni omou," *Hinshitsu kanri* 12, no. 1 (January 1961): 1; Mori and
Matsushima, *Nihon rōmu kanri,* 40–55; Noda, *Gendai keieishi,* 317–24.

[110] Hoshino Yoshiro, "What Technology Has Postwar Japan Learned from the U.S.?" *Japanese Economic Studies* 17, no. 1 (Fall 1988): 71, 74.

[111] Ishikawa Kaoru, "Bōeki jiyūka to MR," *Hinshitsu kanri* 11, no. 9 (September 1960): 1; see
also Ishikawa Kaoru, "Bōeki jiyūka ni wa hinshitsu kanri de," ibid., no. 4 (April 1960): 1; Nonaka, "QC saakuru," 83–84.

[112] On the increasing number of managers in postwar Japan, see Tsuda Masumi, "Study of
Japanese Management Development Practices II," *Hitotsubashi Journal of Arts and Sciences* 18,
no. 1 (September 1977): 9–10.

jiyoshi's *Keieigaku nyūmon* (Introduction to Business Administration)[113]—a mania for modern (and especially American) management techniques swept the media and business circles. The following years witnessed a rapid, even frenzied, process of importation, experimentation, and infatuation. Japan, Takamiya Susumu declared, "has studied and absorbed modern principles and methods with a desire and energy bordering on greed."[114] Like quality control, most of the imports celebrated by journalists and executives—Human Relations, operations research, automation, the work of Peter Drucker—were nothing novel to Japanese management experts. Yet the full postwar panoply of American managerial fashions—including QC—gained tremendous new exposure and cachet in the heyday of the "management boom."[115]

The feverish enthusiasm of the late 1950s boom was too intense to sustain, however, and by the early 1960s the craze for imported management models had subsided. Two American management experts observed that "The top managerial structure of many [Japanese] firms simply is not adequate to assimilate the new processes, techniques and personnel which are introduced, often in a rapid and quite uncoordinated fashion." The result, these Americans concluded, was "managerial indigestion."[116] The more apt term, however, may be "backlash": in the Japanese business press, the raves for U.S. management methods gave way (starting in about 1959) to the disparagement of indiscriminate borrowing, faddish emulation, and slavish devotion to unworthy imported approaches. "Will American management models go the way of the hula hoop?" was the rhetorical question one business journal posed for its readers.[117] Hitherto silent voices of dissent—arguing that American methods were not consistent with Japanese conditions and that time-honored, home-grown approaches were more appropriate—soon proliferated in the discourse of managerial reform. In remarkably short order, the industrial community turned on its former infatuation with American ideas and bristled with what Nakase Jūichi has described as a new sense of nationalism in management thought.[118] Only three years after the publication of his bestseller extolling

[113] James Abegglen, *The Japanese Factory: Aspects of Its Social Organization* (Glencoe, Ill.: Free Press, 1958); Sakamoto Fujiyoshi, *Keieigaku nyūmon* (Kōbunsha, 1958).

[114] Takamiya Susumu, "Background, Characteristics and Recent Trends in Japanese Management," in *Modern Japanese Management* (London: Management Publications/The British Institute of Management, 1970), 107.

[115] On the "management boom," see Noda, *Gendai keieishi,* 82–87; Onitsuka Mitsumasa, "Sengo Nihon ni okeru seisan kanri no hatten," in Sengo Nihon keiei kenkyukai, *Sengo Nihon no kigyō keiei* (Bunshindō, 1991), 230 ff.; Nihon nōritsu kyōkai, *Keiei to tomo ni* (1982), 70 ff.; Nakase Jūichi, *Sengo Nihon no keiei rinen shi* (Kyōto: Hōritsu bunka sha, 1967), 56 ff.; "Teidan: Amerika-shiki keiei kanri no juyō to fukyū," *Keiei to rekishi* 10 (July 1987): 14 ff.

[116] Frederick Harbison and Charles Myers, *Management in the Industrial World: An International Analysis* (New York: McGraw-Hill, 1959), 253–54.

[117] "Tokushū: Keiei ni okeru Amerikanizumu no hansei," *Kindai keiei* 4, no. 5 (1 April 1959): 5.

[118] Nakase, *Sengo Nihon,* 62 ff. See also "Tokushū: Keiei ni okeru Amerikanizumu no

American management as the only model for Japan, Sakamoto Fujiyoshi began a new 1961 study of business trends with Kipling's words, "East is East and West is West. . . ."[119]

Quality control rode the surge of "management boom" fervor, but did not suffer seriously when the wave crested in the early 1960s. One reason for this was that QC, with an institutional base in JUSE and a considerable track record in Japan, was not easily repudiated as a passing fad. But quality control was also well placed ideologically for the backlash against the uncritical Americanization of management. Even in the late 1950s, Japanese quality proponents had begun referring to the statistically minded Deming approach as "American" QC, while the more broadly defined, systematic strategy was styled "Japanese." By the early 1960s, the crucial contributions of Juran and Feigenbaum were increasingly effaced by selective organizational amnesia, and a process of ideological renovation—in which TQC was constructed as a distinctively Japanese variant on quality control—was set in motion.[120] On the most superficial level, JUSE attempted to rechristen TQC, whose name too closely reflected its American origins, as "QC by all" (*minna de yaru hinshitsu kanri*).[121] The Deming medal, a once ubiquitous symbol of the quality movement, was rarely seen in JUSE publications during the 1960s. Moreover, in a symbolically charged decision, QC leaders altered the original designs for an official quality banner, changing the color of the insignia from United Nations blue to the red of the *hinomaru*—Japan's "rising sun" flag—on a white field.[122] By thus emphasizing the "Japaneseness" of quality, and by promoting a somewhat exaggerated dichotomy between American QC and Japanese efforts, the quality movement dodged the nationalist backlash against the "management boom" and began fabricating a new ideological legitimacy for QC reforms.

Beyond these stirrings in the "Japanization" of QC, there was another significant factor contributing to the quality movement's success in weathering

---

hansei"; Michael Yoshino, *Japan's Managerial System: Tradition and Innovation* (Cambridge, Mass.: MIT Press, 1965), 107, 270–71.

[119] Sakamoto Fujiyoshi, *Nihon no keiei kakushin* (Mainichi shinbunsha, 1961), 3.

[120] *Minna de yaru hinshitsu kanri,* 117; *Hinshitsu kanri to hito no mondai,* 133 ff.; Ishikawa, "Nihon no hinshitsu kanri (1)," 6; Nishibori Eizaburō, "Hinshitsu kanri wa Nihonjin no tame ni aru," *Hinshitsu kanri* 16, no. 3 (March 1965): 8–10. On contemporary manifestations of this process, see Sasaki Naoto, *TQC shinwa to no ketsubetsu* (Chūō keizaisha, 1989) and Ishikawa, *What is Total Quality Control?* esp. 23–36.

[121] See the 1962 JUSE compendium, *Minna de yaru hinshitsu kanri*. The articles which made up this collection were originally published in *Hinshitsu kanri* in 1960. Despite this attempt at renaming (and the later promotion of the title "company-wide quality control"), the pithier tag TQC remained the most common referent.

[122] Ishikawa, "Dai-ikkai hinshitsu gekkan ni tsuite," 1. Ishikawa later explained that this change was due to the fact that the quality of blue dyes available in the 1960s was poor (Ishikawa, *What is Total Quality Control?* 4). At the time, however, it was only reported that "general opinion" supported the change.

the managerial tumult of the early 1960s. In the time since Juran's visit, QC proponents had endeavored to broaden not only their audience, but also their message. Many of the management models imported to Japan during the peak of the "boom" were highly sophisticated and technically specialized, and consequently were often ill understood, incompletely applied, and manifestly unsuccessful in actual practice. Uprooted and decontextualized from the advanced mass production economy that spawned them, many American methods floundered in Japan as alluring but ineffective fads. Yet the quality movement, having already traced this trajectory in its first decade, had significantly retooled its technical arsenal and methodological foundations before the backlash of the 1960s. Under the banner TQC, quality control had moved away from the narrow specialization and sophistication that limited so many of the later managerial imports to Japan. Indeed, from the mid-1950s, quality control as defined by JUSE was no longer solely (or even primarily) about quality per se. Between 1955 and 1965, QC was recast as a comprehensive movement for the modernization of industrial management, and increasingly as an instrument of labor-management accommodation as well.[123]

Responding to the perception that the movement was too focused on statistics, and the sense that Japanese industry needed improvements more elementary than mathematical analysis, QC proponents began to embrace a less-specialized, more basic model of management reform from the mid-1950s.[124] After visiting the United States in 1958, Ishikawa Kaoru concluded that "the biggest problem in Japanese QC" was the low level of Taylorization in most factories: work standards were nonexistent or ignored by workers, engineers had only tenuous control over production routines, rule-of-thumb methods predominated.[125] Faced with this sobering reality, Ishikawa and his fellow QC pioneers recognized that fundamental management reform—specifically the Taylorite rationalization of the work process—was an essential prerequisite to the application of statistical quality control. Thus JUSE and the quality movement were resigned to taking a methodological step backwards in order to keep the QC enterprise moving forward: statistics were to be downplayed and new emphasis was to be placed on the familiar concept of standardization.[126] Quality experts readily acknowledged that the setting and maintenance of work standards were nothing new to management reform, but they stressed

[123] *Minna de yaru hinshitsu kanri,* 4–8; Mori and Matsushima, *Nihon rōmu kanri,* 52 ff.

[124] Morioka and Kumasaka, "QC to hoka no kanri," 14–16; "QC masukomi e," *Hinshitsu kanri* 8, no. 7 (July 1957): 9.

[125] Ishikawa, "Nihon no hinshitsu kanri (1)," 9–10.

[126] Nihon seisansei honbu, *Amerika no hinshitsu kanri,* 26–28, 240; Watanabe Eizō, "QC kōza 1: Hinshitsu kanri no soshiki to un'ei—hyōjunka ni tsuite," *Hinshitsu kanri* 6, no. 10 (October 1955): 56–58; Higashi Hidehiko, "Shanai hyōjunka," ibid., 9, no. 9 (September 1958): 8–9. It should be noted that standardization of the production process was always considered significant in the Japanese QC movement: an early JUSE statement bid QC engineers "Don't forget motion study!" "Hinshitsu kanri no isshishin," ibid., 1, no. 1 (March 1950): 5.

that they were an inalienable part of the QC process: "Quality control starts with standards and ends with standards."[127] As Ishikawa rather ominously put it: "Standardization in Japan is still like a newborn child, an infant not yet at adulthood. If we do not pay extremely close attention to it and carefully nurture it scientifically, there is a chance that, what with Japan's high infant mortality rate, it will die an untimely death. If, however, all of us together can conscientiously rear a fine, mature youth, then [standardization] will become a great foundation for the growth of our national strength."[128]

What was remarkable about the shift in the methodological emphasis of quality control was that, in many ways, the banner of modern QC came increasingly to be flown over the homely old nostrums of the efficiency movement and Scientific Management. Although QC proponents would periodically excoriate Taylorism's dehumanizing tendencies,[129] the conception of standardization embraced in the broadened TQC was fully consistent with the reforms long advocated by the Japan Efficiency Association and its predecessors. By the late 1950s, the discourse of the quality movement was studded not only with the rhetoric of Scientific Management, but also with the basic techniques of Taylorism repackaged as the fundamentals of QC. Indeed, preaching cost reduction, waste elimination, efficiency increase, simplification, specialization, and so forth, quality activists sounded more and more like latter-day efficiency engineers.[130] By 1964, one observer could remark, in what surely was an unobjectionable statement, that "it is generally thought that quality and efficiency are the same sort of thing."[131]

As TQC enveloped the traditional methodologies of Scientific Management, antagonisms between the quality movement and the established purveyors of Taylorism, especially the Efficiency Association, began to swell. As institutional competitors in managerial reform, JUSE and the association enjoyed (at best) a cordial but distant relationship. Occasional cooperation between the two organizations—such as in the staging of Quality Month—could not efface an ongoing subtext of rivalry and even hostility. For instance, in the commemorative hundredth issue of the JUSE journal *Hinshitsu kanri,* amidst celebratory testimonials from industrial and bureaucratic leaders, association president Morikawa offered the following sentiments: "To be blunt, at

[127] Mutō Hideo, "Seizō genba no tachiba kara," *Hinshitsu kanri* 11, no. 12 (October 1960): 19; "Zadankai: Kōgi no QC to kyōgi no QC," ibid., 8, no. 7 (July 1957): 19.

[128] Ishikawa Kaoru, "Wagakuni sagyō hyōjun no mondaiten," ibid., no. 9 (September 1957): 70.

[129] See, for example, Ishikawa Kaoru, "Indasutoriaru enjiniaringu (IE) to kuoritei kontorōru (QC)," *PR* 9, no. 1 (January 1958): 41; Ishikawa, "Wagakuni sagyō hyōjun," 70.

[130] Among other examples, see Ishikawa, *Hinshitsu kanri nyūmon,* 14; Suzuki Hirokazu, "Hinshitsu kanri izen no mondai," *Hinshitsu kanri* 11, no. 1 (January 1960): 8–11; Tomizawa, "Hinshitsu kanri to wa"; Ishikawa, "Nihon no hinshitsu kanri (1)," 6.

[131] "Paneru tōronkai: Hinshitsu kōbōsen bōeki jiyūka to QC (2)," *Hinshitsu kanri* 15, no. 3 (March 1964): 64.

the present time, quality control in Japan doesn't make the grade. That is to say, it doesn't make much of a contribution to management. That one must still conclude this, even after a decade [of the QC movement] is truly regrettable. . . . Before we think of quality control, mustn't we introduce the most primitive aspects of Scientific Management?"[132]

Tensions came to a head at the very end of the 1950s, as a rhetorically charged and unusually public turf battle erupted between JUSE and the old efficiency movement mainstream. The confrontation was precipitated both by TQC poaching of Taylorite methodologies and by the introduction of the concept of industrial engineering (IE), a postwar American repackaging of Scientific Management that was enthusiastically embraced by the Efficiency Association and the JPC.[133] IE proponents—following in the steps of their American counterparts—implied that quality control, having become dependent on traditionally Taylorite techniques, had lost the character of a distinct managerial approach. Consequently, some in the Efficiency Association intimated, QC was no more than a component of industrial engineering, a methodological subsidiary of the integrated, holistic IE approach.[134] Seeing their monopoly eroded by the creeping expansion of QC's technical arsenal, the direct heirs of the efficiency movement thus brandished the new notion of IE to reclaim their methodological turf and subordinate the entire quality control project.

This challenge spurred the advocates of QC to sharpen and articulate their vision of what quality control actually entailed. In the initial stampede to TQC, as the traditional statistical core of quality control was progressively diluted, proponents paid scant attention to the question of what made quality a

---

[132] Morikawa, "Hinshitsu kanri shi," 5.

[133] Japan's lackings in IE were a major conclusion of the 1956 Landes report to the JPC. The Productivity Center, in cooperation with the Efficiency Association, subsequently sponsored considerable efforts to promote this updated version of traditional Scientific Management practices. See Nihon IE kyōkai, *Nihon ni okeru IE no dōkō* (Nihon seisansei honbu, 1965), introd.; "Zadankai: IE ni tsuite," *Hinshitsu kanri* 10, no. 2 (February 1959): 17–31, 35; Noda, *Gendai keieishi,* 172–75. For general introductions to IE, see Shiro Tsutomu, *IE nyūmon* (Nihon nōritsu kyōkai, 1960); Katō Takeo and Takada Shinzō, *Seisan kōgaku sōron,* Seisan kōgaku kōza, vol. 1 (Nikkan kōgyō shinbunsha, 1959); *IE no nyūmon,* IE seminaa, vol. 1 (Nihon seisansei honbu, 1960).

[134] "IE no hanashi o kiku kai," *Hinshitsu kanri* 12, no. 2 (February 1961): 1–7; Fujishiro Yūkō, "QC to IE ni tsuite," ibid., 9, no. 11 (November 1958): 13–15; "Zadankai: Nihon no IE to Amerika no IE o kataru," *IE* 3, no. 9 (September 1961): 746–48; Ōtsubo Mayumi, "Ima koso IE dōnyū no toki," *Manejimento* 19, no. 4 (April 1960): 32–33; Niizaki Kuniyoshi, "Indasutoriaru enjiniyaringu no saikentō," ibid., 17, no. 9 (September 1958): 24–32; Noda Nobuo, "Indasutoriaru enjiniaringu no keiei rironteki kōsatsu," *PR* 9, no. 1 (January 1958): 14–16; Kayano Takeshi, "Nihon ni okeru indasutoriaru enjiniaringu no mondai ni tsuite," ibid., no. 2 (February 1958): 20–22; for a concise graphical presentation of the centrality of IE, see "Keiei kindaika ni kōken shita jinmyaku to shuyō kikan," *IE* 9, no. 6 (June 1967): 611. Much of the debate stemmed from pragmatic concern over which staff unit would control QC and IE methods in firms, the quality control section or the industrial engineering section.

distinct approach to management reform. When confronted by the new claims from the Taylorite old guard, however, QC experts, led by Ishikawa Kaoru (by then the ascendant ideologue of the movement), endeavored to turn the arguments of the industrial engineers on their heads. At the heart of Ishikawa's defense—elaborated in a variety of forums during 1959 and 1960—was the premise that "quality" (along with cost and quantity) was a fundamental goal of production management. Quality control was accordingly defined as a basic component of the managerial function. IE, meanwhile, was merely a "methodological category," a set of technical tools that could be used toward higher ends (like quality) but which was not itself intrinsic to the process of industrial management.[135] In other words, Ishikawa and the JUSE leadership maintained that QC was defined by its very centrality to management, a centrality which bestowed upon quality control virtually unlimited methodological breadth. From this vantage, IE appeared constrained by its inherent technical specificity, and was consequently—inevitably—subordinated to QC. While such arguments were not universally accepted (especially not by those in the Efficiency Association), the credible proposition that quality was an elementary component of production management effectively stole the thunder from the insurgent industrial engineers.[136]

The breadth and audacity of this newly formalized reconceptualization of quality control were staggering. Within a decade, QC had progressed from a statistical regimen to a "management tool" to being tantamount to industrial management itself.[137] In the wake of the "management boom," the leaders of the quality movement and the practitioners of QC greatly expanded their vision of quality control, looking beyond the simple absorption of Taylorite methods and toward the construction of a comprehensive model of managerial reform. As Ishikawa Kaoru declared, "QC is, broadly speaking, the same as business management [and] . . . management must be conducted synthetically [*sōgōteki ni*]."[138] Thus one quality advocate described QC as a "link" drawing together disparate managerial specialties, while another styled it a "bipartisan fusion" of the competing approaches to management reform.[139] The quality control of the past was, as one executive keenly observed in 1958, giving way to a "king-sized QC" that offered holistic solutions to the complex problems of contemporary management.[140]

---

[135] "Zadankai: IE ni tsuite," 23–24; "IE no hanashi o kiku kai," 5. See also "Taidan: Kogure-san no miyagebanashi o kiku," *Hinshitsu kanri* 10, no. 5 (May 1959): 66–70; Ishikawa, *Hinshitsu kanri nyūmon,* 56; Fujishiro, "QC to IE."

[136] Kayano, "Nihon ni okeru indasutoriaru enjiniaringu no mondai ni tsuite," 20–22; "Zadankai: QC to IE no yūwa," *Hinshitsu kanri* 12, no. 4 (April 1961): 32–35.

[137] "Spotlight: Nentō ni," *Hinshitsu kanri* 12, no. 1 (January 1961): 13; Ishikawa, "Nihon no hinshitsu kanri (1)," 7; "Sagyōin-hen ni tsuite," 3.

[138] Ishikawa, *Hinshitsu kanri nyūmon,* 20–21.

[139] Ishikawa, "Nihon no hinshitsu kanri (1)," 2; "Spotlight: QC no kaimei," *Hinshitsu kanri* 11, no. 12 (December 1960): 9.

[140] Fujishiro, "QC to IE," 14; see also *Minna de yaru hinshitsu kanri,* 117.

Over the course of the 1960s, quality control became a melting pot of modern management concepts, as freshly imported managerial models were incorporated into the methodological arsenal and intellectual purview of the QC approach. Many of the fads introduced during the "management boom" years were eventually fused with the theory and practice of quality control. A majority of the newly assimilated ideas—"brainstorming," long-range planning, operations research, etc.—had only limited impact, although their methods and strategies entered the repertoires of Japanese QC experts.[141] Some, notably Drucker's philosophy and his "Management by Objectives and Self-Control," would exert a considerable long-term influence on the evolution of Japanese quality thought.[142] A few—and particularly the teachings of the Human Relations school—were readily embraced and rapidly suffused the movement. Emphasizing the need to "humanize" the practice of QC as it spread through the line to the shop floor, HR (as it was perceived in postwar Japan) left an immediate mark on the rhetoric and awareness of quality advocates.[143] As early as 1960, some QC proponents were already making the bold proclamation that "Quality control is Human Relations."[144]

In short, the emphasis in Japanese TQC came to fall increasingly on the "total" sweep of modern factory management rather than on what was usually considered (in the United States at least) to be the province of quality control. The "king-sized QC" of the 1960s, with its accreted methodologies and mindsets, thus appeared a complex and distinctive hybrid, an amalgam too diverse to be shoehorned into the established conceptions of quality control. In less than two decades, QC had been transformed from an obscure technical creed on the peripheries of managerial thought, to a capacious, synthetic approach at the heart of management reform in high-growth Japan.

The Ideology of TQC

The consolidation of total quality control as mass movement and as melting pot has usually been perceived as a major watershed in the postwar evolution of Japanese industrial management practices. Many observers—both at the

---

[141] See, for example, Ishikawa Kaoru, "QC no chōki keikaku," *Hinshitsu kanri* 14, no. 1 (January 1963): 1–4; "Shin hinshitsu kanri 12-kō 2: Gijutsu kakushin to hinshitsu kanri," ibid., 12, no. 2 (February 1961): 85–94; Ishikawa, *Hinshitsu kanri nyūmon,* 51.

[142] On Drucker, see Noda Kazuo, *Drucker no keieigaku* (Kashima kenkyūjo shuppankai, 1963); Ueno Ichirō et al., *Mokuhyō kanri no un'ei to jissai* (Daiyamondo, 1966); Ishikawa, *Hinshitsu kanri nyūmon,* 35.

[143] See, for example, "QC suishinsha no seikaku," *Hinshitsu kanri* 11, no. 12 (December 1960): 10; Mutō, "Seizō genba," 18–20; "Ankeeto: Genbachō o meguru hinshitsu kanri no mondai ni tsuite," *Hinshitsu kanri* 12, no. 9 (September 1961): 54–58; "Shin hinshitsu kanri 12-kō 10: Hinshitsu kanri to hito no mondai," ibid., no. 10 (October 1961): 60–70; *Hinshitsu kanri to hito no mondai,* 22 ff.; Ishikawa, *Hinshitsu kanri nyūmon,* 51–52.

[144] "QC suishinsha no seikaku," 10.

time and in the years since—have considered the quality movement's turn to TQC a repudiation of Taylorism and, more broadly speaking, of American management methods in general. Emphasizing the flexibility of QC in transcending narrow methodological specialization, as well as the movement's efforts to diffuse "quality consciousness" beyond the technical staff, most commentators have seen in TQC the germination of a distinctively Japanese approach to quality control and production management. Since the early 1960s, few have challenged the assumption that TQC evolved as a humanized, inclusive, untechnocratic, un-Taylorite, non-American (even anti-American) approach to rationalizing the Japanese factory.[145]

As the postwar discourse on total quality control reveals, however, the ideology of TQC was not a major departure from the "revised Taylorite" consensus that had long structured efforts at managerial modernization in Japan. Although JUSE ideologues explicitly rejected the existence of pervasive links between prewar Scientific Management and quality control, an implicit acceptance of Taylorism's assumptions and its methods was evident in the TQC initiative.[146] As noted above, efforts to broaden consciousness of QC, though frequently seen as diluting the Taylorite emphasis on managerial elitism, were actually geared toward confirming and improving the status of technical experts within the firm. Moreover, the emphasis placed on "humanizing" modern management—a theme which suffused the rhetoric of TQC after the integration of HR thought—was directly continuous with the Taishō legacy of "revised Taylorism."[147] In a statement which resounded with long-standing Japanese conceptions of Scientific Management, one quality control proponent affirmed in 1961 that "work standards and Human Relations are like the two axles of a car: without one, the car just will not run. We must bear in mind that by combining both [standardization and Human Relations], work will progress smoothly."[148]

---

[145] For a sampling of orthodox interpretations of TQC, see Ishikawa, *What is Total Quality Control?*; Sasaki, *TQC no shinwa*; Sasaki and Nonaka, "Kagakuteki kanrihō," 274; Mizuno, *Zensha sōgō*, 25–27; *Hinshitsu kanri to hito no mondai*, 140; "Spotlight: Kanri no kyōchō," *Hinshitsu kanri* 10, no. 2 (February 1959): 9.

[146] For contemporary examples of QC critiques of Taylorism, see Ishikawa, *Hinshitsu kanri nyūmon*, 35; Gotō, "Gijutsusha no yakuwari," 2; Fujishiro, "QC to IE," 13–16; Karikomi Ichirō, "Shoku, kumichō to riidaashippu," *Genba to QC* 23 (September 1965): 2–5; Nishibori, "Hinshitsu kanri wa Nihonjin no tame ni aru," 10. For representative recent appraisals, see Sasaki, *TQC no shinwa*, 25, 57–58, 120; Karatsu Hajime, *TQC Wisdom of Japan*, trans. David Lu (Cambridge, Mass.: Productivity Press, 1988), 102–3; Ishikawa, *What is Total Quality Control?* 25–26; Cusumano, *The Japanese Automobile Industry*, 331. It is significant to note that timetables of the history of QC in Japan have usually started with the introduction of Taylorism in the 1910s. See Fujita, "Hinshitsu kanri hatten," 70–71; "Hinshitsu kanri nenpyō," *Hinshitsu kanri* 9, no. 6 (June 1958): 76–77.

[147] See, for instance, Ishikawa, *Hinshitsu kanri nyūmon*, 14, 52–53, 59; Mizuno, *Zensha sōgō*, 45; *Hinshitsu kanri to hito no mondai*, esp. 144.

[148] "Shin hinshitsu kanri 12-kō 10: Hinshitsu kanri to hito no mondai," 70.

Perhaps most conspicuously, the quality movement—like the efficiency, rationalization, and productivity movements before it—reified the concept of science, and sought to legitimate the application of scientific managerial practices by emphasizing their supposed empiricism, objectivity, and neutrality. Quality control, one supporter matter-of-factly stated, was synonymous with "rational" and "scientific."[149] Portrayed as the enemy of superstition and the rule of thumb, TQC was acclaimed as a politically impartial medium for improving efficiency in the production process. As Ishikawa Kaoru once observed, "Shop-floor workers know the facts best. But there is the possibility that prejudice will enter into their decision making."[150] In this short and deceptively simple observation, Ishikawa contrived to express respect for labor, affirm the objectivity of scientific expertise, and provide a justification for managerial authority in the workshop.

The spokesmen of the QC movement worked diligently to protect the concept of quality from any politically charged connotations. From the start of its quality campaign, JUSE concentrated on the technical aspects of production, seldom (indeed hardly ever) addressing potentially divisive topics such as wage systems or labor relations. TQC advocates cultivated a studied vagueness regarding touchy issues like the apportionment of authority on the shop floor and the distribution of rewards. Strikingly, by declaring the objectives of management to be cost, quality, and quantity, Ishikawa and his colleagues endeavored to scrub quality control clean of any association with capitalist imperatives or class divisions in the factory. Although ideologically potent, this sleight of hand was not particularly subtle: when once challenged by an assertive industrial engineer to explain why JUSE did not consider profitability among the paramount goals of industrial management, Ishikawa withdrew into politically expedient silence.[151]

Despite such calculated neutrality, the quality movement clearly shared the general objectives and assumptions of the JPC and its postwar repackaging of the Taylorite "Mental Revolution." JUSE had publicly opposed the founding of the Productivity Center, arguing that the new institution was too provocative politically to be an effective instrument in management modernization.[152] Despite this overt repudiation, JUSE would later cooperate with the JPC (on projects like Quality Month) and its rhetoric would increasingly converge

[149] Mizuno Shigeru et al., *Nihon no hinshitsu kanri no hansei to zenshin,* Tenth Quality Control Symposium (JUSE, 1970), 127. For further examples, see Tomizawa, "Hinshitsu kanri to wa," 13; "Shin hinshitsu kanri 12-kō 10: Hinshitsu kanri to hito no mondai," 62; Imaizumi Masumasa, "Genba 7-kai," *Genba to QC* 2 (June 1962): 2–5; Karatsu Hajime, *QC undō: Naze Nihon de seikō shita ka* (NHK, 1987), 70–71.

[150] Ishikawa, *Hinshitsu kanri nyūmon,* 3.

[151] "IE no hanashi o kiku kai," 6.

[152] Nakaoka Tetsurō, "Senchū, sengo no kagakuteki kanri undō III," *Keizaigaku zasshi* 83, no. 1 (May 1982): 50–51. See also "Nikagiren to seisansei kōjō," *Enjinia kurabu,* 10 February 1955, 1.

with the ideology of productivism. "Profits will be divided rationally among consumers, workers and capital," Ishikawa suggested in 1964; "If QC is used, consumers, employees (including managers), and stockholders can all receive returns."[153] Indeed, by the mid-1960s, the relationship between JUSE and the JPC seemed virtually symbiotic, with the quality campaign appearing a depoliticized—and thus potentially more effective—complement to the productivity drive. As an organization committed to managerial modernization and espousing a model of labor-management reconciliation through scientific reform of the factory, JUSE paralleled the JPC and its mission. Yet by taking refuge in political ambiguity and technical specificity, the quality movement was able to proceed without raising the hackles of organized labor or becoming a lightning rod for worker discontent.

In short, the quality movement embraced the methodologies and absorbed the reformist energy of previous Scientific Management initiatives, but it scrupulously avoided the political taint that had dogged prior efforts. To gain distance from its tarnished origins, quality—and specifically TQC—had to consume its heritage and be constructed as a novel and unprecedented formulation. Yet in so doing, ironically enough, the advocates of QC retraced the steps of their predecessors in management reform: following the path of wartime scientific managers, the quality movement trotted out and disparaged the straw man of "original" Taylorism, thus defining quality control in counterpoint. Further, by inaccurately equating American management practice with the literal application of Taylorism, the supporters of TQC (like the wartime modernizers) could convincingly, though misleadingly, claim that their approach was thoroughly Japanese. Thus even in the way that quality experts sought to camouflage the ancestry of QC—to cover their tracks, as it were—they returned as if by instinct to the strategies long employed by the proponents of efficiency, rationalization, and productivity.

In the end, despite staunch protestations of novelty and nativism, TQC emerged as the latest recasting of Scientific Management, albeit one enriched by post-Taylorite innovations imported from the United States and marketed under the evocative, depoliticized banner "quality."[154] By the 1960s, and especially after the deflation of the "management boom," there were indications that Japanese management thought was departing from the narrow emulation of American models, and that (at the very least) Japanese approaches were advancing parallel to American "best practice."[155] Yet through the middle of

[153] Ishikawa, *Hinshitsu kanri nyūmon,* viii, 4. See also *Hinshitsu kanri to hito no mondai,* preface, 147 ff.; "Shin hinshitsu kanri 12-kō 10: Hinshitsu kanri to hito no mondai," 70.

[154] Nakaoka, *Kōjō no tetsugaku,* 222–24.

[155] Although Japanese experts frequently sought to stress the development of an autonomous Japanese path in QC, even they were consistently struck by the parallelism of U.S. and Japanese approaches in the 1950s and 1960s. Nihon seisansei honbu, *Amerika no hinshitsu kanri,* 41, 85; Ishikawa, *Hinshitsu kanri nyūmon,* 13, 20; Ishikawa Kaoru, "Nihon no hinshitsu kanri (5): QC

the decade, the Japanese drive for management reform—including the quality movement—continued to be characterized by a striking consistency with past practice and an ongoing process of cross-fertilization by imported prototypes. What is significant to note, however, is that managers (and increasingly the general public) seemed inclined to believe that a break had been made and that TQC was tracing a distinctively Japanese trajectory in industrial management. That this was the case testified not only to the rhetorical skills of QC ideologues, but more profoundly to the extent to which the "revised Taylorite" ideology had become internalized as "Japanese" management.

QC Circles and the Taylorite Legacy

Over the past twenty years, quality control circles (QCCs) have been regarded as the definitive manifestation of a uniquely Japanese approach to production and labor management. The system of workshop-based, small-group activities which emerged from the quality movement in the early 1960s has been hailed as "an organizational revolution within the firm," and even "a social revolution" of a sort.[156] The widespread adoption of QCCs in Japanese industry has been taken by many as proof of Japan's rejection of a Taylorite paradigm. As Andrew Gordon has argued, "[Japanese] managers transformed American models of quality control or industrial engineering when they experimented with small-group workplace activities. Because companies insisted that all workers be involved in these groups, they directly challenged the American conception, rooted in Taylorism, that workers should not be drawn into decisions about work lest they use their considerable knowledge to make their life easier and ignore management goals."[157] In the popular imagination, as well as in the professional literature of management, the vision of Japan's empowered workshop teams—armed with advanced statistics, autonomy over the production process, and a passion for quality—is almost inevitably juxtaposed with the nightmarish stereotype of Taylorite hierarchy, deskilling, and alienation.

If, however, the development of small-group activities is placed in the context of Japan's transwar Scientific Management movement, the QCC model appears a far less dramatic departure from Taylorite approaches. Although quality control circles were undeniably a postwar Japanese innovation, they evolved out of long-standing ideological premises and managerial techniques

---

team hōkoku," *Hinshitsu kanri* 9, no. 12 (December 1958): 1–3; Takamiya, "Background," 117; *Minna de yaru hinshitsu kanri,* 117; Joseph M. Juran, "The Changing Pattern of Quality Control," *Hinshitsu kanri* 12, no. 1 (January 1961): 2.

[156] Sasaki, *TQC shinwa,* 26.

[157] Andrew Gordon, "Contests for the Workplace," in *Postwar Japan as History,* ed. Andrew Gordon (Berkeley: University of California Press, 1993), 387.

decidedly Taylorite in origin. Rather than a repudiation of Scientific Management, Japan's QC circles can be more accurately understood as a methodological elaboration and refinement of the "revised Taylorism" which had suffused Japanese managerial thought since the 1920s. QCCs, as one observer has suggested, may well be among "the greatest masterpieces born of the Japanese people," yet their heritage is, it seems, in large part Taylorite.[158]

The direct ancestry of the quality control circle concept is extremely murky. Although a number of authors have tried to link postwar small-group activities to traditional organizational patterns or prewar management structures, the connections posited are at best indirect. Watanabe Osamu's comparison of QCCs to mutual surveillance in village society, and the suggestion by critics in organized labor that circles are a "new edition" of wartime Sanpō units, are evocative but unconvincing historically.[159] Okuda Kenji's assertion of a "self-organizing principle" in Japanese factories is an appealing model, yet Okuda fails to account for the transmission of this "principle" from the interwar workshops of progressive employers to the assembly lines of 1960s Japan.[160] One is tempted to conclude, as Andrew Gordon has, that Japan's postwar "workplace culture"—including quality control circles—"by no means grew directly out of an earlier 'traditional' factory culture. Managers reconstituted [shop-floor practices] as they overcame the briefly powerful first unions of the 1940s and 1950s, rationalized production and revived their authority."[161]

[158] Hattori Rokurō, "QC o kiso ni oita 17-nen," *Hinshitsu kanri* 31, no. 3 (March 1980): 23. Compare Robert E. Cole, "Learning from the Japanese," *Management Review* 69, no. 9 (September 1980): 25; Cole, *Strategies for Learning,* 23. For treatments that stress the Taylorite nature of QC circles, see Frank Webster and Kevin Robins, " 'I'll Be Watching You': Comment on Sewell and Wilkinson," *Sociology* 27, no. 2 (May 1993): 243–52; Mike Parker, "Industrial Relations Myth and Shop-Floor Reality: The 'Team Concept' in the Auto Industry," in *Industrial Democracy in America: The Ambiguous Promise,* ed. Nelson Lichtenstein and Howell Harris (Cambridge: Cambridge University Press, 1993), 249–74. For a fascinating overview of the quality control circle and its implications for Japanese workers, see Kumazawa Makoto, *Portraits of the Japanese Workplace: Labor Movements, Workers, and Managers,* ed. Andrew Gordon, trans. Andrew Gordon and Mikiso Hane (Boulder, Colo.: Westview Press, 1996), chap. 5.

[159] Watanabe Osamu, "Gendai Nihon shakai no ken'i-teki kōzō to kokka," in *Ken'i-teki chitsujo to kokka,* ed. Fujita Isamu (Tokyo daigaku shuppankai, 1987), 193; Ōba Hideo and Nakahara Manabu, *TQC to no tatakai* (Gakushū no tomo sha, 1984), 157; see also Robert E. Cole, *Work, Mobility and Participation* (Berkeley: University of California Press, 1979), 208. Koike stresses the importance of Japanese patterns of skill formation in the success of QCCs yet cannot account for the evolution of the circle concept in Japan. Koike Kazuo, *Understanding Industrial Relations in Modern Japan* (New York: St. Martin's Press, 1988), 151–58.

[160] See Okuda, "Nihon keiei kanrishi no ichi teiryū," 2–12; Robert Cole, "Some Cultural and Social Bases of Japanese Innovation: Small-Group Activities in Comparative Perspective," in *The Political Economy of Japan,* vol. 3: *Cultural and Social Dynamics,* ed. Kumon Shumpei and Henry Rosovsky (Stanford, Calif.: Stanford University Press, 1992), 298. See also Ishihara Shigekazu, Ishihara Keiko, Nagamichi Mitsuo, and Alfredo Pinochet, "Neural Network Simulation of QC Circle Activities," in *The Dynamics of Japanese Organizations,* ed. Frank-Jurgen Richter (London: Routledge, 1996), 132–47.

[161] Gordon, "Contests," 388.

Nevertheless, from the 1920s, Japanese Taylorites had consistently stressed the importance of tapping into the specialized knowledge of shop-floor workers and of mobilizing the factory rank and file behind management goals. Such preoccupations, of course, followed directly from the Taylorite imperative to appropriate craft knowledge for the managerial staff, and from the vision of a transcendent "Mental Revolution." Thus prewar advocates of Scientific Management frequently promoted the use of suggestion systems as a means of commandeering worker expertise and creativity for management ends.[162] Yet prior to the postwar period, Japanese Taylorites seldom promoted shop-floor group activities as a viable strategy for enlisting labor into management reform efforts. Only after the war did Japan's scientific managers begin to recognize the full potential of such grass-roots mobilization in facilitating the Taylorization of the Japanese factory.[163]

For instance, in 1949—well over a decade before the appearance of the first formal QCCs—Taylorite consultant Andō Jirō outlined a system for reforming the production process and boosting efficiency using workplace discussion groups. Seeking a means of institutionalizing the collection and evaluation of worker suggestions, Andō recommended the formation of "work improvement committees" (*gyōmu kaizen iinkai*) in each department of an office or factory. These bodies were to be made up from workers in the unit concerned, although the chair of each committee was to be drawn from middle or upper management. Andō's committees resembled the management councils (*keiei kyōgikai*) adopted by many Japanese firms immediately after the war, yet his vision stressed management control and worker mobilization more than labor-capital consultation.[164] As Andō conceived his program, "The goal of the work improvement committees is to awaken the interest of workers in their everyday tasks, to further the spirit of labor-management harmony, to increase the quality and volume of work, and to consider reforms in the work process. They are not management consultative organs, but rather discussion groups

---

[162] See, for example, Okuda Kenji, *Hito to keiei: Nihon keiei kanrishi kenkyū* (Manejimento-sha, 1985), 184–85; Okuda Kenji, "Byūrokurashii-ka no Nihonteki pataan," *Keizai ronshū* special issue (1985): 67–80; Tessa Morris-Suzuki, *The Technological Transformation of Japan* (Cambridge: Cambridge University Press, 1994), 128–29.

[163] In the United States, where the Taylorization of the production process had already reached high levels by the end of World War II, strategies (like small-group activities) which sought to incorporate workers into Taylorization efforts were apparently unnecessary. Thus, even though American scientific managers—like their Japanese counterparts—had long supported suggestion systems, elaborate structures for mobilizing employees in the service of management reform did not evolve in U.S. industry. This comparative perspective only underlines the fact that QC circles were not figured as a reaction against Taylorism, but were conceptualized in Japan as a means of spreading Scientific Management and solidifying managerial control in an environment where the Taylorization of the workplace was relatively retarded.

[164] See Andrew Gordon, *The Evolution of Labor Relations in Japan: Heavy Industry, 1853–1955* (Cambridge, Mass.: Harvard University Press, 1985), 339 ff.; Lonnie Carlile, "Zaikai and the Politics of Production in Japan, 1940–1962" (Ph.D. diss., University of California, Berkeley, 1989), 276 ff.

for earnestly considering the improvement of work methods, and for bringing together managers and operatives."[165] Andō believed that such a system could provide managers with information otherwise monopolized by the workers, foster a "peaceful" atmosphere in the workshop, and give employees a sense of personal involvement in their duties. Andō's scheme did mark a considerable departure from the orthodox practice of Scientific Management, yet it aimed to deliver decidedly Taylorite results: the appropriation of craft knowledge, the extension of managerial surveillance, and the alignment of worker consciousness with corporate objectives.

Whether such "work improvement committees" were ever put into practice is uncertain, as is any direct connection between Andō's plan and the later conceptualization of quality control circles. What is clear is that Andō's committees—and other workplace discussion groups proposed by postwar Taylorites[166]—closely prefigured the model of QCCs which eventually emerged in Japan. Quality control circles thus coalesced from an intellectual environment in which a link between small-group workplace activities and Taylorite management reforms had already been well established.

The immediate antecedents of quality control circles were shop-floor discussion groups which appeared in certain firms during the late 1950s and early 1960s. The first of these bodies—initially called *genba kentōkai* (workshop study groups)—were organized at Shin-etsu Chemical, although similar structures appeared almost simultaneously at Sumitomo Electric and Tōshiba. Shin-etsu, which was a pioneer in QC and had won the Deming Prize in 1953, founded the "study groups" as part of an effort to spread awareness of quality control throughout the corporate hierarchy. The groups, which had from twenty to thirty members and met two to five times a month, were compulsory for factory operatives and were chaired by QC staff engineers. Discussion topics included quality techniques, production methods, and safety, but the groups had no formal authority to implement changes in the work process. Shin-etsu management saw the bodies as "a forum for promoting quality consciousness, improving operations, and allowing for interchange up and down the organization." The study groups were also heralded as means of inspiring worker creativity, fostering labor appreciation for the challenges facing management, and improving human relations on the front line of production.[167]

---

[165] Andō Jirō, "Jimu nōritsu kaizen no yōten," *Jitsumu techō* 1 (January 1949): 30.

[166] Note, for example, the proposal made by the Management Issues Committee of the Japan Association for the Promotion of Science in 1950. This body—whose members included many prominent Taylorites—supported the creation of workshop-based "production committees" (*seisan iinkai*) designed to educate workers in the need for management rationalization and gain their cooperation in reform efforts. Takase, *Sangyō gōrika,* 13.

[167] "Shin-etsu kagaku: Naoetsu kōjō," *Hinshitsu kanri* 10, no. 7 (July 1959): 38–47; Karikomi Ichirō, "Genba kentōkai haiken," ibid., 11, no. 3 (March 1960): 29–32; "TQC tōronkai (1)," 1–5; Sasaki and Nonaka, "Kagakuteki kanrihō," 277–78.

The Shin-etsu Chemical system provided important inspiration to the quality movement leadership in the Union of Japanese Scientists and Engineers. Appreciating the potential of small-group activities in disseminating QC thought, JUSE began an initiative in the early 1960s to establish workplace groups for discussing, studying, and applying quality methods. First tagged "reading circles" (*dokusho saakuru*), though soon rechristened as "QC circles," the bodies were conceived as voluntary, foreman-led educational organs. In 1962, JUSE began publication of a journal, *Genba to QC* (The Workplace and QC), which was to serve as a text and a basis for discussion in newly formed circles. Priced reasonably and written in a nontechnical style ("light, easy to read, and easy to understand"), *Genba to QC* aimed to encourage foremen and workers to study quality control and establish circle activities as the "core of QC in each workshop."[168]

Quality control circles were originally conceptualized within the larger TQC project of diffusing "quality consciousness" throughout corporate structures. QCCs were seen as a promising device for drawing workers directly into quality control efforts, and for eliciting the willing cooperation of shop-floor operatives in management-directed QC reforms.[169] The point of production was very much the final frontier for TQC proselytizers: under JUSE sponsorship, the "quality spirit" had been diffused up to top management, across to middle management, and out to the consuming public, but had yet to penetrate down to the workshop. The circle concept was thus welcomed as an unprovocative means for injecting QC thought into workplace culture—for lowering the walls around the shop-floor "kingdoms" which had frustrated QC specialists for so long.[170] In this regard, what seemed particularly appealing about QCCs was the fact that circle activities—though nominally voluntary—created formal structures which compelled workers to read QC materials they would otherwise ignore. Such gentle—but calculated—coercion would become a hallmark of the quality control circle movement.[171]

---

[168] "Genba to QC," *Hinshitsu kanri* 13, no. 6 (June 1962): 17; *QC Circle Koryo*, 6–7. A general introduction to the early history of QCCs in given in Cole, "Some Cultural and Social Bases," 307–8.

[169] *Hinshitsu kanri to hito no mondai,* 74–78; Yoshimura Hiroshi, "Wagakuni no kōgyō ni okeru hinshitsu kanri no tenbō," *Hinshitsu kanri* 11, no. 3 (March 1960): 36; "Tōron kiroku: Hinshitsu hoshō ni okeru genbachō no ninmu," *Genba to QC* 1 (April 1962): 4–26; Ishikawa Kaoru, "QC saakuru katsudō 3-shūnen ni atatte," ibid., 18 (April 1965): 2–6; see also Mizuno, *Zensha sōgō,* 154 ff.

[170] Ishikawa, "Nihon no hinshitsu kanri (1)," 9–10; "'Genbachō to hinshitsu kanri' tokushū-gō hakkan ni atatte," *Hinshitsu kanri* 12, no. 9 (September 1961): 1.

[171] Ishikawa, *What is Total Quality Control?* 22; see also Cole, "Learning," 26. JUSE experts consistently had a difficult time balancing the rhetoric of individual worker autonomy (in joining a QCC) and the desirability of complete mobilization: "Supervisors are not supposed to demand participation. They are responsible, however, to sufficiently inform people on the necessity for everyone to participate." *QC Circle Koryo,* 57–58.

From the start, however, managers and QC experts envisioned uses for quality circles that went far beyond employee instruction and edification. QCCs—like the suggestion systems long endorsed by management—offered access to detailed information on the manufacturing process which the workers normally kept to themselves. As Ishikawa Kaoru and others frequently lamented, the balkanization of Japanese workshops meant that engineers lacked the knowledge necessary to control the organization of production.[172] What Japanese QC specialists demanded—and what QCCs apparently offered—was "feedback" from the still shadowy world of the shop floor. The breaching of the walls around factory "kingdoms" by quality circles thus promised managers closer scrutiny over production methods and conditions at the grass-roots level.[173]

From this perspective, at least, the QCC concept was fully consistent with the imperatives of Scientific Management. This is hardly surprising considering that the circle model was formulated during the very period that JUSE was preaching a return to basic Taylorite approaches. Quality movement leaders acutely perceived small-group activities as an inconspicuous means of appropriating craft knowledge from the workers, strengthening the position of staff specialists, and exposing the shop floor to the harsh (and relatively unfamiliar) light of scientific analysis. As Karatsu Hajime has stated, capturing both the essence of Taylorite deskilling and an inner dynamic of QCC activities, "Master craftsmen are people who manage to find the best ways of making things. As long as their craft remains a secret, however, it cannot become the basis of an industry. Quality control can be viewed as a way of teaching these methods to everyone, using the science of statistics."[174]

In the QCC strategy, as in Taylor's original blueprint for Scientific Management, the foreman assumed a crucial role as both the subject of reform and the agent of change. After the war, the shop-floor supervisory stratum, recognized as "the ultimate and vital link between executive management and the opera-

[172] Ishikawa Kaoru, "Nihon no QC to Amerika no QC no shindan (2)," *Hinshitsu kanri* 9, no. 11 (November 1958): 23–26; Ishikawa, "Nihon no hinshitsu kanri (1)," 9–10.

[173] Cole has described this function of quality circles as "opportunistic surveillance"; *Work, Mobility and Participation,* 139. See also *QC Circle Koryo,* 26 ff.; Nakaoka, *Kōjō no tetsugaku,* 26–27.

[174] Karatsu, *TQC Wisdom,* 74. According to a 1965 report in *Genba to QC,* "The supervisor may understand the design of the machine and how to run it, but is probably unaware of its detailed tendencies or weaknesses. The people who know best about the condition of the machine are the workers, and quality circles provide an opportunity to get important information from them." Quoted in Nonaka, "Development of Company-wide Quality Control," 154. See also Shimada Haruo, "Japan's Industrial Culture and Labor-Management Relations," in Kumon and Rosovsky, *The Political Economy of Japan,* 3:274; Cole, *Work, Mobility and Participation,* 181; Sewell and Wilkinson, " 'Someone to Watch Over Me,' " 271–89; Mike Parker, *Inside the Circle: A Union Guide to QWL* (Boston: South End Press, 1985).

tive,"[175] was a focus for concern among managerial experts. Foremen—as the potentates of shop-floor "kingdoms" and key intermediary actors in the unsettled environment of postwar labor relations—were viewed by managers as both obstacles to overcome and resources to exploit. Through the 1950s, companies sought means of ensuring foreman loyalty to management goals and controlling their autonomy over the production process. At the same time, in the interests of maintaining workshop order, managers endeavored to prevent the dilution of supervisory authority in a time of rapid technological change.[176]

The Training Within Industry program was the first salvo in management's battle to capture the hearts and minds of foremen, and the QCC movement continued this project. From the start, quality control circles were designed as a means of educating foremen, improving their effectiveness as managers, and coopting them into the managerial hierarchy. The official English translation of "Genba to QC" was "Quality Control for the Foreman" and, in its early days, the QCC movement was often referred to as FQC (foreman quality control). By placing first-line supervisors in charge of circle activities, JUSE leaders hoped to promote leadership skills, boost morale, and absorb foremen into management QC initiatives. Thus, at the same time that QCCs undermined the independence of shop-floor "kingdoms," they were used to confirm the authority of foremen as the most basic unit in managerial control over the workplace.[177]

Although quality control circles are now widely regarded as vehicles for worker self-expression, the initial emphasis in the QCC literature was on shop-floor discipline and worker responsibility. JUSE put considerable effort into portraying circles as spontaneous and voluntary, yet movement leaders clearly envisioned the groups as management-controlled devices for impressing responsibility upon the workforce. Arguing that operatives had lost a sense of personal accountability as Japan progressed from craft production to the assembly line, managers sought to reinstill responsibility for individual per

---

[175] *Japan Quality Control Circles* (Tokyo: Asian Productivity Organization, 1972), 2.

[176] See, for example, Kuroda Ken'ichi, "Sengo Nihon no rōmu kanri to kyōsōteki shokuba chitsujo," in Sengo Nihon keiei kenkyūkai, *Sengo Nihon no kigyō keiei*, 300 ff.; Onitsuka, "Sengo Nihon," 240–41; Tsuda Masumi, "Study of Japanese Management Development Practices I," *Hitotsubashi Journal of Social Studies* 9, no. 1 (May 1977): 11; "Shokuchō kyōiku to QC," *Hinshitsu kanri* 14, no. 8 (August 1963): 6. For comparative perspectives, see Nelson Lichtenstein, "'The Man in the Middle': A Social History of the Automobile Industry Foreman," in *On the Line*, ed. Nelson Lichtenstein and Stephen Meyer (Urbana: University of Illinois Press, 1989); Barbara Weinstein, *For Social Peace in Brazil: Industrialists and the Remaking of the Working Class in São Paulo, 1920–1964* (Chapel Hill: University of North Carolina Press, 1996), 261–65.

[177] "Aru kikai kōjō," 25–28; "Zadankai: Genbachō o meguru iroiro na mondai," *Hinshitsu kanri* 12, no. 9 (September 1961): 2–16; "Ankeeto: Genbachō," 54–58; Suzuki, "Shokuchō kyōiku kōsu," 1–3; Ishikawa Kaoru, "Makoto no QC saakuru katsudō e no michi," *Genba to QC* 36 (October 1966): 4–5; *Minna de yaru hinshitsu kanri,* 116.

formance through QCC activities.[178] "No matter how good your work standards are," one manager declared in *Genba to QC,* "if your employees are not conscientious, don't have a cooperative spirit, and don't feel responsibility for quality, you won't make good products."[179] Companies were none too subtle in trying to impress this point upon their workers: one firm promoted quality circles under the slogan "Bear Responsibility for Your Own Work."[180]

QCCs—like Drucker's system of "Management by Objectives and Self-Control"—were designed to create an environment where employees would naturally align individual interests with corporate goals and standards. As circle activities flooded the shop floor with official expectations of responsibility, each worker was intended to come, almost inevitably, to embrace management norms and self-police his or her own performance.[181] QCC advocates often affirmed that "The power to decide whether or not to maintain work standards rests with the workers." But small-group activities were intended to curtail, rather than foster, this sphere of autonomy on the shop floor.[182] By stressing worker involvement through the assumption of personal responsibility, QCCs became a means for internalizing structures of control and gaining worker compliance with management-defined yardsticks of quality and efficiency. As Robert Cole has perceptively observed, "Management sought to make participation a responsibility, an obligation, of each employee. Participation was not seen as providing an opportunity for employees to express their individual talents or self-actualize, California-style."[183] QCCs were thus figured as something of a collective conscience for shop-floor workers, and not as a forum for the articulation of employee autonomy.[184]

From its inception, the QCC movement was rich with the rhetoric of "participation," "decentralization," and "motivation," yet Human Relations methods were seen as means, and not as ends in and of themselves. The architects of circle activities in JUSE were strongly influenced by Human Relations thought in the delineation of the QCC concept. Even in the early 1950s, QC leaders had acknowledged the importance of worker morale and

---

[178] Yoshimura, "Wagakuni," 36–37; "TQC tōronkai (1)," 4.

[179] Ishiguro Shigeo, "Hinshitsu kanri to ningen kankei," *Genba to QC* 30 (April 1966): 25.

[180] *Japan Quality Control Circles,* 93.

[181] Ishikawa, *Hinshitsu kanri nyūmon,* 35 ff.

[182] Taguchi Gen'ichi, "Sagyō hyōjun to ningen kankei," *Genba to QC* 23 (September 1965): 28–29. See also Mizuno, *Zensha sōgō,* 154 ff.; Tomizawa, "Hinshitsu kanri to wa," 13.

[183] Cole, "Some Cultural and Social Bases," 296.

[184] In evaluating the results of QCC activity, one manager remarked, with a mixture of surprise and awe, that "Everyone began on his own to supervise and check himself, even without nagging, so that the level of quality automatically rose." *Japan Quality Control Circles,* 28. Kumazawa Makoto stresses the "subversive potential" of QC circles as a site of articulation of "an independent logic of labor." Kumazawa concedes, however, that such potential remains (for the most part) latent. Kumazawa, *Portraits of the Japanese Workplace,* chap. 5.

involvement in attaining quality objectives. "Be conscious of how important human relations are in production," one JUSE report warned: "Be aware that you can't manage just with numbers."[185] FQC, one circle proponent suggested, should stand for "friendship"—as well as "foreman"—quality control.[186] As *Genba to QC* assured its readers, QCC involvement could make each workshop "a bright factory, a factory where one can do pleasant work, a blissful home."[187]

Yet from the start, the JUSE embrace of Human Relations techniques was more functionalist than idealistic. The axiomatic belief that improved human relations would bring improved productivity underlay much QCC thinking.[188] The "personal approach" was conceived as an implement for furthering managerial control and was wielded accordingly. For example, the teaching of basic Human Relations methods to foremen was intended primarily as a means of strengthening supervisory authority and ensuring a compliant workforce.[189] "For the sake of QC," one manager bluntly advised, "always endeavor to control human psychology."[190] Human Relations, another quality expert confided, meant "getting things done through people."[191]

Initially, then, Human Relations objectives like morale and participation figured only indirectly in the conception of quality control circles. As Robert Cole has observed, the original focus of QCC efforts "was on engineers aiming to solve quality and cost problems at the workplace; many of the more uplifting themes were afterthoughts that only came to be explicitly discussed many years later."[192] Human Relations techniques were to be the sugar that made the bitter medicine of standardization and accountability go down more easily on the shop floor. JUSE leaders were seldom explicit in acknowledging this calculated use of psychological approaches, yet the circle concept was undeniably embraced as a "humanized" vehicle for injecting QC methods and basic Taylorite reforms into the workplace. In this light, the quality control circle initiative—as well as the larger QC project—can readily be seen as continuous with the transwar "revised Taylorite" consensus on management reform.

[185] "Ankeeto: Genbachō," 57; see also Hirota Hisaichi, "Hinshitsu kanri no kagi wa netsui to aitagai no yūwaryoku," *Hinshitsu kanri* 4, no. 9 (September 1953): 20–21.

[186] "QC no bunrui," *Hinshitsu kanri* 15, no. 2 (February 1964): 15.

[187] Frontispiece, *Genba to QC* 12 (July 1964); see also "Shin hinshitsu kanri 12-kō 10: Hinshitsu kanri to hito no mondai," 60–70.

[188] See, for example, Kirishima Seiji and Nishigaki Masako, "Seisansei to riidaashippu," *Genba to QC* 20 (June 1965): 12–16.

[189] "Ankeeto: Genbachō," 54–56; "Zadankai: Yaruki o okosaseru ni wa," *Genba to QC* 11 (May 1964): 7–17.

[190] Ishiguro, "Hinshitsu kanri to ningen kankei," 25–27; see also *Japan Quality Control Circles*, 20.

[191] "Shin hinshitsu kanri 12-kō 10: Hinshitsu kanri to hito no mondai," 63.

[192] Cole, "Some Cultural and Social Bases," 296.

Nevertheless, as Cole has observed, quality circles "evolved into more than what had been originally intended."[193] Managers discovered from experience that QCCs were even more valuable as tools of personnel management than they were as components of a TQC regime. For instance, Japanese employers gradually came to recognize the potential of QC circles in cultivating "intra-group" competition among shop-floor operatives. From the late 1960s, firms increasingly used QCC participation as a basis for worker evaluation, integrating small-group activities into what Watanabe Osamu has termed a "competitive order" for spurring "spontaneous obedience" in the workplace.[194] At the same time, as Japan's labor shortage worsened, as automation spread, and as business sought to alter basic tenets of the "Japanese employment system," companies looked to QCCs to stabilize human relations on the shop floor and maintain employee morale. In this environment, circle activities were subtly recast as a cure for worker turnover, an antidote for worker alienation, and a palliative for the introduction of "ability" (*nōryoku*) wages.[195] Thus only in the late 1960s and the 1970s did the now-familiar image of QCCs—as motivational tools, as participative organs, and as a strategy in personnel management—begin to come into focus in Japan.

Yet even as QC circles became increasingly associated with personnel (rather than production) management, they remained firmly rooted in Taylorite premises. Despite the heightened emphasis over time on terms like "participation" and "self-development," the autonomy of QCCs remained closely circumscribed by managers. JUSE's *QC Circle Koryo* (General Principles of the QC Circle), a handbook published in response to the circle "boom" of the late 1960s, stressed the role of workplace groups in solidifying management control, not in fostering worker initiative. QCCs "contribute to the improvement and development of the enterprise," the guide claimed, and they "provide an effective support to digest and implement policies set up by the president or the plant manager . . . to achieve quality assurance."[196]

Self-Taylorization also remained a crucial ingredient in the QC circle formula. In the 1980s, for example, some circles videotaped their members at work, later analyzing the films as a group to suggest ways of simplifying motions and speeding up production.[197] Not only was the circle to become a

[193] Cole, *Strategies,* 295.

[194] Watanabe, "Gendai Nihon," 186–92; Katō Tetsurō and Rob Steven, *Is Japanese Capitalism Post-Fordist?* Papers of the Japanese Studies Centre, Monash University, no. 16 (Melbourne, 1991), 15; Cole, "Learning," 39; *Japan Quality Control Circles,* 12.

[195] Cole, *Strategies,* 21, 57; Cusumano, *The Japanese Automobile Industry,* 355 ff.; Odaka Kunio, *Japanese Management: A Forward-Looking Analysis* (Tokyo: Asian Productivity Organization, 1986), 37; Nakaoka, *Kōjō no tetsugaku,* 216–18.

[196] *QC Circle Koryo,* 1, 18. See also Cole, *Work, Mobility and Participation,* 201–4; Cole, *Strategies,* 19–20; Mizuno, *Zensha sōgō,* 45; John Price, *Japan Works: Power and Paradox in Postwar Industrial Relations* (Ithaca, N.Y.: ILR Press, 1997), 168–72.

[197] Ōba and Nakahara, *TQC,* 31–32.

latter-day incarnation of the efficiency engineer, but so was each worker on the assembly line. A 1982 JUSE textbook on QCC activities—produced in cartoon format and aimed clearly at the shop-floor rank and file—encouraged workers to reform themselves by applying Gilbreth's methods of motion study to their own work.[198] The Taylorite stopwatch, so long the property of the specialist staff, was thus imprinted on the agenda of QC circles and the consciousness of individual workers.

But to argue, as many have, that this diffusion of basic techniques to the shop floor constituted a meaningful "democratization" of management knowledge is ultimately untenable. By the postwar period, the Japanese heirs of Scientific Management—and especially those in JUSE—had realized that the "Mental Revolution" was unlikely to be the spontaneous affair Taylor had predicted. Instead, Japanese management reformers recognized that the only way to gain the workers' full commitment to corporate goals was through the subtle coercion of education. As Ishikawa Kaoru repeatedly affirmed, "Quality control begins with education and ends with education."[199] Yet the information provided through QCC activities did not so much empower workers as channel their perceptions in managerially approved directions. QC circles did give operatives a new vocabulary of work reform, but it was a vocabulary defined by management, premised on the objectivity and authority of scientific analysis, and derived from long-standing Taylorite assumptions. The triumph of this vocabulary as the idiom of the workshop—as well as the boardroom— served to discredit political analysis of the work process and confirm the authority of specialist staff. In the end, circles became the backbone of a workplace order premised on "controlled participation," an order which offered workers a voice, but one which could only speak a language provided by management.[200]

There is a certain irony in the fact that QC circles—which were originally designed to further the orthodox Taylorite goals of standardization, specialization, and improved managerial control—eventually became a means of countering worker anomie on the Taylorized assembly line. As Karatsu Hajime has suggested, "For workers who feel like they are on a treadmill all day, QC circle activities provide an opportunity to think and to be heard and to feel like an important member of the organization. . . . This is the joy of working. Workers have a greater sense of self-worth knowing that their work can serve customers. In this sense, QC circle activities represent a return to the days of craftsmanship or of handcrafted products."[201] It would appear, then, that the popularity and durability of quality control circles as management tools de-

[198] Kitaboshi Kōhei, *QC saakuru manga shinan* (JUSE, 1982), 223.

[199] Ishikawa, *Hinshitsu kanri nyūmon*, 35, 54 ff.; *QC Circle Koryo*, 71; Yamaki, *Hinshitsu kanri*, 64.

[200] Cole, *Work, Mobility and Participation*, 201; Cole, *Strategies*, 278–79.

[201] Karatsu, *TQC Wisdom*, 99.

rived, to a great extent, from their versatility and mutability. QCCs exhibited a remarkable—and somewhat unexpected[202]—capacity for fusing "humanization" and rationalization without giving rise to paralyzing contradictions. Circles could promote Scientific Management while denying the premises of Taylorism, they could become venues for interworker competition as well as sites of cooperative integration, and they could be portrayed as unique outgrowths of Japanese tradition as easily as second-hand reflections of the latest Behavioral Science theories.

Thus quality control circles were not only consistent and continuous with "revised Taylorite" thought, but they ultimately became a concrete—and effective—methodological embodiment of its assumptions and imperatives. With the widespread success of the QC circle concept—as workers and managers alike came to embrace the new gospel of small-group activities—and with TQC as a powerful vehicle for the institutionalization of management reform, it seemed that the realization of the "revised Taylorite" vision of technocratic authority, productive efficiency, and a "humane" approach to labor was at hand. By the 1970s, this postwar reworking of the longstanding Taylorite consensus was celebrated, both in Japan and abroad, as a new standard for production and personnel management. Under the dual banners of TQC and quality control circles, Scientific Management at last suffused the Japanese workplace, and the Taylorite origins of Japanese practice were finally, fully dissolved into a flourishing mythology of "Japanese-style management."

---

[202] Ishikawa Kaoru and Imaizumi Masumasa, "Amerika dayori," *Hinshitsu kanri* 16, no. 6 (June 1965): 47; Mizuno et al., *Nihon no hinshitsu kanri,* 116, 133.

Epilogue

The Taylorite Roots of "Japanese-Style Management"

This study suggests that Scientific Management spread further, remained relevant longer, and penetrated deeper in twentieth-century Japan than previous observers have acknowledged. From its introduction in 1911 through the debates of the Taishō period, the rationalization movement, wartime mobilization, postwar reconstruction, and the decades of high-speed growth, Taylorism was progressively embraced as the most logical and natural model for industrial management in Japan. In this light, the popular presumption that corporate familialism has been the dominant managerial ideology of modern Japan begs reevaluation. Likewise, Japan's experience of Taylorism calls into question simplistic notions of postwar American paternity for "Japanese-style management," as well as the widely held assumption of a superordinate role for culture in the making of Japanese business methods. In Japan, as in the United States and Western Europe, Taylorite approaches provided the fundamental structure for contemporary management thought and practice.

The advance of Scientific Management in twentieth-century Japan can be charted on two levels, first as an expansive ideological framework and second as a concrete shop-floor methodology. As an intellectual template for conceiving the nature of work, social organization, and the structures of political economy, Taylorism spread steadily and profoundly through Japanese society. As occurred internationally, the implications of Scientific Management extended far beyond the factory and the firm, tracing an intellectual trajectory embracing ever larger spheres of Japanese economic, social, and political life. The logic of Taylorism—progress through productivity, "objective" expertism, the primacy of "scientific" solutions, class harmonization based on the "Mental Revolution"—was extended successively from the shop floor (in the Taishō efficiency movement), to the industry level (in the rationalization campaigns of the 1930s), to encompass the workings of the entire national economy (during the wartime "New Order"). In the wake of Japan's defeat, Taylorite ideals were revived and mobilized—under the depoliticized banner of productivity—as a comprehensive framework for accord among capitalists, managers, and workers. At the same time, key aspects of the Taylorite mindset were instilled and institutionalized at the workshop level as Scientific Management was diffused through Japanese industry by the assertive quality control movement and by tenacious individuals like Toyota's Ōno Taiichi. The ideological imperatives of Scientific Management thus fed Japan's wartime authoritarian temper as well as the enduring faith in technocratic political and economic leadership. Perhaps even more significantly, the Taylorite notions systematized in the productivist vision undergirded the postwar social contract on economic growth and formed the intellectual foundations of the contemporary "managed society" (*kanri shakai*) in Japan.[1]

Historians have only begun to explore how Taylorite ideals "trickled down" from the realms of industry and the state bureaucracy to influence other spheres of Japanese life. Clearly, the reach of Taylorite thought—especially in the familiar guise of "rationalization"—has been considerable: as William Kelly notes, "*gōrika* has proved an ideologically potent and semantically slippery rubric for reform of everything from work rules and school texts to kitchen design, traffic flow, and dietary habits."[2] Since the 1920s, for example, a variety of public and private initiatives have endeavored to impress upon the Japanese people the vital, personal importance of efficiency, scientific thinking, planning, frugality, and punctuality. Described by Sheldon Garon as part of a larger process of "social management," campaigns like the postwar "New Life Movement" injected a Taylorite morality into Japanese homes, enjoining all to "eliminate wastefulness in daily life," "modernize" outdated customs, and "conduct themselves efficiently."[3] As was also the case in Europe and the Americas, women were often the focus of such efforts to rationalize the quotidian. Cast as a scientific manager for the family and a "rational consumer" in the marketplace, the ideal Japanese woman was expected to embody an array of Taylorite virtues, in what Sharon Nolte and Sally Hastings have labeled a veritable "cult of productivity" for the home.[4] Indeed, even though much

[1] The persistence of the productivist vision was made clear in a 1979 pamphlet on welfare policy issued by the Liberal Democratic Party, the conservative bloc which has dominated postwar Japanese political life. The pamphlet warned against infection by the "English disease," a dire condition of "economic diabetes" triggered by "slicing up the economic pie (GNP) . . . rather than making it bigger." Sheldon Garon, *Molding Japanese Minds: The State in Everyday Life* (Princeton, N.J.: Princeton University Press, 1997), 223. On the "managed society," see J. Victor Koschmann, "Intellectuals and Politics," in *Postwar Japan as History,* ed. Andrew Gordon (Berkeley: University of California Press, 1993), 415–16; Tessa Morris-Suzuki, *Beyond Computopia: Information, Automation and Democracy in Japan* (London: Kegan Paul International, 1988).

[2] "Perhaps most commonly implied in these multiple usages," Kelly adds, "has been a style of expertise that is empowered by its own formal characteristics: the professionalization of roles, the bureaucratization of institutions, and the systematization of procedures." William Kelly, "Rationalization and Nostalgia: Cultural Dynamics of New Middle-Class Japan," *American Ethnologist* 13, no. 4 (November 1986): 606.

[3] Garon, *Molding Japanese Minds,* 162–77.

[4] Nolte and Hastings contrast the Japanese "cult of productivity" with the Victorian "cult of domesticity." Sharon Nolte and Sally Hastings, "The Meiji State's Policy toward Women, 1890–1910," in *Recreating Japanese Women,* ed. Gail Lee Bernstein (Berkeley: University of California Press, 1991), 151–74. See also Garon, *Molding Japanese Minds;* Kathleen Uno, "The Death of 'Good Wife, Wise Mother'?" in Gordon, *Postwar Japan as History,* 293–322. For comparative perspectives, see Mary Nolan, *Visions of Modernity: American Business and the Modernization of Germany* (New York: Oxford University Press, 1994), chap. 10; Barbara Weinstein, *For Social*

scholarly work remains to be done in tracing Scientific Management's conceptual diffusion, the imperatives of order, hierarchy, and control rooted in Taylorism appear to have touched a number of institutions, practices, and discourses—educational methods, strategies of colonial administration, popular culture and leisure, language and script reform, agricultural policy and rural life, to name but a few—lying well beyond the mills, machine shops, and boardrooms of twentieth-century Japan.[5]

Despite Taylorism's pervading ideological presence and broad social influence, the production techniques of Scientific Management were relatively slow to spread in Japan. Progress prior to World War II was spotty: some methods (like time-and-motion study) saw widespread application, others (like incentive wage systems) were the subject of extensive Japanese adaptation, and a few (like functional foremanship) were ignored or abandoned. The advances in several industries, such as textiles, were impressive, yet other sectors seemed almost impervious to Taylorite reforms. Proponents of managerial modernization constantly berated Japanese manufacturers for their retarded implementation of Scientific Management, but such complaints often reflected rising expectations as much as a sluggish pace of change. Nevertheless, only with the changing economic and political realities of the high-growth years, and with the provision of more effective institutional structures (like JUSE) for promoting management reform, were the technical aspects of the Taylorite model generalized throughout Japanese industry.

Peace in Brazil: Industrialists and the Remaking of the Working Class in São Paulo, 1920–1964 (Chapel Hill: University of North Carolina Press, 1996), chap. 6; Ruth Schwartz Cowan, *More Work for Mother* (New York: Basic Books, 1983).

[5] On the Taylorite qualities of the educational system and the managerialism of Japanese schools, see Norma Field, "The Child as Laborer and Consumer," in *Children and the Politics of Culture,* ed. Sharon Stephens (Princeton, N.J.: Princeton University Press, 1995), 51–78; Horio Teruhisa, *Educational Thought and Ideology in Modern Japan,* ed. and trans. Steven Platzer (Tokyo: University of Tokyo Press, 1988); Thomas Rohlen, *Japan's High Schools* (Berkeley: University of California Press, 1983); Thomas Rohlen, "Order in Japanese Society: Attachment, Authority, and Routine," *Journal of Japanese Studies* 15, no. 1 (Winter 1989): 5–40. On colonial administration, see Chalmers Johnson, *MITI and the Japanese Miracle* (Stanford, Calif.: Stanford University Press, 1982), 130–32; Mark Peattie, "Japanese Attitudes toward Colonialism, 1895–1945," in *The Japanese Colonial Empire, 1895–1945,* ed. Ramon Myers and Mark Peattie (Princeton, N.J.: Princeton University Press, 1984), 80–127; Carter Eckert, *Offspring of Empire: The Koch'ang Kims and the Colonial Origins of Korean Capitalism, 1876–1945* (Seattle: University of Washington Press, 1991); and the essays in Peter Duus, Ramon Myers, and Mark Peattie, eds., *The Japanese Wartime Empire, 1931–1945* (Princeton, N.J.: Princeton University Press, 1996). On popular culture, see Marilyn Ivy, "Formations of Mass Culture," in Gordon, *Postwar Japan as History,* 239–58. In *The Culture of Consent* (Cambridge: Cambridge University Press, 1981), Victoria de Grazia writes of a technocratic "Taylorizing" of leisure in fascist Italy. On the reform of Japanese script, see Nanette Twine, *Language and the Modern State: The Reform of Written Japanese* (London: Routledge, 1991); J. Marshall Unger, *Literacy and Script Reform in Occupation Japan* (New York: Oxford University Press, 1996). On the rationalization of agrarian life, see Kelly, "Rationalization and Nostalgia."

The touchstone of the Japanese Scientific Management movement was a "revised" interpretation of Taylorite dogma, one that aspired to softening the hard edges of Taylorite rationality while not compromising its basic tenets. Realizing that meaningful change could not be accomplished through coercion alone but required the cooperation and consent of the workers, Japanese reformers sought a means of "humanizing" the austere Taylorite message. Western advocates of Scientific Management, of course, also came to this conclusion, but whereas Western managers eventually came to depend on technological and bureaucratic means of stabilizing labor relations in rationalized workshops, in Japan the "revised Taylorite" consensus was more profound and durable. The perennial problem facing Japan's scientific managers, however, was finding a workable program for attaining their abstract ideals and, in particular, for realizing a credibly "humane" Taylorite regime on the shop floor. Interwar paternalism and wartime spiritualism proved imperfect solutions, but ultimately the postwar combination of a high-wage productivist system and the innovative QC circle concept was endorsed by managers and workers alike as genuinely participative, empowering, and mutually beneficial. By the 1970s, "Japanese-style management" was hailed around the world for demonstrating unique respect for humanity as well as attaining singular levels of efficiency and technical precision. Contemporary Japanese arrangements thus reflect both the transwar intellectual heritage of "revised Taylorism" and the work of the management reformers who long endeavored to reconcile the competing demands of rationalization and humanity in Japan's industrial workshops.[6]

Although scholars have generally assumed that Taylorism proved antithetical to Japanese cultural sensibilities, this study reveals that Scientific Management was smoothly aligned with Japanese conceptions of "tradition." As Eleanor Westney concluded in her study of the Meiji police, post office, and popular press, "What we see in these three organizations is a reshaping of the Japanese traditions to fit the needs of the organizations rather than a reshaping of the Western models to fit the traditions of Japan."[7] Such a pattern appears to have held in the case of industrial management as well. The consensus on a "humanized" Taylorism forged during the 1920s and 1930s was internalized

---

[6] The embedding of the "revised Taylorite" ideal at the core of "Japanese-style management" was shown graphically in a study by Hosotani Katsuya. On a chart depicting "Company Character and Performance," Hosotani labelled one axis "Emotion, Humanity, Solidarity"; the other axis reflected "Intelligence, QC, Scientific Attitude, Rationalism." A "good company" showed "improvement and expansion" by balancing these two sets of values, charting a path which simultaneously promoted "humanity" and "rationalism." Hosotani Katsuya, *Japanese Quality Concepts: An Overview,* trans. Glenn Mazur and Japan Business Consultants Limited (White Plains, N.Y.: Quality Resources, 1992). The Japanese-language version of this study (*QC-teki mono no mikata, kangaekata*) was originally published in 1984 by JUSE.

[7] Eleanor Westney, *Imitation and Innovation: The Transfer of Western Organizational Patterns to Meiji Japan* (Cambridge, Mass.: Harvard University Press, 1987), 219.

as something "Japanese" by management reformers, business leaders, and workers over the subsequent decades. Central to this process was a deft ideological sleight of hand: Scientific Management was embraced as a model yet simultaneously constructed as a bogeyman, serving both as a blueprint for reform and as a foil for defining what was "Japanese" about modern industrial management. While a caricatured "textbook" version of Scientific Management could be vilified as cold and inhumane by generations of Japanese managers, the politically and culturally denatured provisions of "revised Taylorism" could be championed as authentically "Japanese" and almost seamlessly integrated into notions of indigenous practice. Thus Taylorite doctrines—as well as postwar imports like Human Relations and quality control—were rooted in "tradition" and almost effortlessly recast as "Japanese-style management" when they were imported and applied in Japan. In the end, extensive cross-fertilization by American ideas and a broad parallelism with Western practice, rather than a culturally specific and autonomous course of development, characterized the Japanese experience of Scientific Management.

Nevertheless, the process of introducing modern management thought into Japan was profoundly affected by the particular context of Japan's twentieth-century political economy. Factors such as relatively inexpensive and plentiful labor, scarce capital, uncertain markets, and low levels of technological development all shaped the manner in which Scientific Management was received and implemented in Japan. Most notably, this environmental perspective helps account, in large part, for the fact that Japanese industrialists did not embrace the Fordist model of production with the enthusiasm that their American or European counterparts did. Taylorism offered Japanese managers an economical yet potent prescription for rationalizing the factory: under Scientific Management, the production process could be reformed without the expense of large investments in machinery, a corporate commitment to higher wages, or the uncertain promise of a mass consumption economy. Even in the postwar decades of high-speed growth, when the changing economic and political context appeared increasingly conducive to a Fordist settlement, the long-standing managerial commitment to a "revised Taylorite" agenda of reform remained strong.

In Japan as elsewhere, among the most significant external influences on evolving managerial practices and the experience of Taylorite reform were the involvement of the state and the attitudes of workers and their unions. Despite widespread scholarly presumptions of bureaucratic omnipresence in Japan, direct state intervention in the process of managerial modernization was remarkably limited. As in the United States and Europe, the government participated in reform initiatives yet the state did not take the lead in promoting Scientific Management. Rather, the process of change was propelled by a diverse coalition of shop-floor managers, corporate executives, engineers, academics, and self-proclaimed experts. Bureaucratic participation in the Rationalization Bureau and the Japan Productivity Center notwithstanding, the ideological embedding and technical diffusion of Taylorism were not the "top-down" accomplishments of an activist Japanese state, but were orchestrated "from the middle out" by an emergent stratum of management intellectuals and professional practitioners.

Labor, like the bureaucracy, played a surprisingly small role in the construction of Japan's contemporary production management regime. From prewar mill-hands and machinists to postwar operatives on the Toyota assembly line, worker opposition to Scientific Management was muted. More often than not, the foot-dragging of middle managers and workplace supervisors—rather than the resistance of the shop-floor rank and file—proved the greatest barrier to systematic reform. The "humanized" appeal of the "revised Taylorite" strategy may have conditioned labor's apparent receptiveness: Japan's scientific managers did learn from the early struggles of their American counterparts and tried to alter their approach to the workers accordingly. In this process, some scholars have argued, Japanese reformers stood the Taylorite model on its head: "In Japan, the introduction and development of Taylorism was not linked with depriving workers of skill but rather promoted the full utilization of their productive potential."[8] Yet as this study suggests, instead of such romanticized appraisals, understanding labor's acquiescence to managerial reform demands due consideration of an intertwined complex of factors: the historic weakness of craft-based loyalties among Japanese workers, the extent of managerial authority in the factories of both prewar and "miracle economy" Japan, labor's distinctive preoccupation with gaining societal respect and "full membership" in Japanese enterprises, and, perhaps most significantly, the fundamental persuasiveness of the ideology of "revised Taylorism" to workers as well as managers.[9]

Emerging from such a context, Japanese conceptions of modern management were, needless to say, not entirely derivative from imported models. Although Japan's "revised Taylorite" approach remained broadly consistent with the mainstream of American managerial ideology throughout the twentieth century, Japan's management reformers were hardly content with "translated mimicry." Japanese strategies for modernizing industrial practice did not ossify with the introduction of Scientific Management, but evolved in tandem with the changing circumstances of depression, war, occupation, and rapid growth. "Revised Taylorism" remained the ideological backbone of the movement, yet Japanese reformers experimented with a variety of institutional, rhetorical, and technical forms to spread the good news of modern manage-

---

[8] Morioka Koji, "Introduction: Japanese Capitalism Today," *International Journal of Political Economy* 21, no. 3 (Fall 1991): 6. See also Okuda Kenji, *Hito to keiei: Nihon keiei kanrishi kenkyū* (Manejimento-sha, 1985).

[9] For an interesting reappraisal of the notion that industrial labor is inevitably resistant to Taylorite reforms, see Weinstein, *For Social Peace in Brazil*, 1–4, 38–50, 197.

ment. In the postwar years, a series of significant methodological advances—notably the Toyota production system, total quality control, and the QC circle concept—marked the culmination of this long process of trial and error. Thus, in the Japanese experience of Taylorism, as Westney observed more broadly in Meiji patterns of organizational transfer, emulation ultimately gave rise to innovation.[10]

In this light, the ranks of scholars who now seek to label Japanese industry as "neo-Fordist" or "ultra-Fordist" would do well to reflect on Japan's heritage of Scientific Management. The pervasive influence of Taylorism and the frustrated career of Fordism in Japan suggest that a label like "non-Fordist"—or, better yet, "revised Taylorite"—best captures the nature of contemporary Japanese production arrangements. By going beyond dehistoricized taxonomies of hyphenated Fordisms and alluring monocausal explications—and by thus conceiving "Japanese-style management" as the result of a century-long dynamic of importation and adaptation, of defining and generalizing the "revised Taylorite" ideal—a refined, coherent understanding of the nature and origins of the Japanese paradigm can be attained. In short, this study suggests that an ongoing process of digesting, adjusting, and internalizing Taylorism—and not the perfection, enhancement or corruption of the Fordist archetype—lay at the vital core of the evolution of "Japanese-style management."

Since the early 1980s, Japanese production management techniques have been acclaimed as the optimal model for revitalizing America's moribund industry and outmoded Taylorite practices. Yet, as this study has demonstrated, not only is the distinction between "Japanese-style management" and Taylorism a false dichotomy, but for the far greater part of this century, it has been the Japanese who have looked to the United States for inspiration in factory management. In considering the recent trans-Pacific reversal of teacher and student roles, what is striking is that those qualities which Japanese observers traditionally esteemed so highly in American practice are virtually the same as those which Americans now profess to admire most in "Japanese-style management."

In 1959, for instance, the Japan Productivity Center's quality control mission returned from its tour of the United States gushing with praise for American managerial techniques. The scale and efficiency of American enterprises were, of course, much admired. But the Japanese observers also extolled U.S. industry for the close cooperation between line and staff, for the emphasis placed on education and training, for the nurturing of good human relations, for a responsiveness to customer concerns, and for a diffusion of basic statistical skills to the shop floor. One mission member marveled at the work of office receptionists in the United States: not only were they more motivated

---

[10] Westney, *Imitation,* 224.

and compliant than their Japanese counterparts, but they performed a wide variety of clerical tasks with great efficiency and flexibility.[11] Another Japanese expert noted enviously that even American factories with outdated machinery were more productive than the most modern Japanese installations: a major reason, it seemed, was that American operatives freely offered suggestions and cooperated with management in streamlining the work process.[12]

The fact that Japanese quality experts once lauded American industry for practices which are now considered unique aspects of "Japanese-style management" should not be surprising. The significance of this observation is not—as many have argued—that American business has forgotten the basics of good management while the Japanese have diligently learned and applied them. Rather, it shows the extent to which, throughout this century, both American and Japanese management experts have been speaking in the same idiom, an idiom premised on a "humanized" revision of Scientific Management. What was traditionally a one-way conversation—with the Americans expounding and the Japanese absorbing—has now become a more balanced dialogue of managerial thought and practice across the Pacific.[13]

Contrary to popular assumptions, however, the presence of a Japanese voice in the international discourse of industrial management will by no means guarantee a meaningful reappraisal of the long-standing Taylorite orthodoxy. In Japan as in the West, managerial commitment to the humanization of work has remained shallow and, for the most part, rhetorical rather than practical: even Japanese innovations like quality control circles, so widely praised as models of democratic and compassionate management, were born of the perennial managerial drive to Taylorize the shop floor. Although a few scholars have detected latent revolutionary implications in contemporary Japanese arrangements—some optimistically seeing QC circles as new forums for mobilizing labor, others envisioning "lean production" as salvation from the Fordist nightmare[14]—such potential is, and appears likely to remain, deeply repressed. As this study suggests, "Japanese-style management" may provide American business with a new arsenal of tools and strategies, but it cannot offer an alternate paradigm for conceptualizing the managerial function in modern industry. Over the past century, Japanese and American ideologies of management have traced distinct evolutionary paths, yet their differences—no

---

[11] Nihon seisansei honbu, *Amerika no hinshitsu kanri,* Productivity Report 65 (1959), 207.

[12] Ibid., 78–79.

[13] As Taylor disciple King Hathaway noted presciently in 1929, "The time may come when America will receive from Japan as much or more than it has given." Horace King Hathaway, "Scientific Management in Japan," *Bulletin of the Taylor Society* 14, no. 4 (August 1929): 186.

[14] See, for example, Kumazawa Makoto, *Portraits of the Japanese Workplace: Labor Movements, Workers, and Managers,* ed. Andrew Gordon, trans. Andrew Gordon and Mikiso Hane (Boulder, Colo.: Westview Press, 1996), chap. 5; James Womack, Daniel Jones, and Daniel Roos, *The Machine That Changed the World* (New York: Rawson Associates, 1990).

matter how stridently affirmed by today's scholars and practitioners—have generally remained more superficial than substantive. Drawing on a common heritage of Taylorism, neither "Japanese-style management" nor contemporary American practice has transcended the intellectual confines of Scientific Management.

Bibliography

Works in Japanese

Place of publication is Tokyo unless otherwise noted.

Akamatsu Tokuji. *Toyota zankoku monogatari.* Eeru shuppansha, 1982.

Andō Jirō. "Jimu nōritsu kaizen no yōten." *Jitsumu techō* 1 (January 1949): 22–31.

Andō Masakichi. "Kessenka ni okeru nōritsu-seikatsu-chingin." *Shakai seisaku jihō* 258 (March 1942): 463–90.

Andō Yaichi. *Kōjō kaizen—Nihon no kagakuteki kōjō kanri.* Daiyamondo, 1940.

"Ankeeto: Genbachō o meguru hinshitsu kanri no mondai ni tsuite." *Hinshitsu kanri* 12, no. 9 (September 1961): 54–58.

Arai Mitsuzō. "Soren no nōritsu shōkai." *Kōgyō to keizai* 99 (March 1941): 2–9.

Araki Tōichirō. "Kagakuteki kanrihō to rōdō sōgi." *Tokyo kōjō konwakai kaihō* 42 (June 1929): 59–72.

———. *Nōritsu ichidaiki.* Nihon nōritsu kyōkai, 1971.

———. *Seisan kanri kaizen no chakuganten.* Keirishikai, 1942.

"Aru kikai kōjō no 4-nin no kumichō no taikendan." *Hinshitsu kanri* 11, no. 3 (March 1960): 25–28.

"Atarashii kōjō keiei e no kibō." *Kōgyō to keizai* 90 (June 1940): 1.

Awaji Enjirō. "Keiei kanri jō no hyūman rireeshonzu." In *Hyūman rireeshonzu,* ed. Odaka Kunio et al. Daiyamondo, 1952.

Bae Boo-gil. *Keieigaku hattatsu shi.* Gakubunsha, 1990.

"Chingin no Nihonshiki kazoku hon'i chingin e no hyōjunka." *Sangyō nōritsu* 12, no. 3 (March 1939): 258–60.

Chokki Toshiaki. *Nihon no kigyō keiei.* Hōsei daigaku shuppankai, 1992.

———. "Teiraa shisutemu no dōnyū." In *Nihon keieishi o manabu* 2, ed. Kobayashi Masaaki et al. Yuhikaku, 1976.

Dai Nihon sangyō hōkokukai. *Kikai jitsudōritsu zōshin undō: Dōfuken jisshi jōkyō hōkokushū.* Dai Nihon sangyō hōkokukai, 1942.

"Dōchō-fuken-shi ni okeru sangyō gōrika shidō kikan shisetsu kanbi gutai an." *Sangyō nōritsu* 7, no. 4 (April 1934): 247–55.

"Dōyūkai 20-nen no rinen to genjitsu." *Gendai no me* 7, no. 9 (September 1966): 96–109.

Eto Saburō. "Rōmu kanri no kindaika ni tsuite." In *Rōmu kanri kindaika no jitsurei,* ed. Noda Nobuo and Mori Gorō. Daiyamondo, 1954.

Fujibayashi Keizō. "Kōkoku kinrōkan to keiei rōdōsha seisaku." *Shakai seisaku jihō* 272 (May 1943): 19–57.

———. "Rōdō mondai." In Keizai dōyūkai, *Rōdō mondai.* Keiei kiso kōza, vol. 5. Daiyamondo, 1953.

Fujishiro Yūkō. "QC to IE ni tsuite." *Hinshitsu kanri* 9, no. 11 (November 1958): 13–16.

Fujita Tadashi. "Hinshitsu kanri hatten no rekishiteki kōsatsu." *Hinshitsu kanri* 5, no. 11 (November 1954): 69–74.

Fukushima Matsuo. "Rōmu kanri to seisan kanri." In Noda keizai kenkyūjo, *Shin kinrō kanri no jissai*. Noda keizai kenkyūjo, 1943.

Furukawa Eiichi. *Shin keieisha*. Moriyama shoten, 1948.

"Gaijin gishi o kakomu seisan gijutsu." *Nihon nōritsu* 1, no. 7 (December 1942): 2–16.

"Genba to QC." *Hinshitsu kanri* 13, no. 6 (June 1962).

"'Genbachō to hinshitsu kanri' tokushū-gō hakkan ni atatte." *Hinshitsu kanri* 12, no. 9 (September 1961): 1.

Gōshi Kōhei. "Seisansei kōjō undō." In Ekonomisuto henshūbu, *Shōgen: Kōdo seichō ki no Nihon,* vol. 2. Mainichi shinbunsha, 1984.

———. "Seisansei to kindaiteki keiei." *Seisansei no riron to jissai* 1 (February 1956): 14–17.

Gotō Masao. "Gijutsusha no yakuwari." *Hinshitsu kanri* 2, no. 4 (April 1951): 2–4.

———. "Hinshitsu kanri shi shodai henshū kanjichō no koro." *Hinshitsu kanri* 16, no. 3 (March 1965): 1–2.

Hara Akira. "Taiheiyō sensō ki no seisan zōkyō seisaku." In Kindai Nihon kenkyūkai, *Senji keizai*. Kindai Nihon kenkyū nenpō, vol. 9. Yamakawa shuppansha, 1987.

Hara Yasusaburō. "Keiei no seishin." *Hinshitsu kanri* 15, no. 1 (January 1964): 13–15.

Harada Shūichi. "Sangyō gōrika to shin rōshi kyōchō." *Shōgaku hyōron* 7, no. 4 (March 1929): 1–41.

Hashimoto Jurō. "1955-nen." In *Nihon keizai shi 8: Kōdo seichō,* ed. Yasuba Yasukichi and Inoki Takenori. Iwanami shoten, 1989.

Hattori Rokurō. "QC o kiso ni oita 17-nen." *Hinshitsu kanri* 31, no. 3 (March 1980): 22–23.

Hazama Hiroshi. *Nihon ni okeru rōshi kyōchō no teiryū*. Waseda daigaku shuppanbu, 1978.

———. *Nihon no shiyōsha dantai to rōshi kankei*. Nihon rōdō kyōkai, 1981.

———. *Nihon rōmu kanrishi kenkyū*. Daiyamondo, 1964.

———. *Nihonteki keiei no keifu*. Bunshindō, 1989 [1963].

Higashi Hidehiko. "Shanai hyōjunka." *Hinshitsu kanri* 9, no. 9 (September 1958): 8–11.

———. "Wagakuni ni okeru hinshitsu kanri." *Hinshitsu kanri* 1, no. 2 (April 1950): 5–7.

"Hijō jikyoku ni taisuru sengen." *Sangyō nōritsu* 11, no. 1 (January 1938).

"Hinshitsu kanri nenpyō." *Hinshitsu kanri* 9, no. 6 (June 1958): 76–84.

"Hinshitsu kanri no isshishin." *Hinshitsu kanri* 1, no. 1 (March 1950): 5, 17.

Hinshitsu kanri shi henshū iinkai. *Hinshitsu kanri to hito no mondai*. JUSE, 1966.

———. *TQC kōza: Minna de yaru hinshitsu kanri*. JUSE, 1962.

Hirai Yasutarō. *Sangyō gōrika*. Kobe: Guroria sosaete, 1930.

———. *Sangyō gōrika zuroku*. Shunyōdō, 1931.

Hirao Hachisaburō. "Keieisha taru shikaku." *Kōgyō to keizai* 79 (July 1939): 1–2.

Hiroshige Tetsu. *Kagaku no shakaishi: Kindai Nihon no kagaku taisei*. Chūō kōron sha, 1973.

Hirota Hisaichi. "Hinshitsu kanri no kagi wa netsui to aitagai no yūwaryoku." *Hinshitsu kanri* 4, no. 9 (September 1953): 20–22.

Hōchi shinbun keizaibu. *Nōritsu zōshin jidai*. Chikura shobō, 1930.

Horie Kiichi. "Kagakuteki keieihō to rōdō kumiai." *Mita gakkai zasshi* 14, no. 7 (1920): 82–96.

Horie Masanori. "Seisansei kōjō undō hihan." *Chūō kōron* 70, no. 10 (October 1955): 144–55.

Horime Ken'ichi. "Nihon kōgyō kyōkai no koro o kataru." *IE* 9, no. 6 (June 1967): 556–63.

Hyōdō Tsutomu. *Nihon ni okeru rōshi kankei no tenkai.* Tokyo daigaku shuppankai, 1971.

"Hyūman rireeshonzu no Nihonteki genjitsu." *Seisansei* (June 1959): 8–15.

"Ibara no michi ni manabu kanri gijutsu no shimei." *Seisan nōritsu* 4, no. 6 (September 1949): 1.

Ibe Masakazu. "Shūsei shihonshugi e no michi." *Keizai* 1, no. 10 (December 1947): 9–11.

"IE no hanashi o kiku kai." *Hinshitsu kanri* 12, no. 2 (February 1961): 1–7.

IE no nyūmon. IE seminaa, vol. 1. Nihon seisansei honbu, 1960.

Ikeda Tōshirō. *Kagakuteki keieihō.* Jitsugyō no sekaisha, 1923.

———. *Muda seibatsu no hiketsu.* Shūbunkaku shobō, 1930.

Ikezawa Tokio. "SQC no reimeiki." *Hinshitsu kanri* 41, no. 1 (January 1990): 73–78.

Imaizumi Masumasa. "Genba 7-kai." *Genba to QC* 2 (June 1962): 2–5.

Ina Masao. "Deming hakase no erementarii kōsu o jukō shite." *Hinshitsu kanri* 2, no. 9 (September 1951): 9–13.

Inoue Yoshikazu. "Nihon nōritsu shihō no genri to sono kōsei." *Sangyō nōritsu* 12, no. 4 (April 1939): 379–82.

———. "Osaka ni okeru nōritsu undō o kaerimite" (1950). In *Kagakuteki kanrihō no dōnyū,* ed. Hazama Hiroshi. Nihon rōmu kanrishi shiryō kashū, vol. 8. Gosandō shoten, 1987.

Ishida Mitsuo. "Chingin taikei to rōshi kankei" (parts I and II). *Nihon rōdō kyōkai zasshi* 27, no. 8 (August 1985): 3–14; 27, no. 9 (September 1985): 39–49.

Ishiguro Shigeo. "Hinshitsu kanri to ningen kankei." *Genba to QC* 30 (April 1966): 25–27.

Ishikawa Ichirō. "Fukkō e no michi . . ." *Enjinia kurabu* 12 (May 1949): 1.

———. "Gijutsusha no shinboku to renraku." *Enjinia kurabu* 1 (June 1948): 1.

———. "Sōkan no kotoba." *Hinshitsu kanri* 1, no. 1 (March 1950): 2.

Ishikawa Kaoru. "Bōeki jiyūka ni wa hinshitsu kanri de." *Hinshitsu kanri* 11, no. 4 (April 1960): 1–2.

———. "Bōeki jiyūka to MR." *Hinshitsu kanri* 11, no. 9 (September 1960): 1–3.

———. "Dai-ikkai hinshitsu kanri gekkan ni tsuite." *Hinshitsu kanri* 12, no. 7 (July 1961): 1–4.

———. *Hinshitsu kanri nyūmon.* QC series, vol. 1. JUSE, 1964.

———. "Indasutoriaru enjiniaringu (IE) to kuoritei kontorōru (QC)." *PR* 9, no. 1 (January 1958): 36–41.

———. "Juran hakase wa shachō, jūyaku ni nani o hanasareta ka." *Hinshitsu kanri* 5, no. 8 (August 1954): 5–7, 17.

———. "10 shūnen o mukaete." *Hinshitsu kanri* 11, no. 3 (March 1960): 1.

———. "Kongo no QC to hinshitsu kanri shi." *Hinshitsu kanri* 9, no. 6 (June 1958): 23.

———. "Koyanagi-san no omoide." *Hinshitsu kanri* 16, no. 2 (February 1965).

————. "Makoto no QC saakuru katsudō e no michi." *Genba to QC* 36 (October 1966): 2–11.

————. "Nihon no hinshitsu kanri (1): QC team hōkoku." *Hinshitsu kanri* 9, no. 8 (August 1958): 1–10.

————. "Nihon no hinshitsu kanri (2): QC team hōkoku." *Hinshitsu kanri* 9, no. 9 (September 1958): 89–99.

————. "Nihon no hinshitsu kanri (5): QC team hōkoku." *Hinshitsu kanri* 9, no. 12 (December 1958): 1–3.

————. "Nihon no QC to Amerika no QC no shindan (2)." *Hinshitsu kanri* 9, no. 11 (November 1958): 20–26.

————. "QC no chōki keikaku." *Hinshitsu kanri* 14, no. 1 (January 1963): 1–4.

————. "QC saakuru katsudō 3-shūnen ni atatte." *Genba to QC* 18 (April 1965): 2–6.

————. "Shōhisha no minasama e no onegai." *Hinshitsu kanri* 11, no. 3 (March 1960): 69–70.

————. "Taidan: Nihonteki hinshitsu kanri no tenkai." *Keiei to rekishi* 9 (September 1986): 18–29.

————. "Wagakuni hinshitsu kai no mondai." *Hinshitsu kanri* 2, no. 1 (January 1951): 3.

————. "Wagakuni sagyō hyōjun no mondaiten." *Hinshitsu kanri* 8, no. 9 (September 1957): 68–70.

Ishikawa Kaoru and Imaizumi Masumasa. "Amerika dayori." *Hinshitsu kanri* 16, no. 6 (June 1965): 45–47.

Isobe Kiichi. "Teiraa shisutemu to sono genkai II." *Shōgyō oyobi keizai kenkyū* 47 (September 1927): 166–84.

Jinjiin. *Jinji gyōsei 20-nen no ayumi.* Ōkurashō insatsukyoku, 1968.

Juran, J. M. "Nihon ni okeru hinshitsu kanri ni taisuru inshō." Trans. Koyanagi Ken'ichi. *Hinshitsu kanri* 5, no. 9 (September 1954): 1–4.

"Juran hakase raichō." *Hinshitsu kanri* 5, no. 8 (August 1954): 18.

JUSE TWI kenkyūkai. *Kaisha, kōjō ni okeru TWI jisshi no keikaku to kōka no hakki.* Nihon kagaku gijutsu renmeikai, 1951.

"Kagaku gijutsu undō no tōitsu sensen no kyūmū." *Nihon kagaku gijutsu renmei nyūsu,* 25 July 1946, 2.

"Kagaku no fukkō, gijutsu no jūjitsu." *Enjinia kurabu* 20 (January 1950): 1.

"Kaichō aisatsu." *Nihon nōritsu* 1, no. 1 (June 1942): 4–6.

Kanda Fuhito, ed. *Shiryō Nihon gendai shi 7: Sangyō hōkoku undō.* Ōtsuki shoten, 1981.

Kanda Kōichi. *Jissen kōjō kanri.* Kōbunkan, 1912.

————. *Kōjō kanri kenkyū.* Dai Nihon kōgyō gakkai, 1938.

————. "Nihon sangyō no gōrika to sangyō seishin no sakkō." *Tokyo kōjō konwakai kaihō* 55 (April 1931): 2–14.

————. *Rōdō nōritsu kenkyū.* Tōjō shoten, 1922.

Kaneko Hiroshi. "Shokuba moraaru no bunseki." *Rōmu kenkyū* 2, no. 5 (May 1949): 18–20.

Kaneko Rihachirō. *Kōjō jimu kanriron.* Chikura shobō, 1937.

Karatsu Hajime. *QC undō: Naze Nihon de seikō shita ka.* NHK, 1987.

Karikomi Ichirō. "Genba kentōkai haiken." *Hinshitsu kanri* 11, no. 3 (March 1960): 29–32.

————. "Shoku, kumichō to riidaashippu." *Genba to QC* 23 (September 1965): 2–5.

"Karuizawa no hinshitsu kanri seminaa: Jūyaku tokubetsu kōsu no tanjō to omoide." *Hinshitsu kanri* 41, no. 10 (October 1990): 49–56.

Katō Takabumi, ed. *Nihon keiei shiryō taikei 3: Soshiki, gōrika.* San-ichi shobō, 1989.

Katō Takeo. *Keiei no hanashi, keiei kaizen no kyūsho.* Manejimento kyōkai, 1950.

Katō Takeo and Takada Shinzō. *Seisan kōgaku sōron.* Seisan kōgaku kōza, vol. 1. Nikkan kōgyō shinbunsha, 1959.

Kawakami Hajime. "Rōdōsha kara mita sangyō gōrika." *Chūō kōron* 45, no. 6 (June 1930): 3–31.

Kayano Takeshi. "Nihon ni okeru indasutoriaru enjiniaringu no mondai ni tsuite." *PR* 9, no. 2 (February 1958): 17–22.

"Keiei kindaika ni kōken shita jinmyaku to shuyō kikan." *IE* 9, no. 6 (June 1967): 611–16.

Keizai dōyūkai. *Keizai dōyūkai 15-nen shi.* Keizai dōyūkai, 1962.

————. *Keizai dōyūkai jūnen shi.* Keizai dōyūkai, 1956.

Keizai dōyūkai kigyō minshūka kenkyūkai. *Kigyō minshūka shian.* Dōyūsha, 1947.

"Keizai fukkō keikaku to yūso, seisan, gijutsu." *Enjinia kurabu,* 3 October 1948, 2.

Kimura Kihachirō. "Seisan gōrika no shinkadai." *Tōsei keizai* 4, no. 5 (May 1942): 41–49.

Kinoshita Otoichi. *Amerika no sangyō gōrika undō o miru.* Tenjinsha, 1930.

Kiribuchi Kanzō. "Hito no katsudō kara mita keiei." In *Keiei no sōgō kanri,* ed. Kiribuchi Kanzō. Kōjō keiei jitsumu kōza, vol. 1. Nihon keizaisha, 1952.

————. "Kagakuteki kanri no jūten to sono dōkō." *Keiei kenkyū* 3, no. 2 (September 1934): 47–59.

————. *Kōgyō kanri yōran.* Yoshida kōmujō shuppanbu, 1934.

————. *Kōjō keiei no jissai.* Iwasaki shoten, 1951.

Kirishima Seiji and Nishigaki Masako. "Seisansei to riidaashippu." *Genba to QC* 20 (June 1965): 12–16.

Kishi Nobusuke. "Ōshū ni okeru sangyō gōrika no jissai ni tsuite." *Sangyō gōrika* 4 (January 1932): 27–67.

————. "Senji-ka no nōritsu zōshin." *Nihon nōritsu* 1, no. 1 (June 1942): 15–21.

Kishimoto Seijirō. "Tōsei keizai to sangyō nōritsu." *Shakai seisaku jihō* 258 (March 1942): 1–13.

Kitaboshi Kōhei. *QC saakuru manga shinan.* JUSE, 1982.

Kitagawa Yoshikazu. "Sangyō gōrika to wa nani ka." *Kagaku to gijutsu* 9 (August 1948): 16–21.

Kitazawa Shinjirō. "Kagakuteki kanrihō to rōdōsha." *Kaihō* 4, no. 3 (March 1922): 52–58.

Kobayashi Shigeyuki. "Nōritsu to chingin to no kanren ni tsuite." *Shakai seisaku jihō* 258 (March 1942): 491–519.

Kobayashi Yasuo. *Kagakuteki kanri to rōdō.* Osaka: Nunoi shobō, 1953.

"Kōdō nōritsu no kaitaku e." *Sangyō nōritsu* 15, no. 3 (March 1942): 1–2.

Kogure Masao. "Nihon ni okeru QC shisō no hensen." *Hinshitsu kanri* 5, no. 10 (October 1954): 4–6.

————. *Nihon no TQC.* JUSE, 1988.

————. "TQC e no taidō to tanjō." *Hinshitsu kanri* 41, no. 7 (July 1990): 58–65.

Kogure Masao et al. "Juran hakase ni yoru hinshitsu kanri kōshūkai ni sanka shite." *Hinshitsu kanri* 5, no. 8 (August 1954): 19–21.

"Kōgyōhin kikaku tōitsu oyobi shōhin tanjunka ni tsuite." *Sangyō gōrika* 2 (January 1931): 133–216.

Kojima Kenji. "Gijutsusha no risō." *Seisan* 1, no. 1 (November 1946): 31.

Kojima Seiichi. *Sangyō gōrika*. Chikura shobō, 1929.

———. *Shin sangyō gōrika*. Chikura shobō, 1942.

"Kōjō mo mata hitotsu no shakai." *Seisan nōritsu* 4, no. 5 (August 1949): 1.

Konno Kōichirō. "Kokutetsu kōsaku kōjō ni miru kagakuteki kanri no ayumi" (parts I, II, III and IV). *Rōmu kenkyū* 29, no. 10 (1976): 24–30; 29, no. 11 (1976): 31–35; 29, no. 12 (1976): 27–32; 30, no. 1 (1977): 45–52.

———. "Kure kaigun kōshō ni miru kagakuteki kanri no ayumi" (parts I, II, III and IV). *IE* 17, no. 6 (1975): 53–56; 17, no. 7 (1975): 87–92; 17, no. 8 (1975): 90–93; 17, no. 9 (1975): 90–96.

Kosuge Toshitaka. *Tashu shōryō seisan no tankyū*. Osaka: Seikōsha, 1988.

"Kotoshi ni oite wagakuni no ryoku o itasu kokusaku ni taiō suru nōritsu mondai." *Sangyō nōritsu* 12, no. 2 (February 1939): 145–47.

Koyanagi Ken'ichi. "Atarashii minshū sekai o gijutsusha no nichijō." *Enjinia kurabu* 1 (June 1948): 2.

———. "Dr. Deming to tomo ni." *Hinshitsu kanri* 2, no. 9 (September 1951): 5–8.

———. "Joshiki no sekai o kaerimiru." *Hinshitsu kanri* 2, no. 1 (January 1951): 29–32.

Kuroda Ken'ichi. "Sengo Nihon no rōmu kanri to kyōsōteki shokuba chitsujo." In Sengo Nihon keiei kenkyūkai, *Sengo Nihon no kigyō keiei*. Bunshindō, 1991.

Kurokawa Toshio and Satake Gosaku. *Nihon seisansei honbu*. Aoki shoten, 1970.

Landes, William S. *Nihon no keiei o shindan suru*. Nihon seisansei honbu, 1956.

Matsuoka Kinpei. *Sangyō gōrika ni maishin seyo*. Manejimento-sha, 1930.

Minami Manshū tetsudō. *Naichi ni okeru kōjō chingin seidō no chōsa kenkyū*. Minami Manshū tetsudō, 1930.

Minoguchi Tokijirō. "Doitsu ni okeru sangyō gōrika no keizaiteki oyobi shakaiteki kokka." *Shakai seisaku jihō* 91 (April 1928): 11–22.

Mitsumaki Akiko. "QC to korekara no shōhisha undō." *Hinshitsu kanri* 16, no. 11 (November 1965): 1–3.

Miura Shin. "Hinshitsu kanri sōgyō jidai no kaiko." *Hinshitsu kanri* 31, no. 3 (March 1980): 28–29.

———. "Shinnen ni omou." *Hinshitsu kanri* 12, no. 1 (January 1961): 1.

Miura Toyohiko. *Rōdō to kenkō no rekishi*, vol. 6. Kawasaki: Rōdō kagaku kenkyūjo, 1990.

———. *Teruoka Gitō*. Minkan Nihon gakusha, vol. 31. Riburopōto, 1991.

Miyamoto Takenosuke. "Sangyō nōritsu no zōshin ni tsuite." *Kōgyō to keizai* 102 (June 1941): 3–13.

Mizuno Shigeru. "Deming hakase no sokuseki." *Hinshitsu kanri* 2, no. 10 (October 1951): 7–8.

———. "Nihon ni okeru hinshitsu kanri shisō no hensen." *Hinshitsu kanri* 5, no. 10 (October 1954): 1–3.

———. *Zensha sōgō hinshitsu kanri*. JUSE, 1984.

Mizuno Shigeru et al. *Nihon no hinshitsu kanri no hansei to zenshin*. Tenth Quality Control Symposium. JUSE, 1970.

Mizutani Masaichi. "Wagakuni ningen kankei kanri no genjō to mondaiten." In Nikkeiren, *Hyūman rireeshonzu.* Nikkeiren, 1957.

Mori Gorō. *Sengo Nihon no rōmu kanri.* Daiyamondo, 1961.

Mori Gorō and Matsushima Shizuo. *Nihon rōmu kanri no gendaika.* Tokyo daigaku
shuppankai, 1977.

Morikawa Hidemasa. *Nihon keieishi.* Nihon keizai shinbunsha, 1981.

Morikawa Kakuzō. "Hinshitsu kanri shi: 100-gō kinen ni yosete." *Hinshitsu kanri* 9,
no. 6 (June 1958): 5.

———. *Keiei gōrika no soshiki.* Daiyamondo, 1950.

———. "Nihon nōritsu kyōkai hossoku ni tsuite." *Nihon nōritsu* 1, no. 2 (July 1942):
81–90.

———. "Sōkan no ji." *Nihon nōritsu* 1, no. 1 (June 1942): 1–3.

Morioka Shirō and Kumasaka Hiroshi. "QC to hoka no kanri to no kanren oyobi
chōsei." *Hinshitsu kanri* 8, no. 5 (May 1957): 14–16.

Morito Tatsuo. "Kagakuteki kanrihō no shakai seisakuteki kachi" (parts I and II).
Kokka gakkai zasshi 30, no. 11 (1916): 77–86; 30, no. 12 (1916): 89–114.

———. "Shihonshugi to nōritsu mondai." *Shakai seisaku jihō* 258 (March 1942): 14–
49.

Mukai Shikamatsu. *Shin keieisha gaku.* Nihon hyōronsha, 1929.

Murai Tsutomu. "Seisan gijutsu kōza 1: Sensō to seisan zōkyō ni tsuite." *Nihon nōritsu*
2, no. 6 (June 1943): 414–25.

Murakami Motohiko. *Seisansei to wa nani ka.* Nihon seisansei honbu, 1986.

Muramoto Fukumatsu. "Horie hakase oyobi Teruoka gakushi no kagakuteki keieihō ni
kansuru hihan o yomite." *Shōgyō oyobi keizai kenkyū* 20 (October 1920): 15–35.

———. "Sangyō gōrika no hihan kijun to shite no tōsei no jūyōsei." *Shakai seisaku
jihō* 116 (May 1930): 239–52.

Mutō Hideo. "Seizō genba no tachiba kara." *Hinshitsu kanri* 11, no. 12 (October 1960):
18–20.

Nagaoka Yasutarō. "Sangyō no gōrika to rōdō kaikyū." *Shakai seisaku jihō* 91 (April
1928): 1–10.

———. " 'Senji seisanryoku kōyō tokushū' hakkan ni saishite." *Shakai seisaku jihō*
258 (March 1942): 1–4.

Nainen kikan henshūbu. *Sangyō nōritsu zōshin ni kansuru shomondai.* Sankaidō, 1943.

Nakagawa Seisa. *Amerika no sangyō gōrika.* Tenjinsha, 1930.

———. "Beikoku no sangyō gōrika o miru." *Tokyo kōjō konwakai kaihō* 51 (December 1930): 2–7.

Nakamura Seiji. *Nihon seisansei kōjō undō shi.* Keisō shobō, 1958.

Nakamura Takafusa. "Jun-senji kara senji keizai taisei e no ikō." In Kindai Nihon
kenkyūkai, *Senji keizai.* Kindai Nihon kenkyū nenpō, vol. 9. Yamakawa shuppansha,
1987.

Nakaoka Tetsurō. *Kōjō no tetsugaku: Soshiki to ningen.* Heibonsha, 1971.

———. "QC Nihon no shūhon de." In *Sengo Nihon o kangaeru,* ed. Hidaka Rokurō.
Chikuma shobō, 1986.

———. "Senchū, sengo no kagakuteki kanri undō" (parts I, II and III). *Keizaigaku
zasshi* 82, no. 1 (May 1981): 10–27; 82, no. 3 (September 1981): 43–61; 83, no. 1
(May 1982): 43–57.

Nakase Jūichi. *Sengo Nihon no keiei rinen shi.* Kyōto: Hōritsu bunka sha, 1967.

Nakatsumi Tomokata. "Kagakuteki kanrihō ni taisuru gensei hihan." *Kokka gakkai zasshi* 36, no. 2 (1922): 117–36.

Nakayama Ichirō. "Seisansei kōjō undō hihan o hanhihan suru." *Chūō kōron* 71, no. 1 (January 1956): 46–52.

———. "Seisansei mondai no shozai." *Chūō kōron* 71, no. 13 (December 1956): 96–101.

Nakayama Takasachi. *Shin nōritsu soshiki no tatekata.* Sangyō keiri kyōkai, 1947.

Neagari Kōichi. "Sangyō hōkoku undō to nōritsu zōshin mondai." *Shakai seisaku jihō* 258 (March 1942): 572–82.

Nihon denki tsūshin kōgyō rengōkai, Keiei kanri kenkyūkai. *CCS keiei kōza.* 2 vols. Daiyamondo, 1952.

Nihon IE kyōkai. *Nihon ni okeru IE no dōkō.* Nihon seisansei honbu, 1965.

Nihon keizai renmeikai chōsaka. *Sangyō nōritsu to seishin shidō.* Sankaidō, 1943.

———. *Sangyō nōritsu zōshin undō no genkyō.* Nihon keizai renmeikai, 1942.

———. *Taryō seisan hōshiki jitsugen no gutaisaku.* Sankaidō, 1943.

Nihon kōgyō kyōkai. *Senji ni okeru kōjō seisanryoku kakujū narabini sengo no taisaku.* Dai-13 kai kenkyūkai shiryō. Nihon kōgyō kyōkai, 1938.

"Nihon kōgyō kyōkai no jigyō hōkoku." *Kōgyō to keizai* 112 (April 1942): 24–39.

"Nihon kōgyō kyōkai no ninmu to sono jigyō." *Nihon kōgyō kyōkai kaihō* 4 (April 1933): 1–5.

Nihon nōritsu kyōkai. *10 nenkan no sokuseki.* Nihon nōritsu kyōkai, 1952.

———. *Keiei to tomo ni.* Nihon nōritsu kyōkai, 1982.

"Nihon nōritsu kyōkai setsuritsu shuisho." *Kōgyō to keizai* 112 (April 1942).

Nihon nōritsu rengōkai. *Nihon kōjō kanri no shomondai.* 3 vols. Daiyamondo, 1941–42.

Nihon nōritsu rengōkai annai. Nihon nōritsu rengōkai, 1931.

Nihon sangyō keizai seikeibu. *Seisan sen.* Itō shoten, 1943.

Nihon sangyō keizai shinbunsha. *Zenkoku mohan kōjō shisatsuki.* Kasumigaseki shobō, 1943.

Nihon seisansei honbu. *Amerika ni okeru indasutoriaru rireeshonzu.* Productivity Report 50. Nihon seisansei honbu, 1958.

———. *Amerika no hinshitsu kanri.* Productivity Report 65. Nihon seisansei honbu, 1959.

———. *Han'ei keizai to keiei: Toppu manejimento shisetsudan hōkokusho.* Productivity Report 1. Nihon seisansei honbu, 1956.

———. *Hyūman rireeshon.* Productivity Report 12. Nihon seisansei honbu, 1957.

———. *Rōshi kyōei e no michi.* Productivity Report 28. Nihon seisansei honbu, 1957.

———. *Seisansei undō 10-nen no ayumi.* Nihon seisansei honbu, 1965.

———. *Seisansei undō 30-nen shi.* Nihon seisansei honbu, 1985.

Niizaki Kuniyoshi. "Indasutoriaru enjiniyaringu no saikentō." *Manejimento* 17, no. 9 (September 1958): 24–32.

"Nikagiren to seisansei kojō." *Enjinia kurabu* 81 (10 February 1955): 1.

Nikaidō Shōji. "Nihon kōgyō kyōkai no koro o kataru." *IE* 9, no. 7 (July 1967): 698–705.

Nikkeiren. *Nōritsu kyū no gendaiteki kōsatsu: Nōritsu kyū no kindaika no tame ni.* Nikkeiren, 1956.

———. *Wagakuni rōmu kanri no gensei.* Dai 2-kai rōmu kanri shoseido chōsa. Nikkeiren, 1965.

————. *Wagakuni rōmu kanri no gensei.* Dai 3-kai rōmu kanri shoseido chōsa. Nikkeiren, 1971.

Nikkeiren and Kantō keieisha kyōkai. *Nōryokushugi kanri ni kansuru kigyō no jittai chōsa.* Rōmu shiryō, vol. 89. Nikkeiren, 1968.

Nikkeiren nōryokushugi kanri kenkyūkai. *Nōryokushugi kanri.* Nikkeiren, 1969.

Nikkeiren sōritsu jūshūnen kinen kigyō iinkai. *Jūnen no ayumi.* Nikkeiren, 1958.

Nishibori Eizaburō. "Deming-san to Ete-san." *Hinshitsu kanri* 9, no. 6 (June 1958): 25.

————. "Hinshitsu kanri wa Nihonjin no tame ni aru." *Hinshitsu kanri* 16, no. 3 (March 1965): 8–10.

————. "Juran hakase ni manabu mono." *Hinshitsu kanri* 5, no. 8 (August 1954): 1–4.

————. "Nihon kōgyō no chōsho to tansho." *Hinshitsu kanri* 5, no. 10 (October 1954): 7–8.

Nishinarita Yutaka. *Kindai Nihon rōshi kankeishi no kenkyū.* Tokyo daigaku shuppankai, 1988.

Noda Kazuo. *Drucker no keieigaku.* Kashima kenkyūjo shuppankai, 1963.

————. "Shin keiei gijutsu wa Nihon ni sodatsu ka?" *Kindai keiei* 4, no. 5 (April 1959): 6–9.

Noda Kazuo, ed. *Gendai keieishi.* Nihon seisansei honbu, 1969.

————. *Sengo keieishi.* Nihon seisansei honbu, 1965.

Noda Nobuo. "Amerika ni okeru seisansei no kongen." *Seisansei no riron to jissai* 2 (February 1956).

————. "Amerika-shiki kagakuteki keiei." In *Amerika no keiei gijutusu,* ed. Noda Nobuo et al. Daiyamondo, 1951.

————. "Ekonomisuto 50-nen o kaerimiru." *IE* 10, no. 11 (November 1968): 92–96.

————. "Indasutoriaru enjiniaringu no keiei rironteki kōsatsu." *PR* 9, no. 1 (January 1958): 14–18.

————. "Kagakuteki kanrihō kara seisansei undō e." *Keiei to rekishi* 9 (1986): 2–17.

————. "Kagakuteki kanrihō to rōdōsha no fukuri." *Shakai seisaku jihō* 41 (February 1924): 48–76.

————. *Kindaiteki keiei ni okeru ningen mondai.* Daiyamondo, 1953.

————. *Kōgyō keizai shinron.* Daiyamondo, 1943.

————. "Nenkō chingin." *Seisansei* 2, no. 5 (May 1960): 58–59.

————. "Nihon no gijutsu." *Seisan* 1, no. 1 (November 1946): 2.

————. "Rōmu kanri no genjō to shōrai no arikata." In *Rōmu kanri kindaika no jitsurei,* ed. Noda Nobuo and Mori Gorō. Daiyamondo, 1954.

————. *Seisansei dokuhon.* Nihon seisansei honbu, 1957.

————. "Zōsan kessen to taryō seisan." *Nihon nōritsu* 2, no. 5 (May 1943): 322–26.

Noda Nobuo and Mori Gorō, eds. *Rōmu kanri kindaika no jitsurei.* Daiyamondo, 1954.

Noda Nobuo et al. *Seisansei kōjō no hōhō.* Daiyamondo, 1955.

Noguchi Hisashi. *Toyota seisan hōshiki o tsukutta otoko: Ōno Taiichi no tatakai.* TBS Buritanika, 1988.

Nonaka Izumi. "SQC no dōnyū (2)." *Hinshitsu kanri* 41, no. 3 (March 1990): 55–62.

————. "QC saakuru no tanjō." *Hinshitsu kanri* 41, no. 9 (September 1990): 77–84.

Nōritsu tenrankai shi. Osaka: Nōritsu tenrankai sōmubu, 1924.

"Nōritsu zōshin no igi." *Kōgyō to keizai* 111 (March 1942): 1.

"Nōritsu zōshin no shuppatsuten." *Nihon nōritsu* 2, no. 4 (April 1943): 241.

Ōba Hideo and Nakahara Manabu. *TQC to no tatakai.* Gakushū no tomo sha, 1984.

Odaka Kunio. "Keiei ni okeru ningen no mondai." *Rōmu kenkyu* 2, no. 5 (May 1949): 7–11.

———. "Kōjō kanri no gōrisei ni kansuru jakkan no mondai." *Mita gakkai zasshi* 35, no. 8 (August 1942): 77–92.

———. *Sangyo ni okeru ningen kankei no kagaku.* Yūhikaku, 1953.

Odaka Kunio et al. *Hyūman rireeshonzu.* Daiyamondo, 1952.

Ōike Hisato. "Shokumu hyōka to jinji kōka." *Rōmu kenkyū* 3, no. 7 (July 1950), 15–19.

Ōkōchi Masatoshi. *Tōsei keizai to keizai sen.* Kagakushugi kōgyōsha, 1940.

Okuda Kenji. "Byūrokurashii-ka no Nihonteki pataan." *Keizai ronshū,* special issue (1985): 67–80.

———. "Datsu-koten no jidai ni okeru hito to keiei: Sōhosei complementarity no genri ni tsuite," *Keiei shigaku* 30, no. 4 (January 1996): 1–31.

———. *Hito to keiei: Nihon keiei kanrishi kenkyū.* Manejimento-sha, 1985.

———. "Nihon keiei kanrishi no ichi teiryū." *Nihon rōdō kyōkai zasshi* 29 (May 1987): 2–12.

———. *Rōmu kanri no Nihonteki tenkai.* Nihon seisansei honbu, 1972.

Onitsuka Mitsumasa. "Sengo Nihon ni okeru seisan kanri no hatten." In Sengo Nihon keiei kenkyūkai, *Sengo Nihon no kigyō keiei.* Bunshindō, 1991.

Ono Tsuneo. "Seisan gijutsu ni okeru kihon bunsekihō to seisan kanri no shohōshiki to no kankei ni tsuite." *Seisan* 1, no. 1 (November 1946): 3.

Ono Tsuneo, ed. *Mōshon-maindo: Horime Ken'ichi tsuitōroku.* Nihon nōritsu kyōkai, 1970.

Osaka furitsu sangyō nōritsu kenkyūjo. *Nōken 50-nen shi.* Osaka: Sangyō nōritsu ken-kyūjo, 1976.

———. *Wagakuni ni okeru sangyō tōsei ni tsuite.* Osaka: Sangyō nōritsu kenkyūjo, 1931.

Ota Hidekazu. "Sangyō gōrika no shin-igi." *Sangyō* 7, no. 2 (February 1930): 38–39.

Ōtsubo Mayumi. "Ima koso IE dōnyū no toki." *Manejimento* 19, no. 4 (April 1960): 31–36.

Ōuchi Tsuneo. "TWI to kantokusha kyōiku." In *Amerika no keiei gijutsu,* ed. Noda Nobuo et al. Daiyamondo, 1951.

———. "Wagakuni ni okeru TWI undō ni tsuite." *Rōmu kenkyū,* 3, no. 7 (July 1950): 2–5.

"Paneru tōronkai: Hinshitsu kōbōsen bōeki jiyūka to QC (2)." *Hinshitsu kanri* 15, no. 3 (March 1964): 55–68.

"QC kōza 1: Hinshitsu kanri no soshiki to un'ei—hyōjunka ni tsuite." *Hinshitsu kanri* 6, no. 10 (October 1955): 56–58.

"QC masukomi e." *Hinshitsu kanri* 8, no. 7 (July 1957): 9.

"QC no bunrui." *Hinshitsu kanri* 15, no. 2 (February 1964): 15.

"QC suishinsha no seikaku." *Hinshitsu kanri* 11, no. 12 (October 1961): 10–25.

Rinji sangyō gōrikyoku. "Seisankanri kaizen saku to chūō kikan setsuritsu an." *Tokyo kōjō konwakai kaihō* 55 (April 1931): 46–49.

Rinji sangyō gōrikyoku, Seisankanri iinkai. *Jugyōin tagaikawari seido.* Pamphlet 2. Osaka: Nihon kōgyō kyōkai, 1930.

———. *Chingin seido.* Pamphlet 11. Osaka: Nihon kōgyō kyōkai, 1935.

————. *Sagyō kenkyū*. Pamphlet 13. Osaka: Nihon kōgyō kyōkai, 1936.

————. *Seisankanri iinkai teian no konpon shushi*. Pamphlet 0. N.p. December 1930.

————. *Seisankanri no kaizen o mokuteki to suru chūō kikan setsuritsu an*. Pamphlet 24. Osaka: Nihon kōgyō kyōkai, 1931.

"Risō kōjō no igi." *Kōgyō to keizai* 91 (July 1940): 1–2.

"Rōmu to nōritsu." *Sangyō nōritsu* 15, no. 4 (April 1942): 319–20.

"Rōmusha ni wa tekishita shigoto o ataeyo!" *Seisan nōritsu* 5, no. 5 (May 1950): 10.

Saguchi Kazurō. *Nihon ni okeru sangyō minshūshugi no zentei*. Tokyo daigaku shuppankai, 1991.

"Sagyōin-hen ni tsuite." *Hinshitsu kanri* 11, no. 3 (March 1960): 3.

Saitō Takenori. *Ueno Yōichi—hito to gyōseki*. Sangyō nōritsu daigaku, 1983.

Sakai Tokutarō, ed. *Ei-bei hōmon jitsugyōdan shi*. Nihon kōgyō kurabu 11-nen kai, 1926.

Sakamoto Fujiyoshi. *Keieigaku nyūmon*. Kōbunsha, 1958.

————. *Nihon no keiei kakushi*. Mainichi shinbunsha, 1961.

Sakamoto Shigeharu. *Nōritsu gishi Ninomiya Sontoku*. Kenseisha, 1936.

Samada Mutsuo. "Seikatsukyū taikei kara nōritsukyū taikei e." *Nihon nōritsu* 8, no. 2 (February 1949): 10–12.

Sangyō gōrika shingikai sōgōbukai. *Wagakuni sangyō gōrika ni tsuite*. Tsūshō sangyō shō, tsūshō kigyō kyoku, 1951.

Sasaki Naoto. *TQC shinwa to no ketsubetsu*. Chūō keizaisha, 1989.

Sasaki Satoshi. "Mitsubishi denki ni miru kagakuteki kanrihō no dōnyū katei." *Keiei shigaku* 21, no. 4 (January 1987): 29–60.

————. "Shibaura seisakujo ni miru waaren-shisutemu dōnyū no kokoromi," *Keiei shigaku* 30, no. 2 (July 1995): 48–71.

————. "Tokyo bankoku kōgyō kaigi ni okeru kagakuteki kanri mondai." *Meiji daigaku daigakuin kiyō* 22, no. 6 (February 1985): 129–41.

Sasaki Satoshi and Nonaka Izumi. "Nihon ni okeru kagakuteki kanrihō no dōnyū to tenkai." In *Kagakuteki kanrihō no dōnyū to tenkai—sono rekishiteki kokusai hikaku*, ed. Hara Terushi. Kyōto: Shōwadō, 1990.

"Seisanryoku no kakujū to sangyō nōritsu no zōshin." *Kōgyō to keizai* 61 (January 1938): 1.

Shimazaki Hikojirō. "Beikoku no sangyō gōrika o miru." *Tokyo kōjō konwakai kaihō* 50 (November 1930): 2–9.

"Shin hinshitsu kanri 12-kō 2: Gijutsu kakushin to hinshitsu kanri." *Hinshitsu kanri* 12, no. 2 (February 1961): 85–94.

"Shin hinshitsu kanri 12-kō 10: Hinshitsu kanri to hito no mondai." *Hinshitsu kanri* 12, no. 10 (October 1961): 60–70.

"Shin keiei gijutsu no shippai rei to seikō rei." *Kindai keiei* 4, no. 5 (April 1959): 12–15.

"Shin sangyōdō." *Nihon nōritsu* 1, no. 4 (September 1942): 241–43.

"Shin-etsu kagaku: Naoetsu kōjō." *Hinshitsu kanri* 10, no. 7 (July 1959): 38–47.

Shingō Shigeo. *Seisan kanri no kaizen*. Nihon keizaisha, 1951.

Shinme Shinshichirō. *Kōjō kanri*. Kyōritsusha, 1941.

Shinomiya Masachika. "Senzen Nihon ni okeru kigyō keiei no kindaika to gaishikei kigyō." *Keiei shigaku* 29, no. 3 (October 1994): 35–72.

Shiro Tsutomu. *IE nyūmon*. Nihon nōritsu kyōkai, 1960.

Shōji Yukihiko. "Sangyō gōrika no sagyō shūdan to rōmu seisaku." *Keizaigaku kenkyū* 33, no. 3 (December 1983): 107–32.

Shōkōshō, Seisankanri iinkai. *Shin keizai taisei ka ni okeru kikai kōgyō no shinkōsaku.* Pamphlet 36. Nihon kōgyō kyōkai, 1941.

"Shokuchō kyōiku to QC." *Hinshitsu kanri* 14, no. 8 (August 1963): 6–7.

"Spotlight: Kanri no kyōchō." *Hinshitsu kanri* 10, no. 2 (February 1959): 9.

"Spotlight: Nentō ni." *Hinshitsu kanri* 12, no. 1 (January 1961): 13.

"Spotlight: QC no kaimei." *Hinshitsu kanri* 11, no. 12 (December 1960): 9.

Sugiyama Kōichi. "Taryō seisan hōshiki to setsubi no nōritsuteki kaizen" (parts I and II). *Nihon nōritsu* 2, no. 4 (April 1943): 267–73; 2, no. 5 (May 1943): 341–44.

Suzuki Hirokazu. "Hinshitsu kanri izen no mondai." *Hinshitsu kanri* 11, no. 1 (January 1960): 8–9, 11.

Suzuki Takeshi. "Juran hakase no kanri shisō to wagasha no soshiki." *Hinshitsu kanri* 5, no. 10 (October 1954): 32–35.

———. "Shokuchō kyōiku kōsu: Shokuchō no rikai shita hinshitsu kanri." *Hinshitsu kanri* 6, no. 10 (October 1955): 1–3.

Suzuki Tsunesaburō. *Kōjō kanri jitsugaku.* Daiyamondo, 1916.

———. *Rōdō mondai to onjōshugi.* Yōrokusha, 1915.

Taguchi Gen'ichi. "Sagyō hyōjun to ningen kankei." *Genba to QC* 23 (September 1965): 26–29.

"Taidan: Kogure-san no miyagebanashi o kiku." *Hinshitsu kanri* 10, no. 5 (May 1959): 66–70.

Takahashi Kō. *Gendai Nihon no chingin kanri.* Nihon hyōronsha, 1989.

Takahashi Mamoru. *"Kagakuteki kanrihō" to Nihon kigyō.* Ochanomizu shobō, 1994.

———. "Sangyō gōrika seisaku ni okeru kigyō tōsei." In *Nihon shihonshugi—tenkai to ronri,* ed. Hoshi Makoto. Tokyo daigaku shuppankai, 1978.

———. "Shōwa 20-nendai no sangyō gōrika seisaku." In Sangyō seisaku shi kenkyūjo, *Sangyō seisaku shi no kadai to hōhō.* Sangyō seisaku shi kenkyūjo, 1978.

———. "Shōwa shonen ni okeru sangyō gōrika seisaku dōnyū no keiki." *Seikei ronsō* (Hiroshima University) 24, no. 6 (January 1975): 75–106.

Takamiya Susumu. "Jinji kanri no hatten." *Keizai* 1, no. 3 (April 1947): 9–11.

———. "Keiei gōrika to shitsugyō mondai." *Jitsumu techō* 3, no. 11 (September 1949): 26–31.

———. "Seisansei kōjō to keiei kanri." In *Wagakuni kigyō to seisansei,* vol. 1, ed. Yamanaka Tokutarō et al. Tōyō keizai shinpōsha, 1958.

Takase Shōtarō, ed. *Sangyō gōrika to keiei seisaku.* Moriyama shoten, 1950.

Takezawa Shin'ichi. "Nihon ni okeru keiei kyōiku." *Sangyō kunren* 31, no. 363 (November–December 1985): 44–55.

Takita Minoru. "Seisansei o meguru shin nendo no kadai." *Seisansei no riron to jissai* 7 (April 1958): 96–98.

Tanaka Kunio. "Watakushi wa hinshitsu kanri o kō kangaeru." *Hinshitsu kanri* 3, no. 8 (August 1952): 2–3.

Taniguchi Yoshihiko. "Fukushi undō to shite no gōrika undō." *Shakai seisaku jihō* 116 (May 1930): 161–76.

"Tankō gōrika undō no tenbō." *Seisan nōritsu* 4, no. 4 (July 1949): 1.

Tawara Magoichi. "Sangyō gōrika seisaku yōkō." *Shakai seisaku jihō* 116 (May 1930): 1–6.

————. "Sangyō no gōrika to genseifu no kikaku." *Ekonomisuto,* 1 April 1930, 14–16.

Taylor, Frederick Winslow. *Gakuriteki jitsugyō kanrihō.* Trans. Hoshino Yukinori. Sūbunkan, 1913.

"Teidan: Amerika-shiki keiei kanri no juyō to fukyū." *Keiei to rekishi* 10 (July 1987): 2–27.

Teruoka Gitō. " 'Gōriteki rōdō' no kenchi yori mitaru Taylorism no hihan." *Chūō kōron* 35, no. 5 (May 1920): 29–36.

————. "Rōdō kagaku ni tsuite." *Rōdō kagaku kenkyū* 1, no. 1 (1924): 1–38.

————. "Sangyō gōrika no konpon mondai." *Shakai seisaku jihō* 116 (May 1930): 145–60.

Tōjō Hideki. "Shukuji." *Nihon nōritsu* 1, no. 1 (June 1942): 8–9.

Tokunaga Hisatsugu. "Seisansei kōjō undō no fukyū hōhō o kangaete hoshii." *Seisansei no riron to jissai* 1 (February 1956): 6.

"Tokushū: Keiei ni okeru Americanizumu no hansei." *Kindai keiei* 4, no. 5 (1 April 1959): 5–25.

Tokyo kōjō konwakai. *Kōjō muda nashi shūkan jisshi gaiyō.* Tokyo kōjō konwakai, 1931.

————. *Seiton shūkan jisshi gaiyō.* Tokyo kōjō konwakai, 1934.

Tomizawa Hiroshi. "Hinshitsu kanri to wa." *Hinshitsu kanri* 11, no. 3 (March 1960): 4–13.

Tomizawa Kiichi. "Hikōki kōgyō no rōdō jijō to kinrō shisaku." *Shakai seisaku jihō* 272 (May 1943): 211–25.

"Tōron kiroku: Hinshitsu hoshō ni okeru genbachō no ninmu." *Genba to QC* 1 (April 1962): 4–26.

Toyota jidōsha kōgyō kabushiki kaisha, Shashi henshū iinkai. *Toyota jidōsha 20-nen shi.* Koromo, Aichi-ken: Toyota jidōsha kōgyō kabushiki kaisha, 1958.

"TQC tōronkai (1)." *Hinshitsu kanri* 11, no. 10 (October 1960): 1–5.

"TQC tōronkai (2)." *Hinshitsu kanri* 11, no. 12 (December 1960): 4–8, 28.

Tsuru Gorō. "Jigu oyobi kensagu no hyōjunka." *Nihon nōritsu* 1, no. 2 (July 1942): 117–24, 147.

Tsūshō sangyō shō. *Nenpō 1949.* Tsūshō sangyō shō, 1949.

————. *Shōkō seisaku shi 9: Sangyō gōrika.* Tsūshō sangyō shō, 1961.

————. *Shōkō seisaku shi 10: Sangyō gōrika II.* Shōkō seisaku shi kankōkai, 1972.

Tsuzaki Masanosuke. "Watakushi no nōritsudō (sono 1)." *IE* 11, no. 1 (January 1969): 116–20.

Uchida Hoshimi. "Gijutsusha no zōka, bunpu to Nihon no kōgyōka." *Keizai kenkyū* 39, no. 4 (October 1988): 289–97.

Ueda Takehito. "Omoidasu mama ni—nōritsudō 50-nen." *IE* 10, no. 7 (July 1968): 90–94.

Ueda Teijirō. "Beikoku no han'ei to sangyō gōrika." *Kigyō to shakai* 21 (December 1927): 633–34.

Uenaka Kōdō, ed. *Nōritsu dokuhon.* Chūgai sangyō chōsakai, 1926.

Ueno Ichirō et al. *Mokuhyō kanri no un'ei to jissai.* Daiyamondo, 1966.

Ueno Yōichi. "Amerika ni okeru gōrika undō." *Shakai seisaku jihō* 86 (November 1927): 101–10.

————. "Naigai ni okeru nōritsu undō no genjō." *Sangyō nōritsu* 12, no. 4 (April 1939): 357–60.

————. *Nōritsugaku genron.* Kihōdō, 1956.

————. *Ueno Yōichi den.* Ed. Misawa Hitoshi. Sangyō nōritsu tanki daigaku, 1967.

————. *Ueno Yōichi senshū.* Chōbunkan, 1941.

Ueno Yōichi, ed. *Nōritsu handobukku.* 3 vols. Dōbunkan, 1939.

————, ed. *Sangyō nōritsu kenkyū ni kansuru naigai no jōkyō.* Sangyō nōritsu ken-kyūjo, 1925.

Ueno Yōichi, ed. and trans. *Taylor zenshū.* 2 vols. Dōbunkan, 1932.

Wakabayashi Yonekichi. "Seishinteki dōsa no gōrika." *Shakai seisaku jihō* 116 (May 1930): 211–24.

Watanabe Eizō. "QC kōza 1: Hinshitsu kanri no soshiki to un'ei—hyōjunka ni tsuite." *Hinshitsu kanri* 6, no. 10 (October 1955): 56–58.

Watanabe Eizō and Miura Shin. "SQC no dōnyū (1)." *Hinshitsu kanri* 41, no. 2 (February 1990): 67–73.

Watanabe Osamu. "Gendai Nihon shakai no ken'i-teki kōzō to kokka." In *Ken'i-teki chitsujo to kokka,* ed. Fujita Isamu. Tokyo daigaku shuppankai, 1987.

Watanabe Tetsuzō. "Rōdō no gōrika." *Shakai seisaku jihō* 116 (May 1930): 35–41.

Yabe Yōzō. "Keizai dōyūkai no kessei jijō ni tsuite." *Keizai shūshi* (Nihon University) 48, nos. 3, 4 (October 1978): 91–107.

————. "Kesseiji ni okeru keizai dōyūkai no seisan kōzō." *Keizai shūshi* (Nihon University) 51, no. 3 (October 1981): 85–108.

Yamabe Takashi. *Seisansei kōjō undō no rironteki shomondai.* Nihon seisansei honbu, 1957.

Yamakawa Hitoshi. *Sangyō gōrika no hihan.* Shunyōdō, 1930.

Yamaki Naomoto. *Hinshitsu kanri.* Seisan kōgaku kōza, vol. 15. Nikkan kōgyō shin-bunsha, 1960.

Yamamoto Kiyoshi. *Nihon ni okeru shokuba no gijutsu, rōdō shi.* Tokyo daigaku shup-pankai, 1994.

Yamamoto Yasujirō. *Nihon keieigaku 50-nen shi.* Keizai shinpōsha, 1977.

Yamashiro Akira. "Keiei gōrika no kako, genzai, shōrai." *Jitsumu techō* 3, no. 11 (September 1949): 2–8.

Yamashita Okiie. *Gijutsusha no kokoroe.* Sankaidō rikōgaku ronsō, vol. 24. Sankaidō, 1942.

————. "10 nenkan no kaiko." *Kōgyō to keizai* 101 (May 1941): 1–4.

————. "Senji seisanryoku no kakujū." In Nihon kōgyō kyōkai, *Sensō to kōgyō.* Nihon hyōronsha, 1939.

Yamazaki Hiroaki. "Nihon sensō keizai no hōkai to sono tokushitsu." In Tōkyō daigaku shakai kagaku kenkyūjo, *Fashizumu-ki no kokka to shakai 2: Senji Nihon keizai.* Tokyo daigaku shuppankai, 1979.

Yamazaki Toshio. *Gijutsushi.* Nihon gendaishi taikei. Tōyō keizai shinpōsha, 1961.

Yasuda Hiroshi. "Kanryō to rōdōsha mondai." In Tokyo daigaku shakai kagaku ken-kyūjo, *Gendai Nihon shakai 4: Rekishiteki zentei.* Tokyo daigaku shuppankai, 1991.

Yokouchi Tatsuo. "TWI jukō oyobi kunren jisshi no kansō." *Rōmu kenkyū,* 3, no. 7 (July 1950): 32–39.

Yoshida Masaki. "Seisan kanri no keieishi—senzen no jūdenki seisan o chūshin ni." *Keiei shigaku* 5, no. 1 (October 1970): 41–67.

Yoshimura Hiroshi. "Wagakuni no kōgyō ni okeru hinshitsu kanri no tenbō." *Hinshitsu kanri* 11, no. 3 (March 1960): 36–39, 65.

Yoshino Shinji. *Nihon kōgyō seisaku*. Nihon hyōronsha, 1935.

———. *Wagakuni kōgyō no gōrika*. Nihon hyōronsha, 1930.

———. "Waga sangyō gōrika no ni-daijūten." *Ekonomisuto*, 1 April 1930, 16–18.

"Zadankai: Deming hakase no shidō ni manabu." *Hinshitsu kanri* 2, no. 9 (September 1951): 9–14.

"Zadankai: Genbachō o meguru iroiro na mondai." *Hinshitsu kanri* 12, no. 9 (September 1961): 2–12, 16.

"Zadankai: IE ni tsuite." *Hinshitsu kanri* 10, no. 2 (February 1959): 17–31, 35.

"Zadankai: Kōgi no QC to kyōgi no QC." *Hinshitsu kanri* 8, no. 7 (July 1957): 16–21, 34.

"Zadankai: Nihon no hinshitsu kanri no ayumi o kaerimiru." *Hinshitsu kanri* 9, no. 6 (June 1958): 34–48.

"Zadankai: Nihon no IE to Amerika no IE o kataru." *IE* 3, no. 9 (September 1961): 736–48.

"Zadankai: QC to IE no yūwa." *Hinshitsu kanri* 12, no. 4 (April 1961): 32–35.

"Zadankai: Shufu no mita shin seihin." *Hinshitsu kanri* 10, no. 5 (May 1959): 56–65.

"Zadankai: Yaruki o okosaseru ni wa." *Genba to QC* 11 (May 1964): 7–17.

Works in English

Abegglen, James. *The Japanese Factory: Aspects of its Social Organization*. Glencoe, Ill.: Free Press, 1958.

Adler, Paul. "Time-and-Motion Regained." *Harvard Business Review* 71, no. 1 (January–February 1993): 97–108.

Aguayo, Rafael. *Dr. Deming: The American Who Taught the Japanese About Quality*. New York: Lyle Stuart, 1990.

Aitken, Hugh. *Scientific Management in Action: Taylorism at Watertown Arsenal, 1908–1915*. Princeton, N.J.: Princeton University Press, 1960.

Allen, G. C. "Japanese Industry." In *The Industrialization of Japan and Manchukuo, 1930–1940*, ed. E. B. Schumpeter. New York: Macmillan, 1940.

———. *A Short Economic History of Modern Japan*. New York: St. Martin's Press, 1981.

Aoki Masahiko. *Information, Incentives, and Bargaining in the Japanese Economy*. Cambridge: Cambridge University Press, 1988.

Asahi Isoshi. *The Secret of Japan's Trade Expansion*. Tokyo: International Association of Japan, 1934.

Ballon, Robert. "Lifelong Remuneration System." In *The Japanese Employee*, ed. Robert Ballon. Tokyo: Sophia University, 1969.

Banta, Martha. *Taylored Lives: Narrative Productions in the Age of Taylor, Veblen, and Ford*. Chicago: University of Chicago Press, 1993.

Barnhart, Michael. *Japan Prepares for Total War: The Search for Economic Security, 1919–1941*. Ithaca, N.Y.: Cornell University Press, 1987.

Bartholomew, James. *The Formation of Science in Japan*. New Haven, Conn.: Yale University Press, 1989.

Bedeian, Arthur, and Carl Phillips. "Scientific Management and Stakhanovism in the Soviet Union: A Historical Perspective." *International Journal of Social Economics* 17, no. 10 (1990): 28–35.

Beissinger, Mark R. *Scientific Management, Socialist Discipline, and Soviet Power.* Cambridge, Mass.: Harvard University Press, 1988.

Bendix, Reinhard. *Work and Authority in Industry: Ideologies of Management in the Course of Industrialization.* New York: Wiley, 1963.

Bisson, T. A. *Japan's War Economy.* New York: Institute of Pacific Relations, 1945.

Boltanski, Luc. "Visions of American Management in Post-War France." *Theory and Society* 12, no. 3 (May 1983): 375–403.

Borden, William S. *The Pacific Alliance: United States Foreign Economic Policy and Japanese Trade Recovery, 1947–1955.* Madison: University of Wisconsin Press, 1984.

Brady, Robert. "The Meaning of Rationalization: An Analysis of the Literature." *Quarterly Journal of Economics* 46 (May 1932): 526–40.

———. *The Rationalization Movement in German Industry.* Berkeley: University of California Press, 1933.

Braverman, Harry. *Labor and Monopoly Capital: The Degradation of Work in the Twentieth Century.* New York: Monthly Review Press, 1974.

Burawoy, Michael. *The Politics of Production.* London: Verso, 1985.

Campbell, Joan. *Joy in Work, German Work.* Princeton, N.J.: Princeton University Press, 1989.

Carew, Anthony. *Labour Under the Marshall Plan: The Politics of Productivity and the Marketing of Management Science.* Detroit: Wayne State University Press, 1987.

Carlile, Lonny. "Zaikai and the Politics of Production in Japan, 1940–1962." Ph.D. diss., University of California, Berkeley, 1989.

Cohen, Jerome. *Japan's Economy in War and Reconstruction.* Minneapolis: University of Minnesota Press, 1949.

Cohen, Theodore. *Remaking Japan: The American Occupation as New Deal.* New York: Free Press, 1987.

Cole, Robert E. "Learning from the Japanese." *Management Review* 69, no. 9 (September 1980): 22–42.

———. "Some Cultural and Social Bases of Japanese Innovation: Small-Group Activities in Comparative Perspective." In *The Political Economy of Japan,* vol. 3: *Cultural and Social Dynamics,* ed. Kumon Shumpei and Henry Rosovsky. Stanford, Calif.: Stanford University Press, 1992.

———. *Strategies for Learning.* Berkeley: University of California Press, 1989.

———. "What was Deming's Real Influence?" *Across the Board* 24, no. 2 (February 1987): 49–51.

———. *Work, Mobility and Participation.* Berkeley: University of California Press, 1979.

Cowan, Ruth Schwartz. *More Work for Mother.* New York: Basic Books, 1983.

Cusumano, Michael A. *The Japanese Automobile Industry: Technology and Management at Nissan and Toyota.* Cambridge, Mass.: Harvard University Press, 1985.

———. "'Scientific Industry': Strategy, Technology, and Entrepreneurship in Prewar Japan." In *Managing Industrial Enterprise: Cases from Japan's Prewar Experience,* ed. William Wray. Cambridge, Mass.: Council on East Asian Studies, Harvard University, 1989.

Daitō Eisuke. "Railways and Scientific Management in Japan, 1907–1930." *Business History* 31, no. 1 (January 1989): 1–28.

de Grazia, Victoria. *The Culture of Consent*. Cambridge: Cambridge University Press, 1981.

Deming, W. Edwards. *Out of the Crisis*. Cambridge: Cambridge University Press, 1982.

Dobyns, Lloyd. "Ed Deming Wants Big Changes, and He Wants Them Fast." *Smithsonian* 21, no. 5 (August 1990): 74–82.

Dobyns, Lloyd, and Claire Crawford Mason. *Quality or Else: The Revolution in World Business*. Boston: Houghton Mifflin, 1991.

Dohse, Knuth, Ulrich Jurgens, and Thomas Malsch. "From 'Fordism' to 'Toyotism'? The Social Organization of the Labor Process in the Japanese Automobile Industry." *Politics and Society* 14, no. 2 (1985): 115–46.

Dore, Ronald. *British Factory—Japanese Factory: The Origins of National Diversity in Industrial Relations*. Berkeley: University of California Press, 1973.

Duus, Peter, Ramon Myers, and Mark Peattie, eds. *The Japanese Wartime Empire, 1931–1945*. Princeton, N.J.: Princeton University Press, 1996.

Eckert, Carter. *Offspring of Empire: The Koch'ang Kims and the Colonial Origins of Korean Capitalism, 1876–1945*. Seattle: University of Washington Press, 1991.

Edwards, Richard. *Contested Terrain: The Transformation of the Workplace in the Twentieth Century*. New York: Basic Books, 1979.

Ewen, Stuart. *Captains of Consciousness*. New York: McGraw-Hill, 1976.

Feigenbaum, Armand V. *Total Quality Control: Engineering and Management*. New York: McGraw-Hill, 1961.

Field, Norma. "The Child as Laborer and Consumer." In *Children and the Politics of Culture*, ed. Sharon Stephens. Princeton, N.J.: Princeton University Press, 1995.

Fletcher, William Miles III. *The Search for a New Order: Intellectuals and Fascism in Prewar Japan*. Chapel Hill: University of North Carolina Press, 1982.

Fruin, W. Mark. "From Philanthropy to Paternalism in the Noda Soy Sauce Industry: Pre-Corporate and Corporate Charity in Japan." *Business History Review* 56, no. 2 (Summer 1982): 168–90.

———. *The Japanese Enterprise System: Competitive Strategies and Cooperative Structures*. Oxford: Clarendon Press, 1992.

———. *Kikkoman*. Cambridge, Mass.: Harvard University Press, 1983.

———. *Knowledge Works: Managing Intellectual Capital at Toshiba*. New York: Oxford University Press, 1997.

Fucini, Joseph J., and Suzy Fucini. *Working for the Japanese*. New York: Free Press, 1990.

Fujimoto Takahiro. "A Note on the Origins of the 'Black Box Parts' Practice in the Japanese Motor Vehicle Industry." In *Fordism Transformed: The Development of Production Methods in the Automobile Industry*, ed. Shiomi Haruhito and Wada Kazuo. Oxford: Oxford University Press, 1995.

Fukasaku Yukiko. *Technology and Industrial Development in Pre-war Japan: Mitsubishi Nagasaki Shipyard 1884–1934*. London: Routledge, 1992.

Funahashi Naomichi. "The Industrial Reward System: Wages and Benefits." In *Workers and Employers in Japan*, ed. Ōkōchi Kazuo, Bernard Karsh, and Solomon Levine. Princeton, N.J.: Princeton University Press, 1974.

Gabor, Andrea. *The Man Who Discovered Quality*. New York: Penguin, 1990.

Garon, Sheldon. *Molding Japanese Minds: The State in Everyday Life*. Princeton, N.J.: Princeton University Press, 1997.

―――. "Rethinking Modernization and Modernity in Japanese History: A Focus on State-Society Relations." *Journal of Asian Studies* 53, no. 2 (May 1994): 346–66.

―――. *The State and Labor in Modern Japan*. Berkeley: University of California Press, 1987.

Garon, Sheldon, and Mike Mochizuki. "Negotiating Social Contracts." In *Postwar Japan as History*, ed. Andrew Gordon. Berkeley: University of California Press, 1993.

Gillespie, Richard. *Manufacturing Knowledge: A History of the Hawthorne Experiments*. Cambridge: Cambridge University Press, 1992.

Gordon, Andrew. "Araki Tōichirō and the Shaping of Labor Management." In *Japanese Management in Historical Perspective*, ed. Yui Tsunehiko and Nakagawa Keiichirō. Proceedings of the Fifteenth International Conference on Business History. Tokyo: University of Tokyo Press, 1989.

―――. "Contests for the Workplace." In *Postwar Japan as History*, ed. Andrew Gordon. Berkeley: University of California Press, 1993.

―――. *The Evolution of Labor Relations in Japan: Heavy Industry, 1853–1955*. Cambridge: Harvard University Press, 1985.

―――. *Labor and Imperial Democracy in Prewar Japan*. Berkeley: University of California Press, 1991.

Gordon, David M., Richard Edwards, and Michael Reich. *Segmented Work, Divided Workers*. Cambridge: Cambridge University Press, 1982.

Gospel, Howard F., ed. *Industrial Training and Technological Innovation*. London: Routledge, 1991.

Graham, Laurie. *On the Line at Subaru-Isuzu: The Japanese Model and the American Worker*. Ithaca, N.Y.: ILR Press, 1995.

Gramsci, Antonio. *Selections from the Prison Notebooks*. Ed. and trans. Quintin Hoare and Geoffrey Smith. New York: International Publishers, 1971.

Greenwood, Ronald, and Robert Ross. "Early American Influence on Japanese Management Philosophy: The Scientific Management Movement in Japan." In *Management by Japanese Systems*, ed. Sang Lee and Gary Schwendiman. New York: Praeger, 1982.

Guillen, Mauro. *Models of Management: Work, Authority, and Organization in a Comparative Perspective*. Chicago: University of Chicago Press, 1994.

Haber, Samuel. *Efficiency and Uplift: Scientific Management in the Progressive Era*. Chicago: University of Chicago Press, 1964.

Hanley, Susan. *Everyday Life in Premodern Japan: The Hidden Legacy of Material Culture*. Berkeley: University of California Press, 1997.

Hannah, Leslie. "Comments." In *Government and Business*, ed. Nakagawa Keiichirō. Proceedings of the Fifth International Conference on Business History. Tokyo: University of Tokyo Press, 1980.

Harbison, Frederick, and Charles Myers. *Management in the Industrial World: An International Analysis*. New York: McGraw-Hill, 1959.

Harris, Howell. *The Right to Manage: Industrial Relations Policies of American Business in the 1940s*. Madison: University of Wisconsin Press, 1982.

Hathaway, Horace King. "Scientific Management in Japan." *Bulletin of the Taylor Society* 14, no. 4 (August 1929): 182–86.

Havens, Thomas. *Valley of Darkness*. New York: Norton, 1978.

Hayashi Shuji. *Culture and Management in Japan*. Trans. Frank Baldwin. Tokyo: University of Tokyo Press, 1988.

Hazama Hiroshi. *The History of Labor Management in Japan*. Trans. Mari Sako and Eri Sako. Basingstoke: Macmillan, 1997.

Hazama Hiroshi, with Jacqueline Kaminski. "Japanese Labor-Management Relations and Uno Riemon." *Journal of Japanese Studies* 5, no. 1 (Winter 1979): 71–106.

Hein, Laura. *Fueling Growth: The Energy Revolution and Economic Policy in Postwar Japan*. Cambridge: Harvard University Press, 1990.

———. "Growth Versus Success: Japan's Economic Policy in Historical Perspective." In *Postwar Japan as History,* ed. Andrew Gordon. Berkeley: University of California Press, 1993.

———. "In Search of Peace and Democracy: Postwar Japanese Economic Debate in Political Context." *Journal of Asian Studies* 53, no. 3 (August 1994): 752–78.

Herf, Jeffrey. *Reactionary Modernism: Technology, Culture, and Politics in Weimar and the Third Reich*. Cambridge: Cambridge University Press, 1984.

Hirschmeier, Johannes, and Yui Tsunehiko. *The Development of Japanese Business*. 2d ed. London: George Allen and Unwin, 1981.

Hogan, Heather. "Scientific Management and the Changing Nature of Work in the St. Petersburg Metalworking Industry, 1900–1919." In *Strikes, Wars and Revolutions in an International Perspective,* ed. Leopold Haimson and Charles Tilly. Cambridge: Cambridge University Press, 1989.

Homberg, Heidrun. "Scientific Management and Personnel Policy in the Modern German Enterprise 1918–1939: The Case of Siemens." In *Managerial Strategies and Industrial Relations,* ed. Howard Gospel and Craig Littler. London: Heinemann, 1983.

Hopper, Kenneth. "Creating Japan's New Industrial Management: The Americans as Teachers." *Human Resource Management* (Summer 1982): 13–34.

———. "Quality, Japan and the U.S.: The First Chapter." *Quality Progress* (September 1985): 34–41.

Horio Teruhisa. *Educational Thought and Ideology in Modern Japan*. Ed. and trans. Steven Platzer. Tokyo: University of Tokyo Press, 1988.

Horioka, Charles Yuji. "Consuming and Saving." In *Postwar Japan as History,* ed. Andrew Gordon. Berkeley: University of California Press, 1993.

Hoshino Yoshiro. "What Technology Has Postwar Japan Learned from the U.S.?" *Japanese Economic Studies* 17, no. 1 (Fall 1988): 65–92.

Hosotani Katsuya. *Japanese Quality Concepts: An Overview*. Trans. Glenn Mazur and Japan Business Consultants Limited. White Plains, N.Y.: Quality Resources, 1992.

Hounshell, David A. *From the American System to Mass Production, 1800–1932*. Baltimore: Johns Hopkins University Press, 1984.

Howe, Christopher. *The Origins of Japanese Trade Supremacy*. Chicago: University of Chicago Press, 1996.

Hughes, Thomas. *American Genesis*. New York: Penguin, 1989.

Ishihara Shigekazu, Ishihara Keiko, Nagamichi Mitsuo, and Alfredo Pinochet. "Neural

Network Simulation of QC Circle Activities." In *The Dynamics of Japanese Organizations,* ed. Frank-Jurgen Richter. London: Routledge, 1996.

Ishikawa Kaoru. *What is Total Quality Control? The Japanese Way.* Trans. David Lu. Englewood Cliffs, N.J.: Prentice-Hall, 1985.

Ivy, Marilyn. "Formations of Mass Culture." In *Postwar Japan as History,* ed. Andrew Gordon. Berkeley: University of California Press, 1993.

Jacoby, Sanford. *Employing Bureaucracy: Managers, Unions and the Transformation of Work in American Industry, 1900–1945.* New York: Columbia University Press, 1985.

James, Harold. *The German Slump.* Oxford: Oxford University Press, 1986.

Japan Management Association. *Kanban: Just-In-Time at Toyota.* Trans. David Lu. Rev. ed. Cambridge: Productivity Press, 1989.

Japan Productivity Center. *The Productivity Program in Japan.* Tokyo: Japan–U.S. Operations Mission to Japan, 1960.

Japan Quality Control Circles. Tokyo: Asian Productivity Organization, 1972.

Johnson, Chalmers. *MITI and the Japanese Miracle.* Stanford, Calif.: Stanford University Press, 1982.

Jordan, John M. *Machine-Age Ideology: Social Engineering and American Liberalism, 1911–1939.* Chapel Hill: University of North Carolina Press, 1994.

Juran, Joseph M. "The Changing Pattern of Quality Control." *Hinshitsu kanri* 12, no. 1 (January 1961): 2.

Jurgens, Ulrich, Thomas Malsch, and Knuth Dohse. *Breaking from Taylorism: Changing Forms of Work in the Automobile Industry.* Cambridge: Cambridge University Press, 1993.

Kamata Satoshi. *Japan in the Passing Lane.* Trans. Akimoto Tatsuru. New York: Pantheon, 1982.

Kaneko, Y. "Employment and Wages." *The Developing Economies* 8, no. 4 (December 1970): 445–74.

Kanigel, Robert. *The One Best Way: Frederick Winslow Taylor and the Enigma of Efficiency.* New York: Viking, 1997.

Karatsu Hajime. *TQC Wisdom of Japan.* Trans. David Lu. Cambridge: Productivity Press, 1988.

Kasza, Gregory. *The Conscription Society: Administered Mass Organizations.* New Haven, Conn.: Yale University Press, 1995.

Katō Tetsurō and Rob Steven. *Is Japanese Capitalism Post-Fordist?* Papers of the Japanese Studies Centre, Monash University, no. 16. Melbourne, 1991.

Kelly, William. "Rationalization and Nostalgia: Cultural Dynamics of New Middle-Class Japan." *American Ethnologist* 13, no. 4 (November 1986): 603–18.

Kenney, Martin, and Richard Florida. "Beyond Mass Production: Production and the Labor Process in Japan." *Politics and Society* 16, no. 1 (March 1988): 121–58.

———. *Beyond Mass Production: The Japanese System and Its Transfer to the U.S.* New York: Oxford University Press, 1993.

Kilian, Cecelia S. *The World of W. Edwards Deming.* 2d ed. Knoxville, Tenn.: SPC Press, 1992.

Kinmonth, Earl. *The Self-Made Man in Meiji Japanese Thought.* Berkeley: University of California Press, 1981.

Kinzley, W. Dean. *Industrial Harmony in Modern Japan: The Invention of a Tradition*. London: Routledge, 1991.

Knapp, James. *Literary Modernism and the Transformation of Work*. Evanston, Ill.: Northwestern University Press, 1988.

Koike Kazuo. *The Economics of Work in Japan*. Tokyo: LTCB International Library Foundation, 1995.

————. *Understanding Industrial Relations in Modern Japan*. New York: St. Martin's Press, 1988.

Kosai Yutaka. *The Era of High-Speed Growth*. Trans. Jacqueline Kaminski. Tokyo: University of Tokyo Press, 1986.

Koschmann, J. Victor. "Intellectuals and Politics." In *Postwar Japan as History*, ed. Andrew Gordon. Berkeley: University of California Press, 1993.

Koyanagi Ken'ichi. *The Deming Prize*. Rev. ed. Tokyo: JUSE, 1960.

Kuisel, Richard F. *Seducing the French: The Dilemma of Americanization*. Berkeley: University of California Press, 1993.

Kumazawa Makoto. *Portraits of the Japanese Workplace: Labor Movements, Workers and Managers*. Ed. Andrew Gordon. Trans. Andrew Gordon and Mikiso Hane. Boulder, Colo.: Westview Press, 1996.

Kurosawa Kazukiyo. "Some Considerations on Productivity Schemes." *Keizai shūshi* (Nihon University) 48, no. 2 (July 1978): 103–18.

Large, Stephen. *Organized Workers and Socialist Politics in Interwar Japan*. Cambridge: Cambridge University Press, 1981.

Levine, Solomon B. *Industrial Relations in Postwar Japan*. Urbana: University of Illinois Press, 1958.

Lichtenstein, Nelson. "'The Man in the Middle': A Social History of the Automobile Industry Foreman." In *On the Line*, ed. Nelson Lichtenstein and Stephen Meyer. Urbana: University of Illinois Press, 1989.

Maier, Charles. "Between Taylorism and Technocracy: European Ideologies and the Vision of Industrial Productivity in the 1920s." In Charles Maier, *In Search of Stability: Explorations in Historical Political Economy*. Cambridge: Cambridge University Press, 1987. Originally published 1970.

————. "The Politics of Productivity: Foundations of American International Economic Policy After World War II." In Charles Maier, *In Search of Stability: Explorations in Historical Political Economy*. Cambridge: Cambridge University Press, 1987. Originally published 1978.

Marsh, Robert M., and Mannari Hiroshi. *Modernization and the Japanese Factory*. Princeton, N.J.: Princeton University Press, 1976.

Marshall, Byron. *Capitalism and Nationalism in Prewar Japan*. Stanford, Calif.: Stanford University Press, 1967.

Mason, Mark. *American Multinationals in Japan: The Political Economy of Capital Controls, 1899–1980*. Cambridge: Harvard University Press, 1992.

Mass, William, and Andrew Robertson. "From Textiles to Automobiles: Mechanical and Organizational Innovation in the Toyoda Enterprises, 1895–1933." *Business and Economic History* 25, no. 2 (Winter 1996): 1–37.

Merkle, Judith. *Management and Ideology: The Legacy of the International Scientific Management Movement*. Berkeley: University of California Press, 1980.

Meyer, Stephen III. *The Five Dollar Day*. Albany: State University of New York Press, 1981.

Minami Ryōshin. *The Economic Development of Japan*. New York: St. Martin's Press, 1986.

Miyake Yoshiko. "Doubling Expectations: Motherhood and Women's Factory Work under State Management in Japan in the 1930s and 1940s." In *Recreating Japanese Women, 1600–1945*, ed. Gail Lee Bernstein. Berkeley: University of California Press, 1991.

Monden Yasuhiro. *Toyota Production System: An Integrated Approach to Just-In-Time*. 2d ed. Norcross, Ga.: Industrial Engineering and Management Press, 1993.

Montgomery, David. *The Fall of the House of Labor*. Cambridge: Cambridge University Press, 1987.

Moore, Joe. *Japanese Workers and the Struggle for Power, 1945–1947*. Madison: University of Wisconsin Press, 1983.

Morioka Koji. "Introduction: Japanese Capitalism Today." *International Journal of Political Economy* 21, no. 3 (Fall 1991): 3–7.

Morris-Suzuki, Tessa. *Beyond Computopia: Information, Automation and Democracy in Japan*. London: Kegan Paul International, 1988.

———. *The Technological Transformation of Japan*. Cambridge: Cambridge University Press, 1994.

Murata Kazuhiko. "Personnel Management in Japanese Business Enterprises." *Hitotsubashi Journal of Commerce and Management* 25, no. 1 (December 1990): 35–46.

Nakamura Takafusa. *Economic Growth in Prewar Japan*. Trans. Robert A. Feldman. New Haven, Conn.: Yale University Press, 1971.

———. *The Postwar Japanese Economy*. Trans. Jacqueline Kaminski. Tokyo: University of Tokyo Press, 1981.

Nakaoka Tetsurō. "Production Management in Japan before the Period of High Economic Growth." *Osaka City University Economic Review* 17 (1981): 7–24.

Nakase Toshikazu. "The Introduction of Scientific Management in Japan and its Characteristics." In *Labor and Management*, ed. Nakagawa Keiichirō. Proceedings of the Fourth International Conference on Business History. Tokyo: University of Tokyo Press, 1977.

Naruse Tatsuo. "Taylorism and Fordism in Japan." *International Journal of Political Economy* 21, no. 3 (Fall 1991): 32–48.

Nelson, Daniel. *Frederick W. Taylor and the Rise of Scientific Management*. Madison: University of Wisconsin Press, 1980.

———. "Industrial Engineering and the Industrial Enterprise, 1890–1940." In *Coordination and Information: Historical Perspectives on the Organization of Enterprise*, ed. Naomi Lamoreaux and Daniel Raff. Chicago: University of Chicago Press, 1995.

———. *Managers and Workers*. Madison: University of Wisconsin Press, 1975.

———. "Scientific Management and the Workplace, 1920–1935." In *Masters to Managers*, ed. Sanford Jacoby. New York: Columbia University Press, 1991.

Nelson, Daniel, ed. *A Mental Revolution: Scientific Management Since Taylor*. Columbus: Ohio State University Press, 1992.

Nelson, Daniel, and Stuart Campbell. "Taylorism Versus Welfare Work in American Industry: H. L. Gantt and the Bancrofts." *Business History Review* 46, no. 1 (Spring 1972): 1–16.

Noble, David F. *America by Design: Science, Technology and the Rise of Corporate Capitalism*. New York: Knopf, 1977.

Noda Nobuo. "How Japan Absorbed American Management Methods." In *Modern Japanese Management*. London: Management Publications, Ltd./The British Institute of Management, 1970.

Nolan, Mary. *Visions of Modernity: American Business and the Modernization of Germany*. New York: Oxford University Press, 1994.

Nolte, Sharon, and Sally Hastings. "The Meiji State's Policy Toward Women, 1890–1910." In *Recreating Japanese Women, 1600–1945,* ed. Gail Lee Bernstein. Berkeley: University of California Press, 1991.

Nonaka Izumi. "The Development of Company-wide Quality Control and Quality Circles at Toyota Motor Corporation and Nissan Motor Co. Ltd." In *Fordism Transformed: The Development of Production Methods in the Automobile Industry,* ed. Shiomi Haruhito and Wada Kazuo. Oxford: Oxford University Press, 1995.

Odaka Kunio. *Japanese Management: A Forward-Looking Analysis*. Tokyo: Asian Productivity Organization, 1986.

———. *Toward Industrial Democracy: Management and Workers in Modern Japan*. Cambridge: Harvard University Press, 1975.

Ogawa Eiji. *Modern Production Management: A Japanese Experience*. Tokyo: Asian Productivity Organization, 1984.

Ohno Taiichi. *Toyota Production System: Beyond Large-Scale Production*. Cambridge: Productivity Press, 1988.

———. *Workplace Management*. Trans. Andrew P. Dillon. Cambridge: Productivity Press, 1988.

Okamoto Hideaki. "Management and Their Organizations." In *Workers and Employers in Japan,* ed. Ōkōchi Kazuo, Bernard Karsh, and Solomon Levine. Princeton, N.J.: Princeton University Press, 1974.

Okazaki Tetsuji. "The Japanese Firm Under the Wartime Planned Economy." *Journal of the Japanese and International Economies* 7 (1993): 175–203.

Okazaki-Ward, Lola. *Management Education and Training in Japan*. London: Graham and Trotman, 1993.

Okita Saburo, ed. *The Postwar Reconstruction of the Japanese Economy*. Tokyo: University of Tokyo Press, 1992.

Okuda Kenji. "Managerial Evolution in Japan" (parts I, II and III). *Management Japan* 5, no. 3 (1971): 13–19; 5, no. 4 (1972): 16–23; 6, no. 1 (1972): 28–35.

Ono Tsuneo. "Postwar Changes in the Japanese Wage System." In *The Labor Market in Japan: Selected Readings,* ed. Nishikawa Shunsaku, trans. Ross Mouer. Tokyo: University of Tokyo Press, 1980.

Oshima, Harry T. "Reinterpreting Japan's Postwar Growth." *Economic Development and Cultural Change* 31, no. 1 (October 1982): 1–43..

Ōtake Hideo. "The *Zaikai* Under the Occupation." In *Democratizing Japan: The Allied Occupation,* ed. Robert Ward and Sakamoto Yoshikazu. Honolulu: University of Hawaii Press, 1987.

Ouchi, William G. *Theory Z*. New York: Avon Books, 1981.

Parker, Mike. "Industrial Relations Myth and Shop-Floor Reality: The 'Team Concept' in the Auto Industry." In *Industrial Democracy in America: The Ambiguous Promise,* ed. Nelson Lichtenstein and Howell Harris. Cambridge: Cambridge University Press, 1993.

———. *Inside the Circle: A Union Guide to QWL*. Boston: South End Press, 1985.

Pascale, Richard T., and Anthony G. Athos. *The Art of Japanese Management*. New York: Warner Books, 1981.

Peattie, Mark. "Japanese Attitudes toward Colonialism, 1895–1945." In *The Japanese Colonial Empire, 1895–1945*, ed. Ramon Myers and Mark Peattie. Princeton, N.J.: Princeton University Press, 1984.

Pempel, T. J. "The Tar Baby Target: 'Reform' of the Japanese Bureaucracy." In *Democratizing Japan: The Allied Occupation*, ed. Robert E. Ward and Sakamoto Yoshikazu. Honolulu: University of Hawaii Press, 1987.

Piore, Michael, and Charles Sabel. *The Second Industrial Divide: Possibilities for Prosperity*. New York: Basic Books, 1984.

Price, John. *Japan Works: Power and Paradox in Postwar Industrial Relations*. Ithaca, N.Y.: ILR Press, 1997.

QC Circle Koryo: General Principles of the QC Circle. Tokyo: QC Circle Headquarters, JUSE, 1980. Original Japanese-language edition, 1970.

Rabinbach, Anson. "The Aesthetics of Production in the Third Reich." In *International Fascism*, ed. George Mosse. London: Sage Publications, 1979.

———. *The Human Motor*. New York: Basic Books, 1990.

Rohlen, Thomas P. *For Harmony and Strength*. Berkeley: University of California Press, 1974.

———. *Japan's High Schools*. Berkeley: University of California Press, 1983.

———. "Order in Japanese Society: Attachment, Authority, and Routine." *Journal of Japanese Studies* 15, no. 1 (Winter 1989): 5–40.

Romero, Federico. *The United States and the European Trade Union Movement*. Trans. Harvey Fergusson II. Chapel Hill: University of North Carolina Press, 1992.

Rowlinson, Michael. "The Early Application of Scientific Management by Cadbury." *Business History* 30, no. 4 (1988): 377–95.

Rupert, Mark. *Producing Hegemony: The Politics of Mass Production and American Global Power*. Cambridge: Cambridge University Press, 1995.

Sakuma Ken. "Changes in Japanese-Style Labor-Management Relations." *Japanese Economic Studies* 16, no. 4 (Summer 1988): 3–48.

Samuels, Richard J. *Rich Nation Strong Army: National Security and the Technological Transformation of Japan*. Ithaca, N.Y.: Cornell University Press, 1994.

Sasaki Satoshi. "The Introduction of Scientific Management by the Mitsubishi Electric Engineering Company and the Formation of an Organised Scientific Management Movement in Japan in the 1920s and 1930s." *Business History* 34, no. 2 (1992): 12–27.

———. "The Rationalization of Production Management Systems in Japan during World War II." In *World War II and the Transformation of Business Systems*, ed. Sakudō Jun and Shiba Takao. Proceedings of the Twentieth International Conference on Business History. Tokyo: University of Tokyo Press, 1994.

———. "Scientific Management Movements in Pre-War Japan." In *Japanese Yearbook on Business History: 1987*, ed. Yasuoka Shigeaki and Morikawa Hidemasa. Tokyo: Japan Business History Institute, 1987.

Scherer, James. *Japan's Advance*. Tokyo: Hokuseido Press, 1934.

Schonberger, Richard J. *Japanese Management Techniques: Nine Hidden Lessons in Simplicity*. New York: Free Press, 1982.

Searle, G. R. *The Quest for National Efficiency*. Oxford: Blackwell, 1971.

Sewell, Graham, and Barry Wilkinson. "'Someone to Watch Over Me': Surveillance, Discipline and the Just-In-Time Labour Process." *Sociology* 26, no. 2 (May 1992): 271–89.

Shiba Takeo. "Business Activities of Japanese Manufacturing Industries During World War II." In *World War II and the Transformation of Business Systems,* ed. Sakudō Jun and Shiba Takao. Proceedings of the Twentieth International Conference on Business History. Tokyo: University of Tokyo Press, 1994.

Shillony, Ben-Ami. *Politics and Culture in Wartime Japan.* Oxford: Clarendon Press, 1981.

Shimada Haruo. "Japan's Industrial Culture and Labor-Management Relations." In *The Political Economy of Japan,* vol. 3: *Cultural and Social Dynamics,* ed. Kumon Shumpei and Henry Rosovsky. Stanford, Calif.: Stanford University Press, 1992.

Shingō Shigeo. *The Sayings of Shigeo Shingō: Key Strategies for Plant Improvement.* Trans. Andrew P. Dillon. Cambridge: Productivity Press, 1987.

———. *The Shingō Production Management System: Improving Process Functions.* Trans. Andrew P. Dillon. Cambridge: Productivity Press, 1992.

———. *A Study of the Toyota Production System from an Industrial Engineering Viewpoint.* Rev. ed. Trans. Andrew P. Dillon. Cambridge: Productivity Press, 1989.

Shirai Taishirō. "Collective Bargaining." In *Workers and Employers in Japan,* ed. Ōkōchi Kazuo, Bernard Karsh, and Solomon Levine. Princeton, N.J.: Princeton University Press, 1974.

Smith, Thomas. *Native Sources of Japanese Industrialization, 1750–1920.* Berkeley: University of California Press, 1988.

"Statistical Techniques as a Natural Resource: A Message from W. Edwards Deming to the Ceremony for the Annual Award of the Deming Prize." *Hinshitsu kanri* 6, no. 12 (December 1955): 2–3.

Stone, Katherine. "The Origins of Job Structures in the Steel Industry." In *Labor Market Segmentation,* ed. Richard Edwards, Michael Reich, and David Gordon. Lexington, Mass.: Lexington Books, 1975.

Sugayama Shinji. "The Bureaucratization of Japanese Firms and Academic Credentialism: A Case Study of Hitachi, Ltd." *Japanese Yearbook on Business History: 1991.* Tokyo: Japan Business History Institute, 1991.

Sumiya Mikio. "Contemporary Arrangements: An Overview." In *Workers and Employers in Japan,* ed. Ōkōchi Kazuo, Bernard Karsh, and Solomon Levine. Princeton, N.J.: Princeton University Press, 1974.

Suzuki Yoshitaka. *Japanese Management Structures, 1920–1980.* London: Macmillan, 1991.

Taira Koji. "Factory Legislation and Management Modernization during Japan's Industrialization, 1886–1916." *Business History Review* 44, no. 1 (Spring 1970): 84–109.

Takamiya Susumu. "Background, Characteristics and Recent Trends in Japanese Management." In *Modern Japanese Management.* London: Management Publications, Ltd./The British Institute of Management, 1970.

Takeuchi Johzen. *The Role of Labour-Intensive Sectors in Japanese Industrialization.* Tokyo: United Nations University Press, 1991.

Taylor, Frederick Winslow. *The Principles of Scientific Management.* New York: Harper, 1911.

———. *Scientific Management.* New York: Harper, 1947.

Thompson, Paul. *The Nature of Work: An Introduction to Debates on the Labour Process.* 2d. ed. Basingstoke: Macmillan, 1989.

Tichi, Cecilia. *Shifting Gears: Technology, Literature, Culture in Modernist America.* Chapel Hill: University of North Carolina Press, 1987.

Tokunaga Shigeyoshi. "A Marxist Interpretation of Japanese Industrial Relations, with Special Reference to Large Private Enterprises." In *Contemporary Industrial Relations in Japan,* ed. Shirai Taishirō. Madison: University of Wisconsin Press, 1983.

Tomlinson, Jim. "The Failure of the Anglo-American Council on Productivity." *Business History* 33, no. 1 (1991): 82–92.

Toyoda Eiji. *Toyota: Fifty Years in Motion.* Tokyo: Kodansha International, 1987.

Toyota Motor Corporation. *Toyota: A History of the First 50 Years.* Toyota City: Toyota Motor Corporation, 1988.

Trades Union Congress (U.K.). "Greater Industrial Efficiency." *Seisan* 4, no. 8 (November 1949): 5.

Tsuda Masumi. "Study of Japanese Management Development Practices I." *Hitotsubashi Journal of Social Studies* 9, no. 1 (May 1977): 1–12.

———. "Study of Japanese Management Development Practices II." *Hitotsubashi Journal of Arts and Sciences* 18, no. 1 (September 1977): 1–19.

———. "Study of Japanese Management Development Practices III." *Hitotsubashi Journal of Social Studies* 10, no. 1 (April 1978): 14–35.

Tsunoda, Elizabeth P. "Rationalizing Japan's Political Economy: The Business Initiative, 1920–1955." Ph.D. diss., Columbia University, 1993.

Tsurumi, E. Patricia. *Factory Girls: Women in the Thread Mills of Meiji Japan.* Princeton, N.J.: Princeton University Press, 1990.

Tsutsui, William M. "Rethinking the Paternalist Paradigm in Japanese Industrial Management." *Business and Economic History* 26, no. 2 (Winter 1997): 561–72.

———. "The Way of Efficiency: Ueno Yōichi and Scientific Management in Twentieth-Century Japan." *Modern Asian Studies,* forthcoming.

———. "W. Edwards Deming and the Origins of Quality Control in Japan." *Journal of Japanese Studies* 22, no. 2 (Summer 1996): 295–325.

Twine, Nanette. *Language and the Modern State: The Reform of Written Japanese.* London: Routledge, 1991.

Uchino Tatsurō. *Japan's Postwar Economy.* Trans. Mark A. Harbison. Tokyo: Kodansha, 1978.

Unger, J. Marshall. *Literacy and Script Reform in Occupation Japan.* New York: Oxford University Press, 1996.

United States Information Service. "Labor and Management Solve Problems Together." *Keizai* 1, no. 9 (November 1947): 26–27.

Uno, Kathleen. "The Death of 'Good Wife, Wise Mother'?" In *Recreating Japanese Women, 1600–1945,* ed. Gail Lee Bernstein. Berkeley: University of California Press, 1991.

Wada Kazuo. "The Emergence of the 'Flow Production' Method in Japan." In *Fordism Transformed: The Development of Production Methods in the Automobile Industry,* ed. Shiomi Haruhito and Wada Kazuo. Oxford: Oxford University Press, 1995.

Walton, Mary. *The Deming Management Method.* New York: Perigee Books, 1986.

Waring, Stephen P. *Taylorism Transformed: Scientific Management Theory Since 1945.* Chapel Hill: University of North Carolina Press, 1991.

Warner, Malcolm. "Japanese Culture, Western Management: Taylorism and Human Resources in Japan." *Organization Studies* 15, no. 4 (1994): 509–33.

Webster, Frank, and Kevin Robins. "'I'll Be Watching You': Comment on Sewell and Wilkinson." *Sociology* 27, no. 2 (May 1993): 243–52.

Weinstein, Barbara. *For Social Peace in Brazil: Industrialists and the Remaking of the Working Class in São Paulo, 1920–1964.* Chapel Hill: University of North Carolina Press, 1996.

Westney, Eleanor. *Imitation and Innovation: The Transfer of Western Organizational Patterns to Meiji Japan.* Cambridge: Harvard University Press, 1987.

Willson, Perry R. *The Clockwork Factory: Women and Work in Fascist Italy.* Oxford: Clarendon Press, 1993.

Womack, James, Daniel Jones, and Daniel Roos. *The Machine that Changed the World.* New York: Rawson Associates, 1990.

Wood, Robert Chapman. "A Lesson Learned and a Lesson Forgotten." *Forbes,* 6 February 1989, 70–78.

Wood, Stephen. "The Japanization of Fordism." *Economic and Industrial Democracy* 14 (1993): 535–55.

———. "The Transformation of Work?" In *The Transformation of Work?,* ed. Stephen Wood. London: Unwin Hyman, 1989.

Wood, Stephen, and John Kelly. "Taylorism, Responsible Autonomy and Management Strategy." In *The Degradation of Work?,* ed. Stephen Wood. London: Hutchinson, 1982.

World Engineering Congress. *Proceedings,* vol. 38: *Scientific Management.* Tokyo: World Engineering Congress, 1931.

Wren, Daniel A. *The Evolution of Management Thought.* 4th ed. New York: Wiley, 1994.

Wright, Chris. "Taylorism Reconsidered: The Impact of Scientific Management Within the Australian Workplace." *Labour History* 64 (May 1993): 34–53.

Yonekura Seiichirō. *The Japanese Iron and Steel Industry, 1850–1990.* New York: St. Martin's Press, 1994.

Yoshino, Michael. *Japan's Managerial System: Tradition and Innovation.* Cambridge: MIT Press, 1965.

Index

About the Author

William M. Tsutsui is Assistant Professor of History at the University of Kansas. He is the author of *Banking Policy in Japan: American Efforts at Reform During the Occupation.*